W9-CBX-239

1-18-00

DISCARDED

Brooks - Cork Library
Shelton State

CAPITAL MOVES

Brooks - Cork Library
Shelton State
Community College

DISCARDED

Capital Moves

RCA's
Seventy-Year Quest
for Cheap Labor

Jefferson Cowie

CORNELL UNIVERSITY PRESS

ITHACA AND LONDON

Copyright © 1999 by Cornell University

All rights reserved. Except for brief quotations in a review, this book, or parts thereof, must not be reproduced in any form without permission in writing from the publisher. For information, address Cornell University Press, Sage House, 512 East State Street, Ithaca, New York 14850.

First published 1999 by Cornell University Press.

Printed in the United States of America.

Library of Congress Cataloging-in-Publication Data

Cowie, Jefferson R.
Capital moves : RCA's seventy-year quest for cheap labor /
Jefferson Cowie.
p.   cm.
Includes bibliographical references and index.
ISBN 0-8014-3525-0 (cloth : alk. paper).

1. RCA Corporation—History.   2. Electronics industry workers—
United States—History.   3. RCA Corporation—Employees—History.
4. Business relocation.   I. Title.
HD9696.A3U5334   1999
338.7′621381′0973 — dc21   98-49784

Cornell University Press strives to use environmentally responsible suppliers and materials to the fullest extent possible in the publishing of its books. Such materials include vegetable-based, low-VOC inks and acid-free papers that are recycled, totally chlorine-free, or partly composed of nonwood fibers.

Cloth printing   10   9   8   7   6   5   4   3   2   1 *for Jan'r*

CONTENTS

ABBREVIATIONS

AFL	American Federation of Labor
BIP	Border Industrialization Program
CCC	Civilian Conservation Corps
CIO	Congress of Industrial Organizations
CROC	Confederación Revolucionaria de Obreros y Campesinos (Revolutionary Confederation of Workers and Peasants)
CRT	Confederación Revolucionaria de Trabajadores (Revolutionary Workers' Confederation)
CTM	Confederación de Trabajadores de México (Confederation of Mexican Workers)
ECU	Employees' Committee Union
FAT	Frente Auténtico del Trabajo (Authentic Labor Front)
FCC	Federal Communications Commission
GATT	General Agreement on Tariffs and Trade
HDTV	high-definition television
IBEW	International Brotherhood of Electrical Workers
INEGI	Instituto Nacional de Estadística, Geografía e Informática
ISI	import-substitution industrialization
IUE	International Union of Electrical Workers
IUOHP	Indiana University Oral History Project
IWW	Industrial Workers of the World
NAFTA	North American Free Trade Agreement
NLRA	National Labor Relations Act (Wagner Act)
NLRB	National Labor Relations Board
NRA	National Recovery Administration
NRAT	National Radio and Allied Trades
NYA	National Youth Administration
PAN	Partido Acción Nacional (National Action Party)
PRI	Partido Revolucionario Institucional (Institutional Revolutionary Party)

PRONAF	Programa Nacional Fronterizo (National Border Program)
RCA	Radio Corporation of America
RMWIU	Radio and Machine Workers Industrial Union
TCE	Thomson Consumer Electronics
TNC	transnational corporation
TTM	Thomson Televisiones de México
TSUS	Tariff Schedule of the United States
UAW	United Auto Workers
UE	United Electrical Workers
UNAM	Universidad Nacional Autónoma de México
VSA	Victor Shop Association
WLRB	War Labor Relations Board
WPA	Works Progress Administration

CAPITAL MOVES

Introduction

A lot of people have built their dreams and their houses and their families around working for that company." Bill Breeden, a trucker who hauled RCA television sets and parts between Indiana and the Mexican border, had just heard the announcement that the assembly plant in Bloomington was to be shut down permanently. "Those workers have given their life, really, and their blood, many times, under poor working conditions, for years and years to build a television, a product, that made a lot of people rich." Management had given the labor force the option of taking an enormous wage cut in order to save their jobs, but the television makers knew when enough was enough. In 1998, when the factory gates shut for the final time, the last of the Bloomington jobs followed a well-worn trail carved by thousands of other RCA positions that had been slowly shifted to the company's burgeoning factories in Ciudad Juárez since the 1960s. Many workers who were facing hard times in the NAFTA era vented their anger at the Mexicans who were "taking American jobs." But Breeden, who was familiar with the workers of both nations, saw the issue in more complex terms. After all, he explained, "If someone was to come here and bring a plant here and offer us a job now, would we sit back and say, 'Well, we can't take this job because it's somebody else's job'? The fact is, we wouldn't, and they realize that."[1]

Ironically, and unknowingly, the trucker had described exactly what the Indiana workers did when RCA relocated production out of Camden, New Jersey, to Bloomington almost sixty years earlier—they "took" the jobs of others.

This book examines not just RCA's most recent move to Mexico but a whole series of relocations of the company's radio and television manufacturing from the 1930s to the 1990s. Revealing a much longer and more complicated history of capital migration than we tend to hear about in the "global era," the story moves through four very distinct places and cultures as it examines the remarkably similar experiences of all of them with a single industry. Beginning with Southern and Eastern European immigrants in industrial New Jersey during the Great Depression, RCA moved production to employ ethnic Scotch-Irish workers in rural Indiana in 1940, briefly employed a combination of African American and white wage earners in Tennessee during the 1960s, and, since 1968, has employed Mexican workers in the border state of Chihuahua. Taken together, the chapters that follow comprise a comparative social history of industrial relocation that explores community life, gender, and labor organization across time and space. Placing the impact of capital migration on these working-class communities in a context that is both historically and internationally comparative, this book shows how social changes at the local level drive the relocation of capital investment.

Today it is not uncommon for workers to discover that their plant is to be relocated to a low-wage haven carefully selected for its abundance of underemployed people desperate for jobs. Nor is it rare for a corporation to exploit gender identities to create the desired malleability in a workforce on the periphery of the world economy or for a blue-collar community to become embroiled in bitter competition with another place of a different culture where industrial investment has fled. The marketplace, once an actual location for the exchange of goods and services, seems to have grown into a free-flowing torrent of capital and information that threatens to overwhelm workers' grasp on the pace of history. Pacts such as the North American Free Trade Agreement (NAFTA) place an official stamp on the idea that we live in a new era defined by the mobility of capital and the weakening of organized labor and the regulatory state. Symptomatic of the "reformation of capitalism," the "locational revolution" in production, and the "manic logic" of globalization, these new developments, it is often argued, have recast the world economic system at tremendous cost to workers and their communities.

Rather than marking a radical departure from past practices, however, the RCA story suggests that many of the disquieting trends that add up to today's upheavals have parallels deep in twentieth-century labor history. Although the pace and scope of events may have increased as the century waned, industrial capital has been engaged in a continuous struggle to maintain the social conditions deemed necessary for profitability. "Offshore" production may be a focus of political attention today, but neither the causes of the transnationalization of production nor the problems it creates differ dramatically from those of the transregionalization of industry several decades earlier. Moving employment across an international boundary does mark a very important development, particularly as it throws into question the role of the nation-state as overseer of industrial relations, but it nonetheless stands as a continuation of earlier patterns and strategies.

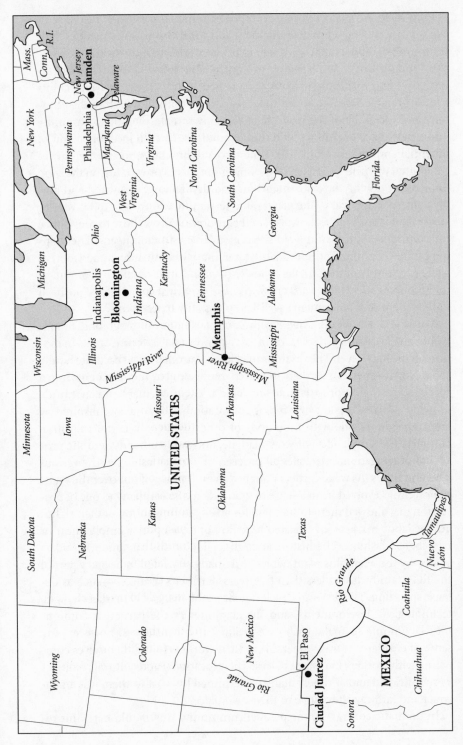

Sites of RCA television assembly operations, 1929–1998

Each of RCA's plant relocations represents the corporation's response to workers' increasing sense of entitlement and control over investment in their community. Capital flight was a means of countering that control as the company sought out new reservoirs of controllable labor. The search for inexpensive and malleable workers that shaped each location decision had its own subversive logic, however: the integration of production into the economy and social life of the new site irrevocably transformed the community into a new place of conflict with the corporation. In each location, a glut of potential employees shrank over time into a tightening labor market, once-deferential workers organized into a union shop, and years of toil on the shop floor recast docility into a contentious and demanding, if isolated and ambivalent, working class. The geographic terrain inhabited by capital was far larger than labor's niche, however, and corporate leaders chose to move once the cultural resources of the old site no longer suited their needs. The shaping of the economic and social landscape, therefore, must be understood as a tale not simply of the unilateral power of capital but, equally important, of the resources wielded by workers who chose over time to fight for a position independent of management's well-laid plans and expectations.

The title of this book, *Capital Moves*, implies not only geographic mobility but an entire series of social changes that industrial investment sets in motion on the local level. The rhythms of change pounded out at each site hardly cause North American workers to march in unison, but they do merge into a sort of staccato beat of social transformation. The excitement and civic pride of being awarded a plant by a major corporation, the initial awe inspired by laboring side by side with thousands of other workers in a vast industrial complex, the simple facts of stress, fatigue, and swollen hands, and the process of organizational struggles all proceed in parallel fashion at the various sites and times. As wage earners punched in and punched out over the years, their feelings evolved from a sense of gratitude to the company to one of possession that allowed them to stand up for an expanding notion of their rights. Yet the labor markets investigated here do not develop in a simple linear or teleological fashion. The historical contingency of this migration is underscored by the Memphis plant, which, originally projected to be a key part of the RCA family, lasted less than five years. Further variations—such as defense spending, Third World development problems, global market changes, technological developments, and the attributes of the particular community—combine to make each case unique. In all instances, however, any sense of entitlement was vulnerable as RCA workers found themselves competing with workers in distant places. Their locational and cultural resources were restricted and at times totally undermined by what to them was an abstract and faraway alternative to their own place.

In dramatic contrast to the parallel community stories told here, this research was originally conceived as a way of illuminating the presumably many and dramatic differences between the experiences of the various communities. By looking at several cities in a variety of periods, I at first thought, I would explore the sharp divide between an old labor relations system and a "new international division of labor," delineate the stark opposition between a seasoned male workforce in the United States and thousands of young women in Mexico, and reveal the gulf between labor-intensive Mexican sweatshops and a well-established, if greatly weakened, U.S. collective bargaining system. I was surprised to find, however, that RCA workers in all the sites exhibited amazingly high levels of shared experience across time and space. In an age in which the political celebration of difference and the intellectual examination of the singular and unique dominate the stage, I found commonality not just in the ways of work but, most important, in the challenges and opportunities RCA workers faced across North America in the twentieth century. One of my hopes, in fact, is that workers may be able to recognize their own experiences across the barriers of national experience, ethnic difference, and geographic distance.

Framed within the overarching tension between the requirements of capital and the social change sponsored by industrial production are several supporting themes that develop as the story unfolds. First, the vast majority of the employees, at least at the opening of each factory, were women. Although a rigid sexual division of labor and the almost exclusive hiring of young female employees are often associated with foreign export-processing zones, they were fundamental industrial relations strategies in the electrical industry from Camden in the 1930s to Juárez in the 1990s.[2] How the gendered labor market was constructed in one locale and then, as it was transformed, rebuilt at a new site forms an important theme. RCA's peregrinations reinforced the difference between highly skilled, high-technology "male" work and low-skilled, labor-intensive "female" work by separating the two labor processes not just on the shop floor but by region and nation as well. The initial importance and the subsequent replaceability of young women workers who built consumer electronics in all of these locations spotlight the need to adjust the popular image of the unemployed male steel or auto worker as the quintessential victim of deindustrialization. Women, whether at the shrinking center or growing periphery of industrial production, have borne the brunt of the process of restructuring both past and present.

Second, I also question labor historians' reliance on the "labor-management accord" as the ruling paradigm for understanding the uneasy truce between labor and capital in the decades of general prosperity after World War II.[3] Though the period of mutual recognition between business and labor formed a golden age for many workers in liberal democracies around the world (including Latin America), it was significantly less stable or uniformly prosperous than many observers believe. Most historians date the disintegration of the pact in the mid-1970s or beyond, but RCA's plant location decisions in the 1930s and 1940s suggest that management may have been significantly less committed to its end of the bargain than many analysts presume. Although manufacturers of consumer electronics faced a much more competitive market than the makers of automobiles and other durable goods, this book adds fuel to the argument that the rust belt began to rust not with the multiple economic problems of the 1970s or the globalization of the 1980s and 1990s but with the complexities of the immediate postwar period.[4]

Another theme challenges the idea that plant location decisions are based on static variables. Although RCA's site selection process may have involved many important issues, the evolving social history of working people was at the center of the story. Traditional location theory points to tangible factors such as geographic proximity to markets, raw materials, and cheap and appropriately skilled labor as key elements in firms' plant-site decisions. Advances in communication and transportation, hastened by interregional rivalries for investment, however, have largely liberated firms from such considerations and allowed capital to evolve from a pattern of centralization into an increasingly dispersed geography of production. In the process the old manufacturing centers have been abandoned to the economic wilds as new factories have cropped up to take their places in green fields around the nation and, later, the globe. As the RCA case demonstrates, however, choices of industrial locations were fundamentally tied to the local history of each site. Labor was not the calculable and static factor of production it appears in plant location theory; workers instead were social actors involved in the very development of economic geography. If laborers can at all be regarded as historical agents — even unintended and contradictory ones — they must be seen as geographic agents as well.[5]

This book, therefore, focuses on the relationship between industrial investment and social change, and it is only peripherally concerned with the well-studied impact of "deindustrialization." The firm that abruptly closes down and abandons its workers to the streets, although perhaps the dominant image of the problem, is actually much less typical than the plant that undergoes a more subtle process of cutbacks, attrition, and the gradual relocation or elimination of industrial jobs. The closure of any plant is of political and social concern, but the final shutdown of a factory — the act that draws the public's attention — usually comes only at the end of a long, silent process of job relocation. These evolutionary changes in the employment structure often mask much of the subtle drama of labor history and hide from the actors themselves both the profundity of the transformations and the continuities in the pattern of events. Such is the case with this history of RCA's radio and television assembly, which can be understood as a "runaway shop" only in the loosest sense, as the corporation shifted employment opportunities over the course of decades rather than simply relocating entire factories wholesale.[6]

My final and broadest argument, developed particularly in the last chapter, questions and complicates the fundamental tool of much of social history, the community study. Years of locally based investigations, the stock in trade of the so-called new labor history, have left the newest generation of labor historians with an ambivalent inheritance. What we have learned is that the rich reservoir of resistance and accommodation to the inequities of the market can often be found in the complex set of relationships, customs, and values established within the community context. The ways workers have mobilized on the local level in the face of both economic change and the political orders developed to support it have formed the core of much of the social and political history of working people. Class, as E. P. Thompson explained, was not a structural determinant but a changing historical relationship. In the United States, Herbert Gutman and his students launched the investigation of local working-class cultures in scores of communities and concluded that the cultural resources of wage earners have been the cement that bonded workers together in countless well-documented locales.[7]

Yet when labor historians venture very far into the twentieth century, their emphasis on culture and community all but disappears as economics, institutions, and the state take center stage. The colorful cultural tapestry of the nineteenth century seems to fade mysteriously into dull shades of gray. Unlike the working-class culture that emerges from analyses of earlier epochs, the historian Leon Fink explains, that of the twentieth century "is used less to account for *capacity* or *empowerment* than for *somnolence* or *passivity*."[8] Clearly, many forces are at work eroding the power of working-class communities in the twentieth century: the homogenizing forces of the market, the pull of the consumer nexus, and the increased role of the state have all served to undermine the uniqueness of communities as oppositional locales. New veins of cultural resistance that parallel those uncovered for the nineteenth and early twentieth centuries may be found when historians dig into the newest waves of immigrants from Asia and Latin America; essentially, however, twentieth-century working-class communities remain uncharted terrain much beyond the New Deal.[9]

One of the goals of this book is to encourage new approaches to labor history by reinvigorating the idea that the shared experience formed within the context of culture and community is often the source of agency and power— even today—while also arguing that community is one of the key limitations and weaknesses of working-class mobilization. Moreover, evolutions in culture are linked to economic transformations. The sources of the changing geography of capitalism and its impact on a community can be found at the local level but can be understood only through a global view of labor-capital relations. The changing nature of space—economic, cultural, and political—can supplement changes over time as a fundamental way of approaching the history of labor. By situating working people on a vast and competitively charged field of industrial location choices, historians find their understanding of class tensions complicated by the problem of a fragmented social geography.

The RCA story exposes how blue-collar communities function as fundamental sources of both power and resistance in industrial relations while simultaneously creating deeply problematic social and political obstacles to the building of solidarity beyond the borders of a shared sense of place. When we expand the analysis beyond the single place that informs the majority of community studies, we are forced to rethink the nature of labor's power when we see "militancy" in one region in competition with "docility" in another. In sum, the community can be understood as one of workers' basic resources in their contest with industry as well as one of the key weaknesses in workers' ability to act on the transnational—or even transregional—level of awareness and organization.

As each community is unique, however, so is each industry. A word on the idiosyncrasies of the consumer electronics industry is therefore in order. This sector suffers most acutely from one of the most enduring problems of free enterprise: overproduction. The constant revolution in materials and manufacturing has produced more goods ever more efficiently with fewer inputs, and this phenomenon has continued to lower prices and undermine the rate of return on investment for firms willing to enter this fiercest of industries. Since the advent of both radio and television, each generation of consumers has been able to purchase a better product at a lower price than the previous one. Crisper pictures, clearer sounds, and more compact sets have all been delivered to consumers with a shrinking price tag. With a relentless downward pressure on production costs, the search for cheap labor has held a pivotal position in firms' strategies to beat their competitors. This pressure has placed the burden of low prices on the shoulders of people toiling on an assembly line that stretches from New Jersey to Chihuahua. Because of the particularly brutal competition that shapes this market, the RCA story offers a more compressed and heightened example than is likely to be found in other industries. The tale of this company's flight, rather than emblematic of larger trends, might more appropriately be regarded as a bellwether for the broader path of industrial employment.[10]

Chapter 1 demonstrates that the struggle to organize the massive RCA Victor complex in Camden, New Jersey, during the 1930s was an instrumental push factor in the company's decision to decentralize its production. In a classic CIO-era battle, the company met the United Electrical Workers' effort to win a contract in Camden with determined resistance. When the workers nevertheless prevailed, RCA still held the trump card: to escape the costs of the union contract, it relocated the manufacture of goods that faced particularly sharp competition to the Midwest. Since the experiences of workers in the old northeastern industrial belt, such as those of Camden, inform a disproportionate share of our understanding of twentieth-century labor history, Chapter 1 also offers an interesting point of departure and comparison for the less-studied locations to follow.

Chapter 2 follows RCA to Bloomington, Indiana, and analyzes both that community's attractiveness as a plant site in 1940 and the subsequent changes brought about by the presence and growth of the factory. Bloomington had many of the characteristics that made the U.S.-Mexican border attractive decades later, but the social conditions of the plant itself slowly ate away at the docility and cheapness that RCA originally found so alluring. By the 1960s, a newly aggressive labor force created problems that began to resemble, in muted ways, the tensions at the original site in Camden.

Before crossing an international boundary, RCA moved across another border, the Mason-Dixon Line. Chapter 3 turns to RCA's short-lived expansion into the southern United States during the tumultuous 1960s. The timing and choice of Memphis as a plant site proved to be disastrous: market pressures pushed the workforce beyond its limits and the obedience the company expected to nurture in Tennessee failed to materialize. RCA shut the plant less than five years after it opened and found workers more appropriate to its needs in the developing world.

The second half of the book marks the beginning of binational production as Chapter 4 moves to Ciudad Juárez and analyzes the border economy's reorientation toward the global market. Many analysts point to a new system of industrial relations and plant location theory in the border zone, but in fact the same factors that shaped RCA's choice of Bloomington and Memphis went into the decision to open production in Juárez. Spurred by the presence of RCA, the growth of foreign-owned factories (maquiladoras), however, initiated a dramatic departure for the local economy of northern Mexico and laid the groundwork for what would soon grow into one of the most industrialized regions in North America.

Returning to Bloomington, Chapter 5 reveals how the draining of employment to Mexico turned the tide on the Hoosiers' demands upon the company. As in Camden, changes in the geography of production forced dwindling numbers of RCA employees in Bloomington to surrender many of the gains they had won during the height of the company's employment in

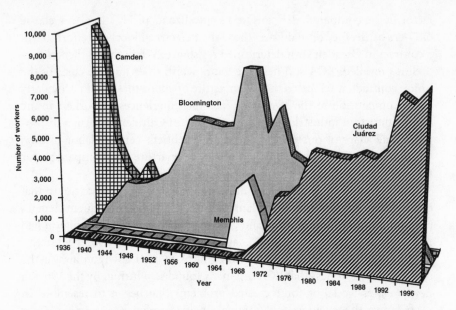

Figure I.1. RCA employment in consumer electronics production, Camden, Memphis, Bloomington, and Ciudad Juárez, 1936–1998. The figures for Camden include all employment there (including workers on assembly, cabinetry, and parts production) before 1939; figures during and after World War II include only workers on consumer electronics. Total figures for Camden after 1940, which included defense workers, are higher than those shown.

the community. The specter of a complete shutdown of the operation loomed over labor-management relations until the plant closed permanently in the spring of 1998 (see Figure I.1).

Chapter 6 traces the growth of employment by transnational corporations along the Mexican border and explores the tremendous obstacles workers faced in their efforts to improve their economic well-being and democratize their union. Although many of the changes evident in the other cities could be found in Juárez, working-class politics in the city were inextricably tied to Mexico's economic and political crises. Nonetheless, despite the obstacles they faced, the RCA workers achieved power and success there too.

Finally, Chapter 7 investigates the spaces in between the four locations. Here we see how workers perceived their counterparts in other cities, the obstacles to transregional and transnational organizing, and the tensions between the needs of communities and the demands of capital.

What follows is a migratory history of which even the participants could grasp only parts. By discussing workers caught up in similar situations at different times and in different places, I attempt to explain how workers' collective efforts, in painful and ironic ways, helped to shape the geography of an industry. Rather than offer a dour tale of shutdowns, I redirect the emphasis toward a hopeful story of plant openings in which sweeping historical transformations can be traced to a myriad of seemingly minute changes among thousands of unknown workers. First the wage earners of Camden, then those of Bloomington and Memphis, and finally those in Juárez were swept by the winds of plant location and relocation into place-bound struggle over private investment. The new locales were always sites of tremendous optimism for women and men eager to work for a living wage. Looking beyond the specific problem of capital migration, I hope this book will also serve as an introductory tour to many of the complexities faced by a broad spectrum of working people throughout the twentieth century. Even more ambitiously, I hope that readers may gain a sense of how the aspirations of workers across the continent shaped, however ironically, at least one slender slice of history.

CHAPTER ONE

In Defiance of Their Master's Voice:
Camden, 1929-1950

Smoke from hundreds of factories along the river on both sides fell like a blanket to the surface of the stream," wrote a ferry passenger in 1920 while crossing the Delaware River on a centuries-old route from Philadelphia to Camden, New Jersey. The industrial pollutants were so thick that they left "all moving craft in a complete shroud of mist."[1] When the view was not completely obstructed, however, the scene visible from the ferry revealed the strength and vitality of Camden's many manufacturing establishments. By the 1920s, the South Jersey city contained a variety of textile mills and leather processors, a huge ironworks, the Campbell's soup cannery, cigar factories, a pen manufacturer, paint and chemical processing plants, and, particularly obvious on the river front, the bustling docks, shipyards, and four thousand workers of the New York Shipbuilding Company. The most prominent symbol of Camden's industrial might, however, was the 205-foot tower hovering over the Victor Talking Machine Company's sprawling complex of factories. Shining through the industrial haze from each of the four sides of the tower could be seen the huge stained-glass windows beaming the trademark featuring Nipper, the black-and-white fox terrier with his head cocked curiously at a phonograph in recognition of "His Master's Voice."[2]

While the back-lit image of Nipper, visible even in Philadelphia, dominated the city's skyline, the imposing presence of the monumental network of RCA Victor factories prevailed over the streets of Camden. By the mid-1930s, after the Radio Corporation of America purchased and enlarged the Victor works, one reporter declared the "monster" complex of plants to be "beyond the imagination" of the lay observer. Twenty-four buildings ranging from one to ten stories in height were linked by over five miles of standard-gauge railroad track that fed raw materials in and finished products out.

Inside the complex, six miles of belt, chain, and overhead conveyor systems shuttled parts around the various plants and set the pace of production for nearly ten thousand workers. To oversee the flow of materials and products through the maze of daily production, engineers drew over 100,000 square feet of blueprints each month. Twenty-four hundred tons of coal and coke fueled the operation each month as workers pumped 54 million cubic feet of compressed air through drills, guns, presses, and other pneumatic machinery. The corporation owned its own wharf on the Delaware River, where employees unloaded materials from around the world and shipped out a long list of consumer electronics goods—records, phonographs, broadcasting stations, photophone machinery, motion picture recording and playing appliances, aircraft and police communication equipment, and, most important, three to five thousand radios produced in the plant every workday.[3]

RCA and the "City of Contented Industries"

The corporation that transformed the Victor works into such an industrial giant, the Radio Corporation of America, began in 1919 as a government-supported monopoly financed by the biggest names in the electrical industry. Before World War I, the wireless communications industry had been foreign-owned and chaotically organized, but when the United States committed itself to the war effort, President Woodrow Wilson placed the industry under the monopoly power of the U.S. Navy. Although the government did not, as some people advocated, establish absolute control over the industry, it did facilitate the creation of the Radio Corporation of America as a patriotic "marriage of convenience" of private electrical corporations as a way to keep wireless communication in American possession and to develop it for the national good.[4]

Under an agreement to pool patents and capital forged by General Electric's Owen D. Young, the ownership of RCA belonged to GE (30.1%), Westinghouse (20.6%), AT&T (10.3%), and United Fruit (4.1%), with a variety of other holders accounting for the remaining 34.9 percent. The agreement also stipulated that RCA would sell radio equipment manufactured by its principal owners, which the new corporation could purchase from the parent corporations on a simple formula of cost plus 20 percent.[5] As early as 1926 RCA broadened its original plan from "narrowcast" communications to public "broadcast" by organizing the National Broadcasting Company (NBC). The growing network of radio stations formed in the 1920s helped to make RCA one of the key growth stocks during the heady investment years of the Jazz Age, but it was actually manufacturing and licensing of patents that made RCA the instant giant of the communications industry. In a reversal of plans, the corporation's success came when the radio manufacturing "tail" wagged the international wireless "dog." In the decade between RCA's inception in 1919 and 1929, its annual revenues grew from $2 million to $182 million—nearly 90 percent of which represented radio sales and licensing income.[6]

The final act in the formation of RCA was again directed by the U.S. government, but this time in its occasional role as trust buster. After the stock market collapsed in 1929, Congress began to crack down on the more blatant excesses of the business community, and one of the central targets became the ostentatious RCA. As many critics were quick to point out, a government-sanctioned monopoly bequeathed to a combination of the biggest corporations in the country on its way to becoming "a worldwide radio trust" was anything but a clean example of free enterprise. "If anyone can find in the history of Standard Oil or steel a more ruthless example of corporate buccaneering than attended the rise of the Radio Corporation under Mr. Young's enlightened guidance," editorialized an article in *The Nation*, "I should like to hear of them." The government therefore revived dormant antitrust laws, directed them against RCA, and forced powerful GE and Westinghouse to divest themselves of all stock in the corporation. Although the breakup was initially devastating to the hopes and stock value of the corporation, Chairman of the Board David Sarnoff saw it as a chance to chart an independent course for the company, which had gone far beyond the corporation's original mission to protect American wireless communication. As the RCA empire grew and competing members of the consortium fell by the wayside, Sarnoff told friends, "There can be only one captain on the bridge and I happen to be that fellow for this ship at this time."[7]

Yet the manufacture of radios remained in the hands of the original corporate owners of the independent RCA, a fact that Sarnoff was determined to change. Shopping around for an existing manufacturing facility, he proposed that RCA purchase the Victor Talking Machine Company's factories in Camden, which had been producing its famous phonographs since 1901. With the support of GE's Owen Young, the "radio trust," as many observers referred to it, incorporated the RCA Victor Company in 1929 with David Sarnoff as chairman of the board and its stock owned 50 percent by RCA, 30 percent by GE, and 20 percent by Westinghouse. Ultimately confident that Camden and its workers could serve the company's manufacturing needs, RCA invested almost $11.5 million to convert the phonograph plant to radio production. Sarnoff proclaimed the South Jersey city to be the "Radio Capital of the World" during rededication ceremonies in September 1930, and the move marked the beginning of RCA's dominance of the consumer electronics industry for over half a century.[8]

When Sarnoff chose Camden for his new radio plant, he certainly had little to fear from the organized power of the city's workforce. As late as 1931, the

RCA Manufacturing Co., Inc., Camden, N.J.

The 2-million-square-foot RCA complex dominated the "city of contented industries" in 1936. Note the Nipper tower at center left and the Campbell's Soup cannery at lower left. Before the opening of the bridge across the Delaware River in 1926, goods and people moving from New Jersey to Philadelphia had to pass through the streets of Camden en route to the ferry. Afterward one could motor past Camden without even taking notice of it—one of the earliest signs of Camden's troubles. (Hagley Museum and Library.)

city's chamber of commerce still proudly boasted of its industrial peace. "Here the moral is strictly an industrial one and it points directly to the city itself," the chamber proclaimed, "for the leaders of these great industries will attest to Camden's advantages—the home-owning workers, the facilities and improvements which have made her the 'city of contented industries.'" Glorifying the outstanding qualities of the South Jersey wage earners, the city's promoters boasted that "in all its history, Camden has never known a major strike." [9] Labor politics and municipal leadership in Camden, described at the time as "the Citadel of Republicanism," remained safely in the hands of old-guard Anglo-Saxons through the 1920s.[10]

Below the industrial peace, however, dramatic changes were under way. As Camden's industrial skyline expanded, so did the national origins, culture, and politics of the city's working-class population. The city remained relatively insulated from the waves of Southern and Eastern European immigrants throughout the late nineteenth century, but the situation changed dramatically by the opening decades of the twentieth century as new immigrants flocked to industrial Camden. Of the foreign-born inhabitants of the city in 1900, over 65 percent came from Northern Europe—Germany, Great Britain, and Ireland; a mere 10 percent immigrated from Italy, Russia, and Poland. Twenty years later, however, the figures were nearly reversed as Eastern and Southern Europeans who flocked to the industrial jobs in Camden made up 60 percent of the foreign-born. So many "Catholics, Jews, blacks, Poles, Italians, and other new groups" poured into the manufacturing center that they fundamentally transformed what once appeared to many residents as a "stable Protestant, Anglo-Saxon society." As local historians noted, "Newcomers filled jobs, seized political power, and squeezed out older residents."[11]

Federal immigration restrictions in the 1920s helped to stabilize Camden's immigrant population, which, according to the labor historian Robert Zieger, helped to create "an emerging second generation of ethnic workers, committed to life in America, increasingly distanced from old-world customs and familial traditions, and expecting the continuation of rising standards of security, prosperity, and mobility."[12] Not even vicious backlashes against the immigrants, such as a campaign against perceived radicalism during the Red Scare and a resurgence of the Ku Klux Klan's assault on minorities, halted the congealing of working-class politics in the city. Although the incumbent Herbert Hoover won a slim majority of votes in Camden County in the presidential election of 1932, it was the last time the county voted other than Democratic for several decades. During the Great Depression and beyond, the city's residents entered into the urban New Deal coalition of workers, Eastern and Southern Europeans, Jews, and African Americans through a broad range of relief programs and the right to organize unions and bargain collectively.[13]

RCA's choice of Camden, however, was contingent on the city's ability to remain a competitive place to produce radio sets. "The industry I represent," E. E. Shumaker, president of the RCA-Victor Company, lectured the Camden Chamber of Commerce in 1929, "can only grow if we can build cheaper here than elsewhere." The "hard-headed Wall Street directors" to whom he was responsible "will not take any theory for granted in making that decision, but they are willing to be shown that Camden has the best to offer." In exchange for doubling employment in the city from Victor's 5,000 workers to over 10,000 radio makers, he demanded assurances. "That means taxes must be low," Shumaker declared. "It means we must have a Delaware River port, and transportation advantages.... I am hopeful, very hopeful that we will all work together and Camden will take advantage of what is possible." With the Great

Depression deepening and unemployment rising, RCA was certainly not concerned about Camden's ability to provide adequate numbers of workers. The 20,000 residents who remained on relief in the county during most of the 1930s created a ready labor reserve and downward pressure on any attempt to raise wages.[14] Most important, however, RCA would not be competing with the shipyards or other major industrial employers for workers, for the vast majority of its new hires would be young women.

Gender and Electrical Production

Of the 9,800 workers employed at RCA in 1936, approximately 75 percent were women. They did all the wiring, crimping, and soldering on the radio sets. On the main production floor, which stretched the length of two football fields, each female line worker performed the labor-intensive operations on 400 to 800 radio chassis each day. Male inspectors stood at intervals of every ten to fifteen female workers to monitor their performance as the women applied the heavy 200-watt irons to the 300 solder joints necessary to build the average radio in 1935. Women working on an incentive piece-rate system also labored on the feeder lines that built intricate subassemblies and components to be placed on the main assembly lines. In contrast, men's part in the production process was to perform the test and repair procedures, build the large and elaborate wooden radio cabinets, staff the machine shop, and design and build the models and prototypes of products that would soon be rolling off the assembly lines.[15]

The Camden works depended on women workers somewhat more than the radio industry as a whole, but wage discrimination by sex was a fundamental tenet of the entire electrical home-appliance industry. In 1939, 54.2 percent of all employees in radio, radio tube, and phonograph manufacturing in the nation were women. Perhaps just as important, most of them were quite young. "If employing women in lieu of men made good sense in the electrical industry, where wages made up a high proportion of production costs," argues the sociologist Ruth Milkman, "favoring young female workers was even more expedient." In a strategy that would continue all the way to the U.S.-Mexican border in the NAFTA era, the electrical home-appliance industry wrote its employment advertisements specifically to recruit young women and established a variety of formal and informal bans on the employment of married women. As a government investigator explained in the 1930s, "You have to be young and strong to get a job" in the radio industry.[16]

Management's standard explanation for its preference for young female workers typically rested on the idea that women's mental and physical characteristics made them peculiarly suited to the intricacies of electrical assembly work. As *Factory Management and Maintenance* magazine explained, electrical work "requires feminine patience and deft fingers"; only "women can handle these minute parts, and are willing to perform the highly repetitive operations that this type of assembly requires." [17] Despite the filth and toxicity of the solder fumes to which women workers were exposed, advocates of the gendered division of labor also pointed to the cleanliness of electrical assembly, which supposedly made it particularly suited to women. The idea of the docile and nimble-fingered woman worker has had such remarkable staying power in feminized occupations that Milkman called it the "idiom" of sex-typing in her examination of World War II employment in the United States, and Leslie Sklair, investigating Mexico forty years later, simply called it "the litany." [18]

Researchers examining electronics production in today's Third World export-processing zones often associate the industry's dependence on female labor with the "new international division of labor," but light electrical manufacturing has been feminized since its very inception in the early twentieth century. Milkman's comparative history of the auto and electrical industries in the United States offers the most compelling explanation of the roots and development of the division of labor in electrical production. Different types of occupational segregation by sex, Milkman argues, were historically determined by the "economic, political, and social constraints" operating when the methods of controlling a particular labor process initially formed. In the auto sector, for instance, management based its control over labor on the combination of the moving assembly line, which dramatically reduced labor time, and relatively high wages, which offered little incentive to substitute female labor for more expensive male workers. The manufacture of more labor-intensive and economically competitive consumer electronics equipment, in contrast, relied on "elaborately constructed piecework systems" that left labor content high and depended on the hiring of less costly women and girls.[19] The "cheapness" of female labor, therefore, had only slight utility in the auto industry but formed the core of industrial policy in the electrical industry. Once forged, this gender formulation had its own ideology and institutional logic that persists to the present day—wherever the plants may have been relocated. These formulations even had the power to supersede the drive for profit maximization, which would dictate increased hiring of less expensive female workers in all industries.

By 1938, the vast majority of plants in the electrical industry, even those with union contracts, depended on wage discrimination by sex. For instance, the agreement of the United Electrical Workers (UE) with the Philco radio plant across the river from RCA—a contract that the Camden workers would try to make their own in 1936—maintained a 20 percent difference in wages by sex after six weeks on the job. Rather than challenging economic and social divisions in the workforce, the union left sexual segregation in place by simply elevating the wages of workers of both sexes. After several years at the plant, however, aggregate wage differentials by sex throughout the factory would be even more dramatic as men moved into more highly skilled and better-paying positions and women remained segregated in labor-intensive assembly.[20]

The ideology of women's innate characteristics makes little sense except in comparative perspective. The construct of the docile, physically weak, nimble-fingered, and presumably nonunion woman worker simultaneously raised an equally mythological opposite: the clumsy, strong, aggressive, pro-union male employee. Rather than reflecting actual biological or social attributes of either sex, these images spoke of the ideal type of workforce that management desired for its assembly lines. The stereotype of the female worker had less to do with any traits inherent in women than with the type of workers the company sought for the manufacture of particularly competitive goods. In a move unpredicted by anybody and unfathomable by most, however, the RCA employees were about to betray their reputation for tranquillity in what one writer called "labor's giant step" into mass-production unionism.[21]

The Unionization of RCA Camden

"Industrial Camden," as the city's leaders liked to call it, was an integral part of the great manufacturing belt that stretched from the garment sweatshops of New York to the slaughterhouses of Chicago. Heading west from Camden, one would have encountered the coal mines of Pennsylvania, the heavy-current electrical workers in East Pittsburgh, the tiremakers of Akron, the burgeoning auto industry in Flint, the steel mills of Pittsburgh and Gary, and finally the meat-packing towns and steel mills of Chicago before heading into the enormous agricultural plains that fed the industrial heartland. Like Camden, many of these cities grew into industrial powerhouses in the early twentieth century. Between World War I and 1927 alone, iron and steel production in the region grew by 55 percent, autos by 178 percent, and rubber tires by 292 percent. Immense investments in fixed capital increased the amount of horsepower an employee wielded by 50 percent and allowed industrial workers to boost their hourly production by 75 percent over the course of the 1920s.[22] The new industrial workforce, often regarded as unskilled, foreign-born, and slaves to machines by the skilled craftsmen of the American Federation of Labor, remained largely peripheral to organized labor's shrinking strength and agenda throughout the 1920s and early 1930s.

Like many industrial centers across the country, however, Camden erupted in labor unrest during the mid-1930s. The women at the Congress Cigar factory rioted, the cannery industrial union at Campbell's called a strike that turned violent as workers crossed picket lines, the cleaners and dyers smashed windows in local shops, and the Industrial Union of Marine and Shipbuilding Workers of America paralyzed the New York Shipbuilding Company from May to August 1935. The most bitter and divisive conflict, however, grew out of a series of organizing efforts at the Radio Corporation of America. Placing Camden in the spotlight as a symbol of the national project of industrial unionism, the conflict became one of the pivotal strikes in the early formation of the Congress of Industrial Organizations (CIO). The repression unleashed on the RCA workers, according to participants, made the term "Jersey justice" a "byword" in the U.S. labor movement.[23]

The combined effect of the rapid, if uneven, rise of RCA's manufacturing wing and the coming of the Great Depression made the Camden works ripe for labor organizing. Most worrisome to the RCA workers during the 1930s, as to workers across the country, was job security. Even in the best of times, the seasonal nature of radio production caused worrisome swings in employment; as the Depression deepened, however, the company initiated massive layoffs, cut wage rates, required overtime while paying only straight time, and gave no assurance that employees who showed up at the plant would find work available—a particularly acute problem for the large numbers of relatively unskilled laborers. Not only female production employees were threatened. Robert Morris, an RCA employee, portrayed the problems in a letter to President Franklin Roosevelt in 1933: "Yesterday we were informed by our superintendent that we are to be replaced by boys who will work for less money. Their only choice was to agree to a wage reduction from $.51 to $.45 per hour and agree not to complain to the company union." Arguing that this move "was not in the spirit of the National Recover [sic] Act," he urged the president to take immediate action "to curb such practices unless they spread damage to what has been started in the way of restoring this nation to some degree of prosperity."[24]

To those women and men fortunate enough to have jobs, the mismanagement of the factory was almost as worrisome as the vagaries of employment. Rates of pay for similar jobs varied throughout the complex, the incentive system was poorly defined and run, and supervisors who were under pressure to increase productivity often abused the incentive system for their own ends. Exacerbating an already tense situation, the general foremen often went down to the docks to hire itinerant workers and immigrants to fill unskilled and semiskilled positions at wages even lower than those the current employees were earning. This practice further flooded the labor market, fueled competition for jobs, and lowered wages. As a result of these pressures, a variety of fragmented organizing efforts throughout the complex slowly coalesced into a dramatic standoff between the new United Electrical Workers and RCA's company union.[25]

Despite the fact that skill requirements at the radio plant were relatively low, the nucleus of the organizing effort emerged from pockets of relatively skilled workers around the plant.[26] Polish and Italian cabinetmakers launched the drive at RCA when they formed a 900-member cell of the Industrial Workers of the World (IWW) in 1932. Then, as management tried to institute a piecework system for the relatively autonomous tool and die makers—which they felt to be a disguised speedup and an infringement on their independent status—300 of them walked out of the shop in protest. Their action turned out to be so successful that they launched the Victor Shop Association (VSA) in 1933 with the intention of organizing all RCA wage earners. In a separate effort in radio test and repair, about a hundred skilled and semi-skilled employees affiliated with the growing National Radio and Allied Trades (NRAT), which, under the direction of James Carey, had been struggling unsuccessfully since 1929 to gain a charter from the American Federation of Labor. Despite Carey's pleas to launch an industrial union for the entire radio industry, all the AFL offered his group was nonvoting Class B membership in the craft-based International Brotherhood of Electrical Workers (IBEW). The AFL's hostility toward industrially based organizations left unions such as Carey's little choice but to seek alliances with radical independent electrical unions.[27]

Across the country, urban craftsmen and highly skilled industrial workers—often "native" or old-stock immigrants—opposed the drive for industrial unionism. They already felt themselves to be losing ground to the new immigrants flocking to the industrial centers across the country, and they resisted surrendering further power to them at one of their major lines of defense: the AFL and its constituent craft-based unions. The simmering conflict between craft and industrial unionism exploded not far from Camden at the AFL's convention in Atlantic City in 1935, when the rather sizable John L. Lewis of the United Mine Workers punched the even burlier defender of craft unionism, William "Big Bill" Hutcheson of the Carpenters' Union. After the brawl, Lewis marched out of the AFL and launched an alliance of progressive forces called the Committee—later Congress—of Industrial Organizations, which would rapidly become a rival to the AFL.

In an effort to check the growth and militancy of these organizing drives, RCA launched, financed, and dominated a company union called the Employees' Committee Union (ECU) in 1933.[28] The ECU gained a significant number of members among salaried and clerical employees but only a minority of production workers. RCA was far from unique in sponsoring a company union. By 1935 six to seven hundred such unions had been formed across the country, with an estimated two to three million members. About half of the workers who belonged to labor organizations in the middle of the decade, in fact, could be found in company-sponsored unions. The battle between the powerful company organization and the independent unions shaped the entire conflict over union recognition at the RCA works. Opposition from the corporation, rivalry with the company union, and the hostility of the AFL forged the fragmented organizers into an alliance, and together they formed one of the charter unions, Local 103, in the new United Electrical Workers union during its 1936 inaugural convention in snowy Buffalo, New York.[29]

Activism on all levels during 1935 and 1936 added up to one of the most important turning points in the history of organized labor in the United States, and Camden's electrical workers were at the center of the upheavals. With federal support in the form of the Wagner Act, institutional backing on the national level from the CIO, and local organizing efforts united under the UE, the prospects for unionizing the radio and electrical industry looked encouraging in the spring of 1936. A solid one-third of the workers at RCA signed on to Local 103, but further organizing efforts had been checked by the power of the company union. After three years of stalemate between the independents and the company-sponsored organization, however, changes in the national direction of the labor movement made the time right to break the standoff. On 20 May 1936, shortly after the formation of the UE, Local 103's leadership pressed for four fundamental demands: an across-the-board wage increase of 20 percent, a thirty-five-hour workweek, abolition of the company union, and a union shop contract that matched the one enjoyed by RCA's nearby competitor, Philco. The UE-RCA membership gave the negotiating committee a boost when approval of strike action to obtain these demands drew a unanimous show of hands on 13 June 1936.[30]

Five days later the company union gave the RCA workers the chance they had been looking for. Long understood to be the veiled voice of the company, the ECU posted inflammatory notices against the new UE organization, and the union leadership seized the opportunity to put heat on management by calling a sit-down strike, which they claimed shut down 80 percent of production. After only five hours, however, the union called off the strike when RCA agreed to state that it did not endorse the notices put up by the ECU, that all acts of intimidation by foremen (including forcing employees to attend ECU meetings) would end, and that the company would commence negotiations immediately. Union officials later regretted giving up control of the plant, as it soon became clear that the company only wanted to get the workers out of the factory in order to have more time to prepare for the strike. The next morning, as scores of guards took their posts at strategic points to detect and report labor unrest, the plant looked like occupied territory.[31]

The leaders of the American Federation of Labor and its affiliate, the International Brotherhood of Electrical Workers (IBEW), appear to have offered to enter into a sweetheart contract to save the company from the impending battle with the UE-CIO. The back-door proposal floated by the IBEW and endorsed by the AFL's president, William Green, allegedly assured the corporation that a contract with the IBEW would make RCA "safe from any future labor difficulty whatsoever . . . and protect the other plants of the corporation against labor organization." The craft union could marshal only the AFL's official endorsement to legitimize the contract, however, since it had no actual workers signed up. The scheme failed as militancy quickly rose at the Camden works and drove RCA to the bargaining table with the UE.[32]

Negotiations between the president of RCA's manufacturing wing in Camden and the union local rapidly collapsed, and David Sarnoff, head visionary of RCA, took over the task of dealing with the conflict from the towering new RCA office building in New York City.[33] When the union delegation arrived to discuss matters, Sarnoff attempted to demonstrate his sympathy for the workers by telling Horatio Alger stories to the labor representatives in extended detail. His account began with desperate poverty in a shtetl in tsarist Russia in 1891, progressed to the Jewish ghetto of New York, and ended, as his biographer put it, with Sarnoff as a "corpulent, immaculately dressed, manicured, barbered, massaged, chauffeur-driven, cigar-smoking corporate prince, poised and assured, a dominating presence whose steely blue eyes fixed on subordinates could bead their brows and moisten their palms." Since his tales absorbed a considerable amount of time, the UE delegates amused themselves by smoking all of Sarnoff's cigars, and when the stories ended, Carey wryly suggested that Sarnoff should have RCA-Victor record his moving epic for posterity. Although Sarnoff was one of the most respected figures in twentieth-century business history, he had no skills or experience in labor negotiations and had little to offer the leadership of Local 103 other than his ability to filibuster the unionists. He did, however, have an image to protect as a liberal business leader and an immigrant who had made good.[34]

In search of expertise in labor relations, the communications magnate turned to his friend General Hugh Johnson, former chief of the National Recovery Administration (NRA), to oversee the Camden dispute. Johnson declared to the press that Sarnoff chose him because of his "experience and a sympathetic attitude toward the labor side in such arguments"; a more likely reason was Johnson's record as an ardent fighter for an interpretation of New Deal labor legislation that would eliminate exclusive union representation, encourage the open shop, and legitimize company unions. When it came to allowing one union to represent a plant's workers under Section 7a of the National Industrial Recovery Act (NIRA) of 1933, Johnson had argued only one year earlier that "the closed shop contract on a majority vote is not a good contract." As the labor historian Melvyn Dubofsky describes it, Johnson's performance during his tenure at the NRA is reminiscent of his bungled job for Sarnoff and RCA. "The mercurial Johnson forever intruded into disputatious labor conflicts, worsening already bad situations," explains Dubofsky. "He promised trade unionists and employers mutually irreconcilable labor policies, and he persistently engendered conflicts with friends as well as enemies." Indeed, confusion reigned as to exactly what Johnson's position was regarding the UE even after his meetings with the union, with John L. Lewis of the CIO, and with the leaders of the Employees' Committee Union. In essence, the radio king and his labor adviser appeared willing to recognize the UE but not to grant exclusive bargaining rights to the left-led union.[35]

After frustrating and failed attempts to ascertain the company's actual position on the union's initiatives, the membership marched out of the Camden works just after noon on 23 June in an impressive display of solidarity that drew along many workers who had not signed up for the union. Not only did they generate a great deal of enthusiasm among the rank and file, but the project to unionize both sides of the river drew support from a variety of other locals in the area. "RCA workers are not like that pooch!" declared a Philco leader pledging solidarity with the striking workers in reference to Nipper's deference to "his master's voice." Francis McCann, of the shipbuilders' union, promised "100 percent support—both morally and financially" and predicted that the strikers would "win and make Camden a good union town." When the company asked the leaders how many workers they actually represented, however, the union responded vaguely, "The vast majority"; when asked for proof, they taunted, "The only proof we will give you is by the pickets on the street."[36] The UE local was hedging. With the 3,000 official members unanimously united behind the strike and the union's institutional framework in place from local to national levels, a major question remained: What would the remaining 6,000 workers choose to do?

To Break a Strike

The local debate over unionization took place in the public and private spaces surrounding the RCA complex and throughout the city. While the union leadership competed with the combined forces of management and the ECU for the upper hand in the strike, the battle for the hearts and minds of the workers took place in thousands of small, often extremely violent confrontations and negotiations throughout the streets and homes of Camden. The discussion hardly took place under impartial circumstances, however, as the violence fueled by strikebreakers and the company union, RCA's manipulation of electoral procedures, and the heavy hand of Camden's courts far surpassed the repression RCA workers would face at any other time or place, even Mexico.

The drama of the battle could be found in hand-to-hand combat that supplemented extended family conversations at the kitchen table about the cause of unionization at RCA. Before and after work hours, roving bands of workers and thugs attacked each other with razor blades, stones, milk bottles, heavy nuts and bolts, and cans of paint that burst open on target; workers wielded lead pipes, swung their fists, and returned the next morning to hurl eggs and pour pepper on men who dared to cross the picket line. In order to tell friends from enemies, UE members marked their foreheads with black smudges and formed their own 150-member "police" force to defend themselves against the guards hired by the company and to restrain their own members from violent reprisals against workers who crossed the picket lines. As strikers and sympathizers "brought their women folk and children" to the picket lines, the press reported, the police "tore lanes in crowds at each entrance for strikebreakers to pass." Even the audio space around the factory became a war zone as RCA executives blasted recordings over loudspeakers in efforts to drown out the speeches, catcalls, taunts, and Bronx cheers of strikers. The union countered the amplified music with a sound truck that circled the buildings, calling the strikebreakers out into the street. While many peacefully waved signs calling for a "100 percent union town, Americanism, and Unionism," the protest frequently descended into what the press called free-for-all violence, in which the "wildest disorder prevailed, with missiles flying, men shouting and women screaming." [37]

The corporation fueled existing divisions with a well-financed and illegal campaign—backed by the courts and city officials—to break the independent unionization effort. Managers imported hundreds of strikebreakers and guards (including such unsavory characters as a New York wrestler known as Big Swede and a Camden fighter locally famous as Peaches Gray). RCA had at its disposal a variety of methods to undermine the struggle as at least seventeen detective agencies offered their professional services as strikebreakers. The Sherwood Detective Agency, chosen on the recommendation of the governor of New Jersey, claimed to have left old methods of strikebreaking behind. Rather than employ force and violence—which it believed to be "passé and no longer desirable" methods of handling labor disputes—the agency attempted "to organize the community sentiment" by trailing workers home after hours for discussions, door-to-door canvassing, and the financing of radio and newspaper advertisements to "promote a friendly public attitude to support the company." All of these efforts were to be advanced through "citizens' organizations" surreptitiously assembled by the agency "to take the lead in the interest of the company" in the name of employment and community welfare. [38]

The ranks of these new-style strikebreakers turned out to be staffed by characters just as disreputable, yet not so effective, as the old brand of union busters, so RCA returned to more traditional means of labor control. Sarnoff poured $250,000 into guards, while the courts and police did their part by wantonly suppressing the workers' legal rights. [39] To get imported

"Camden Striker Subdued by Police," read the *New York Times* caption beneath this photograph in July 1936. This was just "one of the incidents," explained the *Times*, "in the labor war being waged at the RCA Manufacturing Company's plant in New Jersey." The violence and trickery sponsored by the company and the city contributed to the popularization of the term "Jersey justice" to describe anti-union activities throughout the nation during the formation of the CIO. (New York Times Pictures.)

strikebreakers and scabs into the plant, for instance, the company hired men to provoke pickets at one door so nonunion workers could be ushered in through another. The union accused RCA of importing 700 strikebreakers, hundreds of whom were in violation of the new interstate antistrikebreaking law recently signed by President Roosevelt. On many days the police hauled away hundreds of workers—both men and women—"clubbing and jailing the pickets as if they were handling so many cattle." The behavior of the police, according to the union, made it appear "as if the RCA company had purchased the City of Camden outright, and was trying to develop cowboys from the city police."[40] As RCA's own former chief investigator later explained, authorities "would grab people out of the picket line at different times, just for no good reason at all." An emergency telegram from the strike committee to John L. Lewis captured the urgency: "SITUATION SERIOUS . . . WHOLESALE ARRESTS STRIKERS DENIED ELEMENTARY CONSTITUTIONAL RIGHTS LOCAL AUTHORITIES UNITED WITH COMPANY IN SYSTEM OF TERROR AND BRUTALITY. . . . WE URGE YOUR IMMEDIATE HELP."[41]

The *New Republic* editorialized that the Camden courts and police had embarked on a "mass sacrifice for the open shop." Judge Neutze, presiding over the arrested strikers, seemed to imply exactly the same. Reflecting on strikes at Campbell's Soup and the New York Shipbuilding Yards in 1934 and 1935, he concluded that the failure of the courts to deal severely with labor unrest had only encouraged such behavior at RCA. "Now, it seems to me," he explained, "that the leniency that has been heretofore shown has developed and encouraged these very things. As long as I sit on this criminal bench, I am going to deal with such matters severely so as to discourage them. I am going to make Camden, in so far as I am able, a better place in which to live." [42]

Powers Hapgood, a CIO leader who seemed to be present at all major labor struggles in the 1930s, found himself "heartsick" during his time on the RCA picket line, where he found the people "cowed" as "hundreds of cops" escorted scabs in and out of the plant. "They pick one up here even for breathing," he wrote to his wife after he had been arrested for allegedly "inciting a riot." A federal judge found "not one iota of evidence" on which to hold Hapgood legally, and certainly nothing that warranted the bail of $5,000 set by the Camden court. Inside the jail, Hapgood observed the Camden police bloody the face of a fifteen-year-old boy who had made the mistake of shouting encouragement to the jailed protesters. The hundreds arrested over the course of the strike included not just the CIO's Hapgood and the RCA rank and file but also the UE president, James Carey; Harry Harmer, president of Local 103; and scores of shipbuilders and Philco workers. [43]

Women were clearly present during the month of strike activities, but it is difficult to assess the level of their engagement. The fact that female employees faced "sweatshop conditions" was cited as the reason many were on strike, but the UE leadership—one of the most progressive unions in respect to gender relations—was exclusively male. The core of the strike effort remained in the hands of the skilled workers, but arrest lists showed that one-fourth or more of the people arrested at any given time could be women, and some melees were all-female affairs. The union was not above taking advantage of the violence against women to increase its support. Several women had their clothes ripped off as they attempted to enter the plant in the early days of the strike. The union exploited the situation by sending female union members into the factory with their bathing suits on underneath their clothing in order to impress upon female scabs the danger of being disrobed by strikers the next time they entered the factory. Yet the underhanded strategies of management, according to the union, seemed more repugnant than those attempted by the union. Many "girls" became "so disgusted with the tactics of the company that they walked off the job, went to union headquarters and joined Local 103." The number of women committed to the UE functioned as a gauge of the solidarity of support among the RCA employees. "The strike is well in hand. We are winning!" exclaimed the UE leadership. "Listen to the girls singing on the picket lines."[44]

Fear of Flying

Violence and physical intimidation were not the only weapons in RCA's arsenal—the company's threat to move its investment elsewhere hung over the entire episode. Although at the time it could easily be dismissed as mere posturing, the threat was a constant element in RCA's strategy to break Local 103. The warnings emerged as early as the second day of the strike when Elmer T. Cunningham, president of RCA's manufacturing division, proclaimed in a full-page advertisement in the *Philadelphia Record*, "We want to keep our plants open—we want to continue to provide gainful employment for thousands of families in this area . . . we want the citizens and merchants of the Camden-Philadelphia area to continue to benefit from our industrial activity." Compliance with the union's demands, however, would "result in serious loss to employees, their community and company," as it would lead to "the closing of the Company's plant within a few months . . . the responsibility for which we decline to assume." Despite RCA's posting of over $6.1 million in net profits in 1936, the company appeared to be willing to go to extreme measures to prevent the unionization of the Camden works.[45]

Then the ECU, in its role as company spokesman once removed, took over the threat to abandon the city. The organization issued public pleas to RCA not to remove the cabinet shop and photophone divisions from Camden, as it claimed to have "discovered" the company planned to do. By the middle of the strike the ECU listed machines with removal tags attached that were on their way to the shipping platform, and a variety of major subcontracting efforts that were also under way. In a bizarre twist, the ECU even accused the UE of seeking to encourage the removal of RCA from Camden by "importing shock troops to create disorders which are supposed to influence city commissioners to close the plant and perhaps drive RCA to another community." As the strike dragged on, the threats became more immediate. "Certain departments such as Cabinets, Screw Machine, Punch Press, Coils and others will be eliminated unless you soon return," read an ECU flyer. "RCA now has 7 purchasing agents touring the country lining up factories to make these parts." There is no evidence, however, that the workers or the UE leadership took these threats seriously. More immediate concerns, from heated labor negotiations to street riots, made such abstractions only minor threats in an overwhelming wave of anti-unionism.[46]

One of the reasons the UE activists could hold their ground was the solidarity of what was becoming a union town. In particular, thousands of Camden shipbuilders and UE workers at Philco lent strong support. In correspondence between the editor of the *Camden Courier-Post* and a federal mediator, for instance, the editor explained that although the company believed it had "licked" the union—thousands were rumored to have returned to work—he believed the UE would never give up because of the support and pressure from other area unions. The growing symbolic power of the strike to the expanding labor movement in the area and the Philco workers' eagerness to see their competition organized led the editor to see no chance that Local 103 would return with "its tail between its legs." The company's resolve remained equally strong, however, leaving the federal mediator to conclude that they were headed for "a state of anarchy in Camden and perhaps Philadelphia." The editor concurred; he saw "nothing but violence ahead" and feared that "in the end troops would have to be brought in."[47]

After four weeks of false arrests, violence, intimidation, brutality, and threats of relocation, the stalemate finally broke when the company and the union settled on an election sponsored by the National Labor Relations Board (NLRB). John L. Lewis, who had been negotiating with Johnson throughout the conflict, reached an agreement with RCA just as both the company and the union appeared to be weakening. Four thousand of the 9,700 employees had crossed the picket line when the strike finally ended, and the UE had dropped all its original demands except for exclusive representation of the workers at RCA. As for the company, its name and reputation had been dragged through the mud as the national press made it clear it was sponsoring a company union and engaging in a variety of violent strikebreaking activities. Moreover, RCA's main competitor, Philco, continued to produce and sell radios under a union contract while RCA battled with its workers. The two parties compromised on two particularly sticky issues: Local 103 won the rehiring of strikers without discrimination as to union affiliation and RCA was allowed to keep the company union on the NLRB ballot.[48]

RCA and General Johnson signed the agreement in bad faith, however, for the company and its labor organization continued to do everything in their power to sabotage the vote. The ECU and management launched what James Carey later branded as "a vicious campaign of intimidation" against workers in an effort to force a boycott of the election. Such initiatives exacerbated existing tensions on the shop floor, which was still the scene of "free-for-all fighting" and "rough house with hair pulling, scratching and kicking" between women who had been on the picket line and those who had crossed over to work during the strike. Even election day was carefully staged to management's advantage. Movie cameras filmed everyone who voted, the election was held during a workday so that workers who left the plant to cast ballots could be identified, and, with the violence of the strike fresh in the workers' minds, the ECU's broadsides tried to keep them from the polls by claiming that the election "means violence, bloodshed and perhaps loss of life . . . it means rioting, street fighting and general disorder."[49]

The threat that all or part of the great Camden works would close down and move if the UE were to win switched from a minor theme during the strike to a central strategy before the union vote. "Due to outside contracts entered into by reason of the recent strike," claimed Thomas D. Nessler, secretary of the ECU, the company "projected removal to other locations of several key divisions to prevent repetition of last month's fiasco." He estimated that Camden workers would soon be permanently deprived of close to 2,000 well-paid jobs. "Lay-offs already have started," he proclaimed, "and certain sections will be closed as soon as shipments from outside vendors begin to slow." As the NLRB election approached, ECU handbills promised that "A VOTE TOMORROW MEANS LESS JOBS FOR US IN CAMDEN."[50]

The company's campaign to keep workers from the polls worked almost flawlessly: only the UE faithful dared to turn out for the certification election. Of the 9,752 workers eligible, only 3,163 cast ballots—95 percent of them for UE Local 103.[51] Despite the overwhelming majority of votes for Local 103, the clever words of RCA's agreement with the UE denied the union its victory: the sole bargaining agent would be the candidate that received the majority of the votes "of all those *eligible* to vote in such election."[52] RCA's strategy of keeping the majority of workers from the polls therefore succeeded in denying the UE what it needed to win: a majority of all those qualified to vote.

Fortunately for the United Electrical Workers, the agreement also called for the NLRB to oversee the election, leaving the board with the ultimate authority over the interpretation of the results. The year 1936 happened to be a uniquely progressive and pragmatic period in the development of the National Labor Relations Board, and in a surprise decision it favored the UE over the company. The NLRB ruled that the ECU had set out "to defeat the purposes of the election" through its boycott, and that the Wagner Act required only that the winning party receive the votes of a "majority of the employees," not a majority of those eligible to vote. Arguing that "those not voting are presumed to acquiesce in the choice of the majority who do vote," the board took aim at the strategy of the ECU: "Minority organizations by waging a campaign of terrorism and intimidation could keep enough employees from participating to thwart certification. Employers could adopt a similar strategy and thereby deprive their employees of representation for collective bargaining." Of particular note to the board were the ECU's circulars threatening further violence for those who dared to participate in the election. On 9 November 1936 the NLRB therefore certified the United Electrical Workers' Local 103 as the sole bargaining agent for the production workers at RCA in Camden, New Jersey.[53]

And still RCA did not give up its fight against the independent organization of the Camden complex. Still advised by Johnson, RCA, like many other employers in the 1930s, refused to accept the NLRB's findings in the hope that the Supreme Court would shortly overturn the Wagner Act on constitutional grounds. The ECU even went so far as to try to bully the NLRB in its runaway shop campaign by claiming that "if any attempt is made to enforce this decision, RCA has declared that it will REMOVE ALL ACTIVITIES FROM CAMDEN." While the company stalled in expectation of rescue by the Court, tensions continued on the shop floor, where "industrial guerrilla warfare" between the UE and the ECU continued for months. Work stoppages, strife between opposing workers on the same line, and sporadic violence plagued the plant. Exacerbating an already difficult situation was a decline in demand that slowed the rehiring of the striking workers. And, in an effort to crush activism, the company refused to rehire the promised five hundred foreign-born strikers who had been particularly active in the strike. In response to City Hall's demand that the Immigration Bureau investigate the foreign-born workers, Local 103's president, Harry Harmer, exclaimed, "As long as the foreign-born citizens slaved away in the plant of the RCA Manufacturing Company, [city prosecutor John] Reiners had nothing to say about deportation proceedings, but now that the workers are on strike for decent living conditions, they suddenly become undesirable aliens." [54]

Contrary to the hopes of business leaders across the country and the expectations of many others, the Supreme Court sustained the constitutionality of the Wagner Act by a slim margin in April 1937. Prodded by the parade of militant workers to the CIO, Roosevelt's 1936 landslide victory, and the president's threats to enlarge the Court with his own appointees, the justices broke with precedent to render a ruling that fundamentally changed the course of U.S. labor law. They based their decision on the "stream of commerce" doctrine, which states that since industrial production enters the flow of interstate trade, industrial relations are subject to federal regulation. By the time manufacturing entered the stream of *international* commerce in an important way in later decades, however, it would be much more difficult to apply that logic to a transnational regime of labor regulations. [55]

Blocked by the dogged determination and organizational power of the UE local, its national leadership, the support of other unions in the area, and the labor movement's pivotal support from the Wagner Act, the NLRB, and the Supreme Court, Sarnoff finally capitulated to the UE in August 1937—well over a year after the union demanded a collective bargaining contract with the company. In place of General Johnson he selected Edward F. McGrady, former legislative representative for the AFL and former assistant secretary of labor in the Roosevelt administration. McGrady moved rapidly to reverse the

course and tenor of labor relations in Camden. Although a successful nego-
tiator who did not concede anything easily to Local 103, McGrady, unlike his
predecessor, bargained in good faith and ultimately signed a collective bargaining agreement with the union in October 1937. James Matles, the radical
UE leader who helped the RCA rank-and-file committee negotiate the contract, movingly described the uproar at the contract ratification meeting at
the Camden Armory:

> Quite a scene. And quite a meeting. The president of Local 103 [Harry
> Harmer], chairman of the negotiating committee, reported on the agree-
> ment article by article, each one punctuated by prolonged cheers. He had
> to ask constantly for quiet in order to proceed. One minute, thunderous
> cheers in the air. The next minute, absolute quiet, so everyone could hear
> what came next. Finally he announced reinstatement of the five hundred
> fired strikers, news which just about tore the roof off. Then the president
> added: All strikers would be going back to their jobs with full back pay for
> the months they were out. Pandemonium, nothing but, broke out at that
> point.[56]

The contract included all of the fundamentals of collective bargaining: layoffs, transfers, and rehirings would be determined by seniority; work sharing preceded layoffs; grievance and arbitration procedures were instituted;
and, most important, the company agreed not to deal with any other labor
organization, not even the company union. The contract also pledged "as
high wages, under as favorable hours and working conditions, as prevail in
the Camden-Philadelphia manufacturing establishments engaged in similar
classes of work" and a thirty-six-hour week, which placed the RCA workers
on an even footing with the employees of the Philco plant. The contract was
an absolute victory for the membership of UE Local 103. Two years later, furthermore, the AFL-affiliated IBEW and the company union joined forces to
try to oust the UE again, but this time, under a fair and free election, the UE
won with 84 percent of the vote.[57]

Forced by organized labor and the state to accept collective bargaining after doing almost everything possible, legal and illegal, to defeat it, RCA embarked on a two-pronged labor strategy. The first approach to the problem,
as the appointment of McGrady suggests, was the complete acceptance of
collective bargaining in Camden. The UE leadership gave McGrady, who
stayed on as vice president in charge of labor relations until 1951, "unanimous approval" because of his unqualified acceptance of organized labor's
role in industrial production, his inclusion of labor leaders in a variety of decisions, and his desire to keep the channels of communication open between
management and labor at all times. Moreover, the company did not try to

block efforts to organize nonproduction workers. The truck drivers, mechanics, and helpers organized first under the UE, then under the Teamsters; the technicians joined together under the American Federation of Technical Engineers; and even the plant engineers organized as the Association of Scientists and Professional Engineering Personnel.[58]

The reason RCA felt it could afford to accept the unionization of the Camden works, and the second and most dramatic component of the company's two-part strategy, was its determination to make good on its threat to move production out of Camden. The institutional memory among managers recorded the strategy as waving the white flag and running. An RCA plant manager a generation removed from the events in Camden recalled that General Sarnoff was "a very, very fine man, who loved his employees and wanted the best for all of his employees," but found the strike very "distasteful." The word went through the personnel department that the UE workers constituted "a bad portion" within the RCA family, and that management had no choice but "to make the peace at any price"—to bring in McGrady and recognize the union. "Of course," he continued, "you can't have that, you gotta have what's right." So the company decided to relocate home instruments production "as an easy way of sidestepping" the problem. "If we couldn't fix [it]," he concluded, "we moved."[59]

The Regional Division of Labor

The result of Camden's transformation from a "city of contented industries" to a union town resulted in a wholesale dispersal of competitive consumer electronics production out of Camden. In the mid-1930s, when the struggle between RCA and the union began, Camden accounted for all of RCA's manufacturing operations except for a small vacuum-tube plant in Harrison, New Jersey, which had been open since 1929. Ten years after the strike, the South Jersey city produced only one-fourth of the total dollar value of RCA's manufacturing output. Before, during, and after World War II, all products that allowed for high-volume and low-cost mass-production techniques—radios, television sets, phonographs, records, projectors, tapes, cabinetry, and various components—were shifted away from the banks of the Delaware. Records went to Hollywood in 1942; the cabinet shop shifted to Pulaski, Virginia, in 1947; tubes moved to Lancaster, Pennsylvania, in 1940; a small motion picture equipment shop opened in Detroit, and car radios went to a short-lived plant in Chicago. The bulk of household electronics production went to several plants in Indiana. A component plant opened in Indianapolis in 1936, a radio plant in Bloomington in 1940, a tube plant in Marion in 1942, and a cabinet shop in Monticello. Of the nearly 10,000 jobs involved in consumer electronics during the 1930s, only 700 remained in Camden by 1953.[60]

Today many analysts refer to the movement of assembly jobs from the center of the world economy to developing nations as the "new international division of labor."[61] What developed out of the economic changes, the political struggles, and the expansion and diversification of production at RCA can be regarded as an earlier but parallel regional division of labor. Camden became the center for declining numbers of high-tech, high-wage, male, and government-financed defense and aerospace communications production, largely insulated from the competitive economy but vulnerable to the flows of postwar public spending. The Midwest, much like the Mexican border decades later, became a low-wage region for the production of competitive-sector, female-made consumer electronics equipment.

For RCA workers, the shift in production was almost invisible at first, as it was replaced by the $1.5 billion in defense procurements pumped into Camden during World War II. RCA alone won contracts for $7.5 million in radio receivers and other communications equipment. By 1942, nearly 100 percent of the company's production staff was engaged in defense production. Far from a calamity, the period of relocation was actually one of unprecedented prosperity as the boom in defense production drew 44,000 additional people into Camden's shipyards and manufacturing establishments.[62] Women assembly workers, whose jobs were to build goods destined for an extremely competitive market and therefore were the first to be shipped out of South Jersey, could readily find even better positions in defense work as men left to fight overseas.

Although the defense boom temporarily masked much of the impact of the decentralization of consumer electronics production, at the end of World War II the problem become painfully obvious. In 1948, after postwar layoffs had come to an end and reconversion was complete, Local 103 remained "deeply concerned with the amount of work which is being transferred to other RCA shops or to sub-contractors" but had little means to combat it. As the union was well aware, movement of production allowed both lower wages and greater management control over production. The UE's informal survey of the new RCA shops indicated that in Indiana, for instance, testing on television sets could be done twice as quickly as the work rules allowed in Camden and at a wage that was 46 cents per hour less. Repairs in Indianapolis ran at a rate 30 percent higher than in New Jersey, but unskilled female assembly operatives in Camden made $1.46 per hour, significantly more than the skilled male repair workers in Indianapolis, who earned only $1.11. Such savings in wages and production rates lured many jobs away from industrial Camden. "Large-scale layoffs at the Camden Plant of RCA-Victor have seriously affected the entire community," the union reported to the mayor.

"Cutbacks at the plant have imposed hardships on the families of the un-employed, have sharply decreased the business of our merchants and have increased the burden placed on our welfare agencies." During a period of rapidly expanding employment for the company as a whole, Local 103 had dwindled to 5,500 members by October 1949 from a prewar high of nearly 10,000 workers and a wartime peak of 13,000.[63]

What remained in Camden were high-technology communication goods for military purposes and research and production on new products that re-quired higher levels of skill.[64] "The RCA plant in Camden will devote most of its capacity to turning out transmitters, studio equipment, communication apparatus, and other electronic products," announced Meade Bruenet, vice president in charge of the Engineering Products Department. "Receiver manufacturing will be carried forward largely in the company plants at Indi-anapolis and Bloomington, Ind." In essence, all that would be left at the Cam-den works would be the "high technology engineering-oriented businesses." Unfortunately, this production had "comparatively modest space require-ments as compared with the consumer products for which the plant was originally intended," recalled one executive, so that the company ended up with "more space than we need."[65]

The high-technology end of RCA continued to sustain the reduced Cam-den works through much of the postwar period. Production ebbed and flowed along with the tides of Cold War spending to include satellite com-munications, the coordination of the Ballistic Missile Early Warning System, and a variety of projects for the National Aeronautics and Space Agency. Tele-vision manufacturing and broadcast, however, continued to be the company's bread and butter.

The new spatial division of labor may have helped to place RCA in a strate-gic position to avoid the massive postwar strike wave that rocked the country. As workers sought job security and wages lost between the squeeze of infla-tion and the controls set by the National War Labor Board, the UE demanded a wage hike of $2 a day in January 1946 at all of the major electrical firms— General Electric, Westinghouse, the electrical division of General Motors, and, of course, RCA. The battle turned fierce and protracted. In pivotal strikes that shaped the postwar settlement in the electrical sector, GE work-ers settled for an increase of 18 cents an hour after almost two months on strike; Westinghouse workers stayed out another two months for 19 cents. Raises for women electrical workers were often the sticking points. As 200,000 electrical workers across the nation pounded the pavement for a raise in early 1946, however, RCA workers got their raise of 17 cents an hour (retroactive to October) without a strike. The corporation could afford to give raises to its most skilled workers in Camden, where "constructive and peaceful" collective bargaining became a central institution, while it farmed out labor-intensive work to the hinterlands, where organizing efforts remained in their infancy.[66]

The regional division of labor also recast the sexual division of labor. Having betrayed their "cheapness" by endorsing a union contract and having undermined their "docility" by partaking in street battles during the strike, Camden women would be replaced with female workers from rural Indiana. In contrast to the national trend, few jobs were open to Rosie the Riveter in an RCA defense plant; there the percentage of women workers actually declined dramatically during the war. By July 1942, although the plant employed 11,774 production workers, only 3,381 were women—a decline to 29 percent from a high of 75 percent only six years earlier. The slack in "female" work was taken up by the midwestern plants, where the proportion of female employees equaled that of Depression-era Camden. At the new Bloomington plant, for instance, 80 percent of the workers were women in the 1940s. By the spring of 1946, women workers in Camden had been reduced to 31 percent of the 6,500 employees; the employment level of women at the Camden complex continued to dwindle to a mere 20 percent of the manufacturing force by 1962.[67]

None of these developments was lost on Local 103. Acutely aware that their best hope for survival lay in organizing the runaway shops, the rank and file pressured the UE to organize the new factories in the RCA chain in order to check the company's tactic of "farming out work to unorganized shops." The UE reported back to the Camden local that union representatives had established contacts with workers at both the Bloomington and Indianapolis plants. "It is too early to tell yet how successful a campaign can be launched," reported the field organizer from Indiana after the war, but he hoped "the UE policy of getting into RCA everywhere and staying there until the organization is completed holds true for these plants." Despite the UE's best efforts to follow production westward, the union would not have a direct role in the changing social relations of RCA's investments in Indiana. The internal logic of industrial capitalism itself, however, would transform the cultural content and labor traditions in the locations to which RCA fled.[68]

The Camden workers' demand to be respected as bargaining partners had the ironic result of pushing the company onward in search of cheaper and more docile labor supplies. David Roediger's succinct portrayal of the NAFTA-era crisis in labor relations, in which corporate flight has "tended to redefine the labor problem as one to be solved in space (by moving) rather than in time (by responding to labor's demands)," clearly had precedents. As the social geographer Doreen Massey argues, "spatial structures are established, reinforced, combated and changed through political and economic strategies and battles on the part of mangers, workers and political representatives." The making of RCA's regional division of labor must therefore be understood in the light of the power its workers wielded over the politics of production in one particular place and the company's ability to escape the geographic confines of Camden and the entire industrial Northeast. The economic terrain of world development—the "mosaic of unevenness," according to the geographers Michael Storper and Richard Walker—provided ample locations for solving local problems and subverting local struggles while hiding the consequences of community forms of resistance.[69]

Camden Aftermath

When scholars and activists examine the decline of one of the most dynamic and radical unions in the United States, the United Electrical Workers, they typically direct their attention to the "orgy of interunion conflict" sponsored by the Cold War. Concerned about communist influence in the UE, particularly among two of its leaders, Julius Empsak and James Matles, President James Carey bolted from the union and, with the gleeful endorsement of the CIO leadership, launched the International Union of Electrical Workers (IUE) as a right-wing alternative to the left-led UE. Workers were forced to decide whether they belonged to a "red" union or an "American" union as elections were called at electrical plants across the country. The right- and left-wing electrical unions won about equal numbers of certification and re-certification elections in 1950 NLRB polling, but as plants of the same company voted for different unions, "a crazy quilt of bargaining" divided and weakened the electrical workers. As working-class power in the electrical industry fragmented under the pressures of anticommunism, the once creative and militant UE fell from about 500,000 workers in the late 1940s to only 58,000 by 1960.

The right/left split among electrical workers also bitterly divided the RCA workers between 1949 and 1952. In the 1950 contest between the two unions at the Camden works, the IUE received 2,857 votes to the UE's 2,532, edging out the left-led union with 52 percent of the vote. Right-wing unions raided the other three RCA plants under UE contracts as well. The factories in Hollywood, California, and Lancaster, Pennsylvania, went to the craft-based IBEW, and the cabinet shop in Pulaski, Virginia, went to the IUE. By the end of 1950, the UE had no members who worked for the Radio Corporation of America.[70]

The Cold War–politics explanation of the fragmenting of labor's power in the postwar period, however powerful, must be supplemented by an interpretation that takes into account capital's command of the spatial economy. The regional division of labor that RCA launched in the late 1930s and 1940s had sown the seeds of the UE's eventual decline years before the employees of

RCA workers in Camden rally in favor of the United Electrical Workers over the anticommunist International Union of Electrical Workers in late 1949 or early 1950. Once the third largest union in the CIO and the most powerful left-wing institution in the country, the UE was nearly destroyed during the raids launched by the IUE after World War II. (UE Archives, University of Pittsburgh, copyright *UE News*.)

the electrical giant succumbed to the ugliness of red-baiting. With the financial core of the company moved elsewhere, the bargaining power of the remaining workers in New Jersey was radically reduced. Between layoffs and the fear of losing the government contracts on which the complex had become dependent, the RCA workers lost most of their hard-earned power; for management, the Camden works "ceased to be an Achilles' heel for strike action." Clearly, as Nelson Lichtenstein shows, in the postwar period "shop-floor activism atrophied, union bureaucracy flourished, and the power of management renewed itself." In seeking to explain these developments fully, however, we must look beyond the politics of state and shop floor and turn our attention to the broadest geographic terrain of industrial conflict.[71]

Moreover, it was not just RCA that was in decline; nearly every major industry in Camden had shut down or relocated by the late postwar period. In the 1950s, Highland Mills, Armstrong Cork, Howland Croft, Allied Kid,

Quaker Shipyard, and the C. Howard Hunt Pen Company had all abandoned or announced plans to relocate out of the city. The New York shipyard permanently shut down in 1967, partly as a result of "labor-management bitterness," and, between automation and a new plant in California, Local 80-A of the Packinghouse Workers at Campbell's Soup lost 1,500 members between 1957 and 1962. RCA, in fact, actually lingered longer than many firms. Although plagued by constant layoffs as the corporation won and lost defense contracts, the high-tech RCA workers continued to number in the upper five thousands until the 1960s, when the IUE membership fell to 3,700 members. "Things are shaky all over Camden RCA. . . . They're laying off people right and left," worried Local 103's president, Ed Checkley, in 1969. "We feel that RCA is expanding at the expense of the people here in Camden who made the company what it is." By 1975 the company had torn down or donated many of its buildings to Rutgers University; all that was left by 1975 was what the press described as a "think tank" amid the urban decay.[72]

Like other abandoned industrial monuments of the great CIO-era battles across the rust belt, several of the once-sprawling series of red-brick buildings still stand near the banks the Delaware River, now vacant, floating like an enormous postindustrial carcass in a sea of poverty. Panes of glass are broken and missing from the lightless, stained-glass image of Nipper that once beamed the company's logo all the way across the river to Philadelphia. The lifelessness even permeates the surrounding area: houses are boarded up, bars are permanently shut, and one of the worst unemployment rates in the country places Camden on the list of the ten most desperate cities in the nation. Deindustrialization has had an impact on Camden's racial climate as well. Fifty percent of the city's population today are African Americans. These are workers or the children of workers who migrated north to take advantage of the wartime demand for labor, but they arrived just as the industrial train was leaving the station. "A drive through the city is nightmarish," wrote a reporter in 1979. "Block after block of crumbling homes, an occasional black or elderly white face staring out a cracked window. Vacant lots. Interminable junkyards. A few hundred yards from a church, a pile of human waste from an unfinished sewage treatment plant; the stench has made people in nearby homes sick." In contrast, the white ethnic working-class identity that fueled much of the organization of the CIO has melted into the affluence and homogeneity of the suburbs.[73]

"I dream'd in a dream I saw a city invincible to the attacks of the whole of the rest of the earth," wrote Camden's most famous and optimistic resident, Walt Whitman, about the city in which he lived out his final years.[74] Confirming the poet's faith in the South Jersey city, today among the ashes of the RCA complex the state has fanned a small high-tech operation into an ember that may someday rekindle Camden's economic flames. By 1994, Lockheed Martin, a firm several corporate buyouts removed from its original incarnation as RCA, employed 1,100 defense and aerospace contract workers. The corporation's presence in Camden, however, was dependent on $13 million in county money and $21 million in state funds granted on the condition that the work would stay put.[75] The huge investment in the small number of aerospace jobs has had little relevance to the majority of the residents of Camden today. The high-tech employees carefully flee to the safety of the suburbs through the empty and silent streets that once rang to the clash of the electrical workers' battles with the company. Visitors even have trouble finding Lockheed Martin's small, glimmering building nestled in the shadow of the tower on which Nipper, now blackened and missing panes, still responds to his master's voice above the deserted red-brick complex of former RCA factories.

CHAPTER TWO

"Anything but an Industrial Town": Bloomington, 1940-1968

Bob Doty looked as though he had just fallen in a flour bin. Stationed above the pulverizing jaws on the big crusher, he picked out the mud, lost drill heads, and other articles that would destroy the machine if they got caught in the mechanical jaws that converted rock into marketable lime dust. Like many workers in southern Indiana's stone belt, he carried a collapsible aluminum cup into which the water boy could pour relief from the hot and dirty work. On one of the boy's passages, Doty accepted his water ration and began to roll a cigarette for himself. As he put tobacco to paper, however, the overseer barked, "You ain't got time to be rolling cigarettes. Buy hard rolls."

One cross word led to another. The nineteen-year-old Doty was not about to let the foreman push him around.

"You see all them guys standing right out there across the creek there by the office?" the boss demanded. "They're every one wanting your job."

It was 1939, toward the end of the Great Depression, and Doty's patience had worn thin with the ten-hour days, meager pay, no overtime, and even less respect. "Mr. Dobson," he responded, "you'd better get one of them because I'm going home right now. . . . You can mail my check because I'll not even come after it. That's just how much I think of you and this outfit."

Doty knew the economic hardships he faced without a job during the hard times that plagued rural Indiana, but "I was always standing up for my own rights, I always have been. I guess I'd argue with the President if I thought he was wrong." [1]

During the latter half of the 1930s, at the same time the Camden workers' struggles helped to transform the course of U.S. labor relations in the twentieth century, limestone workers in southern Indiana were fighting for simple dignity and survival. Even in the late 1930s, Monroe County had an un-employment rate above 40 percent, one of the highest foreclosure rates in the state, and one of the largest percentages of people dependent on relief in the nation.[2] Finding the coffers empty, the state government abdicated all responsibility for relief, with the exception of some administrative costs, to the local and federal governments. Facing no alternative, Doty turned for as-sistance to the amalgam of programs that made up the New Deal.

Born in 1920, he managed to get through a few years of high school "but didn't have the money for clothing and for books and stuff like that" and had to support his father "to the best of my ability, which," he confessed, "wasn't very good." Hoping to find a position with the Works Progress Administra-tion (WPA) when he left high school, he was disappointed to learn that the agency was hiring only people with families to support. He then turned to the refuge of many young people during the 1930s, the Civilian Conservation Corps, where he spent the maximum allowable two years, from 1937 to 1939. From there Doty moved on to the stone mill. After his run-in with the fore-man, he finally managed to land a WPA job, cutting and laying limestone for the community and cleaning the roads and ditches of southern Indiana. "We did a lot of good," he recalled of his work for the WPA, but he endured fre-quent layoffs because he was single and there were workers with families to feed. Drifting from odd job to odd job after leaving the limestone mill, Doty, along with over two million other young people, ultimately gained a slot in the vocational training program of the National Youth Administration (NYA). There he hoped to acquire the skills necessary to become a machin-ist.[3] He never enrolled in the New Deal program, however, for the struggles of the Camden workers delivered new opportunities to Bloomington.

"One of the greatest forward advances in the history of the city" appeared to relieve the community's otherwise dismal employment picture in Febru-ary 1940, when the local press announced plans for the opening of a Radio Corporation of America factory. Presenting the new venture as a grand "op-portunity to many now on the pittance of WPA payrolls," the city leaders pro-jected that the plant would provide for permanent income, create a demand for new homes, bring economic stability to the community, and draw other national corporations to the area. According to the local papers, which filled the entire front pages with the news, the new plant promised to pull Monroe County out of the Great Depression and to create "A New Bloomington!"[4]

Recruited by a reinvigorated chamber of commerce and aided by the gov-ernor's efforts to relieve the acute unemployment situation in south-central Indiana, RCA moved into the three-block-long space abandoned by the fal-tering Shower Brothers Furniture Company's cabinet shop on the southwest corner of town. Unwilling even to consider a gift of money or land, the cor-poration was determined to pay its own way in order to deserve the "good will of Bloomington people." Pouring $3 million into renovation of the old cabinet works, the company planned to employ between 800 and 1,000 local workers.[5] The reality, however, would be much more dramatic and meaningful to the history of Bloomington. The arrival of RCA in 1940 not only saved many families from destitution; it launched a dramatic departure from Monroe County's earlier path of economic development as the factory grew to employ more than 8,000 workers by the 1960s and became the industrial core of southern Indiana.

One of the thousands who signed up at the new plant was Bob Doty. The first day he reported for work, the personnel director told him to sit on a bench and wait to be called. By noon, when nobody had said anything to him and he had done no work at all, he gave up and walked home. The next day, however, his family doctor, who had become the new physician for RCA, came out to his house to find out why he had left. When Doty had explained the situation, the doctor said, "Get cleaned up and get your clothes on. I'll take you down there. You've got a job. . . . They was paying you yesterday."[6]

In an era when, as Doty described it, "you couldn't buy a job," the number of men lingering outside the gates of the stone mill waiting for someone to be fired or to quit on that day in late 1939 remained a haunting testimonial to the scarcity of employment in southern Indiana and across the country. Being paid by a major corporation to sit and simply wait only a few months later indicated a fundamental change for Bloomington. For decades to come, workers remembered that it was RCA *and* World War II that pulled Bloomington out of the Depression.

Bloomington before RCA

Clearly what made Bloomington so attractive to the corporation was the population's desperation for work. The core of the economic crisis could be found in the way the Depression severed the linkages that generations of Monroe County workers had with the land that nurtured the hardwoods they converted into furniture, produced the crops they ate and marketed, and harbored the stone they cut into building material. The processing of the area's natural resources would never support a significant portion of Monroe County's labor force after the 1930s, but the story had been much different only a decade earlier. Just five years before the stock market crashed in 1929, the Bloomington press optimistically announced that "with Showers [Furniture Company] spending a million dollars and moving scores of new families to Bloomington, with Indiana University spending hundreds of thousands, and with the stone belt developing a great national market for its product, the coming year promises to be the best which has ever fallen to Bloomington."[7]

Showers Brothers Furniture Company, which inhabited a sprawling complex of factories in downtown Bloomington, had grown from a small woodworking shop that made coffins during the Civil War to what its secretary-treasurer claimed to be the largest furniture factory in the world by 1913. Vertically integrated—"From the tree to the trade" was the company's slogan—Showers became the industrial center of Bloomington as it expanded from one plant in 1910 to four distinct operations by 1919. By 1929, Showers's payroll pumped over $1.5 million into the community each year. The Depression "tore savagely" into this core of Bloomington, however, as the 1932 annual payroll fell to less than 28 percent of the 1929 figure. Per capita income from furniture making in the Bloomington area declined from a high of $1,430 in 1926 to a mere $516 in 1934 as the number of hours worked was cut and the hourly wage crumbled. The average number of days worked per month sank to a mere eight, while the hourly wage tumbled from 48 cents to 22 cents. The number of workers at the furniture factory continued to decline throughout the 1930s to a low of 393 in 1939, or less than one-fourth of the furniture makers employed in the 1920s. For six months in 1938, the entire complex and its workers lay completely idle. Townspeople of a variety of economic backgrounds agreed that the major owners of Showers Brothers paid themselves large dividends rather than reinvest in the plant. After the company analyzed the shift of the furniture industry to the South, Showers decided against trying to compete with factories employing cheaper labor in North Carolina and finally closed its doors for the last time in 1954.[8]

Another economic pillar of Monroe County, the limestone industry, did not fare much better than the furniture sector. When the railroad reached Bloomington in 1853, it allowed the rich deposits of limestone, which lay in a concentrated five-mile-wide band stretching thirty miles southward from Bloomington, to be shipped out to distant markets. With limestone of quality unequaled elsewhere in the Midwest, the Indiana stone belt grew to supply over 80 percent of all the building stone used in the United States by the 1920s. Executives at the quarries and mills estimated that peak employment during the mid-1920s at times reached as many as 5,000 workers, and with labor scarce, wages crept steadily upward. By the end of the 1930s, however, employment in the stone industry had all but collapsed; only 503 workers remained at the mills and quarries of Monroe County. Further pinched by the moratorium on nonessential building during World War II, the industry had ground virtually to a halt by 1942. The only commodity of any value that emerged from the stone belt during the war was excess machinery that could be sold for junk or converted to defense use.[9]

Even the land could no longer produce the crops that once sustained the local farm families. Located at the southern terminus of the vast Mitchell

Workers in southern Indiana's limestone belt break blocks after a quarry channeling machine (upper right) cuts the stone. The limestone industry, a furniture company, and Indiana University formed the core of the region's economy before RCA arrived. At the depths of the Depression, however, well over half of the quarries that had been operating in 1926 had shut down. (Indiana Limestone Institute of America, Inc.)

Plain and the breadbasket of Indiana, the wild hills and rocky land of Monroe County never developed much beyond subsistence agriculture. The small plots carved between the wooded hills and deep ravines stood in dramatic contrast to the vastly more productive land just to the north. As one novelist described the terrain, "it was a countryside neither rugged nor savage . . . only ragged, desolate, unkempt, cold . . . neither completely wild nor completely cultivated."[10] The government concurred, finding that "many of the so-called farmers are at the subsistence level," working "submarginal" plots of land. Monroe County farmers also faced severe erosion problems caused by decades of overuse and the cutting of trees to supply the furniture industry. Their problems compounded by the challenges offered by the more easily mechanized and capital-intensive forms of agriculture on the plains, locals found they could not compete in an already glutted agricultural market. As a spokesman for the Purdue University Department of Agricultural Economics explained, "The southern section of the State has the poorer resources and consequently the folks with lower incomes, lower levels of living, and communities and institutions of less acceptable standards."[11]

Rural families continued to identify themselves as farmers throughout the first few decades of the twentieth century, but they looked increasingly to industry for their cash. Farming was an activity for the end of the day, after working hours, and during layoffs. By the onset of the Depression, wage labor had replaced agricultural work as the mainstay of the local economy, and farms were reduced to "a few acres of corn and other crops, or more frequently, simply to a garden to provide for personal needs." As the state employment service explained and RCA understood, the decline in agricultural opportunity in the area "provided a constant reserve of labor for industrial demands."[12]

One local economic institution remained relatively insulated from the ravages of the Great Depression: Indiana University, located right in Bloomington. According to Henry Boxman, president of the local chamber of commerce during the late 1930s, the year-round work offered by the university was a key element in protecting the area's residents from absolute devastation. In addition to actual jobs with the university, boardinghouses for students, domestic work for faculty members, and restaurants catering to students sustained many workers during the 1930s. Jane Chestnutt remembered that her family, whose income was tied to the university, was considerably better off than other Bloomington families. Her father had been fortunate enough to move from quarry work to a more stable job at the university's powerhouse, and she contributed to the household income with her job as a waitress at a local restaurant frequented by students. To her father's continued amazement, however, her mother constantly gave away groceries to families with less stable sources of income.[13]

If farming, furniture, the university, and the stone industry offered only limited opportunities to area men, they offered even less hope to blue-collar women. The limestone quarries and mills employed a small number of women as clerical workers, but the manual labor was almost exclusively the preserve of men. The furniture industry, however, employed a significant number of women. They worked in the sanding room, in the veneer mill, on the glue spreader, on the tape machines, and even in the machine room. One supervisor remembered that eleven of the ninety employees he managed in the veneer mill were female, and there were higher concentrations of women in other departments at Showers Brothers.[14] Undoubtedly farming and gardening for home consumption with a bit left over for the market occupied many women as well. Just as for men, the university offered women the most coveted work. Secretarial jobs at the university paid $7.50 to $10.00 a week, significantly more than a local women could get elsewhere.

The vast majority of wage-earning women in the area, perhaps as many as three-quarters of them, did not work for any of these key local employers, however; they got jobs as domestic workers at $3 to $5 a week. Alyce Hunter, for instance, got a job cleaning boardinghouses three days a week after she left high school in the late 1930s; she did baby-sitting and helped her mother do laundry the rest of the week. Then she got a live-in job, doing the cleaning, cooking, and washing for $3 a week plus room and board. Other possibilities—work in a small glassworks, a basket factory, an office—were numerous but equally circumscribed. Ruth Ann Greene, whose father worked the quarries, held a part-time job in a grocery store after school and on the weekends; in her spare time she worked in the family's garden and canned the vegetables they grew. As Greene recalled, "The Depression was on, honey, and it was hard times. Everyone just had to pull their load—regardless of who they were."[15]

Labor Traditions and Working-Class Politics

Even without the ravages of the Depression, Bloomington would have been an extremely attractive location for an industrial plant. Since few people in the area had any experience with factory work, the RCA employment director, Mary Frances Roll, explained, company executives "figured that we would stand to have good labor relations here for a long time because people hadn't been embittered or involved." And she was right. In 1930, before the Depression completely undermined the industrial economy, the combined output of all of Indiana's forty-two southern counties (out of a total of ninety-two counties in the state) accounted for a mere 14.3 percent of the state's industrial production. Moreover, the organization of labor in Monroe County had been minimal, and the most active unionists were in the conservative building trades. A mob was even said to have confronted the president of the Indiana CIO and beat him up on the steps of the courthouse during his visit to Bloomington in the late 1930s.[16]

Although organized labor was generally weak in Monroe County, the key area industries did have some experience with trade unions. The skilled stone carvers and quarrymen had belonged to various craft unions since before the turn of the century and had struggled continuously to control the competitive pressure of the market and the intrusion of technological innovations, such as the air hammer, onto their skilled domain. Aside from some violent confrontations with immigrants before World War I (the native workers eventually drove them out of the limestone district), the quarry workers had very few labor disputes before the Depression. During the 1920s, however, the cutters' union lost its ability to regulate the use of machinery, failed in its attempt to restrict competition among the firms, and even lost recognition in the majority of the Indiana firms. Production increased rapidly throughout the 1920s, but with the labor organizations severely weakened, profits far outstripped wage increases. Under the guidance of the National Recovery Administration (NRA), all quarry and mill workers were organized into their constituent craft unions in July 1934 and wage rates rose to their precrash levels. The NRA was too little, too late, however, as the Depression, changes in types of building materials, and later the war all but destroyed the stone belt's economy.[17]

Because limestone workers were spread across three counties, the more centralized Showers Brothers Furniture had a greater impact on Bloomington's labor politics. Industrial unionism did make a brief appearance at the furniture plant in the late 1930s, but after the company repeatedly harassed the local with calls for new elections and the social costs of several strikes became difficult to bear, members rejected the CIO local in favor of an AFL affiliate. Whether unionized or not, many people in Bloomington felt that the furniture company played a strongly coercive role in the labor market. Some folks contended that if Showers Brothers had been able to maintain its economic strength and political clout—"Showers controlled this community," one furniture maker commented—an industrial concern such as RCA would never have been allowed to enter the town and drive up the price of labor.[18]

The limited industrial culture, low levels of unionization, and, most important, the destruction of the local economy made Bloomington a dream town for a capitalist in search of workers for labor-intensive electronics production. The local population's desperation for work and deference to anyone who could provide it allowed RCA to establish very strict guidelines for employment. "The people that we hired when we started RCA was this nice person's son and daughter," the employment director recalled. "You know, a rather high level of clientele." Without the constraints of federal- or state-mandated hiring rules, "you could refuse to hire a person if you didn't like the way they parted their hair. So you had full rein of being very selective." Applicants "were just wild to get a job, and particularly something in industry. . . . Jobs had not been available. *They needed them.*" When workers lined up at the Graham Hotel for an interview, a position "would be so important to them, they would be so nervous, they would shake like a leaf in the wind." Workers were not concerned about how much a job paid, what they had to do, or what their hours would be; "they just wanted that job and wanted to hold that job." Boys applying for stock-handling work typically arrived in their Sunday suits, and even prospective employees who were "very minimal in social and education standards" would show up impeccably dressed and groomed when they submitted their applications. "It sounds like a fairy tale," she recalled about the applicants' desperation, "but it was that important to them."[19]

With deference to employers who could offer work, limited industrialization, dependence on the processing of natural resources, spotty unionization, and a reserve army of labor struggling on subsistence agricultural plots, Bloomington appears to have had many of the attributes that made the South an attractive destination for the runaway textile industry in the 1920s and 1930s and for the host of other manufacturing firms that migrated south after World War II. Many of Bloomington's workers in fact traced their roots to the South. The hills of Monroe County sit at the northern edge of the Ohio Valley, mirroring the hills that rise into the mountains of Appalachia to the south. A long history of migration and labor recruitment from the South had brought Bloomington a large contingent of "the 'common folk' from the Kentucky and Tennessee hills." In fact, the only period in which the community experienced a downturn in population growth was at the outbreak of the Civil War. When Indiana voted to stay in the Union, large numbers of Bloomingtonians expressed their political leanings by returning to the land of their origins, and the sympathies of those who stayed often remained with the Confederacy. Showers Brothers Furniture had been recruiting migrants of Scotch-Irish descent from across the Ohio River since the turn of the century. People from the South "just kept coming," commented one lifelong furniture worker. "Bloomington is half Kentuckians, and they'll tell you so." Management's only reservation about the formula they had found in Bloomington was the possible influence of the coal miners in the region and their deep commitment to unionization. "Well, for years," reported the personnel manager, "we did not hire in that area where you would have the coal miner's daughter."[20]

Bloomington seemingly had little to offer other than an abundance of low-cost and controllable labor. As one student of the city's economic history explains, the place had "no vast water supply, no coal or oil, no rich agricultural [resources], and no important transportation facilities; it offered only a large labor force which was willing to give a good day's work for a fair day's pay." For the thirteen managers brought in from the East, however, it also had the distinct advantage of a major institution of higher learning, Indiana University, which ensured a lively cultural life and quality educational facilities for their children. In fact, Bloomington's main competition for RCA's investment was another college town, Bloomington, Illinois. Such cultural advantages could not be overlooked at a time when, according to the only member of management hired locally, easterners "still thought Hoosiers were carrying tomahawks and that our only entertainment was the medicine show or a chautauqua."[21] Just as executives would one day enjoy the benefits of living on the U.S. side of the border while hiring Mexicans to work in factories they had located on the other side, so RCA found that the combination of a somewhat cosmopolitan town with an abundant supply of inexpensive labor served its interest in 1940.

"High Class Feminine Labor"

When RCA entered Bloomington's economic life, however, it was not the unemployed stonecutters, laid-off furniture workers, marketless farmers, or their sons that management sought to hire. As in Camden, the company went in search of their daughters. Men were hired for the heavy work, such as shipping and stock handling, and for jobs that called for some skill, such as troubleshooting and repair, but the vast majority of the new workers—about 80 percent—were to be women. As the newspapers made clear, the corporation chose Bloomington because it had "a large field" of "high class feminine labor" to fill the assembly lines that would produce the tabletop radio, the Nipper. More than just being female was required, however: recruits had to have a high school education and they had to be between the ages of seventeen and twenty-eight, single, within specified height and weight limits, of "high moral character," and capable of passing a physical exam and a series of dexterity tests. The corporation's employment director, who knew the local labor market extremely well, later claimed with very little exaggeration that RCA delivered the industrial revolution to the women of Monroe County.[22]

In Bloomington, where work for anybody was scarce, underpaid women workers were in abundance. The top of the pay scale for women in Monroe County was $7.50 a week. When RCA opened, it paid 17.5 cents to 19.5 cents an hour, or $7.00 to $7.80 for a forty-hour week. This scale placed entry-level pay in competition with some of the very best wages available to women in the area. Moreover, rates of pay quickly rose to 23 cents and 25 cents an hour, a rate that made factory work much more financially appealing than any other job for working-class women. This tactic RCA called paying a "community wage"—a system of offering marginally better pay than other blue-collar jobs in the area in order to attract the finest workers. The "community wage" concept also cut the other way. When the Bloomington workers sought raises to bring their rate of pay up to those of other RCA workers in the country after World War II, the company rejected their request because their pay was deemed "appropriate in terms of community and industry." In sum, while offering very valuable and much-needed work to Bloomington women, RCA reaped the real financial bonanza, as the female operators in Camden started at between 40 and 50 cents an hour—up to double what Bloomington women could expect.[23]

With the labor force facing so much hardship in Bloomington, one might expect the men to resent the company's hiring policies. The sexual division of labor at the plant, however, simultaneously relied on and complicated the existing gender hierarchy in the area. Both sexes were accustomed to segregation at work, whether at home or on the job, so when the work at RCA was pronounced as "feminine" from the beginning, there was little dissent. This patriarchal common sense, at a time when any job for any member of the family was welcome relief, left the company's hiring policies all but uncontested. One male applicant reflected, "There was just a management directive and, you know, you didn't question things like that. Work was hard to get . . . and you were just happy to get a job."[24]

Elites did their best to assuage a residue of discomfort with the idea of a factory staffed largely by women. One of the local papers sent a reporter up to the four-year-old components plant in Indianapolis to explore what was in store for Bloomington. Upon his return he eased fears that the town's daughters might become hardened under the pressure of factory work. "Even at the end of this day shift we did not see a girl whose makeup had suffered from the afternoon's work," he reported. "An ambitious girl could not ask for a better opening than a job with RCA." From a variety of other quarters came the awkward logic that since the stone and furniture industries employed mostly men, RCA offered the perfect complement to Monroe County's existing male-dominated industries. Few local people made any effort to reconcile these cheerful tidings with the fact that the traditional industries were not employing many men either.[25]

More than just labor market conditions and gender factored into RCA's hold on the local population: the sheer size and technological dazzle of the industry stunned the new workers. The first generation of RCA workers remember their awe at the immensity of the operation and the excitement of learning about something as sophisticated as radio production. "I had a feeling that that was the biggest place I nearly ever seen," remembered Anna Belle

Ooley. "When I walked down through there I was scared to death. Cause you know it's big. It's big!" Each woman began by learning to crimp and solder wires, and those hired very early on built an entire radio set from start to finish. "That was the thrill," remembers Jane Chestnutt. "Of course we didn't get to keep it," she added disappointedly. When the first Nipper model rolled off the assembly line on 17 July 1940, everything in the factory came to a stop as all the workers gathered around to see the first completed set. When they turned the switch and music from the radio broke the silence, everyone in the plant "screamed and clapped" at their success.[26]

The general sense of the early days was a "family feeling" peppered with a variety of complaints about the discipline involved in high-speed production under autocratic managers brought in from the East Coast. Of course, oral history evaluations of RCA's early days in Bloomington must be carefully gauged against the often implicit comparisons between an ideal past and the contemporary problems—buyouts, job losses, speedups—that have engendered bitterness and frustration. Alyce Hunter perhaps best summarizes the workers' feelings toward RCA. Never having seen the inside of a radio—"which hadn't been around for us for a great long time anyway"—she found the experience "fascinating" but life on the line "rough." The women's feelings toward their co-workers were unambiguous, however: they remember RCA in the 1940s as having a "hometown feel." They were a close-knit group of workers who knew each other through a variety of social and familial relations. "It was just like a family, you know. And we got along so," Joska Hoke said. "And if somebody had sickness in the family, you know it seemed like everybody . . . would take up money and help. . . . Any time anybody needed help, it seemed like everybody was always so willing to give and to do things. It was just like a family."[27]

Management applied the family metaphor to the Bloomington workers as well, but did so in contrast to the contentious and unfamilial environment that years of industrial struggle had produced in Camden. "I can tell you unofficially that they certainly appreciated the Bloomington work force as compared to what they had in the East," reported Mary Frances Roll, because "in the East they had considerable labor problems. The labor environment wasn't too healthy, the employees, I don't think, had nearly as high a regard for their work place as our employees." In Bloomington, RCA produced a "feeling of camaraderie between the working force and company that was certainly nonexistent in the East." Echoing the ideas of her employees, she explained, "It was more of a family feel and that family feel kept up for years and years and years. It was the RCA family—very strong." The main factor Roll pointed to in her analysis was the lack of industrial culture in Bloomington. "It will probably be a long time before we would have the adverse feeling develop here as say might on the East Coast," which "has always been industrialized, and we weren't an industrial community. We have not had the things that has poisoned the work force against the work place."[28]

The Unionization of RCA Bloomington

RCA's investment in Bloomington began to recast the "unpoisoned" culture and politics of southern Indiana's workers almost immediately upon its arrival. Few transformations better make the case that capital includes more than equipment, buildings, parts, and raw materials; it embodies also a complex social relationship. The desire for controllable labor that informed management's decision to move to Bloomington (and every other site under consideration) stood in tension with the social relations of industrial production, which served constantly to undermine the very factors management sought in its workers: cheapness and passivity. Since labor power—Marx's "peculiar commodity"—is embedded in living, breathing, conscious workers with an evolving sense of culture, history, and place, the new factory regime had an inevitable impact on the RCA employees' social identity. Although RCA's flight from the insubordinate workers in New Jersey to the seemingly cheap and docile workers in Bloomington appeared successful on every level, the very act of opening a factory in Monroe County initiated a series of changes in the social factors for which management had chosen the site. The pressure of laboring on an assembly line with hundreds, later thousands, of other workers inscribed an incipient class awareness in Bloomington workers, which began to erode the very social control management gained by moving production away from Camden. The "family feeling" of the early years did not prevent cultural changes that would come to parallel, albeit in subdued and muted ways, the industrial strife of Camden.

Although nobody could recall exactly how the idea of unionizing the rapidly growing plant began, all workers could remember why. The simple speed and discipline of the assembly line drove workers to a more antagonistic relationship with management. As Bob Doty recalled, the bosses "couldn't understand why I couldn't keep up. . . . I was just a hick kid. . . . I'd never been inside of a place like that before and these people, a lot of them, had come from New Jersey, see. . . . And they couldn't understand why the people around the Bloomington area couldn't keep up." Alyce Hunter recalled the unrelenting tedium of the line where she held a heavy 200-watt soldering iron all day. "You held that in your hand until you got the break," she explained. "It was just one after another until it come time for the break." The regimentation imposed by a seemingly alien management also left Hunter feeling inimical toward the corporation. They were "company people," she recalled, "and they weren't very friendly. What they said goes, whether it was right or not." The control RCA attempted to wield over the young women was captured on the cover of the Bloomington edition of the company paper, the *RCA Victor Family News*. Sitting on a stool with a dunce cap labeled "I was absent" perched on her head, a young woman wrote "production, production, production" across the blackboard behind her. The possibility of public humiliation implicit in the child-teacher relationship was reinforced by a set of time cards fanning out around the image of the punished employee, with the names of workers who had punched in late clearly legible.[29]

Specific grievances also drove the organizing effort. Women operatives frequently arrived at the plant in the morning only to be sent home after a couple of hours because of shortages of parts or production overruns. The new radio makers felt that if they had been scheduled at the shop, they deserved at least half a day's pay. One manager recalled with nostalgia the days before the union came in with its work rules. "In the beginning women never argued, neither did they give you any sass if they [had to] help out on something else if a line happened to go down or we ran low on parts." More worrisome than not having work for a day or two was the fact that women would automatically be fired if they became pregnant, and that management frowned on employing married women at all. Everyone wanted better rules regulating overtime compensation, felt the need for grievance procedures, and, of course, sought higher wages and better benefits. Ruth Ann Greene explained, "In the early years we wanted the grievance procedures so you couldn't get fired without going through the channels and if you were fired then you had steps you could go to."[30]

Word began to circulate around the plant in early 1943 that workers could sign union cards after hours at Hook's drugstore, on the city square. Most organizing took place outside the plant because management "didn't believe in a union.... If you said something about a union you was fired, just like that," Doty said as he snapped his fingers. RCA tried to block the drive by announcing over the loudspeaker that they would close the doors if the employees voted the union in, and several workers were fired for their organizing efforts. Despite such obstacles and the alleged passivity of the young women workers in the face of authority, most of the women readily signed up for the union. When it came time to build the union, Bob Doty said, "some of the women were worse than men.... Why, they were meaner than snakes, some of them was.... It was a dual thing, you know, where men and women worked together in the union." As "dual" as the effort may have been, no woman was ever elected president or business manager, but women did remain consistent activists. Many were shop stewards and chief stewards, and, reflecting their status on the shop floor, almost always held the lower elected offices of the local, such as recording and financial secretaries. Alyce Hunter, pondering women's role in factory work, explained, "I think they'll always be second-class citizens as far as jobs in plants like that are concerned, but the women, if you didn't like something that the foreman had said to you, he could just tell you to get out, you see, and that happened so much that, well, the women were just as bad wanting the union as the men were." [31]

The drive to organize the Bloomington factory initiated another battle between the United Electrical Workers, the original Camden CIO union, and the International Brotherhood of Electrical Workers, the old AFL craft union. Much as in Camden, the IBEW's position in Bloomington wavered between perfunctory representation of its membership and collusion with the company in its effort to block the growth of the "dual unionist" UE-CIO. The UE organizer who moved out to work with the Bloomington workers reported that "the IBEW and company officials were very friendly" and "spent a little time joking about the money one of the company officials lost in a poker game they had recently." Given the conservative makeup of southern Indiana, the international representative of the left-wing UE admitted that the UE "wouldn't stand any chance in an election" but planned to "be present at the hearing and screw it up as much as possible." Despite RCA's intimidation and the diligent efforts of the UE, the Bloomington workers voted overwhelmingly in favor of the IBEW in 1944 but failed to gain management's recognition of a union shop. [32]

As the war drew to a close, however, the UE sent organizers out to Bloomington and Indianapolis to try once again to bring the entire RCA chain under a single UE contract. Rising wages at the periphery, they reasoned, would help stop jobs from leaving Camden. The pressure produced by the UE's second effort had the reverse effect, however: the company granted the union shop to the IBEW in an effort to check any possible gains by the UE. "The fact is clear," reported the UE field organizer, "that the IBEW and RCA were involved in a backdoor agreement with respect to recognition and contract," and the company granted the IBEW a union shop contract "in the face of the beginning of an organizing campaign by the UE." [33] RCA had much to gain by ensuring that the IBEW remained at the Bloomington works. A comparison of UE and IBEW contracts performed by the UE showed the CIO union's contract to be better than the AFL affiliate's in protection against speedups, union security, dismissals, work hours, seniority, and paid holidays. Moreover, industrial workers remained Class B members of the craft union, were allowed only one vote per fifty members in elections, and were excluded from several benefits. [34]

Although the RCA workers were now affiliated with the AFL, their success in unionization derived largely from the efforts of the CIO unions in the major industrial centers. The labor upheavals of the 1930s and 1940s paved the way for the IBEW in Bloomington, since a militant organization such as the UE posed a dire alternative in the eyes of management. The setmakers became only tenuous members of the labor-management accord that shaped the political economy of the entire industrial belt in the postwar era. Still, as Alyce Hunter pointed out, "sitting across the table and talking over your problems with somebody eye to eye was better than him saying 'you do it or else,' no discussion on the thing." Moreover, Bloomingtonians seemed to have a rudimentary understanding of the larger world of industrial labor politics they had entered. The new radio assemblers, recalled Doty, began to want "better pay because everybody else was getting better pay. . . . Well, big steel . . . got an 18 percent raise the first crack out of the box after the war" (much as the Camden employees did), whereas the Bloomington RCA workers, even with the union, received only 3 percent.[35]

With weak leadership from the International office, the IBEW local remained very much a homegrown affair. One of the first employees to be elected to serve as the union's business manager explained, "That was back in the time you didn't have anything; you had to go from scratch and build it all up." Though the workers had joined the AFL union in 1944, the local did not bargain with RCA through the International until the early 1950s. The fact that "we didn't trust 'em was the biggest reason" they did not negotiate nationally, recalled the local's president, Lew Watson, and many other local officials agreed. When an officer of the International tried to railroad Bob Norris into agreeing to something he was sure the Bloomington workers did not want, Norris had to threaten him to get him to back down. "I told him if he wasn't gonna leave, I was going to throw him through a plate-glass window," Norris remembered. Officials who were not on the job site did not have to be responsible to the membership, Norris explained, but he had to face his fellow workers every day. "See, the International don't have to deal with the people here—they can leave. *You* can't leave, and if the people don't want it, you're here."[36]

Alyce Hunter, who served in several elected offices at IBEW Local 1424 during her four decades at the plant, recalled that many employees distrusted the International, yet they realized that the local leadership lacked experience and training in industrial relations. "There was suspicions about the International officers that they were in collusion with the company on a lot of things. They held things down, as far as benefits were concerned, [more] than they should have. I think there was a little bit of horse trading there due to the friendships that went on at the International level. I don't think we got what we should have got in our group. . . . Our officers were not always as experienced as they should have been in international affairs . . . they could have gotten us a lot more in benefits." Nonetheless, change did come, if slowly. "Each negotiation," reported one female operative, "changed a little bit at a time."[37]

If the company was forced to have a union in Bloomington, another key reason it undoubtedly preferred the IBEW over Camden's UE was that during the war, the UE turned to combating one of the central tenets of industrial relations in the electrical sector: wage discrimination by sex. In 1942, as the defense effort drew increasing numbers of women into the workforce, the UE linked up with the United Auto Workers to challenge gender-based pay at General Motors with a case before the War Labor Relations Board (WLRB). By 1945, the UE had attacked wage discrimination and won at both electrical industry giants, GE and Westinghouse; but as the WLRB's power waned with the end of the war, the companies easily ignored the rulings. The UE's tactic had been carefully designed to minimize tension between male and female employees. The union explained to the membership that low-paying women's jobs threatened men's higher wages because women could always be substituted for higher-priced men. If they were to raise wage rates for men, then, the floor would have to be raised for all wages. The Cold War, which bitterly divided the left-led electrical workers' union, quickly superseded the issue of wage discrimination, but at the end of World War II the UE seemed to be well on its way to establishing equality in the workplace.[38] The UE's offensive against wage discrimination by sex made Bloomington an even safer place to shift more production from Camden, since the gendered division of labor remained secure with the IBEW. Indeed, wage differentials based on sex would not become an issue in Bloomington until the mid-1960s.

The successful organization of the plant did not deter the growth of employment, however, as the Bloomington works expanded rapidly throughout the war and beyond. During the war, the assembly lines were converted to produce a special defense product, the proximity fuse, which everyone was proud to hear was second only to the atomic bomb in importance to the defense effort. Wartime employment reached between 1,600 and 1,800 workers —already over double the employment projections for Bloomington—and by the end of 1948 the number had continued upward to 2,300, between 75 and 80 percent of them women. The expansion provided jobs to all who wanted them, and the unfaltering growth in women's employment stood in stark contrast to the situation at other electrical plants around the country, where women were displaced by men returning from the war and many female jobs were eliminated when defense contracts ended. National employment figures for women in the electrical industry plummeted from 305,600 in 1945 to 181,600 in 1946.[39]

A brief strike in 1950 allowed the union to exercise its growing power and consolidate its gains. Before the walkout, Bob Doty said, "people wouldn't band together . . . everybody was still scared of their job . . . and the union wasn't strong enough to get the people's jobs back for them." [40] By 1950, however, things had begun to change. Rejecting the company's wage proposal, the workers walked out in early August 1950 and stayed off the job for forty-four hours. This short, peaceful walkout resulted in an immediate across-the-board wage increase of 5 cents, to be followed by another raise of 4 cents the next year (average wages were $1.10 an hour); workers were also to get vacation pay and another paid holiday. Most important, they gained insurance benefits from the company of their choice rather than the one RCA preferred. The specifics of the agreement aside, the quick strike served to consolidate Local 1424's position with the company and to make it a legitimate bargaining agent. As the president and business manager explained, when you're negotiating, "they've got to know you're not jiving. They've got to know you'll strike . . . that's the power, the strike." [41]

The Arrival of Television

Visitors to the 1939 World's Fair in New York flocked to the RCA exhibit to hear David Sarnoff announce, "Now we add sight to sound. . . . A new art and a new industry, which eventually will provide entertainment and information for millions and new employment for large numbers of men and women, are here." At that time only about two hundred rich and curious people owned television sets (a receiver cost about as much as a new car), and all of them lived in the New York metropolitan area. RCA had pumped $2.7 million into television research during the 1930s and another $2 million into patents. The war postponed television's growth and availability, but in 1946 a television set with a 10-inch screen became available for $375. The definitive postwar consumer product meshed neatly with postwar consumer affluence and suburban isolation. As one enthusiastic set owner proclaimed, TV guaranteed the ability "to enjoy ourselves, relax in our own living room to the accompaniment of smokes, cool drinks, shoes off, and minimum dress . . . that's the kind of television enjoyment that is awaiting everyone in all of the 30 million American homes that now have radios and who will eventually be seeing as well as listening." Banking on television manufacturing "to blossom into one of the most enormous businesses this country has every known," RCA devoted its resources and facilities to the mass production of television receivers. [42] Most important, the new industry meant that thousands of new workers would receive the same benefits of postwar prosperity that made the television receiver the very symbol of a new American affluence.

The introduction of color slowly pushed the frenzy for television even further. RCA had developed a color television system in the late 1940s, but the Columbia Broadcasting System (CBS) already had a system that delivered a higher-quality picture than the RCA system. RCA's technology, however, had the unique advantage of being compatible with existing black-and-white sets. With so few television receivers in operation, however, the Federal Communications Commission (FCC) approved the CBS system because of its higher performance. RCA focused its efforts on improving the quality of its picture and, with great political fanfare, led a group of twenty receiver manufactures in an appeal of the FCC's decision. With many more monochrome receivers in use and the notable improvement in the quality of RCA's picture by the time the appeal was heard, the FCC reversed its decision and granted approval to the RCA system. The FCC's decision not only opened up a huge market for RCA's receivers, but also made the sale of parts, tubes, and receivers and the lease of patent rights to other receiver manufacturers key elements in the company's postwar growth.[43]

The initial investment in monochrome was paying off well by the 1950s, but color took off very slowly. In the first half of 1954, only 8,000 color sets had been sold. Bob Hope joked that his color broadcast had a "tremendous" audience: "General Sarnoff and his wife." Contrary to the company's projections, consumers did not buy a new color model as a second set, but waited until they were ready to replace their old black-and-white receivers. Color was, as RCA's business historian described it, merely "an improved version of an existing technology that while interesting hardly was a pressing need." The company did not turn a profit on color until 1959, and the complete turnaround did not really come before 1960, when prices fell, buyers were ready to replace their old monochrome models, and a wider variety of color programming became available. By 1962 RCA could claim to have 70 percent of the booming market for color television sets, and it was Bloomington workers that the company chose to build them.[44]

The arrival of television production in Bloomington, once an obscure corner of the RCA empire, signaled fundamental changes for the workers of southern Indiana. After World War II, suspicions lingered that the Bloomington works might remain a marginal unit of the RCA chain, vulnerable to layoffs with every downturn in the economy. Only the university remained immune to adverse business conditions. Permanent employment there reached 2,100 in 1948, about the same as at RCA, but the university's payroll was boosted by another 1,050 part-time workers. What Bloomingtonians perceived as RCA's tenuous tie to their community emerged as a strong commitment when the company announced in 1949 that the prize of the light end of the electrical industry, television, would be manufactured there. The day the new products began to roll off the assembly lines, 6 September 1949, was proclaimed to be TV Day in the city, and billboards outside of town announced that travelers were entering the "Color Television Capital of the World."[45]

Building a television receiver was not a simple process, and the choice of Bloomington suggested not only that RCA had found a successful labor relations formula there but also that the workers had advanced considerably in skill and proficiency in electrical assembly. As the industry press explained, production of TV sets was extremely complex; "by comparison ordinary radio set production is simplicity itself, [and] will eventually pale to peanut proportions."[46] Elizabeth Shelton recalled that the introduction of television to Bloomington required intensive training:

> A group of ten women and one foreman were selected and they went to a place in the plant all by theirself and they each person built the entire television set from beginning to the end . . . one person, one set. And the foreman read the instructions from the process sheet over a microphone and . . . we would look at our charts, . . . And then we would place the part in the television set until we completed one entire television set which took about three to four days for one set. And we did that about—oh, maybe six months. Then they broke the process down into smaller operations and I think when they finally put the television on the production line it took about 100 people to finish one set.[47]

The Bloomington workers mastered their trade, and by 1950 three assembly lines had been devoted to the new product. Radio production was dropped completely in 1952, the first commercial color set rolled off the assembly line in 1954, and by the latter half of the 1950s, all color and monochrome production was in Bloomington. With virtually all TV manufacturing centered in Bloomington by 1960, the company payroll swelled to $13 million annually for the workers of Monroe County.[48]

Several other electrical industries followed RCA to Bloomington. A former engineer for RCA, Sarkes Tarzian, went into business for himself after the war, manufacturing television tuners to supply to the large receiver producers, and eventually he moved into a variety of consumer electronics products and other components. As his shop grew from 900 employees in 1948 to more than 3,000 workers by the 1960s, again most of them women, organizing Tarzian's operation became a perennial goal for Local 1424 and the IBEW International office. Although they got close on several occasions, the union never won a certification election. Mrs. Tarzian was notorious for her extraordinary efforts at keeping the union out of the factory. She promised to build a swimming pool for the employees if they agreed not to vote for the union, and she was known to sit outside of union organizing meetings in an ineffective disguise to take note of the workers who attended.[49]

Energized by their success in recruiting RCA and by the flourishing of spin-off industries such as Tarzian's, the city elite formed the Bloomington Advancement Association in 1953 to lure even more firms to the city. The nonprofit corporation sold shares in the venture, and with the proceeds invested in 450 acres of land for an industrial park beyond the city limits. Their first recruit, Westinghouse—another corporation successfully organized by the UE in East Pittsburgh—came to Bloomington to make high-voltage distribution parts. Unlike Tarzian and RCA, however, Westinghouse employed mostly men, required significantly higher skill levels of its employees, and by the early 1960s employed only about 600 workers. The Bloomington Advancement Association also enticed the Franklin Manufacturing Company, a large producer of freezers, to open its sixth plant in Bloomington—a factory that would eventually become a branch plant for General Electric. Later, in 1965, Otis Elevator, en route from its home in Yonkers, New York, opened a plant in the industrial park to build hydraulic and machine elevators. The Westinghouse, Franklin, and Otis plants were organized by the IUE, the CIO union launched as an anticommunist replacement for the UE. The managements of these manufacturing concerns entered into "a loosely knit organization" of their own to discuss "mutual problems" in the Bloomington labor market.[50]

Monroe County's success in attracting electrical firms was actually a small part of the amazing growth of the sector in Indiana as a whole. In an effort to recruit clean industry, Indiana advertised to prospective firms its new right-to-work law, the lack of any corporate tax, and the facts that the state had had only one tax increase in twenty-eight years, had no debt, and was conveniently located in the center of the country. Between 1958 and 1967, the share of Indiana's manufacturing workforce accounted for by electrical production rose from 13.6 percent to 18.5 percent, and the sector's payroll jumped 109 percent while all of manufacturing in the Hoosier state grew only 73 percent. Value added in the electrical sector increased by 142 percent during the same period, as opposed to 80 percent in manufacturing as a whole. By 1966, the electrical industry led all other Indiana industries in total employment, payroll, value added, and capital expenditures. With a wage rate in electrical work 13 percent below the national average in the early 1960s, Bloomington still maintained a competitive advantage vis-à-vis more industrialized areas.[51]

The geographers Michael Storper and Richard Walker argue that the relocation of industry does not follow the logic of "core and periphery," according to which branch plant locations such as Bloomington function as appendages to centers of innovation such as Camden. Instead, they conclude, industrial location follows a path toward "growth peripheries." What may begin as one of a series of decentralized branch plants can, as the optimal conditions for economic growth congeal, become a new center for industrial design and production. An industry new to a region, whether it has been "pulled by market penetration, pushed by labor militancy, propelled by technological standardization, facilitated by large-scale factory integration, or forced by pressures," is slowly transformed into an integrated production center, a new industrial nucleus in its own right. Following the pattern these geographers have laid out, a significant portion of the state's boom in electrical manufacturing can be traced to RCA's choice of Indiana as the new geographic hub of its Home Instruments Division. By 1961 the corporation employed over 12,000 people in the state. Marion, Indiana, had over 2,000 workers making picture tubes, Monticello had 600 employees building cabinets for the products, and Indianapolis, where records, tubes, and components were produced, employed thousands more. The company had substantial additional economic linkages to the region, for it claimed to pay more than $14 million annually for materials, components, and services supplied by five hundred firms in the Hoosier state.[52]

Indiana's status as a new innovating center rather than a branch of the old was confirmed in 1960, when the headquarters of both the Home Instruments Division and the RCA Sales Corporation were relocated from Camden to Indianapolis. No longer just manufacturing, but administration, engineering, sales, design, advertising, personnel, finance, and marketing—and several hundred engineers and executives—all moved to the Indiana capital to oversee the largest division of the corporation. In addition to the reasons RCA gave publicly for its move to the Hoosier state—a desire to centralize operations, Indiana's prime location for transportation, and its educational opportunities—interviews with managers point clearly to the organization of the engineers and technical workers in Camden as an important reason for the relocation of design and engineering. A rare example of successful white-collar unionization, the American Federation of Technical Engineers (AFL-CIO) and the Association of Scientists and Professional Engineering Personnel (independent) had been organized in New Jersey, and the RCA executives, one manager recalled, were "having trouble with the union of engineers back then—they wanted to get them out." Thus the same lack of control evident in the UE struggle with blue-collar workers drove the firm to rid itself of its white-collar workforce as well.[53]

After the entire Home Instruments Division had moved to Indiana, RCA embarked on the largest expansion program in its history in order to meet the projected demand for television sets. In June 1965 the company announced the investment of $51 million in new and expanded factories in an effort to double the production of television receivers in two years. Marion, Indiana, received $24.7 million to improve color tube operations, Indianapolis drew $4.7 million, and Bloomington enjoyed an additional $5.9 million to build another 400,000 square feet of production space. At the end of the year the corporation announced a new Canadian tube plant, a new plant in Circleville, Ohio, and plans for a $20 million assembly plant in Memphis to perform the same television assembly work as the Bloomington complex. With employment in Bloomington already hitting record numbers, the further expansion squeezed the local labor market and fostered a fundamental reorientation of labor politics at the plant.

Labor Market and Social Change in Bloomington

According to Mary Frances Roll, the employment manager, the arrival of television meant a "big jump" in the number of workers required at the growing Bloomington assembly complex, and the ready availability of employment transformed the industrial culture of Monroe County. Although the small size of the area's labor market fitted RCA's needs in many ways, growing demand for labor required an intensification of recruitment efforts. "Do you have a girl friend, sister or daughter between the ages of 16 and 35 who would like to work at the RCA Victor Bloomington Plant?" asked management in the company newspaper after the war. "These girls will be interested to know about the many advantages offered by RCA Victor"—"fluorescent lighting, the excellent ventilation, the rest periods in clean lounge areas, our modern Cafeteria and music programs they will enjoy while working." Recruiters could also boast of a variety of plant activities—a camera club, a rod and gun club, basketball teams, softball teams, and a bowling league. Forty-six percent of the workers in 1950 already came from outside the city, so even with current employees pulling their friends and family onto the shop floor, the demand for workers could not be met unless management took to the road to find them.[54]

Armed with a recruitment film that gave a rosy view of a young woman going through the various steps of getting a job, receiving training, and working at RCA Bloomington, Mary Frances Roll traveled throughout southern Indiana in search of workers. She showed her color movie in all the high schools in seven surrounding counties and set up interviewing stations for other young women at post offices and other public buildings. Eventually her recruitment drive even pushed her into mining country, for by then the area coal industry was in decline and the militancy she feared seemed to have declined along with it. "It was a deprived area that depended on the coal mines," she explained, "and basically most of those big mines were down, and that's where people most needed jobs." As RCA was to do after it moved to Ciudad Juárez, the company paid for buses to pick up workers all over the region. "Well, everybody wanted to come up here to work . . . but they didn't have cars so I had to subsidize buses. That was against corporate rules, to subsidize. But it was the only way."[55]

As the reservoir of labor shrank, the company had to accept workers they would have sifted out only a few years earlier. Recruiting in the old coal mining areas of southern Indiana, Roll confessed, "had opened up another kettle of worms, because we got a completely different type individual," people whose families had been "indoctrinated" in the "extreme" views of the United Mine Workers. "We had people that had long before learned how to scheme and to malinger and so forth that got introduced at the time." Bob

Kitty Murray poses dreamily during the filming of a color movie used to recruit workers for the RCA factory where she worked in 1947. The film, shown at high schools and civic organizations throughout southern Indiana, portrayed a new employee applying for a job, undergoing the interviewing process, and being tested, trained, and assigned to her exciting new job on the assembly line. (*RCA Victor Family News*, March 1947.)

Doty, though, remembered the introduction of the miners into the plant with respect, even awe, for the strength of their labor traditions. "You know the United Mine Workers is a pretty strong union," he said, "and them boys out of the coal fields, they wasn't afraid to talk, either. . . . I think they actually made our union stronger because they just talked right up [and] . . . wasn't afraid to talk back to the company, and a lot of them became shop stewards due to that fact that they had the moxie to stand up to the company."[56]

Not only did the type of worker recruited by RCA change but so did the consciousness of the older workers. A growing awareness of shared fate and power emerged. Deference gave way to a sense of entitlement. As RCA's roots sank deeper into the soil of Monroe County, the company also became firmly planted in the memory and experience of the area, and an incipient sense of prerogative and even ownership evolved in the workforce. As in Camden, however, any sense of entitlement was always vulnerable to competition from workers in the vast terrain of the world labor market.

The widespread availability of employment had one of the most significant impacts on the area's workers: "When you get a scarce labor market," Roll concluded, "everything changes." When RCA first opened in Monroe County, she recalled, the possibilities for carefully selecting her workforce were "very wide open," but by the 1960s she had seen "the labor market die and go" as the control the company enjoyed upon its arrival had all but vanished. The early memories of Ken Beasley, who was part of the second generation of workers that joined RCA in the 1960s, were very different from those of the workers who had come to RCA in the early 1940s. "When I hired in, you could go literally anywhere and get a job making nearly identical wages," he explained. "There was just a choice of where am I going to go to work? . . . It was understood that you could go here, go there, get a job, no problem."[57] Although the employment opportunities represented an economic windfall for area workers, management saw them as a loss for the company, since they made for a significantly more unruly and uncontrollable labor force. "As jobs became more plentiful," explained Roll, "we got more affluent, and people got more selective, and more choicy, and more independent, and I think possibly a lot of young people had a very exaggerated idea of their importance." The timid and deferential worker of 1940 had become demanding and uncontrollable in the 1960s. "Instead of you interviewing them, in the later years, they would interview you." No longer could the company depend on appearing benevolent as it granted jobs to the unemployed of Monroe County. By the 1960s, the workers were not asking "What can I do for you?"; it had become a "what-the-hell-can-you-do-for-me? type of thing."[58]

Arguably, the forced regimentation and rigor of the assembly line had the single most profound effect on the workers' sense of their relation with the company. An RCA worker's every motion on the line had been broken down into its smallest elements by a sophisticated version of Taylorism known as the work factor system, developed at RCA Camden and exported to the other shops. The system, based on extensive research designed "to eliminate human judgment in setting output rates," classified the distance any part of a worker's body needed to move, the body part or parts used, the type and degree of manual control involved in each motion, and the weight or resistance encountered in the operation. Each motion segment had been quantified into a "work factor unit" that equaled 1/10,000 of a minute. Using an intricate formula that compensated for the time required for a worker's body part to change directions, the time necessary to synchronize different motions, the degree of visibility of an operation to the worker, the amount of control and dexterity required, and the amount of "mental process" involved, the manager could "objectively" determine the time required to complete any task from values derived from reams of tables without recourse to a stopwatch. The time required for a given movement could vary with the obstacles or cautions involved. All of the work factor calculations for each movement in the assigned job could then be added up to a single aggregate amount of time, or "work process." The assembly of the entire television set consisted of hundreds of separate processes performed by each operative.[59]

"The animating principle of all such work investigations," Harry Braverman explains, "is the view of the human being in machine terms." The pressures to resist such regimentation were quite compelling. Mary Gallagher found work on the line "so tedious it makes you feel like you've lost your mind." Her husband, Rocky, vividly described life on the line as akin to playing the bounce-the-ball-off-the-paddle game for eight hours each day, and getting punished for missing. But drill bits could be broken, air guns could be dropped, hoses could accidentally be cut, and production had to stop. Conversely, a group of line workers could decide to work extremely fast and build up a bank of production so they could take time for a few beers at lunch. Yet in general the Bloomington workers accepted the principles of the system and expressed indignation only when the company violated its rules.[60]

Even though the work factor system had supposedly eliminated the need for a stopwatch, the minutes of Local 1424's monthly meetings reveal an obsession with ensuring that each shop steward had one to keep the pace of the line from being pushed above "objective" limits. Stewards had to circulate every hour to time the lines to prevent the company from raising the rate. The former business manager Bob Norris recalled, "If you didn't watch the company, they were constantly pushing that lever"—the one that controlled the speed of the line. If a worker managed to find a shortcut that allowed her to perform a task faster than the time-study engineers had calculated, the experts came in to reevaluate the process. "That was one of the problems we'd have with this work factor study," explained a process engineer, "trying to figure out where'd I goof? How come they can beat that rate so much? So you'd go back in and reanalyze and see what you'd done wrong." The dehumanizing aspect of the system frightened even the time-study engineers. Working there "would kill me, those rates—maybe fifty an hour, seventy an hour, hundred an hour," said a plant engineer. "To do the same thing a hundred times an hour for an eight-hour day would drive me nuts, putting the same parts in, and you just keep going and going and going. Ugh!" And the line stopped for nothing.[61]

Judy Cross, who hired on in 1963, found her first job simply "terrible"; her hands ached so badly at the end of the day that she couldn't even unscrew the lid from the baby bottle when she returned home to her second shift as a mother. When she was training for a wire-dress job, which entailed connecting fifty wires of various colors and lengths covered with black glue to their appropriate terminals, she thought she was "going to have a nervous breakdown" before she learned the job. Her friends on the line helped her out, but then the time-study man added more work to her job when he found she had some spare time on her hands. "I just psyched myself up to where I just started going as fast as I could," she explained, but she ended up having to take leave because the stress made her sick. She later figured out that the work process rules had been violated. "If I had just been a little smarter—see, I hadn't worked here very long—I would have realized that I didn't have to separate those wires, that wasn't on my process. . . . They should have had somebody doing it for me." This pressure from management pushed workers closer together. "The people on the lines are really great," Cross said. In those years RCA would "supposedly give you two weeks to learn a job but actually only gave you about two or three days." While you were learning, however, "the people on the line, if you would kind of get [behind] a little bit, they would put in a few crimps for you. They were really good back then."[62]

Strike Wave, 1964–1968

"People never talked about strikes at the beginning," Joska Hoke recalled. "People were satisfied with whatever they got."[63] The clearest indication of the sea-change in Bloomington's working-class life was a series of strikes. After only one brief walkout in 1950, the employees struck the plant three times between 1964 and 1967. Two of the walkouts were wildcat actions that violated the no-strike clause in their contract. The labor force grew increasingly impatient with formal contractualism in general and with the company's willingness to use the contract and the union as a way to discipline them in particular. Increased rigor on the line became necessary as the market for television sets grew almost out of control, and workers were pushed not only to meet the demand but to beat the competition as well.

In the late spring of 1964, local and international IBEW leaders, meeting in Hollywood, Florida, had been negotiating for a month over the terms of the new contract, but they had failed to reach an agreement by the time the old one expired. The company and the union agreed to extend the old contract from day to day until a new agreement could be reached. After an anxious week in which the rank and file were left in the dark regarding negotiations, 5,000 employees took matters into their own hands. The word went down the lines in hushed voices: "We're going out at lunchtime."

The wildcat walkout became an occasion to vent anger and frustration over a wide variety of ills. Workers "pointedly criticized union officials and the attitude of management" in an airing of grievances that had "been building up for ten years." The fact that the negotiators were in Florida took on particular symbolic value. One woman carried a sign saying: "Creech on the Beach for Two More Weeks"; another sign proclaimed: "Creech is a Leech." Paul Creech, the local's business agent, was even strung up in effigy on a maple tree across the street from the plant entrance. Workers claimed that union officials had grown distant and uncommunicative, pay increases had been inadequate, production quotas had risen without compensation, and management was generally unsympathetic to their plight. Many emphasized working conditions rather than pay. "I'd say to hell with the raise if we could get some decent working conditions!" exclaimed one set builder. "They're working these poor women to death in there. . . . They tell us how to dress, when to shave, when we can talk, just like a little Russia."[64]

The local leadership branded the strike extremist and irresponsible and urged the workers back onto the lines. "Resist unwise, short-sighted and irresponsible leadership of this radical element," Creech fired back from Florida, "and aid those officers of Local Union 1424 whom you have elected by the democratic process to alleviate the chaos and unrest generated and stampeded by the unwise action of a few." Calling up the specters of communism and anarchy, the business agent warned workers against falling victim to "mob psychology." Employees must remain strong in the face of "evil forces" that are "attempting to undermine and destroy our free and democratic way of life," he proclaimed in a statement to the press. "Labor, Management, and Government officials must remain vigilant in their efforts to subdue these evil forces and preserve the freedom and dignity of man throughout the world." It was exactly such control over their lives that the employees were protesting against.[65]

Despite the seven-day walkout, the rebellious workers ultimately approved the contract by a 2-to-1 margin when union leaders made public the results of the negotiations. Although they did not gain any further control over the shop floor or a union local more responsive to their needs, they won a sufficient bread-and-butter package to persuade them to return to the job. Raises from 1 to 7 cents over the next three years, increased insurance benefits, longer vacations, and an earlier retirement age ensured the success of the new contract. In tune with postwar industrial relations strategies, the company doled out higher wages and more benefits in exchange for labor peace and productivity. Nonetheless, a generational split appears to have been at work between the employees who approved the contract and those who voted against it. "It's a shame," one woman said. "Eighty percent of the plant only got a nickel raise. The people that voted for it were the old ladies over

"RCA workers mill around the nation's 'Color Television Capital' as wildcat strike continues," reported the *Bloomington Herald-Telephone* in 1964. Criticizing both management and the local union leadership, employees refused to work while negotiations between the company and the International Brotherhood of Electrical Workers dragged on for more than a month. The dispute was the first of a trio of walkouts to rock Bloomington. (*Bloomington Herald-Telephone*, June 4, 1964.)

40 — they think they're making big money. The truth is they can't get a job any place else. They're scared to vote anything but yes."[66] Even during the boom times of the early 1960s, employment at RCA served as a lifeline to the middle-aged women whose only other choice would have been the nonunion Sarkes Tarzian.

Only two years later, in October 1966, the workers walked out again in a violent and controversial clash in violation of the very contract they had approved in 1964. Before the strike, the new and more respected business manager, Richard Jean, called a special meeting at the union hall. Many workers still remember it vividly. "He told us the company was doing this, screwing us here, screwing us there, and somebody said something about not going back to work," recalled Bill Cook. Jean, who as business manager could not endorse a wildcat action but still believed the workers needed to protest, reminded them, "You're all free, white, and twenty-one." His remark had a couple of the black members looking at their skin quizzically, but it was the green light the workers had hoped for. After they had marched out, the business agent admitted that the strike was unauthorized, but told the press that "the company has consistently broken the contract the past fourteen months . . . [and] forced the people out by contractual violations and discrimination against many employees such as inadequate relief for operators, mixing of classifications, refusing insurance claims, refusing to recognize doctors' statements, over-processing lines, etc."[67]

A twenty-point list of grievances fueled the strike, but at the core of the dispute was the "mixing of classifications"—the company's attempt to reduce wages by harmonizing all wages down to the level of "women's work," or light assembly jobs. "Men have been hired off the street to do women's jobs at women's wages and women have been doing men's jobs for women's wages," explained an angry spokesman for the picketers at the outset of the strike. When a woman did "male" work, she was supposed to be issued a temporary upgrade and receive the higher pay for the time spent on that job. Men were not supposed to do women's work at all, or if they did, they were supposed to keep their male pay level. This sexual division of labor was breaking down, and it was clear that management was pushing as many workers as possible into the light or female wage category. A shop steward recalled, "I've had blue [upgrade] slips, a stack of them that high, that I'd take up to payroll in order to check out to find out if this person got that money. And about 90 percent of the time the person had never got that money."[68]

For a few days the chaos on the streets around the plant resembled the mayhem in Camden during the UE strike. The stoppage descended into violence on several occasions. Fights broke out, workers disabled the vehicles of people trying to get into and out of the plant, and a few workers punched and pushed down some stairs a company guard trying to protect an RCA photographer. Photographs taken at the time show police in riot gear and clubs raised in pursuit of strikers, and rows of police cars waiting near the plant for the call to mobilize. A riot squad of 150 men sent by the Indiana State Police office was on standby alert at the nearby National Guard armory in case matters spiraled completely out of control. About ten workers were arrested, and many of them complained of abuse and unnecessary brutality while they were in custody. At night, stacked railroad ties fed bonfires as workers sang, laughed, and drank to kill time on the picket line. Like the earlier walkout, however, this one ended quietly when local negotiators got management to agree in writing to cease their violations of the contract. Having walked out on a Wednesday, the workers were back on the job by the following Monday.[69]

When the third strike erupted, the Bloomingtonians quietly expressed exasperation with both the company and the union at the conclusion of contract negotiations in the summer of 1967. This stoppage, officially sanctioned by the IBEW International office and supported by the majority of workers in the IBEW-RCA chain, was in opposition to a recent contract offer, though the Bloomington plant had actually voted in favor of the settlement. During the month-long strike, mismanagement and distrust came to the fore. The promised strike benefit of $25 was distributed only once, and many workers were left without income during the dispute. Yet, knowing the company had only a few days' worth of parts, Local 1424 could have waited those few days until the company had to lay off the workers. They then would have been eligible for unemployment benefits. Following a similar pattern of disenchantment with the IBEW in Indianapolis, the Bloomington workers considered disaffiliating from the union and seeking a more active voice, possibly with the Teamsters. After perfunctory picketing for four weeks, only 1,600 yes votes from a body of eligible workers numbering 7,000 were enough to approve the contract.[70]

The Bloomington RCA workers who remembered the labor unrest of the mid-1960s recalled a long battle against contract violations, job classification mixing, and speedups, but management's recollections were quite different. In the company's eyes, the workers had become spoiled. As the plant manager recalled, "There was full employment, people didn't value a job. You'd have . . . songs like 'Take Your Job and Stick It.' "[71] The availability of jobs in Bloomington, as he saw it, had made the workforce too secure and too aggressive. Commenting after RCA had moved 7,000 jobs out of Bloomington, he remarked, "People feel a little different about a job today." Yet it was never again as good as those earliest days in Bloomington, when Depression-era workers knew the value of a daily wage. "The people who were old employees lived through a period [the Depression] and had some appreciation [for work]." During the 1960s and 1970s "there were many who were too dumb to realize what they were losing when they were in."[72]

The threat of capital flight did little to tame the RCA workers during the years of unrest. As in Camden three decades earlier, management's attempts to coerce the workers by claiming they would relocate production failed to win them anything but further animosity. As the ever-cocky Bob Doty recalled, management frequently voiced the threat of capital flight. "More than once [during negotiations] they said, 'If you don't like to work here, we'll just close her down.' I don't know where they was going to move it. But you know what our comment was? 'Well, you let us know when you want to close it and we'll help you pack it.' Now that's exactly what our comment was."[73] Such bravado was of no use when, one afternoon in 1968, management announced the layoffs of over 2,000 workers, most of them women engaged in the most labor-intensive assembly jobs. The rest of the plant would follow over the ensuing decades.

Most of the production that drained out of Bloomington between 1969 and 1998 ended up in Ciudad Juárez, in Mexico's northern border state of Chihuahua. Before RCA committed its resources to the developing world, however, it experimented with a domestic version of the southern strategy. In the spring of 1965, when the company geared up for its major expansion to meet the predicted television boom, it invested $51 million in plants and facilities, mostly in the Midwest, to produce receivers for the growing market. The largest expansion of production moved outside the state, however, in an experiment launched in Memphis, Tennessee. RCA invested $20 million in a new plant that executives claimed would be the site of future television receiver production. Though RCA's plant location team had been extremely careful in choosing the new site, the promise of industrial growth in the southern United States was never fulfilled.[74]

CHAPTER THREE

Bordering on the Sun Belt:
Memphis, 1965-1971

When David Sarnoff, the aging mastermind behind RCA's tremendous growth, read the investors' report on Memphis during the corporation's search for a new plant site, he concluded, "We can't afford not to move there." Having remained on the margins of the postwar success story, the Mississippi River city embodied the perfect industrial recruitment formula: plenty of underemployed workers at wages below the national average, local elites committed to providing infrastructure and assistance to investors, a controlled and divided local labor movement, and a limited manufacturing base. The corporation moved quickly to capitalize on its new site in the last few weeks of 1965, when massive earth-moving equipment invaded an old cotton field on the outskirts of the City of Hope. As the machinery prepared the field for the foundation of what would soon be the largest factory in the mid-South and a new future for Memphis, the local paper proclaimed: "Even King Cotton Bows to Progress."[1]

RCA banked on Memphis to play a central role in the future of its organization. Management planned to hire 8,000 workers at the new television plant, which would make it more than double the size of the largest current industrial operation in Memphis, the Firestone tire plant. Immediate projections were for the Memphis works to begin by taking over Bloomington's monochrome sets and then expand into color production. As the capacity of the plant expanded, management would shift component production to Tennessee from the aging Indianapolis facilities. In the long term, Memphis's "better" labor market was slated to dwarf—possibly eliminate—color production in Bloomington.[2]

The context that made Memphis the perfect location for an industrial plant, however, changed much more rapidly than any RCA executive, civic leader, or worker could have predicted. Managers made the decision to open the Memphis factory in a largely national context: the United States' borders marked the boundaries of both the labor market and the competitive challenges faced by the firm. Less than five years later, when the $20 million plant shut down, both market pressures and the labor pool from which executives could choose had expanded well beyond the United States. The sun belt industrialization strategy thus met its stiffest competition not from other southern U.S. locations but from the all but infinite terrain of the globalizing labor market that had emerged in the television receiver industry by the late 1960s and early 1970s.

Perhaps equally important was the fact that the cheap and docile workers predicted by city leaders and plant location experts never quite materialized. Whereas the company had started slowly in Bloomington and transformed the community into the "Television Capital of the World," RCA sought immediate competency in mass assembly work from inexperienced employees in Memphis. When a dramatic increase in competition from foreign firms compounded the frantic push to meet the growing domestic demand, the pressure manifested itself on the assembly line, and the workers simply balked. Although plant location experts believed they had found a sea of tranquil labor in Memphis, the global pressures also pushed to the surface undercurrents of racial tensions and an aggressive CIO tradition submerged since the end of World War II. The company found the combination so intolerable that only five years after opening the plant, it shut it down and went in search of new pools of labor in the developing world.

Memphis before RCA

Since the mid-nineteenth century, the processing, shipping, and financing of local commodities—hardwoods, soybeans, and, above all, cotton—had played a decisive role in the town's development. Cotton planters migrated westward and took a firm hold on the small Memphis economy by the 1830s, and only two decades later the growing urban population could boast that its city was the "Biggest Inland Cotton Market in the World." The city grew to become the regional center for farm supplies, the distribution and processing nexus for the vast cotton market, and, most important, the headquarters for trading and banking in the northern part of the rich Mississippi Delta.

At the core of the antebellum cotton economy, of course, were the slaves who planted, tended, picked, and shipped the cotton around the world. Memphis therefore profited from a sizable slave trade in field hands and maintained a substantial population of urban bondmen as well. By the time of the Civil War, slaves made up 30 percent of the urban population and worked as carpenters, mechanics, artisans, and domestic workers. The urban masters often rented their slaves out for construction projects, the building of the railroad, and even factory work in exchange for shares in manufacturing interests. After the Civil War—from which Memphis emerged relatively unscathed—a staggering postwar debt and a vicious yellow fever epidemic destroyed the economy and drained the city of everybody, white or black, with enough resources to get out.

After a slow recovery from these calamities and the collapse of Reconstruction, race riots and lynchings accompanied a return to rigid segregation policies. As the labor historian Michael Honey makes clear, the segregation of the free-labor market along the color line remained the key historical legacy for Memphis's working-class population well into the next century. African Americans, who made up roughly 40 percent of the population of Memphis throughout the twentieth century, staffed the lowest positions in the lumberyards, warehouses, docks, sawmills, cooperages, and paper, furniture, and hardwood flooring operations. For whites, a segregated labor market had the appearance of allowing skilled white workers to maintain their social prestige and higher wages, but in reality, segregation prevented workers from taking a common stand on the basis of class and gave employers access to unskilled white workers at rates only slightly above the pitifully low wages paid to black workers. "Racial fragmentation and workers' disorganization, as well as the South's poverty and isolation from national labor markets," concludes Honey, "helped to ensure that white industrial workers—as well as sharecroppers, tenants, and other 'unskilled' laborers in the surrounding Delta—shared almost equally bad economic conditions with blacks."[3]

As racial tensions prevented the congealing of working-class unity in Memphis, the isolation of the entire labor market stalled the economic development evident in other parts of the nation. Although the international cotton trade knitted Memphis into an economic network of global proportions, the labor market remained socially and economically bound by the limits of the cotton South. As the economic historian Gavin Wright explains, "many of the characteristics of backwardness, such as low-wage, low-skill industry, underinvestment in education, even capital scarcity, were rooted in the regional character of the labor market." Indeed, one of the most important choices black workers made in the twentieth century was to break out of the regional labor market by migrating to higher-wage jobs in northern factories. This migration made Memphis the connection between the Delta's rural lands and major industrial centers such as Chicago and Detroit. Yet, even within the regional context of southern economic development, Memphis lagged behind such cities as St. Louis, Louisville, Atlanta, and New Orleans in industrial production. Although the production of cottonseed oil, timber, lumber, and furniture grew during the early part of the twentieth century, the business historian Robert Sigafoos tells us, these industries continued to depend on "cheap raw materials from the surrounding region, remained locally owned and poorly capitalized, and relied on intensive use of human labor rather than expensive technology to boost production."[4]

The formula of a seemingly inexhaustible supply of cheap and racially divided labor fueled by a migratory flow from the countryside not only lay at the core of the local economy but also became central to Memphis's plan to attract northern industry. As early as 1873, the *Memphis Appeal* editorialized that "the great want of Memphis is home manufacture," and others asked, "Why doesn't the city have manufacturing?" By the end of World War I, a study by the Memphis Industrial Welfare Committee had concluded that "from an industrial view point the Negro labor is one of the best assets of this community," and civic leaders publicized Memphis's attributes as an industrial location site throughout the country. Civic boosters tried to lure northern capital by touting, in addition to the massive labor to be pulled in from the surrounding agricultural lands, the city's central geographic location, its access to river and rail transport, a ready supply of coal from the fields of Kentucky and Alabama, and its inexpensive industrial lands. Even the local branch of the Ku Klux Klan joined the refrain by adopting "A Bigger and Better Memphis" as its slogan in the 1920s.[5]

Labor control in Memphis depended on the same factors that had been at work in Bloomington—a limited industrial tradition, low unionization rates, and high unemployment—exacerbated by deep racial divisions and a history of brutal suppression of civil rights in the name of attracting capital and industry. Memphis's reputation for having a "good labor climate" became one of its prime assets, and the strategy for industrial recruitment found its main voice and political force in the political machine run by Edward Crump from 1915 to his defeat—by a coalition of labor, business, and civic reformers—in 1948. Under Crump, democracy was a farce, civil rights were repressed, and organized labor remained in check. But the city was kept clean, government ran relatively efficiently, the Klan was suppressed, and goods and services were readily delivered in exchange for patronage and obeisance. In a break from southern tradition, even the 40 percent of the population that were African American had been enfranchised within the narrow confines of the Crump machine. Explaining that the "best business is the best politics," Crump sought social peace and low wages as a way to increase the number of jobs in his city. The growing power of the CIO was one of Crump's biggest fears, since the organization's struggle to unionize factory workers would directly undermine his plans for industrial recruitment and development in Memphis.[6]

Boss Crump's plans to use labor peace as an incentive for industrial recruitment had an ironic edge, as increases in the number of factory workers simply brought on increased efforts for labor organization. The city's biggest success in attracting northern investment, the opening of a Firestone plant in 1937, had the unintended effect of helping to transform the labor culture of Memphis. In a preview of RCA's Camden-to-Bloomington dynamic, CIO organizing drives placed new pressures on the rubber tire industry in Akron, Ohio, in the 1930s. Goodyear responded by fleeing to Gadsden, Alabama, and Firestone chose to locate production in Memphis. The Firestone operation became the largest nonunion rubber factory in the country, and despite productivity rates that surpassed those in Akron, its wages remained only half what they were in the North. Within the growing industrial sector, economically marginalized black workers carried the heaviest burdens of organizing at Firestone and many smaller industries, but white workers enjoyed the majority of the benefits of union membership.[7]

Deeply exacerbating racial divisions during organizing drives, as the CIO publicist Lucy Randolph Mason put it, was the fact that there was "no Bill of Rights in Memphis, Tennessee." Unleashing a brutal campaign against industrial unionism, Crump announced, "We ain't gonna have any Chicago, Detroit, or New York in Memphis, Tennessee. We ain't gonna have any niggerloving communist union in Memphis, Tennessee." As in the rest of the country, however, the New Deal and the war brought profound social, political, and economic changes to Shelby County. War production delivered thousands of industrial jobs that made Memphis fertile soil for the CIO organizers Crump feared. One labor leader responded to Crump's protestations: "Mr. Crump, it is not a nigger-loving communist union, and we've got thirty thousand CIO members in Memphis today. You say we aren't gonna have 'em, but we already have 'em." Biracial organizing by the CIO unions won the Firestone plant in 1942, and by 1943 Memphis had 5,000 members in the United Rubber Workers, 4,000 signed on to the United Cannery, Agricultural, Packing, and Allied Workers of America, 2,000 in the United Steel Workers, and 1,500 members of the United Auto Workers. "Crump," Michael Honey concludes, "obviously realized that the industrial sector he had promoted so heavily was becoming a battleground over the assigned role of blacks [and organized labor] in southern society."[8]

Postwar Memphis

Biracial unionism in the South had always been vulnerable to charges of being led by communists, and the postwar red scare provided ample opportunity for anticommunism to become the rallying cry for elites and racially anxious workers throughout the city. Some of the most committed activists were driven out of the Memphis labor movement after the war, segregation reappeared, and the combined labor/civil rights agenda that had informed earlier efforts all but disappeared. After Boss Crump died in 1954, the CIO sought participation in local politics and turned its efforts toward restrained civic reform. "The unions made few subsequent moves to endanger this new-found respectability," explains Honey. "The days of organizing the unorganized were over." The 1947 Taft-Hartley Act, Cold War hysteria, and a hasty retreat from civil rights left one of the most successful biracial organizing drives in the South paralyzed. The labor force once again divided between better-paid and relatively skilled white workers and a subclass of African Americans who were denied access to better jobs and training.[9]

Industrial opportunity in Memphis had grown rapidly during World War II as the number of black men and women with factory jobs doubled. After the war, Memphians welcomed four large manufacturing firms to their city: International Harvester, Kimberly-Clark, Borg-Warner, and General Electric. Less than 7 percent of Memphis residents had industrial jobs before World War II; 20 percent did so by 1950. Despite such industrial growth throughout the rising sun belt, however, by 1961 the South had a smaller union density than it had had in 1950 or 1945. Although the immediate post-war experience proved profitable to Memphis's working class, from the 1950s onward very few new opportunities came to Memphis and many others went away. Mechanization eliminated many industrial jobs, and the mechanical cotton harvesters that swept through the Delta pushed sharecroppers off the land. In 1950, machines harvested only 5 percent of the cotton crop; by the late 1960s mechanization had taken over 90 percent of the harvest. The elimination of cotton work not only drove southerners north, it pushed increasing numbers of undereducated and poorly trained agricultural workers into cities such as Memphis. The wartime demand offered unskilled workers employment as factory labor; the end of the war forced many, particularly African Americans, back into casual jobs, grueling physical labor, or domestic work.[10]

Despite limited blue-collar opportunities, the growth rates of both per capita income and industrialization were higher in the South than anywhere else in the country. In the 1940s, per capita income in the South was only 60 percent of the figure for the United States as a whole, but it had risen to 80 percent of the national average by 1969. Much of this growth was poorly distributed, however, as the South still had 46 percent of the nation's poor persons by the late 1960s, and the absolute gap in income between whites and blacks had actually increased between 1959 and 1969 both in the South and in the United States as a whole. Much of the South's economic "development" was a product of the migration of poor people out of the South and the commitment of local elites to importing northern capital. Moreover, progress for blue-collar women remained dismal. Of the increasing number of new jobs available, black women held between 3.0 and 5.5 percent, whereas they held 17 to 37 percent of the jobs in the South's traditional manufacturing sectors—food, tobacco, wood products, and furniture. Much of the growth in employment associated with the rise of the sun belt, such as that in light manufacturing, was actually quite limited; much larger numbers of jobs were added in the more traditional industrial sectors of the southern economy. For instance, employment in the manufacturing of electrical equipment, the sector with the highest growth in the sun belt, shot up 131 percent during the 1960s, but absolute growth was much larger in traditional sectors such as trade, government, and services.[11]

The Arrival of RCA

The demand for job-creating investment from the North reached fever pitch in the 1960s, fostering what the historian James C. Cobb calls "a decade of torrid interstate competition for industry." Tennessee's Industrial Development Division first contacted RCA in 1961, and the director of industrial development for Memphis Light, Gas & Water, Daniel D. Dale, had been pursuing his connections with the company for many years, but the project had waxed and waned since the early 1960s. Taking care that their competitors knew nothing about their connections with Memphis, RCA executives made the decision to move to Shelby County under what the local papers described as "cloak and dagger" secrecy. Fearing that speculation might drive up land costs or that news of the move would disrupt labor relations at older RCA plants, company representatives went so far as to use pencils embossed with the name of another company and were introduced around the city under fictitious names that they changed regularly. Executives never revealed their identity until the deal had been concluded.[12]

A survey to determine the reasons that electrical firms had selected Tennessee as a production site in the late 1960s suggests the factors RCA probably took into consideration in its choice of Memphis. The top three—low-cost and available labor, cooperative community leadership, and favorable labor relations—had been constant lures throughout the labor history of Memphis. True to the formula, wages for production of durable goods in Memphis during the mid-1960s were only 77 percent of the national average, and a ready reserve supply of workers could be found in the surrounding countryside. Moreover, the wage differentials between Memphis and the average wage in the rest of country could be attributed not to the types of industries present in Memphis but specifically to low wage rates in the same industries everywhere.[13]

Of course, as in Camden and Bloomington and in Juárez to come, it was not just any workers RCA wanted but specifically those who were young and female. "Women's Nimble Fingers" would be sought "to Tickle RCA Executive Pink," declared the *Memphis Press-Scimitar*. "When you have long assembly lines," the plant manager explained, "a woman is better than a man; she has more dexterity. That's one reason we picked Memphis, there was plenty of females possible down there." When "a girl does the same job all day, it soon becomes as automatic as the same stitch of embroidery or crocheting." A Chamber of Commerce official confirmed the conventional wisdom: electronics work "requires a lot of tiny, detail work—men just can't be that confined." Sharing his approach to labor recruitment, another RCA executive explained, "I favor applicants with an agricultural or small town background . . . somebody from the farm who has taken responsibility, learned work habits. I contrast her or him with the city-bred youngster who has seen and done everything." RCA would have no problem attracting young women from the cotton fields around Memphis, although the agricultural system there was far from that of the independent, landowning yeomen he implied he liked to hire. As they always did, the RCA executives sought not only a place with an economically weak labor force and a limited industrial culture but also the most marginal and economically vulnerable workers within that geographic space.[14]

Other considerations important to a plant location decision also made Memphis attractive. Low-cost electrical power could be obtained from the Tennessee Valley Authority, good transportation networks already existed, and Memphis was large and cosmopolitan enough to provide cultural opportunities for management. In contrast to Bloomington, which did not subsidize RCA's new venture, Memphis and Shelby County jointly invested $1.5 million in improving streets at the plant site on the southeastern edge of town. They also installed sewer lines, funded a railway spur to the plant, and increased their commitment to technical courses at local schools. Finally, racial politics—and thus the social and industrial peace—appeared relatively calm in Memphis. Voting rights had been recognized since the early days of the Crump machine and integration had been taking place without major clashes. The relative racial quiescence in Memphis allowed the city leaders to avoid such awkward situations as Governor Terry Sanford's visit to RCA in New York in search of a plant to bring back to North Carolina in 1962. Despite the brutal response of the state's citizens to the lunch-counter sit-ins in Greensboro, his aides urged him to assure the executives that "North Carolina leads the South, has had and will have no strife."[15]

RCA's fate in Memphis was sealed when a New York plant location firm, the Fantus Company, began discussions with the Memphis Chamber of Commerce in concert with the other groups and set up meetings with the executives of the other major manufacturing firms in Memphis to discuss wage rates, labor availability, and the industrial climate. Finally, after weeks of rumors and speculation, RCA authorized Governor Frank Clement to release the news of RCA's choice on 20 December 1965. The governor flew to Memphis for a press conference to read the company's announcement that the new plant would be directly providing between seven and eight thousand new jobs to the people of Memphis.[16]

A "jubilant" city greeted the news with a gush of civic pride that made RCA's arrival in Bloomington twenty-five years earlier pale in comparison. Claiming that there was "no finer hour" for the community, the press echoed RCA management in boasting that it was "irresistible Memphis"—a "clean city with [a] bright future"—that drew the corporation to Shelby County. The local press tracked RCA's every move with awe and reverence for the speed and efficiency with which the television giant could fulfill its destiny in Memphis. "RCA Says 'Go' and Machines Move in High," crowed a typical headline. Governor Clement even decorated both the plant manager and the head of RCA Victor Home Instrument Division as "Tennessee colonels" for their contribution to the state's development.[17]

More than just television assembly jobs captured the city's imagination; projections of more new industries and the multiplier effect that RCA wages would have on the local economy reached outlandish proportions. Chamber of Commerce officials claimed to be in contact with fifty other companies that manufactured parts for RCA televisions, rumors circulated as to which local firms might be able to make wood and metal cabinets for the corporation, and every construction contract became major news. The Chamber of Commerce also fueled speculation with inflated estimates of how much growth the company would deliver to the area: a $27 million boost in retail sales for Memphis businesses, a $5.2 million jump in grocery sales, 107 new automobiles to be sold for every 100 new employees at the plant, and 1.7 more workers to supply the services and goods for every new RCA worker.[18]

If any group had reason for optimism, it was Shelby County's working-class population. RCA's advertised wage of $2.25 an hour for a basic line operator stood at least 30 cents above the rate for any nonunionized job in Memphis. Women could make as much as $1 an hour more at the RCA plant than in other jobs in the area. Moreover, the plant offered job security, a benefits package, union work rules, and an air-conditioned factory—all very uncommon in Shelby County. RCA's policy of nondiscrimination in hiring, the announcement that 75 percent of the workforce would be women, and the news that the plant would be unionized made many area employers nervous. A major corporation that hired a large number of women and blacks threatened the local elite's control over the labor market. Indeed, when a reporter from the *Commercial Appeal* went up to Bloomington, one of his concerns was that the ready supply of electrical assembly jobs in Monroe County forced upward the wages paid to domestic workers. The RCA Memphis plant

Prospective employees are interviewed for jobs at the new RCA factory in Memphis in January 1966. To ensure the employees' loyalty to the IUE rather than the IBEW, the company let the union actually hire the workers. By the time the factory opened, RCA had a pool of over 15,000 applicants from whom to choose. (Mississippi Valley Collection, Memphis University Libraries.)

manager recalled, "I had a little problem with all the bigshots because we were hiring their maids away from them."[19]

Shelby County's workers showed up in droves to apply for jobs at RCA. One month after the announcement of plans for the plant, the Memphis branch of the state employment office announced that more than 10,000 applications had been filed for positions at the TV factory. Slightly more than two weeks later, the head of the Memphis office of the Tennessee Department of Employment Security claimed, "When the Radio Corporation of American starts full-scale employment for its new Memphis plant, it will have more than 15,000 job applicants from which to choose."[20] Management transferred managers for key positions from other RCA sites, but the vast majority of supervisors, technicians, and operatives came from the surrounding area. The positions managers found trouble filling locally were in the area of troubleshooters and electronics technicians. Workers with the skills needed to repair defective sets could not be found in the area, and RCA recruiters traveled from South Carolina to Texas in search of the 250 technicians necessary to get the plant running. The engineering school at Memphis State University and other schools committed themselves to expanding their course offerings to meet RCA's needs.[21]

By June 1966, a mere six months after the announcement of RCA's intentions in Memphis, 1,000 workers staffed the shop floor of the $20 million complex when the first set rolled off the line and was presented to the mayor as a gift. By the end of the year, employment figures had risen to 2,800 workers from Shelby and other nearby counties, and workers churned out color television sets four months ahead of schedule. The opportunities offered by RCA transformed their lives by offering steady employment at a good wage. "There ain't no work in this county," explained a new employee who drove fifty miles each day to work at RCA. "When I got the job I went over to my old boss and told him I didn't have to do all the part-time jobs for him no more." Another woman recalled, "When I hired on at RCA it looked like it was straight from heaven. It was more money than I'd ever seen. The plant was even air-conditioned. And the best thing, it was the first time me and the family had ever had any hospitalization. I thought the world had finally opened up for us."[22]

The Unionization of RCA Memphis

Despite high expectations, RCA's presence in Memphis started and ended in labor controversies. After trying and failing to block organizing efforts in Camden and Bloomington, RCA immediately conceded the unionization of the Memphis plant in order to make sure the workers would choose the union of RCA's choice, the International Union of Electrical Workers (the union launched as an anticommunist answer to the UE), rather than risk having both the Memphis and Bloomington assembly plants organized by the International Brotherhood of Electrical Workers. In the advent of a strike at one of the plants, the operations in the other would continue unaffected. As the International president of the IBEW explained in a letter to the International president of the IUE, "The cause of our present problem is, of course, the Company's massive effort to separate the Home Instrument Division for bargaining purposes so that in the future they can whipsaw us against one another to their advantage and to the disadvantage of our collective members." Despite such clarity of vision as to management's intentions, each union baited the other into an ugly jurisdictional dispute that gave the company the upper hand.[23]

RCA asserted its choice of unions very effectively during the earliest stages of its move to Memphis. Even though government agencies collected employment applications on behalf of the company, management arranged for IUE leaders to do the actual hiring for the shop, a move that ensured loyalty to the union of the corporation's choice. The company then recognized the IUE local without the formality of an NLRB election. The IBEW claimed the act to be illegal and filed charges against the IUE on grounds that it conspired with the company to represent the Memphis workers. Unfortunately, the RCA-IUE contract was signed in June 1966 and did not come to a vote by the membership until December, after the NLRB had sifted through the various charges and countercharges.[24]

The intervening six months gave the two unions plenty of time to tear each other apart. The IUE accused the IBEW of forging signatures on membership cards and misleading the NLRB regarding the size of the bargaining unit; the IBEW accused the IUE of colluding with the company, ramrodding an agreement without an election, and tolerating corruption in the election of International officers. The unions traded accusations of engaging in sweetheart contracts with RCA, and each tried to be more anticommunist than the other. Even though the NLRB found RCA guilty of unfair labor practices in its dealings with the IUE, the IUE had the active support of all the other industrial locals in Memphis, including the UAW at Harvester and the United Rubber Workers at Firestone. Perhaps most important, the IUE, a CIO-heritage union, had tremendous political legitimacy among the majority black workers as part of the labor movement that had taken a courageous stand on race relations since the late 1930s.[25]

The IUE had the vast majority of workers on its side throughout the conflict, and events in Bloomington virtually ensured an IUE victory in Memphis. In late October 1966, the Bloomington membership walked out in their wildcat strike against the IBEW's ineffectual leadership with regard to unprocessed grievances and the abuse of gender-based job classifications, both of which were exacerbated by a tense situation regarding wages and working conditions. The four-day Bloomington walkout gave the IUE organizers in Memphis the ammunition they needed as they distributed photos of one IBEW member beating another who tried to cross the picket line, other workers letting the air out of the tires of an RCA truck, and a man being pushed down the stairs by strikers. If the IBEW mayhem were not enough, an open letter from one of the women wildcatters in Bloomington recommended that the Memphis workers choose the IUE instead of her own IBEW. Her union, she charged, allowed "the Company to break our contract at will by speed-ups, increasing our work load and may other things too numerous to mention." With nearly all of the 2,100 workers turning out for the election in Memphis, the IUE won easily, 1,463 to 581. RCA was now the largest union shop in the region.[26]

On the Shop Floor

Walking onto the line for the first time, a new worker might easily be over-whelmed by the huge space, noise, and apparent chaos of the new RCA works. The stacking and dropping of forklift platforms and crates sounded like someone "slamming a book face down on your desk," according to one new employee. The workers hollered and chattered as they moved material and stock, the power transformers rumbled, the break horns pierced the hubbub with their blasts. The line moved extremely fast, and operatives had to be on constant watch to stop dislodged dollies of TV chassis from rolling into them. What appeared to be chaos to the new workers, however, quickly revealed itself to be the pushing of the new employees beyond their abilities.[27]

Whereas RCA had planned on a small plant in Bloomington but ended up with one of its largest, the Memphis operation started big but never reached its full potential. Problems began when the company required a rapid adjustment to life on the assembly line at speeds even the highly experienced Bloomington workers were finding difficult. The company's brief training sessions may have given its employees the technical skills to build television sets but did not prepare them for the discipline and speed imposed by the line. Shelby County's wage earners had been accustomed to a much less rigorous labor market, where paternalism, casual production standards, irregularity in work patterns, and low pay had been the rule. In contrast, RCA managers set an extremely rapid pace and planned on only a slim margin of profit for each set. Line stoppages, personal breaks, and casual conversation were not tolerated. "Our policy was simple," explained a manager, "manufacturing gets what it wants at all cost."[28]

The pressure to produce prevented Bloomington's "family feeling" from ever developing at the Memphis works. Women on the line, for instance, were disappointed to find absolutely no social space at the factory and found the foremen dictatorial. "I think of a job as a place to meet people, make friends. In the place I worked before RCA, all the girls were always bringing in food they had cooked to share. There was always a lot of kidding going on. We would double up on our jobs so we could have more breaks and have time to talk. RCA had none of that. That line was so fast I could hardly do my own job. It seemed like I was always sitting in the lap of the woman next to me just trying to finish a set before another was coming at me. . . . I was there two years and never got to know anybody." Another line operative complained that "the foremen really thought they were somebody. The bossman would walk through the shop and never speak to anyone." She decided that she would rather have had her old job back sewing seat covers for less money than face the pressure of the line at RCA. "I quit after nine months and worked in a grocery store," she said. "It didn't pay as much, but I had more freedom."[29]

Many workers thought the managers didn't know what they were doing. "They thought they were really bigshots," one worker said, "but they didn't know any more about production than we did." RCA failed to deal effectively with grievances, allowed many minor complaints to proceed all the way to the arbitration level, and foremen even forced the workers to sign up to go to the bathroom. It was not uncommon for a shop steward to file as many as ten complaints in a single shift, and a stack of unresolved grievances dating back eighteen months built up. "There was just such a backlog of grievances," revealed a shop steward, "that we were just a half step from a strike all the time." Many workers skipped sets just to keep up with the line while others damaged work done by other operatives as they struggled to stay with the pace. Even after years of production experience, troubleshooters reported as many as 40,000 defective television sets stacked up around the factory waiting for expensive test and repair procedures. At least partly as a result of the bad feelings on the shop floor and partly because of informal work patterns in the Delta, workers were frequently absent—particularly on Mondays— even after the company resorted to giving out S&H Green Stamps as rewards for good attendance.[30]

Less than a year after the plant opened, in March 1967, these cumulative pressures drove a minority of workers to walk off the job to set up pickets outside the plant in protest against further speedups. "The production rate has been set so high we can't keep up," reported a shop steward. "They've had a time-study man in here but they stall on negotiating grievances." Particularly infuriating, she said, was the requirement to sign up on a waiting list before going to the bathroom. Management, charged another striker, had "intimidated employees for not working to exceed the quota." By early evening the wildcat had spread throughout the plant and production came to a complete halt as almost everyone honored the picket line. Herman Dare, another shop steward walking the picket line, complicated the celebratory pronouncements surrounding RCA's arrival in Memphis by pointing out the "higher rates the company pays in the North." RCA "came South to get cheap Southern labor," he bristled, "but this is the new South." Although the union local's leadership was sympathetic to the walkout, its president, Virgil Grace, under pressure from the International office, reminded the strikers that their action violated the no-strike clause in their contract. The union and the company settled quickly, however, and managed to have the workers back on the job the next Monday. The major complaints—the speedup and bathroom list—were officially resolved in the workers' favor, but conflicts on the shop floor went on.[31]

Confusion and tension not only set labor and management at odds but also deepened the divide between black and white workers. "Nerves are tensed by racial situations" as blacks and whites exchanged accusations of

Memphis police stand by as RCA workers surround the plant in a wildcat strike to protest working conditions in March 1967—less than a year after the plant opened. The pace of the line, a backlog of grievances, and restrictions on bathroom use all fueled the walkout. (Mississippi Valley Collection, Memphis University Libraries.)

discrimination, explained the tester D. H. Bartholomew. "Tempers and emotions are exercised instead of logic and reasoning."[32] In an effort to combat the drudgery of production work, black workers sang and chanted on the assembly line just as they—or their parents—had done in the cotton fields. White workers complained that the chanting interfered with their concentration, decreased productivity, and made "everything a big mess."[33] Clearly singing and chanting served to lighten the burden of crimping wires and soldering terminals all day long, but it may also have worked as a way for the African American workers to assert a little power over the white establishment at the plant.

After almost two years of tension on the shop floor, the company finally took responsibility for the seemingly endless production problems in 1968. RCA replaced the plant manager with a labor relations specialist, sent supervisors off to sensitivity training seminars, and summoned foremen to weekend retreats to learn about handling personnel problems and develop strategies for individual counseling. Management also changed policies so that a larger number of grievances could be handled directly on the line in an effort to prevent the backlogs that had plagued the plant since its opening. These modifications solved a number of production problems and boosted the plant's productivity rate above Bloomington's. The factory even turned profitable in mid-1968. What little hope there was for shop-floor stability at RCA, however, was shattered by the assassination of Dr. Martin Luther King Jr. on 4 April 1968 in downtown Memphis.

Carrying the Man's Garbage

The City of Hope had been spared much of the turmoil of desegregation in the 1950s and 1960s, as most public spaces were integrated relatively peacefully. Despite the outward appearance of peace, however, Memphis's black population remained very much at the bottom of the city's economic and social scale, and frustrations were never far from the surface. Many political tensions remained unresolved since the crumbling of the Crump machinery in the mid-1950s, and a liberal mayor elected with black support in 1963 proved ineffectual in delivering economic change to the African American community. Worsening the situation for black workers, the 1967 mayoral race split the black vote and Henry Loeb was elected mayor of Memphis without African American support at the same time that the labor politics of Memphis burst upon the national stage.

In February 1968, twenty-two of Memphis's black sanitation employees working on sewers and drains were sent home because of rain. Although white supervisors drew pay for the entire day, black laborers were paid for only two hours of work. The pay could be as little as $1.10 an hour to begin with—more than $1 less than RCA operatives received—and served as a key point of contention between the sanitation workers and the city. Only a tiny minority of the sanitation employees had been paying dues to the American Federation of State, County, and Municipal Employees, but a strike meeting called after the incident surprised many people by attracting 400 workers to the Labor Temple, ready to act on the problem. The relatively minor grievance quickly escalated into a series of overdue demands, and only 200 of the 1,300 employees showed up for work on Monday. The strike tapped a deep reservoir of tension as hundreds of the lowest-paid male employees in the city marched with signs declaring, "I am a man."

Mayor Loeb refused to bargain with the sanitation workers and allowed the strike to drag on for sixty-five days. The union's agenda coalesced into a few key demands: union recognition, a contract, grievance procedures, dues checkoffs, merit promotions without regard to race, and pay raises. "The strike is illegal," the mayor myopically declared, "and you can't deal with illegality." [34]

On 29 March 1968, the day after marchers supporting the sanitation workers' strike rioted under Martin Luther King's leadership, National Guardsmen armed with 50-caliber machine guns ensured the peace. King returned to Memphis determined to reclaim the movement's commitment to nonviolence. His assassination on the balcony of the Lorraine Motel, however, sparked outrage and violence not only on the RCA assembly lines but in cities throughout the nation. (Mississippi Valley Collection, Memphis University Libraries.)

Religious, civil rights, black power, and labor groups quickly rallied to the cause of the garbage workers, offering both funding and organizational assistance. Effective boycotts, rallies, and marches took place throughout the late winter, and Martin Luther King Jr. showed up to address a large rally on 18 March. Moved by the energy of the protest and his increased interest in connecting civil rights with poverty and other economic issues, King advocated a one-day general strike and agreed to return to lead a march on the chosen day. Ten days later, he returned to lead a protest of 5,000 people through Memphis. The march turned into a riot. Police turned on the protesters with tear gas and violence, and the march ended in the arrest of 300 people, the injury of 60, and the death of one young African American man.[35]

Many white Memphians regarded the violence as a victory against the strikers, and others across the nation began to question King's ability to lead a nonviolent movement as the slow pace of change pushed so many African Americans toward militancy. King had begun to infuse his civil rights agenda with an appeal to broader class-based issues through his Poor People's Campaign. To succeed, he had to demonstrate his leadership ability to the country, and another demonstration in Memphis would provide that opportunity. This time, however, he gave the younger and more militant protesters a role in planning the demonstration in order to include their ideas and restrain their violence and vandalism.

While King was preparing for his second march to bring dignity and economic justice to the sanitation workers in Memphis, an assassin's bullet took his life as he stood with colleagues on a balcony of the Lorraine Motel. Memphis, in concert with much of the rest of the country, exploded in arson, looting, and gunfire. Clarence Coe, a black worker at the Firestone plant, recalled that the event signaled nothing short of Armageddon. "I told some of the other guys out there that we'd probably never see each other again," he said. "I just expected to go to war. I mean, that's what I came home for, that's what I was planning on. And I thought that would just happen all over the world."[36]

In the heat of the civil rights and black power movements, and after years of denied reform and stagnant economic progress, King's murder signaled the further racialization of already tense labor relations at RCA. When the devastating news of the civil rights leader's assassination reached the assembly lines, such pandemonium broke out that all of the workers had to be sent home and the factory temporarily closed as foremen abandoned all hope of getting workers to return to the line. After King's assassination, African American workers became increasingly aggressive in their demands against the company, and disputes often raged over broad social problems rather than issues specifically addressed in the contract. In an assertion of power over the shop floor, workers often followed the rules to the letter and pushed minor grievances all the way through the arbitration machinery. Workers sought to correct a variety of problems throughout the plant, and the black workers unified their votes in order to replace many union officials and most of the shop stewards with African American candidates.[37]

Little more than two months after the slaying of Dr. King, Virgil Grace, IUE Local 730's black president, penned a manifesto that reflected the new militancy. "This Local Union has, for almost a year and a half," he wrote, "explored every avenue searching for evidence to substantiate the theory that the management of RCA Memphis is even remotely interested in the individual employee, his problems or his welfare." Unable to "uncover even a shred" of evidence to substantiate this idea, the local leadership found management to be "masters of deception" who "have been weaving tangled webs, trying desperately to thwart the responsible efforts of the IUE Local 730 to prevent our members from being raped of their dignity and pride." The membership had ordered him to tell the company that the "day of reckoning is at hand." He took the company to task for violating not just the spirit of the contract but the fundamental rules of human decency as well:

> The days of slavery and all its attendant misery was abolished a century ago. We will not allow RCA to institute it all over again. RCA must realize that our foreman is not our lord and master and the Corporation does not own us body and soul. We have stood by too long and watched the grievance machinery choke up with garbage, which should have been settled without a grievance. We have been content with crumbs, when the whole cake was rightfully ours. We are not convinced [that] the no strike clause in our National Agreement prohibits this Local Union from taking action against a Company who would not stop short of anything in their mad dash to attain the almighty production quota and, in many cases, more. . . . We do not hold to the theory that a Company can, because of a no strike clause, do anything it wishes without regard for contractual obligation, moral obligations or the basic principles by which all members of society are governed.[38]

Over a year after the King assassination, life at the plant began to settle down. Interviews with operatives and supervisors suggest that the majority of production problems had been resolved by 1969. The plant became increasingly profitable, and production rates higher than those at the Bloomington factory seemed to suggest the future might again belong to Memphis. It was the calm before another storm, however.

National contract negotiations in the spring of 1970 progressed slowly as workers pushed for wage increases under the squeeze of inflation. On 3 June 1970 all IUE-RCA members rejected a contract similar to the one signed by the IBEW in Bloomington and walked off the job. The bitter strike lasted eleven weeks. The operatives who returned to work in August 1970 earned just under $3 an hour.[39]

The Shutdown

Although color production had already been shifted back to Bloomington during the IUE strike, company officials flatly denied that the dispute had anything to do with the announcement, made two months later, that the Memphis plant would be closed. Management stated that it made its decision "to meet the rising costs of materials and manufacturing" and in response "to increasingly competitive conditions in the industry." The news surprised very few in the Memphis business or labor communities; rumors had been circulating for months. In August 1967 the 4,000 workers produced their millionth television set. That point represented the company's employment peak in Memphis; from then on, employment figures dwindled. "We first started hearing rumors that the plant would close about a year ago," explained a worker in December 1970. "At first we didn't pay much attention. Then the layoffs started." In October 1969 RCA "temporarily" laid off 600 of the remaining 3,000 workers but had no intention of rehiring them, as the reduction accompanied the termination of lucrative color production at the factory. A year later, when executives recommended closing the plant, only 1,600 production workers remained—a far cry from the 8,000 projected for the factory on the southern edge of the City of Hope. By December 1970, when the plant actually terminated production, only 1,200 workers remained to be dismissed.[40]

Roughly 70 percent of the workers who lost their jobs in the final shutdown were heads of households and most were women. Low-skilled assembly work had rescued many of those women from poverty. When RCA announced the plant's closure, creditors who had loaned money to its employees started demanding payment in full. "When I got that final notice just before Christmas I was mad as hell," one woman said. Having been drawn into consumer debt by the security of a factory job, she worried about how she would pay her way. "I had more bills than when I had gone to work. Worst of all, I lost my hospitalization for my kids. All I could think, if I didn't find another job, we'd have to go back down to that City Hospital if anything happened." Moreover, the skills learned at RCA were not transferable to any other job in Memphis. Return to the low pay of the secondary labor market was all that remained. "Man, I can't tell you how I felt. I felt a lot worse when I tried to find another job," said a former line operative. "Who wanted a woman that could solder TV terminals? Nobody. The only thing available was a cook's helper in a nursing home paying less money than I got from unemployment." Doug Payne echoed, "RCA was the best thing to ever come to Memphis. I hate to see it go."[41]

Although many rallied to try to save the factory, the corporation could not be influenced. Five years earlier, David Sarnoff had proclaimed a partnership for the future between RCA and Memphis. Since then Robert Sarnoff, his son, had taken over the helm of the company, and the mayor could not even get his secretary to return his calls. Paul Jennings, International president of the IUE, blasted the company for abandoning Memphis. "This is a cruel blow to the thousands of workers affected. It is a case of increased profits for the corporation [and] lost jobs for your employees." RCA blamed the closure on a sales slump, but, queried Jennings, "assuming this is sufficient explanation for laying off 1,600 workers during the Christmas season, let me ask if RCA will build plants in America when domestic consumption rises? Or will you continue to move off-shore at our expense?"[42]

The cause of RCA's shutdown in Memphis became a focus of speculation that resulted in a great deal of finger-pointing throughout the community. The Memphis elite blamed the workers for closure of the plant. Rumors had made their way around Memphis that the workers talked back to managers, that they lacked the basic skills to do their assigned tasks, and most important, that the International Union of Electrical Workers had spoiled them. Although the Memphis plant had actually surpassed Bloomington in production rates and RCA had never suggested that its employees were at fault, locals accused the former workers of poor productivity, bad work ethics, and plain laziness. Two researchers who have examined the shutdown conclude that "local businessmen were bitter that RCA had increased wage rates in the area." A few workers blamed management for making poor decisions and pushing the workforce too hard too soon. The majority of the black women, the majority of the workforce, however, more accurately pointed to international competition as the reason for the closure.[43]

From National to Transnational Markets

RCA and other receiver producers faced a double pinch in the second half of the 1960s. First, the television boom that the corporation invested millions of dollars to exploit turned out to be sluggish at best; second, U.S. producers faced a dramatic upsurge in foreign competition.[44] Throughout the first half of the 1960s, consumption of receivers followed a general upward trend, but it dropped from 13.0 million sets in 1966 to 11.2 million in 1967. Moreover, the value of purchases declined from $2.4 billion in 1966 to $1.8 billion in 1970. In sum, total consumption was down 6 percent from 1966 to 1970, but the value of that consumption had fallen by a dramatic 26 percent. As the domestic market declined, moreover, a wave of imports (mostly monochrome but color too) drew a larger percentage of a shrinking market away from domestic producers. The competitive threat of the Japanese electronics industry, efficiently guided by an industrial policy geared toward winning the export market, stunned the television receiver industry as consumption of lower-priced, high-quality imports jumped from 12 percent to 37 percent in quantity and from 5 percent to 18 percent in value between 1966 and 1970. Challenged by a flood of imports, U.S. producers failed to make any inroads into the export market, as Figure 3.1 indicates.[45]

With the downturn in consumption and a dramatic upturn in competition, RCA sought to widen its market share by lessening labor costs. Hence its insistence on pushing the new workers beyond their capabilities and their

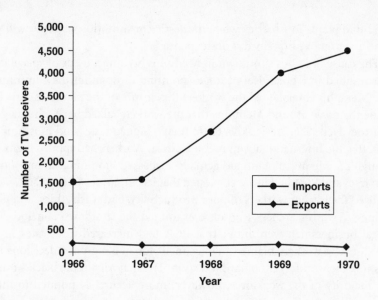

Figure 3.1. Television receivers imported to and exported from the United States, 1966–1970 (millions of receivers). (U.S. Tariff Commission, *Television Receivers and Certain Parts Thereof: Report to the President on Investigation No. TEA-I-21*, Publication 436 [Washington, D.C.: GPO, 1971], A-56.)

subsequent unruliness. With the failure of this tactic, the firm sought new workers. Color production was recentralized back in Bloomington before being parceled out to Mexico, while all compact black-and-white production went to Taiwan until those sets became unfashionable and production proved cheaper in Mexico. Meanwhile, electronics workers in Memphis shouldered the burden of the global pressures on both the assembly lines and the unemployment lines. RCA, in contrast, could maintain its competitive position by relocating production to even less expensive and (it hoped) more docile labor markets.

Such moves were facilitated by the U.S. government. With the assistance of tariff provision 807, a company that exported raw materials and parts, had them processed or assembled abroad, and reimported the finished goods paid a tariff only on the value added outside of the country. The only stipulation—and a vague one—was that the products could not have "lost their physical identity . . . by change in form, shape, or otherwise" while abroad. Provision 807 was perfect for the television industry, in which distinguishable parts were assembled into larger components and products. Foreign value added to TV sets under provision 807 grew from $3 million in 1967 to $35 million only three years later, at the time of the shutdown, and would continue to grow in importance for decades to come. Without the tax loophole, argued U.S.

producers, it would be impossible for them to maintain a foothold in the domestic market in the face of foreign competitors.[46]

The Trade Expansion Act of 1962, which lowered tariffs up to 50 percent, also made readjustment and retraining funds available to workers affected by trade liberalization. The act stipulated that if a specific set of criteria were met, extensive federal funds would be available for the displaced workers. To qualify, workers had to show that imports of similar products were increasing, the increases had resulted from trade agreement concessions, and the trade concessions were the major factor in employment reductions. Since tariffs on television receivers had slowly been reduced from 15 percent to 6 percent between 1948 and 1971, proving a direct relationship would be tricky.[47]

The Tariff Commission tied in a 2–2 decision as to whether the Memphis workers fitted the criteria for the retraining benefits. Ruling against the IUE's case, one judge argued that the major duty concessions on televisions had been granted in previous decades and that the minor concessions given in the late 1960s could not account for the impact on domestic producers. The other judge who ruled against the former RCA employees found that the problems of the television receiver industry could be attributed not to any specific trade pact but to Japanese dumping of television receivers on the U.S. market and tariff provision 807. The two judges who affirmed the workers' claim simply argued that had the original 1930 tariff rate of 35 percent still been in effect, the duty on a foreign television receiver would have been $56 rather then the $14 in place in 1970. Given the sharp price competition in the industry, they posited, that duty would have protected the firm and its workers. Although the rulings against the workers followed the letter of the law more precisely, the judges who argued in favor of the IUE may have actually followed the spirit of the act more closely. The tie vote moved the case to the White House. In May 1971, Richard Nixon broke the tie by voting in favor of the Memphis workers and extended retraining funds to the "redundant" RCA employees of Shelby County.[48]

The economics of the plant closure were far more complex than the questions surrounding the workers' eligibility for adjustment assistance. In contrast to the Keynesian formula that supported the postwar boom, the interests of firms, which initiated cheap foreign labor strategies, and those of workers, who wanted to maintain a high employment level, began to diverge. This change in the meaning of "foreign trade" for U.S. labor marked the beginning of the division between the growth strategies of major U.S.-based corporations and the interests of U.S. workers. The postwar boom that briefly embraced so many Memphis women and men began to erode for workers across the country in the late postwar era. "As labor came to be seen more as a production cost to be minimized rather than a source of final demand," explains Patricia Wilson, "the social contract underlying the mass production model was fundamentally undermined."[49]

The Memphis workers did not know the exact statistical story or the precise economic complexities behind the shutdown, but they had their own understanding of events from firsthand experience. Searching for words to capture the abstract global changes engulfing them, the local's leader explained to members during a major layoff, "In life there are many enigimatical, intricate, and perplexing problems, that we sometimes have no control over. To you I know this is one." They may have been only dimly aware of technical details, but the workers knew exactly where production was headed as they crated up test machinery and shipped it to "RCA Taiwan Ltd." Many Memphians even insisted that the company had put assembly equipment on a barge and shipped it down the Mississippi to be sent on to the Far East. Memphis's color production, however, returned to Bloomington, but even that factory's labor-intensive component assembly would soon be shifted out of Indiana to northern Mexico.[50]

Memphis Aftermath

The closure took place at an inopportune time for Memphis workers. The local labor market was weaker than it had been for several months, and the shutdown exacerbated employment problems caused by the 1969–70 recession. Unfortunately, the Trade Readjustment Assistance (TRA) program failed to do much beyond extending unemployment benefits. A government-funded study of the Memphis workers' plight uncovered no evidence "to confirm the hypothesis that extended benefits, counseling, testing and training improved a worker's job search procedure." No correlation between training and reemployment could be found in either the short or long term of unemployment. Workers who received readjustment benefits were actually less satisfactorily adjusted two years after the shutdown than those who did not receive them—their earnings losses were greater than those of a control group of unemployed workers.[51]

As of February 1972, 1,125 former RCA employees had signed up for the special benefits. Approximately 90 percent of them were women, two-thirds of whom were black and had received a high school diploma, and the majority were their families' primary breadwinners. Eighteen months later, 300 former workers had completed the training program for work in a variety of blue-collar occupations and some had found jobs in their new fields. Of the forty-seven who trained to be cosmetologists, for instance, twenty-nine found work in their field. Forty went to clerical programs and twenty-three had found secretarial jobs thirty days after their training. Of the thirty-nine who learned to be keypunch operators, twenty-nine found work. A year after the shutdown, however, 1,000 of the 1,600 workers were still on the active list at the unemployment office. Of those fortunate enough to find steady employment in any field, very few ever worked again in a unionized plant.[52]

With the failure of the government assistance program, the most powerful variables for explaining successful readjustment were directly related to skill, sex, race, and education. Skilled white men, who already had a relatively privileged place in the Memphis labor market, maintained their earnings much better than black women with less skill. With few alternatives, the majority of the African American women slipped back to their old positions in the secondary economy. Inasmuch as training had no effect on opportunity in Memphis, the former line operatives tended to treat the extended benefits available through the TRA as simple income maintenance, and many enrolled in the approved courses merely as a way of extending unemployment benefits.[53]

Another possible solution to unemployment, which the government report suggested might have been the best strategy, was an age-old one: the redundant workers should consider moving out of the Memphis labor market. Former RCA employees, however, whether for financial, familial, or emotional reasons, showed a strong attachment to place. Geographic mobility among them was only 7 percent—about half the national average—and of those who migrated, most were older white males. Nonetheless, the main improvement to the TRA program that the researchers had to suggest was an increase in stipends for relocating out of Memphis. As the researchers concluded, employees who had "held jobs as factory operatives, enjoying the benefits of a union contract, had as their next best work opportunity relatively menial service jobs, perhaps as household workers." When RCA left Memphis, the move "foreclosed their opportunity to work as electronic assemblers; neither training, counseling nor an extended job search could prevent this loss."[54]

To make matters worse, the former RCA workers' reputation for being "undisciplined and difficult" locked them out of many jobs in Memphis for years to come. Employers told the Department of Employment Security not to send any applicants who had worked for RCA—they were all known as "troublemakers" and "pro-union." Pat Hanna, an administrator for the Tennessee employment programs, found that workers "cursed with the RCA taint" were simply considered undesirable. "You couldn't tell the employer they worked at RCA or you couldn't get an interview for them."[55]

For awhile it appeared as if General Motors might turn the situation around when it purchased the 1.2 million-square-foot building constructed for RCA with the intention of producing light trucks and campers there. As the energy crisis cut demand for larger vehicles, however, GM too abandoned its plans for Memphis. After the assassination of Dr. King, the increase in racial strife and a variety of economic problems earned Memphis a reputation as a "southern backwater," a "decaying river town," and ultimately the "dark spot in the Sunbelt." Despite the occasional opening of major firms such as Federal Express in the City of Hope, and the efforts of boosters who pleaded with investors to "Start Something Great in Memphis," Memphis did not keep pace with other southern cities in economic growth in the 1970s. The unemployment rate of African Americans, typically over three times that of whites, regularly rose into double digits—officially as high as 17 percent during 1982 and 1983. "Poverty and people's situations are worse now than they were in the Depression," the Memphis worker Hillie Pride said. "The Republicans cut all the jobs out and ran all of the best plants away. . . . The jobs people do have, they can't hardly live on them. There's nothing here anymore." [56]

The corporation's social relationship with its community was stormier in Memphis that it had been in Bloomington or than it would be in Juárez. Seemingly objective findings by the company's plant location experts clearly showed Memphis to be the perfect site for the new television operation, and the community's enthusiastic reception of the news seemed to point toward a bright future. Had RCA executives achieved the level of social control they had hoped, it is reasonable to assume—as management claimed when it built the complex—that the future of production would have been in Tennessee and not in Bloomington. Had the inexperienced Memphis RCA workers not been pushed so hard and so quickly to keep up with global economic pressures, had the demand for television sets kept up with expectations, had the company not inadvertently tapped into a racially tense labor market, and had Memphis not had such a strong historical undercurrent of working-class struggle, it might have been the Bloomington workers who faced the earlier shutdown.

Counterfactual history aside, neither Tennessee nor Indiana won, for sites in the developing world grew to become the new industrial cities of the late twentieth century. Competition with "so-called Third World nations where industrial workers often earned considerably less than a dollar an hour," observes James C. Cobb, made the traditionally low-wage South, "by comparison at least, a high-wage region." The globalization of labor markets created a new type of colonialism: the modern South, as Gavin Wright argues, became a colony not "to any other geographic entity but to placeless global organizations and markets." RCA itself was not harmed by the decline of industrial manufacturing in the United States, of course, but the loss of the nation as a geographic site for production cost workers high-wage manufacturing jobs that often meant the difference between economic security and anxiety, between material comfort and survival. Although the last vestiges of the Old South died as globalization made Memphis's working conditions into the norm rather than the exception, the mobility of capital made the region resemble the old slave economy in at least one disquieting way. Drawing a parallel between the flight of industrial capital and the western migration of cotton planters, Wright observes that "in this one respect, all economies are coming to resemble the economy of the antebellum South, where slave owners were ruthless and footloose because their wealth [the slaves] was portable."[57]

CHAPTER FOUR

The New Industrial Frontier:
Ciudad Juárez, 1964-1978

On any clear night, the border between Mexico and the United States stands in sharp relief where the sprawling pale-green city lights of Ciudad Juárez abruptly change into the dense orange glow of El Paso along a distinct line dividing people between south and north. The desert dawn reveals the skyline of El Paso set against the arid Franklin Mountains dissolving into the sprawl of single-story homes and squatter *colonias* along the southern bank of the Rio Grande. The built environment spilling out in both directions from the narrow trickle of water that legally separates the two cities and their respective nations suggests a stark difference between the developmental histories of First and Third worlds. The message is driven home most dramatically by the concrete-lined, chain-link-flanked river that seems to form an impenetrable barrier between the two societies. Even with the ever-increasing militarization of the border, however, the Rio Grande continues to be less an absolute line between two nations than a crossroads that for centuries has been filled with obstacles and opportunities for migrants in search of a better life.

Indeed, *juarenses* can often be seen loitering along the river as they await their chance to cross to the higher wages and abundance of consumer goods on the other side when the border patrol's attention is diverted elsewhere. When the periodic crackdowns on immigration have not pushed the field hands, domestic servants, and shoppers to other crossing sites, a man piloting a small *lancha* or raft will even ferry them across the river in the cool shadow of the international bridge that connects the commercial centers of the two cities. The authorities' struggle to defy centuries-old migration patterns has failed, leaving the region as much a social frontier as an international boundary. The borderlands, according to the Chicana poet and writer Gloria Anzaldúa, is a place where "the Third World grates against the first and bleeds"; there the lifeblood of the two worlds converges in a unique "border culture."[1]

Many analysts agree that a distinct culture is shared among the people in the region that straddles the 2,000-mile boundary. They have long debated the meaning of the social space of *la frontera norte*, however, arguing whether it is best understood as a simple political boundary, a frontier of two conflicting social systems, or even, as some borderlands nationalists argue, a separate nation.[2] From the perspective of Mexicans, the meaning of the border zone varies from region to region. For those in the impoverished rural areas of Mexico, it is a land of opportunity after a long journey from the southern state of Chiapas or Oaxaca or, more likely in the case of Juárez, a shorter trip from the northern state of Zacatecas or Coahuila, either of which is followed by a perilous crossing to *el otro lado*. Those from the nation's capital, in the central part of the country, often view the region as tragically lost to the United States—a place where an alien culture and economy have sprung up to offend their strong sense of *mexicanidad*. Finally, northerners view themselves as deeply Mexican—a fact driven home to them by their daily resistance and accommodation to Anglo culture and economic power as tourists flock across the line to what critics describe as "an illusionary, anachronistic place where merchants cater to tourists' expectations by marketing a vision of Mexico that is a product of history, myth, reality, and fantasy."[3] All of these perspectives, however, are defined by the border cities' proximity to the wealth of the United States and their geographic distance from central Mexico.

Few developments capture the complexities of life on the frontier between First and Third worlds more than the flood of U.S. industrial capital into northern Mexico since the late 1960s. During the last third of the twentieth century, the forces of history and geography that simultaneously melded and divided the people of two nations also produced the ideal formula for industrial location for RCA and hundreds of other transnational corporations (TNCs). The same factors so evident in Bloomington and Memphis—a glut of available labor, a history of economic underdevelopment, a weak and divided labor movement, meager industrial traditions, and political elites dedicated to the interests of capital investment—could be found in unprecedented abundance on the Mexican side of the border. By 1968, when RCA made its cautious move to Juárez, the promise of cheap and docile labor in Juárez stood in stark contrast to the rising unruliness management confronted in Bloomington and Memphis. The logic of an early promoter of border industrialization echoed down the entirety of RCA's migratory path: "The paramount reason for foreign firms to participate in Mexico's Border

Industrialization Program," argued Donald Baerresen, "is the availability of large supplies of relatively inexpensive, unskilled labor located close to the United States."[4]

Although the factors that made the U.S. cities so attractive to the company were much the same in Juárez, they were intensified by the complexities of Third World development. The process of social change—the growing resistance to the prerogatives of capital engendered by industrial labor—could be more easily contained by local elites and managers of capital in Ciudad Juárez than in the other cities under consideration. Important elements of social control, such as the manipulation of gender, the checking of union power, and reliance on a flooded labor market, placed restraints on expressions of social change in Juárez beyond what the political and economic situation allowed in U.S. sites. The many restrictions placed on the factory workers' power to redefine the terms of their employment were therefore extremely attractive to foreign industrial capital. By 1991, when the U.S. Congress approved the Fast Track process for expediting the vote on the North American Free Trade Agreement, more than 124,000 workers were already employed by foreign capital in Ciudad Juárez alone. By the following year, over half a million maquiladora workers made Mexico's northern border states one of the most significant industrial zones in North America.[5]

Yet the system of labor control exercised in the border zone was neither as perfect nor as authoritarian as many observers liked to believe. Mexican workers' gratitude to transnational capital for the job opportunities it provided slowly dissolved into an expanding notion of their rights as they struggled to remove the most oppressive edges from the system that employed them. Like the workers of Camden, Bloomington, and Memphis, those at the border possessed a unique working-class culture engaged in the universal experience of industrialization. The severity of poverty and unemployment in Juárez could slow the social changes that developed in the other three locations, but it could not stop them.

El Paso del Norte

The conquistadors of New Spain knew of a low spot in the Great Divide where the Rio Grande could easily be forded and game and vegetation could be found to fuel the journey northward into the Spanish empire's far northern frontier. El Paso del Norte, or the North Pass, as the location became known, may even have been used by Cabeza de Vaca in 1535 during his epic eight-year trek across the Americas. Spanish expeditions crossed the desert pass throughout the sixteenth and seventeenth centuries and eventually colonized the area in 1659, when the mission of Nuestra Señora de Guadalupe was founded on the site where Ciudad Juárez now stands. With water flow from the Rio Grande offering a contrast to the surrounding desert, the valley supported a growing population sustained by corn, beans, and even grapes— a crop that gave the area a reputation for wine and brandy production. Spain built a sizable presidio, or fortified settlement, to safeguard the assemblage of pueblos and missions on the outskirts of its empire, and by the mid–eighteenth century the population of El Paso del Norte—including Native Americans incorporated into the settlement—numbered about 4,000.[6]

Distance, isolation, and a scarcity of labor defined the historical development of the desert outpost. The complex remained on the margins of both New Spain and, after independence in 1821, Mexico, since it was located a brutal six-month journey from the cultural and economic heart of a weakly centralized country. In other areas of New Spain, the *encomienda* system drew laborers into peonage, but the loosely organized bands of Native Americans in the north did not offer the large pools of labor the system required. Extensive ranch-style production did exist in the region, but it was generally worked by a paid labor force that exhibited substantially more geographic mobility than the population of Mexico's rich central plateau. Here the social system was less firmly based on racial and class stratification than it was in other areas of the country.[7]

Not until the end of the Mexican-American war did an international border divide the settlements on the north and south banks of the Rio Grande. Before the war, Americans—the "illegal aliens" of the day—aggressively snapped up land in sparsely populated northern Mexico and ultimately defeated an unstable Mexican government in a war fought to determine who would possess the territory.[8] In essence, the signing of the Treaty of Guadalupe Hidalgo in 1848 reflected the reality of an Anglo-occupied territory. The new geopolitical boundary running through El Paso del Norte, however, meant very little to the frontier settlements; they continued to remain isolated and economically self-contained. The remoteness of the community and its vulnerability to attacks by both Native Americans and outlaws kept north–south trade connections to a minimum. Settlements lower down the Rio Grande, particularly the cities of Tamaulipas, won the majority of international commerce.

Toward the end of the nineteenth century, El Paso del Norte came increasingly to be defined by its location on the frontier between two worlds, with the population south of the border in a constant struggle for a viable economic and cultural path between the two societies. Too far from Mexico City to sustain commercial and social contact, the population was forced to look northward for easily obtained American goods, services, and employment. The arrival of four railroad lines on the northern side of the border in the early 1880s brought the area out of isolation and deepened U.S. penetration of the regional economy through an even greater influx of cheap American goods. As a result, the northern side of the pass received the economic benefits of rail connections to the United States, while the Mexican side, renamed Ciudad Juárez in 1888, after the great liberal president Benito Juárez, slipped into further economic dependency on the north.[9]

To help the border area contend with the high cost of shipping goods in from the interior of Mexico and to prevent the region from drifting further under U.S. domination, the federal government made the entire border region a tariff-free zone, or *zona libre*, in 1885. The government designed the free-trade provision to allow European goods to enter free of tariff in order to compete with U.S.-made products. Local and federal officials hoped this strategy would keep Mexicans from migrating across the border to live, where goods were cheaper and jobs more readily available. Business leaders on the U.S. side reacted vehemently, however, arguing that the arrangement served as "a mill stone around the neck of every merchant in El Paso" as less expensive foreign goods began to outsell U.S. products. Propounding arguments that would still resonate a century later, the *Lone Star* complained that under the rules of the *zona libre*, "foreign wines and liquors, China ware, imported groceries and, indeed, all articles of necessity and luxury can now be purchased on the other side much cheaper than here. If this continues it will not be long before we will see our merchant tailors with their cutters and workmen [on the Mexican side of the border] turning out custom made clothing from ten to fifty percent cheaper than the same could be bought for on this side, or in fact, anywhere in the United States, or in Mexico, outside of the boundaries of this Free Zone." The tariff-free provisions became subject to increasing debate, pressures, and restrictions from the interior and received substantial U.S. protest until 1905, when federal officials eliminated them under the premise that improved transportation from the central part of the country now made possible the consumption of Mexican goods—always the preferred option, in the government's view.[10]

Contrary to Mexico City's hopes, the increased efficiency of transportation between the capital and the border did not solve *juarenses*' competitive problem with El Paso. The ending of trade coincided with the collapse of agricultural production when water supplies dried to a trickle because Americans upstream diverted the Rio Grande to their cotton fields. By the turn of the century, the end of trade and the dwindling of agriculture cost Juárez much of its population: the number of inhabitants of the *municipio* fell to fewer than 9,000 from a nineteenth-century high of 29,000. Thousands of people flocked across the border to work in the "instant city" of El Paso, where employment in smelters, railroads, commercial establishments, and agriculture grew dramatically. By 1920, the U.S. city had almost 100,000 inhabitants— half of them Mexican.[11]

To survive, Juárez turned to catering to the interests of American tourists in search of alcohol and an exotic atmosphere. The collapse of commerce and the crippling of agriculture in Juárez happened to coincide with American reformers' efforts to curtail alcohol consumption and other vices during the Progressive Era. These pressures simply pushed many entrepreneurs interested in indulging the American appetite for sin and vice across the border. To attract tourists, Juárez constructed a bull ring and race track, but much of the activity was significantly less respectable. What was once an outpost on the fringe of the Spanish empire quickly evolved into a center for gambling, bullfights, cockfights, boxing, and prostitution to entertain Americans who could not find similar amusements in the United States.[12]

Having hosted and barely survived key battles of the Mexican Revolution, Ciudad Juárez grew notorious and wealthy during Prohibition as a center for Americans looking for a variety of disreputable recreations. "Juárez is the most immoral, degenerate, and utterly wicked place I have ever seen or heard of in my travels," proclaimed American Consul John W. Dye in 1921. "Murder and robbery are everyday occurrences and gambling, dope selling and using, drinking to excess and sexual vices are continuous. It is a Mecca for criminals and degenerates from both sides of the border." The moral scourge of *norteamericanos* aside, the deeper problem lay hidden in the fact that the more economic benefits the city reaped from tourist dollars, the more dependent it grew on its northern neighbor, until it had been reduced, in the words of the Juárez Chamber of Commerce, to "a mere barrio" of El Paso.[13] The trap of Juárez's relationship with the North became most obvious during the Great Depression. The tourist industry all but collapsed, U.S. officials dumped massive numbers of Mexicans back across the border, and the city was used as a rest stop for unemployed migrant workers trekking back to the interior.

The Regulated Border

The onset of the Great Depression, as the anthropologist Josiah Heyman suggests, marked the transition from the "open" border to the era of the "regulated" border as the state's attempts to control flows of labor and goods became increasingly aggressive. The evolution from an ill-defined and sparsely settled region with little governmental control toward a precise line of demarcation between two countries crystallized the social and economic significance of the boundary for the entire population of the borderlands. As the line separating the two cities became ever more distinct, it never managed to divide the "transboundary urban spaces" from Tijuana in the west to Matamoros in the east. In the twentieth century, El Paso and Juárez grew to be unequal but fundamentally interdependent socioeconomic partners.[14]

Certainly the most important aspect of the north–south relationship was migration. Throughout the twentieth century, agricultural interests in the United States relied on the massive reservoir of labor available just across the border, and Juárez served a dual function as springboard to launch migrants from the interior into the United States and a receptacle for them during periods of repatriation.[15] Until the Depression, the government barely, if at all, interfered with migration, and people from the Western Hemisphere were even exempt from the 1924 National Origins Act, which closed off the stream of immigrants from other parts of the world. As employment collapsed in the United States in the 1930s, however, authorities attempted to stop the flow of job seekers from Mexico, and a nativist backlash sent those already in the United States back south. World War II transformed the border economy, however, as U.S. demand for raw materials and labor from Mexico sparked dynamic, if grossly uneven, growth. The city became a crossroads for workers heading north either illegally or under the auspices of a new guest worker program designed to provide cheap labor for American agriculture during the wartime emergency.

Faced with a sudden labor shortage during the war, U.S. growers turned to the mobilized federal government to legalize and regulate immigration to meet their needs. Launching a federally run guest worker or bracero program, the government entered the business of supplying U.S. agricultural interests with inexpensive, mobile, and controllable labor. As one critic put it, the system offered agribusiness the "dream" of "a seemingly endless army of cheap, unorganized workers, brought efficiently to their doorstep by the government." The formal program, initiated in 1942 and terminated in 1964, funneled 4.5 million people legally into the United States, but in a move that suggests the number of workers crossing without documentation, the Immigration and Naturalization Service (INS) deported another 5 million workers during the same period. "Mexicans from all walks of life," explains one student of the program, "literally inundated recruiting depots, paid sizable bribes, risked imprisonment and even death by illegal border crossing, and literally fought one another for the 'privilege' of becoming a temporary migrant to the United States." Working conditions, according to the assistant chief border patrol inspector for the INS, were abysmal. "Slaves are treated better than the men on some of the farms we have visited," he remarked. "Peonage conditions under which the wetbacks frequently live, eat, and sleep are horrible."[16]

Increased immigration also supported the sexual division of labor along the border. Men went in search of work in *el norte* while women eked out a living on the Mexican side of the border or, quite frequently, commuted across to work as domestics in the middle- and upper-class homes of El Paso. The local newspaper reported, "Even though they risk being overworked, swindled, and even sexually abused, [domestic workers] come to El Paso by the thousands, taking off their shoes, rolling up their pants and wading the Rio Grande in the early morning hours." Crossing over early on Monday, Mexican maids cleaned house and cooked the food all week and then returned to their families in Juárez for the weekend. In 1953 Anglo housewives even tried to obtain a bracero-style program for their domestic workers. Forming the Association for Legalized Domestics, they sought to contract Mexican women to perform specific tasks in certain households, but the Department of Justice refused to consider the proposal. With about 10 percent of El Paso's homes employing domestic workers, between 15,000 and 20,000 private household workers were employed in the city by the early 1980s. Mike Trominski, deputy director of the INS, said, "People think that it is a God-given right in El Paso to have a . . . maid that they can pay a few dollars and will do anything they want." [17]

One observer of Juárez's urbanization process explains, "The news that there are many jobs and opportunities in Ciudad Juárez is real in the minds of the peasants and transients who come from the states on the north-central plateau of Mexico. . . ." Moving northward, migrants took advantage of kinship networks to find food, shelter, and employment upon arrival at the border and slowly carved out lives for themselves there. Many became squatters or bought small parcels of municipally owned land on the dusty, barren terrain ringing the developed part of the city. The family often began with a one-room dwelling made of cement blocks, adobe, scrap wood, or even cardboard; as the collective income increased, they added rooms, spread cement on their dirt floors, and brightened the exterior with layers of plaster and paint. Eventually, through negotiations and pressures brought to bear on municipal authorities, utilities—particularly water—even reached the new subdivisions. When RCA began its operation in the border town in the late 1960s, thirty-eight sprawling *colonias populares*, or poor people's neighborhoods, spread across the eroded hillsides of Juárez; 72 percent of the dwellings in them had been built solely by the family and friends of the occupants. Many family members shared the cramped space in the tiny houses: 54 percent of *juarenses* lived in households of five or more and another 29 percent in homes with seven or more.[18]

Juárez's dual role as tourist attraction and labor depot transformed the city into a major urban center after the war, yet one with extremely high rates of unemployment and a growing dependency on its twin across the river. In 1940 the city had 55,024 people; ten years later the population had more than doubled, to 131,308, and it had doubled again to 276,995 by 1960. Such dramatic rates of urbanization and in-migration made Juárez the fourth largest city in Mexico by the 1960s. Of the people who lived there in 1961, however, an estimated 20,000 heads of households remained jobless, and the vast majority of those who had work were dependent on Juárez's proximity to the United States for their jobs.[19]

Although the United States labor market defined much of Juárez's working-class life and drew many of the new residents into the city, the border town did offer some industrial employment—in fact, more than any other border city. According to official figures, almost 30 percent of the economically active labor force could be considered to work in industry, another 36 percent in service, and the rest in agriculture, transportation, and commerce. Yet the existing transformative industries in Juárez, as in early Bloomington and Memphis, offered no jobs involving high technology, sophisticated materials, or high skill; all focused on labor-intensive production for local consumption. Distilled spirits, beer, soft drinks, vegetable oil, and meat supplemented the footwear, garments, construction materials, and furniture produced in Juárez. The largest plant in the city was the Cruz Blanca brewery, with only a few hundred employees. Lack of quality primary materials and skill was a constant obstacle to the creation of new industries in the desert community, and for the most part the local population consumed goods made in other areas of the country or, most likely, in the United States.[20]

The local economy's dependency on El Paso for goods and services was of genuine concern to the city's leaders in the postwar era. In 1956 more money came into the state of Chihuahua from the remittances of migrant workers than from any other single source besides the state's mainstays: mining, cotton, and beef. In 1960, the city's trade with the United States amounted to nearly 21 billion pesos while it exchanged a total of only 830 million pesos with the rest of Mexico. Ten years later, 70 percent of all residents who visited El Paso still did so to shop, where they spent $57.9 million annually on food, clothing, and furniture, or 62 percent of all expenditures on such items by Juárez families. Even the U.S. tourist dollars earned in Juárez were quickly returned across the border in exchange for goods and services; Mexican border towns together spent almost 400 million pesos ($32 million) more in purchases in the United States than they made in sales. Just as important as the outflow of capital northward, over three-quarters of the city's working population, according to a study performed by concerned border leaders, were dependent on "foreign-oriented" activities.[21]

The National Border Program

From the point of view of Mexico City and the local elite, the booming border metropolis had slipped unacceptably far into the orbit of the United States and urgently needed to be reclaimed from its humiliating dependency on the "colossus of the north." The political concern over recovering the border for the good of Mexico, however, can be understood only in the context of projects launched by many developing nations to attain self-sufficiency. Beginning in the early 1940s, Mexico, like many other Latin American nations, looked to import substitution as a means to pull the nation away from a debilitating dependency on goods made in the First World. Using a combination of high tariffs, direct import controls, and a variety of restrictions designed to channel foreign direct investment, the government sought to fill national demand with domestically manufactured durable goods and intermediate products. By protecting fledgling national industries from international markets, leaders in the developing world hoped to break their countries' reliance on foreign-made goods, which had locked them into a cycle of exporting unprocessed commodities in exchange for foreign manufactured goods.[22]

The strategy of import substitution industrialization (ISI), as it was known, had widespread support in the government and the popular sectors. Domestic manufacturers enjoyed a protected market and organized labor had room to push for state action—even the nationalization of industries—to promote economic development with the hope of social justice. A key element in the import substitution formula was therefore an alliance among organized labor, the federal government, and Mexican capital based on the idea that protected industries could afford to raise wages, maintain prices, and keep inflation down in exchange for a general climate of stability in labor-management relations. The result, the so-called Mexican miracle, was an average annual increase in the gross domestic product of 6.3 percent in real terms between 1940 and 1965.[23] In the midst of this "miracle" of national growth, however, the northern border appeared to be wandering outside the control of the federal government on a mischosen path that took it ever closer to foreign domination.

A Juárez community leader, Antonio Bermúdez, personally undertook the mission to recover the entire border market for his country. Having served as director general of the Mexican national oil monopoly, Pemex, as a federal senator, as mayor of Juárez, and as president of the Juárez Chamber of Commerce, he was selected by the president of Mexico to lead the crusade. "We must strive to consolidate our economy," he argued, "consuming what we produce, investing in Mexico what we earn in Mexico . . . since we have no right to squander willfully or unwittingly what our country needs at a time when there is so much poverty and, in some areas, destitution." In sum, he sought to remold the border economy along the lines President Gustavo Díaz Ordaz had adopted for the country. "Let us make our country economically free so that it may be politically free," he was fond of quoting the president as saying.[24]

In order to deliver the national ISI model of development to the border, Bermúdez and the government launched the National Border Program (Programa Nacional Fonterizo, or PRONAF) in 1961. In remarkable contrast to

NAFTA-era goals, the effort called for Mexicans in the border area to reduce the consumption of imports while increasing the purchase of Mexican-made goods, to increase the sale of Mexican products and crafts to foreigners, and to improve the appearance of their area and the living conditions there. With Bermúdez in charge and his city the largest on the border, Ciudad Juárez received almost one-third of all the PRONAF funds slated for improvement of the entire region. Installing modern entry points, shopping malls, museums, and cultural centers, the government hoped to make the city a showcase for foreign tourism and to create jobs for the embarrassingly large number of people hoping to find work in the United States. Overall, officials hoped the program would transform the border cities into "outposts of the country's decorum, grandeur, and technical abilities."[25]

The funds, allocated through a variety of public works programs and subsidies, were still not enough to transform the border cities into "the gateways to Mexico" of proponents' hopes. Increased tourism of a more respectable sort was the most successful project as PRONAF set out to control gambling, stop prostitution, and end the quickie divorce industry that had done so much to sustain the tourist trade. The goal of increasing the consumption of Mexican goods failed miserably, and the emphasis on tourism proved woefully inadequate to meet the basic goals of promoting employment, improving living conditions, and strengthening domestic industry.[26]

The lack of basic employment for *juarenses* and the massive numbers of migrants flooding into the city presented the most chilling picture. As the mayor noted in 1963, braceros, "having no employment and no means of subsistence, have become a social and economic burden on the city. They go on hoping to be called [to work in the United States] at any moment and bed down anywhere; they invade private property, they live outdoors, and most of their sizable families beg and steal, driven by the need to eat. They present a sad and shameful spectacle in the local streets and parks, aside from the health problem caused by the unwholesome conditions they live in."[27]

This dismal picture went from misery to crisis in 1964, when the United States unilaterally canceled the Bracero Program, thereby appeasing organized labor and eliminating a project that was out of synch with the glittering pretensions of President Kennedy's New Frontier. The termination of the program and repatriation of the braceros triggered massive unemployment all along the border. In 1964 the program still employed 178,000 Mexicans (only 40 percent of the maximum annual figure achieved in 1956). When those repatriated workers joined the people still hoping to gain access to the United States, the border cities found themselves inundated by as many as 250,000 people without income. Unemployment rates in the area topped 20 percent and rates of underemployment soared as high as 50 percent. Militant organizing efforts by desperate *campesino* groups along the border placed further pressure on city leaders. Farmworkers, former braceros, and peasants began to join the Independent Peasants' Central, an organization that steered a course outside the corporatist structure of the ruling party and the government-dominated peasant union. Guerrilla activity among squatters in Chihuahua also appears to have threatened the stability of the region. Peasants and farmworkers with few employment options even attacked military outposts and occupied private lands, occasionally facing violent retaliation.[28]

The Border Industrialization Program

Hard-pressed for solutions to the employment crisis and having failed to do more than give the border a face lift, PRONAF leaders came up with a master stroke. They would invite multinational firms across the border to take advantage of the city's most abundant commodity: cheap labor. When the bracero program was canceled, two PRONAF strategists recalled, community leaders were forced to take "a hard look at what the city was all about." What they found was tourism, the divorce trade, agricultural land disappearing under urban sprawl, "no industry to speak of," and "no hope of Juárez merchants competing in any way, shape or form with El Paso." Moreover, "we were too far from any markets and there was nothing available here to export to the United States."[29] The local industrialists, financed by Bermúdez, decided to contract a major international consulting firm, Arthur D. Little, to study the problem.

The 1964 Arthur D. Little report proposed a "twin plant" concept—an assembly operation with facilities on both sides of the border—which would be exempt from all Mexican tariffs and could offer to the developed world Juárez's overabundance of unskilled workers.[30] The result was, as James Givens, secretary of the Central Labor Union in El Paso, explained, "a Bracero Program in reverse. . . . Where we used to bring low-pay Mexican labor to our country . . . we now take the work to them." Ironically, the program launched to "recover" the border zone for Mexico ended up marketing it to U.S.-based transnational corporations. Instead of drawing the border into the national consensus of economic development, the program allowed "offshore" assembly plants to get a foot in Mexico's door. And Bermúdez and company, instead of making money developing protected domestic capital, gained even more riches as facilitators for transnational investors. Bermúdez's nephew later commented that the creation of the Border Industrialization Program (BIP) was "the logical thing to do. It made sense. American companies saved money. Mexicans got jobs. Everybody won."[31]

Richard Bolin, the author of the Arthur D. Little report, who had helped Puerto Rico to set up a similar program, aimed his pitch at U.S. companies "currently hard-pressed by imported products at low prices." Promoting the benefits of a minimum wage of about U.S.$2 a day, Bolin argued that with migration to the border zone continually flooding the labor market, employers could expect wages to remain low indefinitely. The "twin plants" that Bolin advocated—a plant devoted to labor-intensive work on the Mexican side and another for higher-skilled production on the U.S. side—turned out to be quite rare in reality; most companies were interested only in the cheap-labor side of the equation.[32] To U.S. managerial staff, however, promoters touted the city's proximity to El Paso, "which offers the living and cultural conditions of a United States city" but the benefits of "opportunities for travel, new associations, and language development" just across the border. "Of advantage to the housewife," they explained, "are freely available domestic help in El Paso at affordable prices."[33]

One major obstacle to the entire concept remained: the high tariffs designed to protect Mexican industry, which would interfere with U.S. transnationals' ability to import materials and machinery from the United States. Multinational firms had a long history in Mexico—the Ford Motor Company, for instance, had been making cars in Mexico since the 1920s—but the old multinationals did not worry about tariffs because they were manufacturing products for domestic consumption. The PRONAF planners had a new idea: firms would use local workers to form an export platform for goods to be consumed in the United States. As a way around the high tariffs, therefore, the Arthur D. Little Company proposed a "bonded manufacturing zone" along the border. Raw materials and semifinished products would be allowed to enter Mexico duty-free on condition that all finished products would be exported back out of the country. In fact, one major corporation was already taking advantage of Juárez's inexpensive workers: A. C. Nielsen, which sorted coupons for grocery stores and other retailers. The import and export of canceled coupons were not subject to tariff restrictions and therefore offered the perfect commodity to be processed by *juarenses*.

The administration of President Adolfo López Mateos had not acted on the idea of a bonded manufacturing zone by the time López left office, but his more pro-American successor, Díaz Ordaz, wasted no time before moving on the concept.[34] Octaviano Campos Salas, his secretary of industry and commerce, returned from a fact-finding tour of assembly plants in Asia to announce to Juárez business leaders in May 1965: "After careful study of border business and industrial problems, and to relieve the severe explosion of growth along the border, Mexico will permit you the free importation of machinery and raw materials for the establishment of factories and to manufacture products for export to world markets." The audience greeted the news with a standing ovation that lasted for several minutes. As Campos Salas later made clear, the government now sought to place the border zone in competition with other locations in the growing global network of factories.

"Our idea," he reported, "is to offer an alternative to Hong Kong and Puerto Rico for free enterprise."[35] The government had just taken the first step on a path that would lead to an eventual rejection of the import-substitution-industrialization strategy and the beginning of a neo-liberal development model.

Unsure of the course the program would take, Mexico City left the guidelines for the Border Industrialization Program relatively open, treating each application individually. The plan essentially created an enclave in which U.S. industry could use low-wage Mexican labor to produce goods for the U.S. market free of Mexican tariff restrictions. Manufacturers could set up plants along a 12.5-mile strip adjacent to the northern border, and the Mexican government would allow them to import machinery, raw materials, and components duty-free. The companies merely had to guarantee that everything brought into the country or produced there would be reexported so as not to compete with Mexican economic development. Technically referred to as "in-bond" industry or "twin plants" in the United States, they were called "maquiladoras," or "maquilas" for short. A term used earlier to describe various workshops, it derives from the verb *maquilar*, to exact a toll in flour for the miller's service of grinding a grower's corn or grain. By analogy, the Mexican plants assembled clothing and electronics for U.S. corporations and charged a fee in the form of wages in return for the service. The program required no official action from the U.S. government—other than the key subsidies already offered through the tariff exemptions of provisions 806 and 807—but does appear to have had a nod of approval from the Lyndon Johnson administration.[36]

RCA and the Maquiladoras in Juárez

In 1968, two years after the program officially began, ten maquiladora plants employing 1,502 workers had taken advantage of BIP incentives in Juárez. The largest was Acapulco Fashions, with 450 workers; second was A. C. Nielsen de México, with 364 employees.[37] Most of the early operations, however, were small shops that inhabited old converted buildings, had minimal capital requirements, and needed relatively simple operations performed. One exception was Fabricantes Técnicos, a subsidiary of the piano maker D. H. Baldwin, which made piano and organ components with a sizable $3.5 million investment in fixed capital.[38] But the majority of the earliest plants dealt in woodworking, a dramatic contrast to the high-technology electronics firms and huge garment makers that would dominate the city in the years to come.

After originating as an ad hoc experiment, the Border Industrialization

Program exploded into the fundamental strategy for sopping up unemployed workers in the border zone when RCA and other transnationals arrived in the city in the late 1960s and early 1970s. Jaime Bermúdez, Antonio's nephew, later recalled, "A few small factories came first. Then came RCA in 1968, and that was the breakthrough, the first big company, a household name."[39] The Bermúdez group hired a U.S. citizen, a retired military officer named William Mitchell, to sell the "maquila in the park" plan to *Fortune* 500 companies in the United States, and RCA was his first major victory. RCA spent a short period in a small facility elsewhere in Juárez while the Grupo Bermúdez built its first park around the new RCA factory, where the corporation planned to begin the labor-intensive wiring of yokes for the television receivers assembled in Bloomington. The city leaders' original nationalist-entrepreneurial impulses were easily assuaged as the Bermúdez family and their allies became the most important developers of industrial parks and facilitators for U.S. capital in the entire border region.

Perhaps as a result of the Memphis catastrophe or uncertainty about the stability of the BIP, management moved very slowly in developing the size and scope of the plant. Beginning with only a couple of hundred workers wiring receiver yokes in 1968, the plant still had only 350 workers by 1971, and RCA hired no workers at all in El Paso. With fears ranging from nationalization of their facilities to poor productivity and workmanship, many firms shared RCA's tentative commitment to the region. The productivity figures that William Mitchell quoted to his corporate recruits seemed too good to be true. "They don't believe it," Mitchell boasted. "They always underestimate the amount of material to keep the people busy. Productivity is comparable to the U.S. during the Great Depression, back when workers still had the 'work ethic.'"[40]

The U.S. ambassador to Mexico, Fulton Freeman, feared that "substantiated charges of 'run-away industries' . . . could lead to retaliatory measures in the United States that might well damage the Border Industrialization Program and the harmonious developments between the two nations." The U.S. government therefore urged Mexico to screen applicants to the BIP carefully so as to keep the border from becoming a haven for migrant factories. Mexican officials, according to the State Department, agreed to avoid runaway shops and claimed to have "refused to accept one such U.S. firm." In reality, however, neither the Mexican government nor the State Department took plant closings or employment reductions seriously except during the occasional campaign waged by organized labor against tariff provision 807. The main defense against criticisms of capital flight became the largely illusory concept of the "twin plants" that BIP advocates claimed promoted development on both sides of the border.[41]

The image of respectable firms like RCA flocking to sites in industrial parks like the new Parque Bermúdez gave the BIP the stamp of legitimacy and presented a genuine alternative to the Far East. As early as 1971, according to *Fortune* magazine, 54 percent of black-and-white TVs, 18 percent of color TVs, 32 percent of phonographs, and 91 percent of radios were being manufactured abroad for import back into the United States, and much of this production landed in the border cities. Mexico's exports to the United States under tariff provision 807 rocketed from only $7 million in 1966 to over $145 million in 1969, when it far surpassed those of other leading export processing countries—Hong Kong, Taiwan, South Korea, and the Caribbean nations. Wage rates were often higher in Mexico during this period than in many popular Asian assembly sites, but proximity to the U.S. market saved significant transportation costs. Wielders of capital, however, had prejudices to overcome. "The exotic world beyond his own border was one that the businessman hesitated to enter," opined the *Columbia Journal of World Business*. Even when investors did venture abroad, they tended to look east rather than south. "Taipei is justly famous for its day-and-night industriousness," declared *Forbes* magazine, with no shortage of assumptions, "while Tijuana—and other small towns along the border—are better known for daytime siestas and tequila excesses at night." [42]

A joke among maquila executives was that Mexico's nearness to the United States beat out the "slow boat to China" for transnational production. By 1973, 168 electronics plants had opened along the border—a figure that surpassed the number of such plants in either Taiwan or Hong Kong. Among them, in addition to RCA, were Fairchild, Litton Industries, Transitron, Texas Instruments, Zenith, General Instruments, National Semiconductor, Motorola, Sylvania, General Motors, Chrysler, TDK, Warwick, and Bendix. For workers in minor centers of electrical manufacturing such as Bloomington, the problem of capital flight to the border became a major problem. Of the electronics operations in existence in Bloomington alone—General Electric, Westinghouse, Sarkes Tarzian, and RCA—all had shops in the border cities by the end of the 1970s. Even Otis Elevator, which opened in Bloomington in 1965, had a plant in Juárez by the 1980s. [43]

Competitive Pressure, Resistance, and Flight

Obviously, we must take into account more than the unique circumstances and developments in the RCA cities when we seek to understand the exodus of so many firms in the electrical sector of the United States. Resistance to high wages in the face of simple price competition from Japan is the obvious explanation, but the matter may be more complex than that. As we saw in Chapter 2, the social changes engendered by RCA's investment in Indiana had taken a weak, unorganized, and overflowing labor pool that was "not poisoned against the work place" and transformed it, in the plant manager's terms, into a workforce with a "take your job and stick it" attitude. As the workers in both Bloomington and Memphis were aware, the combination of international competition and offshore production created a vicious circle of local conflicts over production, which in turn engendered management's urgent searches for cheaper and more malleable labor supplies. In both locales, workers bore the pressure of international competition as management pushed them to extremes in its effort to cut the costs of production. The wage earners fought the drive to increase production at their expense through a variety of shop-floor struggles and formal organized protests. Their unruliness, in turn, increased management's determination to search out more controllable and less expensive pools of labor. Much as they had done in New Jersey after the Camden workers organized their UE local, managers retrieved the control they had lost in Bloomington by migrating to the developing world.

That pattern may have had parallels in shops across the country. The strike rate in the U.S. electrical sector, after remaining constant for ten years, skyrocketed over 250 percent between 1964 and 1969—approximately the years of the wave of strikes in Bloomington (1964, 1966, 1967) and Memphis (1967, 1970). The simultaneous increase in work stoppages across the United States suggests a pattern of market pressures and resistance throughout the industry—at least, as Figure 4.1 suggests, until the labor politics of the Reagan era undermined the legal foundations of the right to strike in the United States.[44]

Whether or not the forces that were pushing firms out of the United States were similar everywhere, the local factors that attracted managers to Chihuahua were remarkably similar to those that drew corporations to the southern states. A survey of electronics firms considering locating in the border zone reveals that the top factors match those reported in a similar study in Memphis: (1) availability of labor, (2) low unit labor cost, and (3) favorable labor relations.[45] The factors of control RCA managers found in Bloomington in 1940 and in Memphis in 1965, however, paled in comparison with the dramatic constellation of variables they found in Juárez in 1968. Every socioeconomic factor that made those sites so inviting—high unemployment, a divided labor movement, a weak industrial tradition—could be found in seemingly inexhaustible abundance in Ciudad Juárez. For industrial capital, the border appeared to be a quantum leap in control of the labor market, fueled by ever-increasing migratory pressures, which added up, as the U.S. Commission for Border Development and Friendship explained, to "a social climate that guarantees uninterrupted production and a high level of output."[46]

Certainly workers who were cheap and plentiful were not a problem in Juárez, where the high level of unemployment among migrants attracted

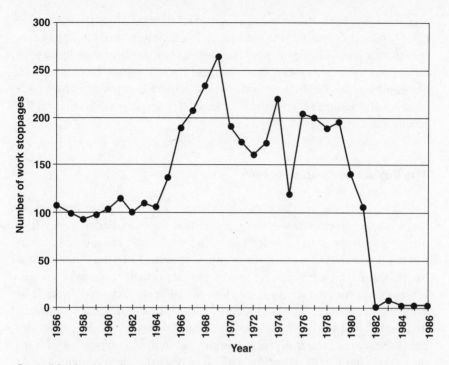

Figure 4.1. Number of work stoppages in the U.S. electrical industry, 1956–1986. (U.S. Department of Labor, Bureau of Labor Statistics, *Handbook of Labor Statistics* (Washington, D.C.: GPO, various years.)

there placed an immediate chill on labor militancy.[47] Indeed, Mexican government officials and other informed observers estimated there were from 30,000 to 60,000 unemployed men and women in Ciudad Juárez in 1970. The local wages spoke for themselves. In 1968, on the eve of RCA's opening in Juárez, the fully burdened wage for a 48-hour week was just over U.S.$20. RCA workers in Juárez, then, made in a day what a typical Bloomington worker might make in about an hour. As in Depression-era Monroe County, the glut of labor ensured the labor peace and reinforced management's freedom to be highly selective in its hiring practices.[48]

In fact, an early guide to setting up factories in the border zone pointed out that the surfeit of workers allowed employers to pick the cream of the crop. "A more stable and even more valuable advantage is the opportunity to select from the top of the labor pool, rather than from the bottom as is the case in other locations," explained the promoter Donald Baerresen. "Because the city is characterized by high underemployment, most of the jobs offered in Juárez are much in demand. Firms who administer standard manual dexterity tests find that well over half of their applicants score in the highest ranges of dexterity with scores seldom found among applicants obtained from the available labor pool at their present locations." Richard Michel, the manager of GE's maquila, explained the situation in less delicate terms. "With a 25 percent to 40 percent unemployment rate you can be extremely selective in your hiring, and we are. For every ten applicants for a job, we may hire one or two. The results of this flexibility give you a productivity improvement over what you probably realize in the States of at least 10 to 15 percent. In addition the quality is extremely good."[49]

The Sexual Division of Labor

Of course, it was not the unemployed braceros, the migrant houseworkers, or the underemployed street vendors that the maquiladoras sought to hire, but their daughters. As in all the other sites under consideration, RCA and the rest of the border factories rigorously pursued a distinctly young, unmarried, and female labor force. In doing so they actually enlarged the wage-labor pool in the city, for they drew into the labor market people with little or no job experience. Equally troubling, the combined size of the numerous firms relocating to the city was so large that the impact of the gender dynamics was even greater in Juárez than in Camden, Bloomington, or Memphis. It was not just RCA, but the equivalent of dozens, later scores, of RCAs competing to hire young women (and overlooking the employment needs of anyone who did not meet their highly selective criteria) that shaped the local labor market.

In the mid-1970s, Rosario Hernández found herself among the thousands of young women heading into the border factories. After her husband of only two years left her, she returned to live with her mother, her young brother, her two aunts, and their two children—all crammed into a leaky two-room house. While her mother tended the children, her aunts worked at a U.S.-owned garment factory sewing clothes for export back across the border. The sewing shops typically employed the older women, while the younger ones flocked to the electronics firms. The working-class neighborhood where they all lived, the Colonia Zacatecas, she explained, was "full of idle bums." Jobs were hard for young men to find, so "they stand at the street corner smoking pot, drinking, playing and occasionally harassing pedestrians. What a curse! They have no jobs." When Rosario's husband, who had faced difficult employment problems himself, deserted her, she followed her aunts into one of the U.S.-owned border factories that were sprouting up all over the city. "When he finally left me there was nothing to do but to look for work at a plant," she said. "I was fortunate to land a job at RCA. They were expanding production and hiring people, all women." Rosario considered herself lucky. "Many could not get placed because they didn't have enough education. But

I went to school for nine years and have some knowledge of typing and short-hand. For a time I thought management would find me a position as a receptionist or secretary but you need to speak English to even be considered for that, so I guess I'll just have to keep on doing assembly work." At the end of the week, she turned half of her wages over to her mother. Much of the rest was taken up by meals, transportation costs, and personal expenses, although, she proudly explained, she was saving some of her wages for a new stereo.[50]

The typical maquila want ad specified that prospective employees must be between the ages of seventeen and thirty (often younger), be single without dependents, have completed primary school but have no more than one year of secondary school, be available to work any shift, and be a resident of the city for more than six months. Many of the recruitment advertisements featured Anglo women, typically with flowing blonde hair, in high-fashion poses to suggest the glamour, beauty, and potential liberation of industrial labor at a transnational corporation. The proportion of female workers in the BIP never dipped below 75 percent between its inception and 1983.[51]

The familiar argument in favor of hiring young women was once again marshaled in Juárez: female employees were somehow uniquely suited for electronics and garment work. But now the paternalistic tones had become more strident and gender as a mode of control had become more explicit. "We know that in all cultures . . . women . . . have the greater manual dexterity," explained a Juárez plant manager. "They have the gift of fine and delicate fingers . . . they don't tire of the same, monotonous operations . . . are patient . . . and are highly productive. . . . This is why we prefer to use female workers in our plants."[52] As an early promoter of the border industries made explicit in his 1971 guidebook to the program, the maquiladoras' strategy of employing working-class daughters also had the effect of bringing the full weight of patriarchal family discipline onto the shop floor. Given the employment practices in the BIP,

> it is often the daughter, working in an industrial plant, who becomes the main source of family income. Some families are supported almost entirely by the income of such a daughter. When the father does work, it happens not infrequently that the daughter earns more. Certainly male egos, of fathers and would-be boyfriends, must suffer some deflation from this dramatic change in the economic influence of these young women. Loss of a woman's factory job can represent a serious financial blow to her family. Thus, we find that members of a worker's family cooperate to ensure that she performs properly. A worker, in turn, is strongly motivated to maintain her job because of her deep sense of responsibility for her family and her desire to retain her new life style. . . . The women are more easily disciplined

and directed, and can develop a spirit of loyalty toward their colleagues and the companies analogous to that which they show toward their families. . . . [They] are very susceptible to flattery and praise . . . they show respect and obedience to persons in authority, especially men. [Equally important, they are] less demanding of convenience than their counterparts in the United States."[53]

Because the maquila sector came to dominate the entire occupational landscape of Juárez and the other border cities, the gendered division of labor was of such magnitude that many observers took it to be something historically unprecedented, although most electronics and garment workers were women in the United States as well. The conflation of the runaway shop and female employment fueled a minor firestorm among social scientists who had shown little interest in women assembly workers in the United States. When the employers moved to less developed countries, gender politics moved to the fore. Leslie Sklair has written, "There is no single topic within the field of maquila studies that has caused as much controversy as the 'women in the maquilas' question."[54] What appeared new at the border and new to transnational capitalism, however, actually had a long history at RCA and in the rest of the electronics industry.

Unionization in Juárez

In addition to segmentation of the labor force by sex, a divided and controlled labor movement served RCA's interests in Juárez. An intense local struggle between two competing national federations, the smaller Confederación Revolucionaria de Obreros y Campesinos (Revolutionary Confederation of Workers and Peasants), or CROC, and the dominant Confederación de Trabajadores de México (Confederation of Mexican Workers), or CTM, defined and weakened labor politics in Ciudad Juárez. The CTM was formed on the national level in 1936 to organize and unify the labor movement, in accordance with President Lázaro Cárdenas's pro-labor policies, and these developments fundamentally changed the structure of the ruling party. Through a variety of political, financial, and legal subsidies, which the government selectively allocated to suit its needs, the CTM grew to play an important role in the governing alliance that ruled postrevolutionary Mexico. However, the durability of the alliance between labor and the state, explains the political scientist Kevin Middlebrook, "increasingly depended upon major labor organizations' willingness to moderate their demands and control rank-and-file participation in exchange for state-provided legal, financial, and political subsidies."[55] In sum, in exchange for participation in national affairs, labor organizations became important mechanisms of political control.

During the 1940s and 1950s, as the labor movement strengthened its "social pact" with the government, the state found itself in search of ways to assert further control over Mexico's unions. The CTM often threatened to break out of the mold cast for it; at times it even appeared to threaten the country's postwar stability. "Under the firm leadership of Fidel Velázquez," writes Victor Manuel Durand Ponte, "the CTM was prepared to charge the Mexican state a high political price for its control of rank-and-file demands." By purging radicals, centralizing the power of union leaders, and facilitating rival labor confederations, the federal government sought to check the influence of the CTM. In 1952, the relatively conservative administration of Miguel Alemán therefore helped to piece together several disparate labor groups into a competing alliance, the CROC. The CROC managed to reduce the CTM's ability to pressure the government by accusing the CTM of corruption and servility to the state. Ever since its launching, the CROC has tried to weave a path between fidelity to the ruling party and vehement opposition to the CTM. Despite its fragmented voice, labor has tremendous political influence with the state and ranks as one of the most powerful constituents of the Partido Revolucionario Institucional, or PRI, which has ruled Mexico since the Mexican Revolution of 1910–1920. The Constitution of 1917 promised some of the most favorable labor rights in the world, and congressmen and senators have often been drawn from the ranks of labor. At the same time, however, organized labor's freedom to act independently is dramatically circumscribed. If Mexican unions made a problematic bargain with the PRI at the cost of their ability to act outside the limits of the state, it has ensured the movement's survival and strong national presence.[56]

Long before the establishment of maquilas in Juárez, the rival labor centrals battled each other to represent the employees of the city's bars, hotels, and factories. In Juárez the CROC organized the small commercial businesses; the CTM had a much more solid presence in local politics and the manufacturing concerns. The power of both centrals within the community had dwindled since the 1950s, but the arrival of the transnationals offered potentially rich new organizing terrain. In June 1969 the CROC launched its first effort in the maquilas at Acapulco Fashions. Rather than boding well for the future of the workers, however, that contract signaled a series of benefits that the labor central would provide to the companies. Over the next ten years the CROC would sign contracts with ten more maquilas covering a total of 5,500 workers, or 33 percent of all the organized workers in Juárez maquilas. Indeed, some companies even found it advantageous to be organized by such a union, often regarded as the quintessential *sindicato blanco*, or white union. Jaime Bermúdez praised the CROC leader's pro-management stance: "Luis

Vidal has always been understanding. He's been a big help to us, and I think it's been to our advantage to have a labor leader like Vidal—very, very advantageous." [57]

The CTM took a more aggressive approach to the maquiladoras during the first ten years of the program. Roberto Delgado Urías ran the labor central in Juárez from 1966 to 1976, the period during which the union gained the majority of its contracts and battled the CROC most intensely for control of labor politics in the city. Delgado Urías, however, centralized his power so well that members had little say in the union or in the companies. His authority grew so immense that he began to fight with the head of the Chihuahua state CTM for control of the local transport union and, it has been suggested, control of the entire state organization. Finally, after selling the CTM headquarters building, he could not account for the money from the sale, was accused of financial mismanagement, and was driven out of the CTM in the fall of 1976. He went on to launch yet another labor central in the city, the Confederación Revolucionaria de Trabajadores (Revolutionary Workers' Confederation), or CRT, but the CTM remained the primary labor central for the organized maquilas in Juárez, though it never again wielded the power it did under Delgado Urías. The fragmentation of labor's voice in Juárez among the three centrals produced situations of almost comic-opera dimensions. In 1983, for instance, four unions were disputing the rights to twenty contracts. For a labor relations system often criticized for being overly centralized at the federal level, it appeared rather fractured at the local level. [58]

True to Juárez labor politics, the CROC and the CTM entered a debilitating fight for the contract with RCA in 1969. At first the CROC appeared to have won the day, but then the CTM argued that the workers should be placed in the RCA Victor National Union (Sindicato Nacional de RCA Victor) with their fellow RCA workers who made records for domestic consumption in Mexico City. Although the CROC contested the title, the CTM won the contract even as control and administration remained in the Federal District. By the mid-1970s, RCA's Mexico City operation folded and the Juárez RCA workers became the Sindicato Único de Trabajadores de la RCA–CTM (Single Union of RCA Workers–CTM), with the seat of operation and arbitration in Juárez. [59]

Workers in all of Mexico's highly centralized labor unions clearly suffered from the authoritarian structure of industrial relations, but there was a key distinction in the role and operation of unions engaged in the growing transnational export market. A leading scholar of organized labor in the maquila zone, Jorge Carrillo, argues that labor relations in national and ISI firms, both oriented toward the internal market, functioned in such a way that management's control over the workers was mediated by the power of the union through a series of negotiations with the company and with the Conciliation and Arbitration Board. The board also served as a buffer between individual workers and the company by providing a place for individuals to file grievances. But a new or "restructured" system of management control emerged in the maquila zone to serve the competitive needs of transnational capital involved in competitive export industries. Now the system functioned to exert more effective control over the labor force and create significantly more "flexible" workers. The union ran interference between the Conciliation and Arbitration Board and the company, insulating the TNCs from complaints filed by the workers. In this restructured model, the company dealt with the workers directly rather than through the union, an arrangement that allowed it more complete control over its labor force. The union functioned almost solely as a weak intermediary between the arbitration board and the company and served to insulate the corporations from rank-and-file demands. Carrillo labels the unique maquila system "regressive and functional"—regressive because it left little room for workers to exert any power at the local level and functional because it served the needs of foreign capital very effectively and minimized differences between organized and unorganized shops.[60]

Despite this "regressive and functional" model of labor relations, control over the workers in Juárez was far from absolute. Despite widespread *charrismo* (corrupt or sold-out unionism), the splintered labor politics in Juárez ensured that the unions were not, as they were widely reputed to be, merely tools of the state devised for the benefit of management and the labor bureaucracy.[61] Clearly, weak bargaining positions, interunion competition, and, in the case of the CTM, intraunion divisions prevented the labor organizations from presenting a unified front to the well-organized maquiladora managers; but there was enough organization to promote a high level of formalistic compliance with Mexican labor law. With no single union wielding control of local politics, as the CTM did in Matamoros, there was no single group with which management could form a single alliance. With about 33 percent of the workers organized into the various unions throughout the early history of the BIP, gross violations of workers' rights would not be in management's best interest. Particularly oppressive actions could spark the unification of existing organizations, decertification of corrupt unions, or a growth in unionization that would work against the corporations. In short, the labor organizations had just enough independent power and presence to keep a check on abuse. The obvious strategy in this situation would be general compliance with labor law in order to minimize the possibility that the rank and file would be galvanized into action and breathe life into the otherwise stolid system.[62]

The Growth of RCA and the BIP

Despite initial ambivalence about the border's new dependency on foreign capital, the swelling numbers of factories moving into the area made debate over the future of the program obsolete. The BIP evolved from an ad hoc plan to revamp the city into the fundamental development strategy for the entire region. In 1969, Clemente Bolio, an attorney, planner, and civic leader, could still argue for the diversification of industry along domestic lines. "Industrialization in Juárez is a must," he remarked. "But we must not depend entirely on twin plant operations. We must develop our own resources under a Federal department of desert resources. We can develop cotton clothing manufacturing plants here, utilizing our cotton resources for Mexican consumption. We have the raw materials for cement manufacturing. We have raw materials for a number of plate glass factories." Two years later, the program graduated from one option among many to what the secretary of industry and commerce called "a necessary evil." By 1975, with 86 plants employing nearly 20,000 people in Juárez alone, Manuel Quevedo, later to be mayor of the city, announced, "Let's not kid ourselves. The twin-plant operations are the economic lifeline of Ciudad Juárez."[63]

Although the recession of 1974–75 in the United States devastated foreign industry in some border cities and labor unrest shut down several plants, Juárez actually maintained its net growth throughout those difficult years. As Nuevo Laredo hemorrhaged jobs, only 300 of the 2,740 RCA workers in Juárez were laid off, and the rest surrendered four days of work each month. The recovery of the U.S. economy and the devaluation of the peso in 1976, which essentially halved the value of the currency for U.S. industry, revitalized the program and drew many more industries into the area. Concern that there would not be enough workers to staff the factories emerged as early as the mid-1970s; such fears were unwarranted, however, as the border labor supply demonstrated remarkable elasticity.[64]

During the 1970s, RCA grew to be the largest maquiladora in the largest maquila city. Yoke assembly worked out so favorably in Mexico that in 1974 management took the plunge into the heart of television manufacturing, the chassis. A research scout sent to Ireland, Portugal, Singapore, and Taiwan in search of the definitive plant site finally concluded that expansion of production in Juárez would be the most profitable decision.[65] Both the building and the staff had to be doubled in size. Employment reached 2,700 by 1973, and by 1979, with chassis production firmly established there, employment rose to include 5,600 workers. The shop had a privileged place in the community, was known respectfully as La Erre (the *R*) , and grew to be one of the most stable and desirable places to work in the entire city.

By the 1980s, the once agricultural Juárez valley was dominated by maquiladoras and sprawling squatter settlements. Here the Bermúdez Industrial Park, the largest industrial park in the world and the home of RCA, is seen from the air. The huge building at the top of the scene is the home of RCA Componentes, the company's original chassis plant. (*El Paso Times*.)

A common explanation for the success of the labor relations system during the early years of the BIP rested on the inexperience of the border workers. A student of the 1970s maquila experience, for instance, pointed out that "the workers' lack of previous wage-labor experience . . . puts them at a severe bargaining disadvantage individually and collectively with supervisors and managers trained in industrial relations practices." This newness to industrial life, echoed another researcher, "is one of the reasons female workers accept adverse working conditions. They have no frame of reference because they have not had the opportunity to gain experience that might enable them to better organize themselves and confront their situation." By definition, however, this relationship could not remain static.[66]

As we shall see in Chapter 6, RCA did not remain immune to the types of upheavals it had sought to escape in the United States. Antonio Bermúdez, responding to criticisms that the maquilas exploited young women and unleashed a variety of social problems, understood many of the changes he saw among the workers in his industrial park. "The girls who have worked at RCA for two or three years, say, are worth more and earn more today than when they began because they have the training and skills to do the job," he explained. "Here it's critical for them to think independently, to be independent, to have economic rights, and to be able to say: 'We're working, we're producing, and we're helping in the development of Ciudad Juárez.'" The changes in social norms pinpointed by Bermúdez could also serve to undermine management's control over its workers. By the 1980s *juarenses* showed an increased tendency to challenge the authority of the maquilas as they grew accustomed to the wage-labor life in the "new industrial city."[67]

CHAPTER FIVE

Moving toward a Shutdown: Bloomington, 1969–1998

Almost three decades after Bob Doty quit the stone mill in disgust and followed the stream of workers through the gates of Bloomington's new RCA plant in the waning years of the Great Depression, he had his first encounter with the company's move toward offshore production. In the late 1960s he and a friend stumbled upon stacks of cartons lining the walls of the warehouse, each containing a small television receiver labeled "Made in Taiwan." At that moment the future trajectory of the Bloomington plant fell into place. "Cecil," Doty remarked, "looks like we're going to be losing out here one of these days." "It sure does," responded his co-worker. In the next few years, lamented Doty, "production just kept going." Expressing the powerlessness and confusion that many workers feel as they watch their ranks dwindle and their livelihood threatened, he continued, "There wasn't nothing we could do about it. I mean, it just seemed like the government or Congress just sat back and looked back and turned their other cheek." Even though job losses began with those portable TVs from Taiwan, the local union leader Bill Cook explained, "Really what dropped our membership down to the level we are now is Mexico." [1]

The International Division of Labor

As a strategy for competing in the marketplace and resisting the authority and wage rates that labor had slowly accumulated at the Bloomington works, RCA embarked on an international division of labor that mirrored the original regional division of labor between New Jersey and Indiana. Much like the Indiana workers of two generations earlier, the population of Ciudad Juárez, desperate for work, stood ready to take over all television assembly if RCA deemed that the current assemblers had stepped out of line. Although the products were very different by the time the company opened in Mexico, the types of work segregated between the new center and the new "growth periphery" were remarkably similar.[2] The green belt plants of Indiana, which in 1960 included the division headquarters in Indianapolis, no longer served as labor-intensive branch plants, but performed the high-tech, high-wage, "male," center-of-innovation role—the type of work that shrinking numbers of employees did in New Jersey during the 1940s and 1950s. Juárez emerged to take over Bloomington's previous position by engaging in the lower-wage, labor-intensive, "female" work—the type that had been relegated to Indiana in the late 1930s and early 1940s.

Although the Bloomington workers lost most of the labor-intensive work during the 1970s and 1980s, the higher-end products and high-technology innovations stayed, for awhile at least, to take advantage of the skills the Hoosiers had accumulated over the decades. This work, however, sustained employment that was only a small fraction of its previous level.

Despite clear regional precedents in the United States, the international segregation of production was commonly understood as something new, either celebrated as "production sharing" by proponents or attacked as the "new international division of labor" by critics.[3] Typically, this division was understood as permanent by both groups. Many economists and political commentators believed the Mexican workers would be indefinitely relegated to the most mundane aspects of industrial production. The developed world's role would be to contribute the high-value technology and skill while the less developed countries contributed the lower-value, low-skill, low-wage labor. Even if the Monroe County workers had been aware of Camden's plight, and all evidence suggests they were not, they did not have to conjure up the image of a dilapidated hulk of a factory on the banks of the Delaware to know where this division of labor could lead. As the infrastructure, labor skills, management systems, transportation, and communication improved south of the border, the neatness of the international division of labor could readily crumble and production would no longer be "shared." In the end, both critics and advocates were wrong: even the highest-end products would not remain safe from relocation, and wages and working conditions in Indiana could readily be whipsawed against the lower standards and pay in Mexico.[4]

In contrast to the swift shutdown in Memphis and the rapid exodus of consumer electronics from Camden, however, Bloomington's television production simply drifted slowly away. "I think the first move was to Tennessee in a very small way," said the RCA worker Elizabeth Shelton in 1979, "but the rumors started as long as twelve years ago that eventually RCA in Bloomington would be reduced to just more or less a shipping point or a final assembly [operation]. And it all happened gradually over a ten–twelve-year period." Although marked by occasional large-scale layoffs, the decline in receiver-manufacturing jobs took place over the course of a generation as employment reductions combined with the early retirement of workers to eliminate 7,000 positions between the late 1960s and the mid-1990s. Judy Cross explained, "We had eight thousand people working here and all the chassis went. . . . [Then] we lost our tuners, we lost our pre-amp, we lost our remote control." Even after the television chassis started arriving from Mexico in the mid-1970s, the Bloomington workers at least performed the tasks of attaching equipment to the core of the set, but then the chassis began arriving in Bloomington with all the components already in place. In sum, according to Sandy Anderson, rather than laying everybody off at once, "they just sort of snuck it out one line at a time." The Bloomington workers were actually more fortunate than many U.S. workers in the consumer electronics industry, for RCA kept some production in the country longer than many of its competitors did.[5]

Bloomington was not alone as the problem of layoffs in the consumer electronics industry reached epidemic proportions across the United States during the 1970s. In the seven years between April 1975 and July 1982, 75,000 electronics workers applied for adjustment assistance. During the same seven-year period approximately 3,500 RCA positions were eliminated in Bloomington. Exact figures are difficult to obtain, as the local press, probably relying on the company's press releases, printed the good news much more often than the bad. A "realignment of manufacturing priorities" meant the layoff of 200 workers for "a number of weeks," according to a typically tiny article in the 1970s. Scattered throughout the papers in the 1970s and 1980s, articles on the incremental reductions in force made the process appear almost painless to the community, and no word of the Mexican operations ever appeared in the press until the company began to threaten the workers publicly with further relocations in the early 1990s. When the elimination of the last 1,100 jobs and the final shutdown were announced in the spring of 1997, the North American Free Trade Agreement (NAFTA) was often at the center of the controversy. Typically, however, commentators neglected to examine the other 7,000 jobs lost long before the implementations of the continental trade pact (see Figure 5.1).[6]

Two major types of shifts abroad became apparent across the entire television industry in the 1970s, and each is clearly seen in the RCA story. First, small-screen black-and-white sets were moved abroad early on. Labor content, as a percentage of the price of the receiver, was significantly higher for monochrome sets than for color sets, so, although much simpler to build, black-and-white sets were actually some of the most labor-intensive products in the TV market. With labor content high, skill requirements low, and

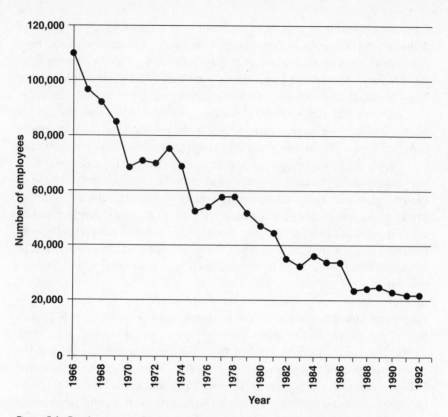

Figure 5.1. Production workers in U.S. television industry, 1966–1992. (U.S. Department of Commerce, *Census of Manufactures* [Washington, D.C.: GPO, 1967, 1982, 1992], SIC 36651.)

transport costs at a minimum because of their small size and weight, the monochrome sets were perfect candidates for offshore production. RCA's commitment to manufacture small black-and-white sets first in Memphis and then in Taiwan was its main contribution to this trend.[7]

The second movement abroad began around 1974, when a similar formula was applied to key labor-intensive portions of the higher-end products. As the Juárez case shows, RCA moved from laborious but simple yoke-winding to the construction of the entire chassis at the border in 1974. By that time the sales of black-and-white sets (and thus the Taiwan jobs) were dwindling to insignificance, and color production had been reduced to the simple process of uniting various subassemblies built both abroad and in the United States. The industry journal *Television Digest* reported in 1980, "Virtually all U.S. plants do no more than marry imported chassis and subassemblies to American tubes and cabinets, and a single line with 25–30 work stations can turn out 150,000 sets annually."[8]

In the 1970s and 1980s, the highways between Ciudad Juárez and Bloomington were choked by trucks moving parts across the Mexican border and finished chassis back up to Bloomington. "I swore RCA almost owned Roadway [trucking company] because you could almost line them up from here to Juárez," said the engineer Emil Pruitt. "No matter where you went between here and there, [you knew] that's goin' to Bloomington, that's goin' to Juárez." In a late-capitalist version of the triangle trade, thousands of tractor trailers went to Indianapolis to get parts, took them down to the Mexican border for the workers there to install in the chassis, and then hauled the chassis up to Bloomington. Once a chassis was in Monroe County, according to the RCA worker Robert Brookshire, "all we do is stick it in a cabinet and throw a pin in and a few knobs on it and the decoration on the package and we've got a set."[9]

Although resigned to their fate, the RCA employees took comfort in the belief that they did better work than foreigners. According to Alyce Hunter, "There was discontent about [the relocation of production] but we had to have jobs, you see, we had to work, [so] we had to go along with it." Some of the bitterness of surrender was alleviated by a psychological wage earned by rejecting Mexican-made goods on the inspection line or reworking defective products shipped in from south of the border. Bob Norris, the union's former business agent, was the last quality inspector on the chain, and he made sure all the finished products were in working order. The Juárez product, he claimed disgustedly, "was the lousiest stuff you've ever seen." He wrote up sixty-five rejects on the first day of running Juárez goods instead of his normal three or four—so many rejects that he ran out of paper. His supervisor's solution was simply to recategorize the major rejects as minor repairs. Pushing inferior products into the warehouse for sale, however, left Norris dejected, even heartbroken. "I took that last set off [the line]", he explained, "and I never felt more emotional in my life. Them jokers down there couldn't make 'em!" The notion that the superior skills and experience of U.S. workers might somehow insulate the Bloomington employees from direct competition with Mexicans may have offered comfort to U.S. workers, but it proved largely false in the long run. As the Juárez workers rapidly gained the relatively simple skills involved in setmaking, it became clear that the notion of a static division of labor between First and Third Worlds rested on the dubious assumption that somehow foreign workers would not be able to adjust to an advanced industrial regime.[10]

Technology and Productivity

Employment problems for Bloomington's RCA workers were not caused solely by the relocation of production; dramatic increases in the use of technology also displaced workers. As an economist who studied the changes in the industry during the 1970s noted, one of the competitive responses to the

Kenneth Wagner lowers a color picture tube into its cabinet in Bloomington in 1980. With the chassis arriving preassembled from Mexico and increased use of automation in Bloomington, production became a simple task of joining picture tube, chassis, and cabinet into a single unit. Wagner repeated his assigned task every 30 seconds. (UPI/ Corbis-Bettmann.)

pressure of imports was for labor to be "wrung out" of the manufacturing process by an increasing commitment to automation and the purchase of prebuilt components. The standardization of production, solid-state technology, automation, and the increased use of subassemblies and chassis from abroad all decreased the investment in U.S. labor required for each receiver. Solid-state circuitry alone allowed for the miniaturization and reduction of parts, the elimination of bulky and fragile tubes, and a dramatic increase in the use of machines that inserted parts automatically.[11]

With such technological innovations, productivity in the receiver industry far outstripped that of U.S. manufacturing as a whole during the 1970s. From 1958 to 1977, productivity in receiver manufacturing increased an average of 8.7 percent per year while manufacturing in general maintained an annual growth rate of only 2.8 percent (see Figure 5.2). By the early 1980s, however, output in the television industry was increasing by an astonishing 18.2 percent per year. In terms more concrete to the individual employee, a production worker in 1958 added $5.65 in value per production hour, but by 1967 that figure had risen to $8.61, and by 1977 it had leaped to $27.71 in real terms. At the same time that each worker added more value, technological improvements reduced the overall labor content of a TV set. In 1954, wages accounted for 12 percent of the cost of a receiver and by 1977 that figure had been reduced to a mere 6.4 percent. Workers on the assembly line in the early 1960s could build a set in eight to ten hours; by 1970 the time required had fallen to six hours, and by the end of the decade only two hours were needed to construct a receiver. The upward trend in productivity continued throughout the 1980s. In 1986, a worker at the Bloomington RCA plant produced 4.63 units per day; that figure rose an incredible 110 percent to 9.72 televisions per worker per day only four years later. Economists and politicians often point to exactly this type of increase in worker productivity and decrease in labor content as the key to winning the game of international competition, but such dramatic gains through technology, work reorganization, and the use of imported components may have only slowed, not stopped, the hemorrhage of jobs in the television receiver industry.[12]

Since the basic television receiver had become something of a generic commodity by the 1980s, competition in the industry came to be based less on the quality of the product than on strategies for beating the competitor's labor costs. "Well, that was the theory back in those days: trying to beat the wages," said the former manager of the Memphis plant and later leader of the plant-location team. "You decided all right, what can I move where?" Thus the globalization of the labor market played as large a part as the Japanese in transforming the industry.[13]

Indeed, many critics pointed to the cheaper labor employed by Japanese firms as the factor behind the relocation of jobs in the consumer electronics

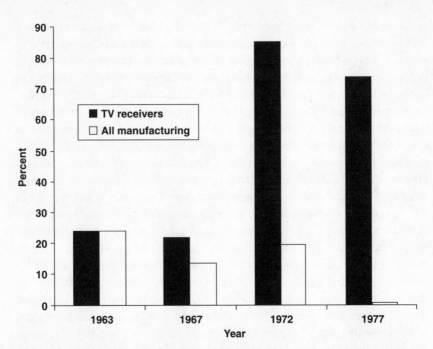

Figure 5.2. Value added per hour per production worker in U.S. television receiver industry and in all manufacturing, 1963–1977 (percent change from previous period). (Vincent LaFrance, "The United States Television Receiver Industry: United States versus Japan, 1960–1980" [Ph.D. diss., Pennsylvania State University, 1985], 318.)

sector, but by the mid-1970s the Japanese advantage in labor costs had almost disappeared. In 1963, U.S. wages were six times higher than those in Japan, but by 1977 the difference between the two had shrunk until U.S. wages were only 1.5 times those of Japan. As early as 1966 *Television Digest* declared that Japan's rapidly developing economy was no longer the "low-cost, high-labor-content bargain basement of [a] decade ago." In 1973 Sony could even claim that the two countries' wage costs were about the same once the elaborate system of Japanese fringe benefits was calculated into the equation. The "Japanese cheap labor" argument for moving U.S. production abroad held what little merit it could claim only until the mid-1970s, when it became clear that the Japanese government's investment in industrial policy, in the form of subsidized and targeted development strategies under way since the 1950s, was what was really paying off. By that time, however, the foreign labor against which U.S. workers competed did not belong to foreign firms but could be found on the payrolls of their own companies. Every U.S.-owned television manufacturer had become a transnational manufacturer by 1977.[14]

The dramatic decline in the number of workers, the technological innovations, and the pressure of global labor markets combined to produce a stressful workplace. As the number and length of operations to be performed on a set declined, the number of sets a worker had to contend with on a given shift rose. When Judy Cross began working at the plant in the 1960s, she saw about 800 sets move past her work station each day; by the 1990s, between 1,700 and 2,100 sets were zipping by her. "Used to we could talk quite a bit and have a good time too while we worked, but now," with a set flying by her every fifteen seconds, "it's kind of hard to have a good time." Whether or not the work load had been adequately lightened to compensate for the increase in speed, as the work factor requirements demanded, the task list seemed disproportionately burdensome. "They lightened the jobs some," Kay Oliver said, "but they're still pretty heavy." [15]

According to Alyce Hunter, so many jobs had been relocated or automated that the occasional figure tending a machine seemed like a ghost. "You don't see much people," she said after three decades at the plant. "It only takes one person to push the button, on and off, mostly." By the late 1980s and early 1990s, after RCA had invested $30 million in further automation, vacuum lifts pulled the picture tubes out of their packaging and placed them on the line, pick-and-place robots put the tubes in the sets, machines automatically screwed the chassis into the cabinets, packaging machines folded and sealed the boxes for the finished sets, and robots on tracks circled the warehouse, automatically unloading and stacking the newly built merchandise. Many of those machines did not even require manual operation; they were triggered by automatic vision systems. "You don't need a highly skilled workforce to produce a high-skilled product," explained Ken Beasley. "All you need are highly skilled machines." [16]

The Gender of Deindustrialization

The days when women workers dominated the RCA shop floor ended with developments in technology and transformations in the geography of production. With the relocation of key parts of the manufacturing process abroad and the automation of other aspects of assembly, Bloomington women, like their Memphis and Camden counterparts before them, carried a disproportionately large share of the burden. Once almost 80 percent of the labor force, by the late 1970s the proportion of women had fallen to barely over half of the plant's workers.[17] Female employees, historically defined as cheap and dispensable, could be readily replaced by machines or young untrained workers in Juárez.

The International Brotherhood of Electrical Workers estimated that of the two major steps in manufacturing a television set—the building of subassemblies and the final assembly of all the components into the cabinet—

two-thirds of the labor content was in the first step and one-third in the second step. The labor-intensive first step—building the chassis, doing the wiring, and inserting components—had historically been regarded as women's work, while the jobs of the second step—putting the bulky and heavy tubes and subassemblies into their final form—had been defined as men's work. The jobs in the first step were the ones moved to Mexico. "It's always been the majority women [at the plant] because originally it was women's work," explained Elizabeth Shelton. "But now since they've changed from chassis production to more or less assembly of the . . . parts into one, why it's more male work now than female." Another woman worker agreed that "there was a lot more women that worked here than men. . . . The chassis, the tuners, all that was women's work, so that's what left."[18]

Technology had a similar impact on women's employment as the labor-intensive aspects of production that were not shifted abroad were simply mechanized. At one time hundreds of women soldered parts together on dozens of lines, but the printed circuit board eliminated the majority of those jobs. The manipulation of the soldering iron, which once required experience and the development of some skill, dexterity, and speed, became a simple act of inserting a wire from a resistor into a hole on a board and passing it over a solder pit so that the solder could automatically adhere to the printed circuit board. "Originally a good solder operator was very essential," one woman remarked, "but now she's like the dodo bird, she's extinct." Yet the elimination of the hot and heavy irons did not make the work any more pleasant for those who managed to remain on the job, for now they had to contend with noxious fumes from the soldering pit. "I have seen [workers] where their eyes were watering so bad and were so bloodshot that they would have to go to their own doctor to get medicine," reported Larry Hatten. "And it was so hot they would pass out and fall over their chairs." Management, according to Jeanette Wilcher, was often "thinking more of the machines than the people who've been working there all these years."[19]

Since work defined as female was shrinking, those women who took the opportunity to upgrade into "men's work" before the layoffs began had a much higher probability of staying employed. The ability to apply for male positions was a product of a decision by the Equal Employment Opportunity Commission that cut straight to the heart of employment strategies in the electronics sector. "An employer cannot justify the refusal to hire women on the basis of an assumption of the comparative employment characteristics of women in general, or stereotype characterizations of the sexes," the commission declared. A "seniority system or line of progression which distinguishes between 'light' and 'heavy' jobs constitutes an unlawful employment practice if it operates as a disguised form of classification by sex." Furthermore, as we have seen, many women at the plant began to complain that they did not receive their temporary upgrade pay after they had been called on to do heavier work. Others grew frustrated with shop-floor segregation and simply applied for men's jobs. "Gradually, you know, the women just started saying, 'OK, we're not gonna do this,'" explained Sandy Anderson, "and we started putting in for their jobs. . . . Then I put in for male inspection, 'cause I got aggravated one day down here. I said, 'If I'm going to do this, I'm just going to get paid for it!'" After the EEOC overturned the company's labor strategy, "light" and "heavy" classifications replaced "male" and "female"; this move technically separated the sex of the operator from the type of work. Scores of women eventually received large checks from the company, as much as $1,000 in back wages, for inadequately compensated work performed at the higher "male" classification.[20]

The gendered division of labor ran so deep in both the factory and the society, however, that many women hesitated to apply for what had traditionally been men's jobs. "When they tried to put me in a man's job, that's when this red hair stood up, because I just didn't approve of a woman taking a man's job away from him, especially a man that's married and got a family," explained Betty Doty. "I think they should hire more men and get them women off of them men's jobs." The rewards for transferring to the heavy classification, however, included much greater job security. "The girls that stayed in the female classification who hired on about the time we did were laid off a few times," explained Sandy Anderson, who hired on in the 1960s, but upgrading to heavy work "saved me from being laid off." Moreover, the daily tasks and working conditions at Judy Cross's new position as a "male" storekeeper "was a lot better than a woman's job."[21]

The seniority system also had a subtle bias against female employees, for women with family responsibilities had a higher turnover rate than men. Once an employee had three years at the plant, she could quit and pick her seniority back up as long as she returned to the job within two years. Many women worked from September to June and stayed home in the summer, when their children were not in school. Such an employment pattern worked in a woman's favor only in respect to retirement benefits and vacation pay; it did not help when the time came for layoffs. As production growth appeared nearly endless in the 1950s and 1960s, layoffs seemed too unlikely to be feared. By the 1980s, however, even people with twenty-five and thirty years of seniority were getting their pink slips, and women who had taken time off to raise children and wanted to return to their jobs had lost their place in the seniority queue. Though at least 75 percent of the employees hired in the early years had been women, when the company honored workers with twenty-five years or more of service in 1971, after the first round of layoffs, only 46 percent of the persons so honored were women.[22] With employment becoming increasingly unstable, a worker of either sex hesitated to leave the plant for any length of time for fear of losing what had become one of the most precious commodities an RCA worker could own: her seniority.

Industrial Decline and Working-Class Power

Just as the flow of industrial capital and jobs into Monroe County transformed the labor culture of the Bloomington workforce, so the ebb of production reversed many of the changes. The transnationalization of production reimposed much of the discipline lost during the height of production in the late 1960s and reestablished many of the factors for which Bloomington had been chosen as a factory site. Much as the company's migration to Indiana had tamed the militancy of the UE in Camden, the movement of production—or merely the threat of it—had a profound impact on the Bloomington IBEW local. "The uncertainty of the future and the uncertainty of whether RCA will even keep producing in Bloomington or not," one worker reported, "has changed the worker from a secure, proud person to an uncertain, unruly, stubborn [one]. It's just not a happy worker at all." Others concurred. The company was "pitting employee against employee and causing a lot of disharmony among our people," said Rocky Gallagher. "They were crunching the people down by taking more and more and more."[23]

First to go was the strike threat; the final walkout took place in 1967. If the workers got too demanding, Elizabeth Shelton concluded, the company would just say, "Well, if you're going to act that way, we'll just go on and take everything to Mexico and everything to Taiwan." Between transnational production and the aggressive turn of the federal government against labor in the 1980s, the workers were in a bind. "We have no position at all right now because we're lucky to have a job," explained Shelton, "I'm telling you. If you go through Plant Three you can see the machinery doing the work and they just don't need the people." Ken Beasley, too, understood their predicament: "When you don't have the right to strike and you have a Third World country on a common border . . . then you're put in a position where you can't say a hell of a lot. It's obvious what the effect is going to be and everybody holds on and hopes to make it to retirement age."[24]

Management also regained complete control over the shop floor. "If you send for a shop steward," reported a line worker, "you might as well forget it because they can't help in any problems hardly now because of the situation." The elaborate work rules established over years of negotiations collapsed as twenty-six job classifications were reduced to five, the speedup left little room for informal forms of shop-floor resistance, and relief breaks were eliminated. With the changes in classifications, a worker could be assigned to almost any job demanded of her—shipper, receiver, storekeeper, forklift operator; or more tasks, such as inspection, could be tagged onto a line worker's assembly operations. Worst of all, the collapse of job classifications could be used to force expensive senior employees to quit. No longer safe in easier positions appropriate to their age, skill, and seniority, older workers were frequently forced to do the most backbreaking work in the plant. "Nobody likes to see a fifty-year-old woman trying to unload a boxcar . . . if you're a human being," Elizabeth Shelton said. "And you say, 'Well, look what's happened to this old woman that's been here thirty years. What's going to happen to me in ten years? I'll be out there trying to unload too and I know I won't be able to do it." [25]

Indeed, the union began to appear more as a retirement club than an advocate for the workers. In 1980, the average tenure at the plant was sixteen and a half years, and by 1994 local union leaders estimated that the average length of service had grown to about twenty-six years and the average age of the workers in the plant to forty-seven. "Those people are very fearful because at forty-seven years old you're getting a little old to be retrained for anything," Ken Beasley said. "By the time you retrain, you're going to be at retirement age." With people biding their time until retirement and the pressure increasing from management, Joska Hoke felt pleased to have made it out of the factory when she did. "Things aren't the same. Wasn't like a family anymore." It became a "dog-eat-dog" environment and "people couldn't get along." [26]

The deindustrialization of Monroe County was palpable outside of RCA's factory gates as well. Steve Tesich's popular 1979 Hollywood film *Breaking Away*, set and filmed in Bloomington, captured many of the tensions produced by the dwindling of blue-collar opportunities. Against the backdrop of competitive bicycling, the film explores the class tensions between local working-class kids facing a deindustrialized future in the midst of a booming economy and a constant influx of well-groomed outsiders flocking to Indiana University. The film focuses on four young men fresh out of high school and dreading their dismal employment options. The boys are the sons of "cutters," skilled stone millers and carvers, who lost their jobs as the mills and quarries shut down. Spending their summer swimming and hanging out in one of the abandoned quarries that dot the county, the young men scheme about ways to find jobs in the same place so they can fulfill their covenant to stick together. The father of the main character, who runs a small used-car lot, speaks nostalgically of his glory days as a stone craftsman. The emphasis on manual skill and the aesthetics of stone carving may have made for engaging Hollywood imagery, but it hid the fact that jobs in the stone industry had long gone by the time the film was made. The young men might as well have been put down for being "setmakers," because in 1979 it was the jobs of RCA workers that were slipping away.

The constant stream of new college students attending Indiana University in *Breaking Away* are an ongoing reminder of what the local boys will never be, and their situation is complicated by the fact that they won't even have the work opportunities lost by their fathers. New students come along every year, never getting fat or out of shape, complains Mike, the former high school quarterback, and the film revolves around the competing worlds of the well-scrubbed fraternity boys and the scrappy working-class locals. "They're gonna keep calling us 'cutters,'" Mike remarks after one of their many confrontations with the college students. "To them it's just a dirty word. To me it's just somethin' else I never got a chance to be." One of the four finally does land a menial job at a car wash, but the boss is arrogant and the job a dead end. When the boss chews him out in front of his friends, demanding that he punch the timeclock properly, he does just that: he smashes it with his bare hands and roars off with his buddies in the muscle car in which they cruise the streets of Bloomington.[27]

Although fictional, *Breaking Away* clearly portrays the underside of Monroe County's much-celebrated economic success. In the steady stream of Frisbee-playing college students we see what shielded Bloomington's economy from the devastation experienced in Camden and Memphis: the astonishing growth of public and private spending in and around Indiana University. With unemployment rates consistently below those of the rest of the state and a population growth of over 10 percent between 1980 and 1990, administrative and managerial employment rose an amazing 49.4 percent, professional specialty occupations grew 21.7 percent, technical support personnel went up 34.4 percent, and sales positions swelled by 39.6 percent. Traditional blue-collar occupations, however, were dwindling. The number of machine operators, assemblers, and inspectors fell by 18.6 percent in the same decade. When the growth of the city's population is taken into account, the percentage of clerical workers, farmers, laborers, equipment handlers, and helpers also showed a net loss during the 1980s. Jobs for college-trained professionals grew to define Monroe County, while locals with little or no higher education shifted from industrial to low-paying service work.[28]

The class divisions evident in the statistics bear out the impressions of RCA employees in the 1980s. When Mary Gallagher signed on in 1968, RCA "was the best income around here if you didn't go to college," and it supported much of her family: her brother and sister-in-law, her mother, her older sister, her husband, his father, his aunt, and his mother had all worked at the factory at one time or another. "It would be hard to go through Monroe County and pick out a family that hadn't had someone work there at one time," she explained. Exactly what workers would do without RCA remained a bit mysterious to all concerned. Where were young working people turning in Monroe County? "I haven't a clue," Chief Shop Steward Ken Beasley said.

"Assembly jobs are paying less and less all the time. The wage pressure on people is phenomenal. Bill Clinton talks about the skilled workforce of tomorrow—well, maybe it's going to be possible to train all those people, but where in the hell are they going to get a job? I don't see that much stuff coming down the road the people in the United States are going to be able to do."[29]

RCA for Sale

David Sarnoff, or "the General," as he liked to be called, aggressively ran RCA until 1966, when he turned the reins of the corporation over to his son and heir apparent, Robert Sarnoff. During the elder Sarnoff's period of leadership, the company designed and manufactured radio, radar, and microwave communications systems and a host of defense- and space-related communications equipment, but its name remained practically synonymous with color television. Under "Bobby" Sarnoff's control, however, the company took a different tack: it diversified by acquiring such wide-ranging companies as Banquet Foods, Hertz Rental Cars, and Random House, the book publisher. The company committed few resources to manufacturing and technology development and made a disastrous venture into computer manufacturing.[30]

The 1970s were difficult times for the company as the combined effects of the recession, foreign competition, and poor management eroded RCA's competitive position. After a dramatic sixty-year history of expanding sales and product innovation, *Fortune* magazine pronounced the corporation one of the worst-managed companies in the United States. Investment in research declined precipitously, a string of relatively short-lived CEOs followed Robert Sarnoff's resignation after his short but disastrous reign, and the company, burdened by nearly $2.9 billion of debt, finally divested itself of its various subsidiaries. "I am anxious to get back to the roots of this company," announced Chairman Thornton F. Bradshaw, who was imported from Atlantic Richfield to restore order to RCA. "We'd like to spend more on our production lines to bring them up to the Japanese level of investment." Some observers believe that if the company had been investing in its productive capabilities rather than buying other companies and searching out cheap labor, both the workers' and the industry's future would have been quite different. By moving production abroad so early in the face of international competition, the industry made an implicit decision to embark on a long-term strategy that would eventually end domestic production. "A decision to battle imports with automation and radical technological change" earlier on, argues one industry analyst, "could have resulted in a dramatically different outcome."[31]

After many years of mismanagement and a string of ineffective CEOs, however, in 1986 RCA ironically returned to its native fold. In the merger mania of the Reagan era, General Electric acquired RCA for $6.4 billion in cash, and the corporation ceased to exist. Overnight the Monroe County workers found themselves employed by one of their major competitors, a company they felt to be autocratic and cruel in its labor relations policies. GE was already committed to fulfilling its 5 percent market share in consumer electronics by producing through Korean subcontractors. So when the buyout took place, the Bloomington workers surrendered several important provisions in their contract and bade farewell to 272 more of their co-workers in an effort to keep their jobs. "GE came through like a buzz saw," remarked Beasley, "pretty much threatened people's jobs, reduced large numbers of people, pretty much told everybody that they really didn't care about them."[32]

GE's CEO, Jack Welsch, was a hero to Wall Street, but nobody in Bloomington had a good word to say about the corporation. The union's business agent characterized GE as "the most underhanded company in the world." One exchange with the company's management stood out in particular for Judy Cross, and many workers shared her assessment of the company: "I felt they treated us like scum." When she argued against the draconian wage cuts proposed by the new owner, an executive told her, "Well, you should have went to college if you wanted more money." In sum, as Ken Beasley said, "everybody just hated GE, whereas before they felt kind of a family relationship with RCA." GE was not yet sure whether domestic consumer electronics production was profitable enough to keep, so even managers were nervous about the pruning of their ranks. "We all knew we were not a full-fledged member of the General Electric family," explained the consumer electronic division's chief executive, Richard W. Miller. "We were on trial."[33]

The Justice Department approved the merger of the two giants with the proviso that GE would sell parts of the company. GE went beyond the government's requirements and kept only NBC and the defense-centered branches of RCA (and, some workers say, the well-stocked RCA pension fund). It sold all the consumer electronics production to the state-sponsored French conglomerate Thomson Consumer Electronics (TCE) less than a year later. Thomson saved RCA workers with a much-needed influx of capital in the aging production facilities, but now they became part of an even larger network of consumer electronics production, which literally spanned the globe. Some workers joked that Nipper, the fox terrier so attentive to "his master's voice," would have to become a French poodle, but most were simply happy to be liberated from GE. "When Thomson bought the business, we were relieved," Ken Beasley said. "We didn't care who bought it as long as we got out from under GE." Bill Hacker, the business agent, echoed Beasley's sentiments. He had no qualms about working for a firm owned largely by the

French government. "If they want to provide job security and wages, that's what we come to work for." As the Cold War wound down, the RCA workers quietly showed up to assemble televisions for a socialist government.[34]

The Bloomington workers' new employer had an odd combination of characteristics. The chairman of the Thomson Group, Alain Gomez, a person said to quote Goethe and Nietzsche with regularity and ease, was the grandson of a Spanish anarchist. Once committed to left-wing politics, he had even started a far-left faction of the French Socialist Party before he took over Thomson in 1982. The one-time radical turned out to play the game of capitalism with the best, however, by slashing thousands of production workers and headquarters staff from the payroll. The year he took over the conglomerate, it lost $142 million; by 1990 he had posted $86 million in earnings and doubled the company's sales volume. "In my political days, we were fighting to modernize the country and its economy," Gomez said. "I decided to help do that in the field, in business. I have no regrets." Understanding Japanese competition in largely military terms, Gomez believed Western firms were free-trade dupes. Japan had asserted complete domination over consumer electronics, and if they were not careful, countless other sectors would fall to its assault. "The Japanese have chosen consumer electronics as their field of battle," Gomez said, "and if that domino falls, a lot of other industries will fall too."[35]

High-Tech Hopes: Videodisc and HDTV

Since the international division of labor dictated that the Bloomington workers would, theoretically, remain in control of high-technology production, both workers and management invested their hopes for recouping some of the community's losses in two major undertakings in the 1980s and 1990s. The first turned out to be one of the most colossal failures in the history of consumer electronics: RCA's decision to build a videodisc player. Industry analysts knew the future of electronics would be in home video reproduction. Although RCA had broken the news about the invention and plans to build the videocassette recorder (VCR) as early as 1973, it chose to apply its resources to a videodisc technology called SelectaVision in 1980. To the consumer, videodiscs were to videocassettes what record albums were to audiocassettes. Viewers with RCA's videodisc technology could buy discs with prerecorded movies on them, but those who owned VCRs could buy tapes and record the television broadcasts of their choice. RCA banked on consumers to choose disc over tape technology. By the end of the decade, the firm predicted in 1981, 30 to 50 percent of all homes that already had color TVs would also own videodisc players.[36]

The corporation gambled on the disc system for several reasons. It believed that the technology required to produce the very close tolerances necessary to manufacture VCRs could not be achieved quickly, and that the prices of the machines would not fall below $500. They also failed to foresee the massive movie-rental market, which would liberate consumers from the need to buy high-priced tapes and eventually would drive down the price of the tapes (a movie that would retail for $80 to $90 on tape at the time would sell for only $10 to $20 on a disc). Although many observers agreed that the picture and sound were better on RCA's SelectaVision machine, which sold for half the price of a VCR, videocassette technology won the contest by a landslide. In fact, RCA barely even entered the video race. The Japanese improved on RCA's original VCR technology, prices fell quickly, and people enjoyed renting and recording their own shows instead of owning a collection of prerecorded discs. Four years into manufacturing the product, the company had lost $582 million and decided to concede victory to the VCR. By the fall of 1984, RCA was quietly buying videodisc players back from customers angry over the company's decision to halt production.[37]

For a few years at the Bloomington works, however, the relationship between skill and job security looked positive as disc technology made people "very hopeful." The manufacturing of the disc players had a skill level that many workers found "refreshing." As one worker explained, "You had kind of a grunt work on the floor and all of a sudden videodisc operations came in and people thought here was a chance of advancement into higher classifications and generating higher skill levels." Workers involved in assembling the products were given special treatment, new uniforms, fancy work spaces, and plenty of fanfare. In 1954, under a similar gamble, color television had slowly taken over the plant, but no such windfall came Bloomington's way now. In April 1984, when RCA terminated its entire adventure in videodisc technology, 550 workers lost their jobs in Bloomington and hundreds more were laid off in Indianapolis, where the company pressed the discs. The product had been a technological success but an unmitigated disaster on the market and another lost hope for the developed skills of Indiana RCA workers.[38]

Expectations that the relationship between skill and job security might deliver tangible results surfaced again in the 1990s with the debate over the development of high-definition television (HDTV). Promising the complete theater experience with rectangular pictures, sharp digital images, compact-disc-quality sound, and enormous sizes, HDTV was predicted to play the same innovative role in the receiver industry that color did in the 1950s and 1960s. As in the case of color, however, a heated battle ensued over which system of standards the Federal Communications Commission (FCC) would accept and which company or group of companies would get to build the machines. Four systems were being advocated by various consortia; the firm whose system won the competition would have a big jump on the other firms in bringing the technology to market. With predictions that the HDTV system selected by the government would be the standard broadcasting system fifteen years after its introduction into consumers' living rooms, the stakes were high.[39]

The Japanese had been working on HDTV since the mid-1980s, and other nations became concerned that they would dominate yet another innovation in consumer electronics. Taking a page from the Japanese economic strategy, which demonstrated the success of publicly guided industrial policy, several members of Congress launched initiatives to promote the new technology with federal funds. The debate rekindled discussions about industrial policy that had been dormant since the early 1980s as various consortia were organized to win FCC approval and, they hoped, government subsidies. General Instrument Corporation and the Massachusetts Institute of Technology formed a consortium with NHK (the Japanese Broadcasting Corporation), and Zenith and AT&T joined together to develop a "U.S.-based" version of HDTV—even though Zenith no longer actually built sets in the United States. The European electronics giants Thomson and Philips of the Netherlands joined NBC, the David Sarnoff Research Center, and Compression Labs to form yet another consortium to build yet another system.

This time, however, U.S. workers based their hopes for HDTV jobs not on theoretical "production sharing" but on concrete plans for a political deal with the U.S. government to build the new sets in the United States. In an effort to win over the FCC and Congress, Thomson's group made one of its most enticing selling points the fact that their sets would be built in the United States. Like the Camden workers who had staked their future on government-funded defense and aerospace projects after World War II, the Bloomington workers relied on government intervention to save them. The IBEW, the IUE, and the AFL-CIO joined the Thomson–NBC–Sarnoff–Philips–Compression Labs group in advocating that the FCC apply a domestic jobs test in awarding its approval.[40]

Whereas the "American" corporations employed no workers in the United States, the European companies could commit to building the HDTV sets in the United States, most likely in the Bloomington factory. The need to choose a combination of either foreign capital and domestic labor or domestic capital and foreign labor sent government leaders through the looking glass into a global wonderland of confused political identities in efforts to figure out, in the words of the former labor secretary Robert Reich, "who is us" and "who is them." The issue was rendered moot when a grand alliance of all the major players took shape. There was no advantage in manufacturing domestically when Thomson lost its hope of exclusive FCC approval, and even HDTV ended up in Mexico. Responding to anger among the rank and file when they heard the news, a company spokesman, Dave Arland, claimed, "It's not reneging when the promise was contingent on the proposed standard that never happened. We realized no exclusive benefit." A political commitment to produce "domestically" may not have been the answer to the workers' problems anyway, since it raised what one RCA manager called "a problem of definition." Clearly there were clever ways around even government-mandated commitments to domestic production. "Are we talking about the final assembly," the RCA manager asked rhetorically, "or are we talking about taking the very first operation and taking it all the way through to the final assembly here in the United States?"[41]

Labor Relations in the NAFTA Era

In 1991, Congress passed fast-track authority for approval of NAFTA. The fast-track process made the free-trade agreement a yes-or-no choice rather than subject its many complicated provisions to a full debate. Spurring a heated national controversy over the meaning of "free trade" and the course of globalization, advocates and opponents alike churned out often inflated predictions of jobs to be gained and jobs to be lost under the final text of the agreement. Unfortunately, the debate rarely focused on the types of jobs, labor standards, and possible regulatory alternatives to the version of regional trade hammered out in secret by official negotiators. Although the range of discussion was often limited, the anger the very idea of the agreement aroused among workers shook U.S. organized labor out of years of political torpor and organizational lethargy. The NAFTA battle raged on until President Clinton finally marshaled enough votes to squeak it through Congress in late 1994.[42]

Although the agreement was of monumental political and symbolic value, speaking as it did to widespread anxieties over job security and declining wages, the actual pact merely formalized decades' worth of "silent integration" that had been taking place between Mexico, Canada, and the United States without the formal cover of an agreement. A "just say no" approach to NAFTA, then, left opponents with nothing more than what they had before the trade agreement. What was needed, and what was blocked politically by the fast-track process and ideologically by opponents' approach to the campaign, was a national discussion of alternatives to the deal, including meaningful labor rights and standards. Missing from the debate was a discussion of what kind of regime would lead to a "high road" harmonization of the three countries' workers rather than the de facto alternative that threatens to reduce wages and standards to the lowest continental common denominator.

Even the bone thrown to NAFTA opponents, the agreement's Side Accord on Labor Rights, is proving to be of more strategic value in shaping the type of arrangement labor advocates would like to see than most observers expected.[43]

Few things demonstrate the process of silent integration more effectively than the fact that about 75 percent of the Bloomington RCA jobs had been lost before the acronym "NAFTA" even entered the political discourse. Indeed, the threat of capital flight had hung over all labor relations at the plant since the late 1960s, but by the 1990s, with global pressures increasing and labor law turned against the workers, it became a weapon wielded aggressively against the dwindling numbers of RCA employees. In 1991, during standard contract negotiations between the Bloomington union local and the company, for instance, RCA-Thomson demanded a wage cut of $2 an hour or it would relocate all of the 20-inch sets, one of the factory's staple products, to Mexico, where it could save nearly $80 on every set produced. Rather than submit to extortion and surrender 20 percent of their members' paychecks, the union representatives decided to call the company on their threat. Their response clearly demonstrated the distance the Bloomington workforce had traveled since the early days. "We caucused back in the room," reported an exasperated Bill Cook, and decided, "Fuck it! Move 'em! And they did."[44]

The union made its bold decision to call the company's bluff in the context of events it had closely observed unfolding at Zenith's operations in Missouri. Their competitor had followed a similar migratory path, moving from industrial Chicago to Springfield, Missouri, and finally to Matamoros and Reynosa, on the Mexican border. Having just witnessed the Zenith IBEW local make painful concessions on the promise that the workers would get to keep what remained of their jobs, only to see them transferred to Mexico six months later, the RCA local was not in the mood to offer much in the way of concessions. "The story going around the [Zenith] plant was, if you didn't give them the wage concession, they were going to move to Mexico," explained a former Zenith employee who had worked at the plant over twenty-four years. All of the concessions they granted to keep the plant open, however, "just gave them an extra five years to finalize their plans to move. We just helped pay for it." In Bloomington, local leaders simply felt "like what they [RCA] were saying didn't mean anything to us either." The union's strategy not to give in to the company's demands was probably wise, as RCA-Thomson had plans to build one of the most advanced high-technology "just-in-time" television factories in the world in Ciudad Juárez—probably whether Bloomington caved in on concessions or not.[45]

The pressure to concede on wages, benefits, and working conditions did not stop with the production of 20-inch sets; it simply moved up the chain of products to higher-end goods. On a sunny day in March 1994, long before the union contract was due to expire, management called all the Bloomington workers out into the parking lot. The warmth of the spring day turned to chill as the company unilaterally demanded a 30 percent cut in pay and benefits or it would relocate assembly of the high-end 31-inch and 35-inch television sets and production of the associated plastics to a new site in the United States. (It still appeared as though HDTV would require domestic workers.) The company's willingness to abandon Bloomington for an unknown location somewhere in the United States where workers were desperate for industrial work, labor costs were cheaper, unionization was unlikely, and benefits were minimal fueled the downward pressure on the income and living standards of the Bloomington labor force. The new location against which they were pitted was rumored to be in Tennessee (again) or possibly Texas, but in reality it was an unknown and abstract point in space that enabled Thomson to reorder class relations in Bloomington, Indiana. In a disturbing speech the company called for "mutual cooperation" while Thomson scrutinized "wages, benefits, work practices, and overhead costs" in the search for a more competitive position in the consumer electronics industry. Essentially, the union local would have to open up its contract for complete renegotiation or lose members' jobs.[46]

Before the company made its demands, events may have led the employees to believe that their jobs were safe for at least a little while. Two years earlier the city of Bloomington had granted the company an "enterprise zone" status that had already saved it over $1 million in taxes. As one city official remarked in the wake of the threat to relocate, however, "You don't buy loyalty when you buy a company through tax breaks." In addition, Thomson had announced substantial profits just the day before the meeting in the parking lot and had recently committed $10 million to have the name of the Indianapolis Hoosier Dome changed to the RCA Dome for the next ten years. The company, however, still talked tough about the need for "bold actions to cut costs" and argued that it had to "think and act globally." RCA-Thomson managers announced that their actions would be "swift" because their options were "limited" and their time "short."[47]

The workers, of course, did not take the threat lightly. The high-end television sets under consideration this time represented Bloomington's last hope. If they lost the manufacture of large-screen TVs—the product with high sales potential and a wide profit margin—then the plant was about to become little more than a warehouse and distribution center, just like Zenith's Missouri operations. As the Thomson spokesman explained, "The future is in the high-end business, and if you take that out of the uncompetitive Bloomington [labor] market, the Bloomington plant becomes even more unattractive" as a production site. Even though the workers took the company's threat seriously, they were tired of threats and concessions. "We're supposed to be one big family here," Bob Griffin said. "Well, today the children are rebelling." Anne Meek, a twenty-nine-year RCA veteran earning a typical wage of $10.29 an hour, expressed her exhaustion with the company's tactics from her mobile home, across the street from the complex of Thomson buildings. "We have already given and given," Meek cried. "And I don't think they will stay no matter what we offer them. They've already got their minds made up." Shay Freeman, who had spent almost three decades at RCA and Thomson, felt similarly—nothing would appease the company. "Even if they got us down to a dollar an hour," she said, "I don't think they would stay." Bill Cook, the union's business agent, cautiously opened the door to negotiations for a reduction in benefits. "If any concessions are to be made, they certainly should not be wages." The employees' resistance to the company's demands partially paid off—at least for the short term. In final negotiations, they gave up future raises, took cuts in health insurance and other benefits, and accepted incentives for early retirement as ways of cutting costs. In exchange for $210 million in concessions, they won a guarantee of four years of employment at the current wage level for every worker who chose to stay on.[48]

The four years guaranteed in the contract exactly defined the length of time the plant lasted before it was finally closed in 1998. On 13 February 1997, at the beginning of each shift, company officials announced that the plant would be closed forever in April 1998. All operations, from warehousing to manufacturing, would be terminated. The remaining 1,100 Bloomington workers and 420 others in Indianapolis would be out of work by the following spring. "We just stood there, stunned," remembered Janice Wilhite, an employee since 1956. "It was very, very quiet. Then you could feel the anger. Some started crying. Some were very upset." Reeling with shock, all employees were given the rest of the day off. Nelda Stuppy, a thirty-one-year veteran, wondered how many employees would even come back to work the next day, a Friday, and, if they did, whether they would even be able to do their jobs. Not only did they show up, but they even surpassed their quota for the shift. "We're from the old school," she explained. "We're paid for a day's work and that's what we've always done. We all went in, started doing our jobs and did it well."[49]

Before the announcement, the corporation floated the idea of a 60 to 70 percent wage cut, but the union leadership refused even to consider it on the heels of the concession package in the last contract. "While we have had a presence in Mexico for more than 25 years," explained Dave Hakala, vice president for manufacturing operations, "we have resisted moving final assembly of larger-screen TVs there, unlike virtually all of our major competitors. . . . But we are out of options." Pointing to the plagues of the industry—overproduction, price erosion, and fierce competition—Hakala proclaimed, "We cannot survive if we don't take dramatic actions." Even after factoring in the cost of shipping the heavy picture tubes from Marion, Indiana, to Mexico, the firm projected an annual wage savings of $60 million. "They've slammed the door in our face, that's the common comment you hear," said Richard Wilhite. "We felt like we were overpowered. For years, it was 'Give in to us or you'll lose your job.' And here we are." [50]

The projected economic impact of the shutdown left the community reeling. Statewide, Thomson had already been granted $6.4 million in tax breaks in addition to the concessions given by the workers. The pullout meant the loss of $2 million in tax revenues, the loss of an additional job in the community for each job terminated at TCE, a direct payroll loss of $34.6 million, and, not to be overlooked in an era when voluntarism was supposed to rush in to fill the void left by the dwindling role of the state, the loss of an annual contribution to the United Way of $117,500. Bloomington, however, was not Flint, Michigan, or, for that matter, Camden, New Jersey. With an unemployment rate between 3 and 4 percent, the city would probably recover, as it had already done after the loss of thousands of other RCA jobs. With a diverse economic base, a strong influx of public spending from Indiana University, and a core of affluent middle-class professionals, the city would not become one of the many rotting, deindustrialized nightmares that dot the landscape of the United States. [51]

Despite the relative prosperity of Monroe County, however, the distance between opportunities for trained professionals and the relatively unskilled blue-collar workers remained vast, and most workers would face a serious decline in income. When Bloomington's Wetterhau food distribution plant closed in 1994, for instance, many workers never regained their former earnings. "We had to cut back awhile till we got back on our feet," reported Chuck and Chris Burleson, whose baby arrived at the same time the plant announced its shutdown. "We both worked odd jobs for awhile. You have to bust your butt sometimes to make it back." Chuck landed a custodial job with the university and Chris became a secretary for the city, but the new jobs barely covered expenses. "Financially, we're making a few dollars less per hour," he said, "but we were able to keep the house and we have good benefits." The Burlesons were untypically young. The average age of the Thomson workers was forty-nine, and their tenure at the plant averaged twenty-six years. Older workers faced an extremely difficult time in a very competitive job market. "To be working here for thirty years," explained fifty-two-year-old Sandy Griffin, " and not be drawing a paycheck after April first, that scared the life out of me." [52]

In view of the fact that many firms shut down with little notice and even less support, the severance package ultimately negotiated by the union for the

Thomson workers offered much comfort. Employees with twenty or more years of service received a lump sum equal to one week of pay for every year of service; those with fewer years got one week of pay for every two years of service. The average worker got about six months' pay, plus government re-training funds available under the Trade Adjustment Assistance Act and special education and training funds set up to sweeten the pot during the NAFTA debate. In addition, Thomson gave the city some property and $800,000 in grants. The complete severance package totaled $41 million, seemingly a generous figure, suggesting that being fired by Socialists may be better than the alternative. The union local's business agent, Bill Cook, however, branded it a mere "drop in the bucket." Putting another spin on the math, he argued, "That money came from less benefits, part-time workers and frozen wages, which amounted to $210 million. Take $41 million [the total cost of the exit package] from $210 million and you have the sum that was used to build a new plant in Mexico, move our jobs and some left over."[53]

Singing "Auld Lang Syne" and "Happy Trails to You," workers marched down the ramp of Bloomington's enormous Plant 2 for the very last time in April 1998. "It's been a pleasure working with you . . . and God bless," read the notice each former employee clutched as she headed out the factory gates and into an unknown future. Few questioned why the firm chose to move to Mexico, but neither the workers nor the media that followed their plight stopped to wonder why Bloomington had been selected in the first place.

The final shutdown was the end of an era for southern Indiana and the consolidation of a new one for Ciudad Juárez. "This is much bigger than the closing of a plant," Gib Apple, a former plant manager, proclaimed with little exaggeration. "This is the end of a chapter in Bloomington history. Heck, it's darn near the whole book." The situation the corporation left behind, however, could not have been more different from the one RCA found on its arrival in 1940. Charles Deppert, president of the Indiana AFL-CIO, summed up the industrial life span of a community: "They got all they could out of us, and now they're going somewhere else." Indeed, the reasons the company had selected the site almost sixty years earlier had all but evaporated into the rhythms of industrial life. Meanwhile, Deppert's counterpart in Chihuahua, Jesús José Díaz, a CTM leader, was as ready to step in as the Bloomington workers had been generations earlier. "We'll receive them with open arms!" he exclaimed when he heard the news that more RCA-Thomson jobs were headed south.[54]

CHAPTER SIX

The Double Struggle:
Ciudad Juárez, 1978-1998

Carmen Ruiz, at the age of twenty, had already worked at RCA for two and a half years in 1978. Citing the need to earn money and a dislike of school, like many young *juarenses*, she finished the sixth grade and turned to the world of wage labor at the age of thirteen. With the recommendation of her sister, who was already a seasoned veteran with an unusually long six years on the line at RCA Componentes de Televisión, she eventually landed a job soldering electrical components among the 5,000 other assemblers of television chassis at the plant. When she clocked out of La Erre on mid-Saturday at the end of a forty-eight-hour week, she met her ride outside the huge complex of industrial plants that made up the Parque Bermúdez. Piling into the car with five or six other tired but chattering workers, she watched the huge tile mosaic representing electronic circuitry on the outer wall of the factory disappear until the following Monday. Expensive and inadequate transportation networks remained a constant headache for the 30,000 maquila workers in the city, and partway on her long journey home she bade her co-workers good-by and switched to one of the small buses known as *ruteras* for the remainder of her trip across the urban desert sprawl.[1]

Back in her neighborhood, Colonia Barrio Alto, Ruiz turned over 600 of the 875 pesos she received weekly (approximately U.S.$34.50) to her mother to help support the family. About 100 pesos went for transportation to and from work, miscellaneous expenses absorbed another 75 pesos, and she tucked the final 100 pesos into the RCA savings plan. The Ruizes' two-bedroom cinder-block house sheltered nine members of Carmen's extended family—her parents, three sisters, two brothers, her paternal grandmother, and herself. Her father worked as an *ambulante*, an itinerant street vendor, specializing in clothing. His three eldest daughters worked in maquilas—the sixteen-year-

Teresa Silva walks with her son through a street in the Colonia Medanos, a few miles from the Thomson Televisiones de México plant, where she works. Houses here typically begin with materials salvaged from the maquiladoras (note the fences made of shipping pallets) or other cheap materials and are improved and expanded as resources permit. (Photo copyright © Mark Hume.)

old at General Instruments, and both Carmen and her older sister at RCA. Only the younger three, all of whom were still in school, and Carmen's mother and her sixty-five-year-old grandmother were exempt from work outside the home. Such industriousness still left more than four people to sleep in each bedroom, but it did afford the family a few luxuries. Like the majority of maquila workers' families, the Ruiz clan enjoyed indoor plumbing, hot water, and even a washing machine. Although the family did not own an automobile or a telephone, they did have what Carmen and her sister spent their days making—a large console TV, which the family purchased on credit.

The dusty streets and foreign customs of the Juárez workers would have seemed very alien to RCA's Bloomington employees, but the clean and modern building in which Ruiz labored would have been very familiar terrain. Except for the guards at the entrance to the plant, one observer noted, "the exterior and landscape architecture of RCA-Juárez looks more like that of a college campus than like that of a postmodern version of William Blake's dark, satanic mills."[2] Although substantially enhanced by new production technologies, the tortuously repetitive jobs at RCA had not changed significantly since the Camden days. The simple tasks would have been familiar to their New Jersey cousins, and the *juarenses* often worked on equipment formerly in the Bloomington operation. On the feeder tables, women built the required subassemblies by doing the delicate but quite tedious work of inserting components onto circuit boards with manual tools. The subassemblies were combined to become the chassis as each worker placed a new piece on the core of the set as the assembly line moved past her to her neighbor's work station for another part or operation. Finally, another small army of workers, facing high temperatures and noxious fumes, made the countless solder joints necessary at all stages of the manufacturing process. Just as the tasks had not changed dramatically since the Great Depression, neither had the sexual division of labor: 78 percent of RCA production workers were still young women. The majority of the group chiefs were also women, promoted from the assembly line, but all work was constantly monitored by male line supervisors, who stalked the shop floor to keep the young women churning out TV chassis.[3]

As in the U.S. RCA factories, the work factor system divided the *juarenses'* workday into minute time-motion components for maximum efficiency. Though the rates had been "objectively" determined from the books of tables developed under the system, the Mexican workers, like their northern counterparts, were hardly mere extensions of management's will. A survey of Juárez maquila workers revealed that a startling 62 percent of them fought what they perceived as a speedup by exploiting the fundamental weakness in mass assembly work: the potential to restrict output. What Frederick W. Taylor, the father of scientific management, identified as "soldiering" among the U.S. workers he studied, BIP employees called *tortuguismo* or *tortuosidad*—working at the stubborn pace of a turtle. "Certain features of output restriction dynamics are 'universal,'" writes Devon Peña, "that is, they occur in Fordist organizational settings regardless of national location or cultural context."[4]

Although the shop-floor experience of Carmen Ruiz and her co-workers was much like that of their Bloomington counterparts, they confronted formidable barriers to the types of social change apparent in the other RCA locations. An unstable currency, high labor turnover, an authoritarian union structure, and employers that colluded to prevent wage increases all served to check the growing sense of investment in the job, entitlement to the company's consideration, and emboldened class awareness that emerged at the other sites. Only the violence, intimidation, company unionism, and economic devastation of the Great Depression in the Camden case could compare with the obstacles faced by workers on the Mexican frontier. In sum, the cluster of factors favorable to the company in Ciudad Juárez allowed RCA to maintain its workforce the way it wanted it—young, fresh, female, and cheap.

Before the Juárez employees could lay claim to greater rights or pay at the plant, they first had to break through the "regressive-functional" model of unionism that buffered corporate investment in the border zone from popular discontent. As we saw in Chapter 4, the CTM local at RCA, like the border unions in general, served to insulate the company against workers' demands, a process that would become increasingly important during Mexico's frequent financial crises in the 1980s. Anything the workers wanted from the company, particularly wage increases above established salary caps, depended on the rather formidable prerequisite of democratizing their union. This was the *lucha doble*, the "double struggle" the maquila employees faced: opposition not only from the company but from their labor representatives as well.[5]

As overwhelming as the barriers to change appeared in Juárez, the experiences of Camden, Memphis, and Bloomington militate against the strident exceptionalism that permeates the literature on maquiladoras and other export-processing zones. Much of our understanding of working-class life on the border is based on anthropological and sociological studies of a specific moment and so cannot capture changes over time or make comparisons with other locations outside of TNC enclaves.[6] Armed with a comparative-historical understanding of labor relations at RCA, however, we cannot see the exploitation of young female workers by ever-mobile capital in search of regions of oppressive poverty and weak unionization as a dramatic departure from previous strategies. Although the formula RCA relied on in Ciudad Juárez did not differ significantly from that used in the other sites, it was of such potency as to guarantee the site's attractiveness to corporations for a very long time.

During the 1980s, national economic crises triggered a series of confrontations as the Juárez RCA workers pushed against the unions' intransigence and entrenched wage controls. By the end of the decade, the same broad transformations in working-class social and political life evident in the U.S. cases were clearly under way in the still young industrial culture of Ciudad Juárez. A sit-down strike in 1995 successfully capped years of struggle to democratize the union and break through the ceiling that local managers had built to contain wages.

Working-Class Life in the New City of Industry

Numerous detailed social and demographic portraits of the maquila employees conducted in the late 1970s and early 1980s confirm that Carmen Ruiz fitted the broad-stroke portrait of the typical electronics worker in Juárez at the time. Seventy-seven percent of all workers in the maquila sector were women. Depending on the data set used, two-thirds to three-fourths of the city's workers were between the ages of sixteen and twenty-four; the average age was between twenty-two and a half and twenty-four years. The factories preferred employees with some education, and 33 to 45 percent of the workers had between one and six years of schooling; an additional 29 to 40 percent had between seven and eleven years of education. The majority of the employees were single and had worked in their plant only about two years, and for about 70 percent of them, their current job was their first experience in paid employment. Depending on the sample, between 56 and 74 percent of the maquila employees were single. Few of them lived alone, and most contributed their earnings to the household and kept only a small portion to pay for their job-related expenses and the occasional luxury. RCA's workers were slightly younger than the city average, but they fitted the general pattern. The earnings of each BIP employee interviewed by Jorge Carrillo and Alberto Hernández in 1978 supported an average of 1.95 family members.[7]

Work at the transnationals offered these families a mixed bag of material benefits. A massive 1979 survey of Juárez households revealed that on a 10-point standard-of-living index, maquila households rated 6.69 and non-maquila households an almost equivalent 6.72. Maquila homes tended to be located in lower-income neighborhoods, had more and younger people crammed into fewer rooms (5.26 vs. 4.95), and included more women. Families with TNC workers owned slightly more consumer goods, such as televisions (96% vs. 91%), but the higher rate may reflect both youth and a rising consumer consciousness as much as the economic benefits of maquila employment. Border-plant workers also faced higher levels of debt than their counterparts employed by local firms, most likely encouraged by a steady paycheck, and faced dramatically higher transportation costs because of the distance of their homes from the industrial parks. One researcher captured some of the pitfalls of TNC work: "While maquila households earn at least minimum wage or better, they tend to have more expense and less 'return' on their income than other households. They exhibit a tendency to live beyond their means, a pattern partly determined by employment and related costs of transportation."[8]

The crucial difference between the two groups, however, was that maquila workers, as employees in the formal sector, received a host of benefits for which workers in the informal sectors were not eligible. Progressive Mexican labor law provided for health care through the Mexican Social Security system, paid vacations, sizable Christmas bonuses, profit sharing, maternity leave, and workers' compensation, among several other benefits. Many of the larger plants also offered subsidized meals, some of them a nursery, and, in lieu of sorely needed wage increases, sizable bonuses. Nonetheless, 26 percent of the BIP employees still had to work extra hours, 12 percent held additional jobs, and another 6 percent worked in family shops. Differences between workers in the transnational and national sectors of the local economy quickly pale, however, in view of the fact that before the arrival of the maquiladoras there were precious few job opportunities at all in Ciudad Juárez.[9]

One might reasonably expect women's economic and social power in the family unit to increase as their incomes rose. In general, however, as young BIP women became their families' financial pillars, their economic clout did not tend to erode traditional patriarchal relations within the family unit. In 75 percent of nonmaquila households, the person declared to be "head of family" was also the primary breadwinner. In only 39 percent of maquila homes, however, was that relationship maintained, and that primary wage earner was likely to be a border-plant worker. Most of the women continued to be responsible for domestic chores in addition to their shifts on the assembly line.[10]

Outside of the home, however, changes were evident in Ciudad Juárez. Female factory employees began to dominate public spaces, such as the Cruz Blanca brewery, on Friday nights, and one of the most popular discotheques, the Malibú, even renamed itself the Maquilú after it became a favorite night spot of the young, single working-class women. Along with the expanding freedom of young women, however, came fears and rumors of prostitution and declining morality. With the city's history as a center of disreputable entertainment, the relationship between prostitution and factory work often took center stage as industry advocates argued that work kept women from prostitution while critics argued that it encouraged it. Local tabloids frequently published sordid tales of sex and power in the maquilas—many of which had at least some basis in fact, since it was not unknown for a supervisor to demand sexual favors from his subordinates.[11]

On the whole, the male members of TNC households continued in the occupations available to them before the arrival of the U.S.-owned plants. Among those men fortunate enough to find work without migrating to the United States, the anthropologist María Patricia Fernández-Kelly found unskilled construction workers (30%), petty clerks (27%), general unskilled workers (15%), and street vendors (7%); another study found that almost half of the male workers could be classified as "intermittent day workers." As the labor market tightened and new industries such as auto parts started arriving in the 1980s and 1990s, however, the TNCs would begin to open up opportunities for men too.[12]

The Woman Worker's Orientation Center

In the face of unresponsive unions, the project to build a cohesive class and gender politics sprang from many points. One of the most innovative and dynamic sources of change was a working-class education and consciousness-raising program at the Woman Worker's Orientation Center (El Centro de Orientación de la Mujer Obrera, or COMO), founded for maquila women in Juárez. A local labor lawyer and political figure described conflict between workers and their companies as analogous to the bickering of a married couple over the quality of the coffee while they ignored the larger problems in their relationship. There was no shortage of class conflict in Ciudad Juárez, he implied, only a shortage of cohesive, organized political opposition based on an understanding of the structural and political issues of life in the border plants.[13] Emerging from the massive RCA factory, COMO was designed to increase class and gender awareness among the maquila workers and bring focus to their discontent. Although the organization could not bargain on behalf of the workers (and showed no interest in doing so), it went a long way toward providing the tools that would enable them to organize themselves. It also created a public forum for clarifications of social issues that conflicted with the news emanating from both the state and the press.

María Villegas, a nurse designated to keep the workers healthy at the RCA plant, played a pivotal role in the founding of COMO. When she began her job in the late 1960s, she believed her role to consist basically of preventing the workers from becoming ill. "After observing the production line," she recalled, "it occurred to me that it was the working conditions and working materials . . . that caused many of these problems. They told me I was being stubborn, and that the things I was asking for were not needed." Over the course of several years of visiting the RCA workers' homes and discussing issues with them on the job, she began to put more pressure on the company to conform with social security regulations and to develop the employees' skills, but her requests continued to fall on deaf ears. Searching for activists with similar concerns, she discovered a dynamic middle-class reformer, Dr. Guillermina Valdés-Villalva, who had been working on women's issues for some time. "I told her that I dreamed of a group that would orient the women workers," recalled the RCA nurse, "not help them like the boss, but rather in their self-orientation. I mean an intrinsic or integral orientation."[14]

Established in the early 1970s and staffed largely by former maquila workers, COMO helped women workers understand their society and families from the standpoint of their positions as female employees of transnational corporations. Since women's issues played such an important role in the maquila city, and the unions at all sites in this story failed to include in their agenda issues of particular relevance to female workers, COMO's strategy was particularly apt. Adopting the grass-roots teaching methodologies advocated by the Brazilian pedagogist Paulo Freire, the organization launched numerous intensive research projects, sponsored many classes in subjects from labor law to English, and pushed for changes in areas such as child care, transportation, and protection against hazardous materials in the electronics plants. "COMO is not a trade union, yet it promotes labor organizing through support and linkage of independent worker coalitions and informal networks," explained one scholar. "COMO is not a political party, yet it promotes political involvement and articulates political demands, sometimes much more effectively than leftist parties."[15]

The organization quickly moved away from its original focus on health and family problems as it sought to make working women aware of the structural factors functioning in their lives and to empower them to act on them. At its height, the organization had a staff of twenty paid employees working on the principle that "the personal is political." With sessions between 5:00 and 8:00 P.M. each day, the complete COMO training program consisted of a full year of instruction and consciousness-raising in the areas of feminism, labor economics, reproduction and family, local and national politics, industrial relations, and global economic structures. The vast majority of the course participants were young (the average age was twenty-two), and 70 percent were from electronics plants. Following a narrow path between reformism and radicalism, the workers typically came out "personally empowered but not politicized," as the critical perspective presented by the center offered neither concrete solutions nor links with any broad-based political organizations or parties.[16]

The efficacy of the COMO educational project in raising workers' consciousness was nonetheless strongly evident in a three-part survey of workers conducted in 1982 and 1983. Questioning three groups—COMO students, workers engaged in a protracted strike, and a control group of workers at an electronics firm—researchers found that those involved in COMO and those involved in the labor dispute had a greatly enlarged concept of their roles as women, while the control group continued to profess what the researchers called the "stereotype of the ideal Mexican female." With its emphasis on education, consciousness-raising, and the connections between workers' lives and the political economy they inhabited, the organization's training program had the same impact on the workers' sense of themselves as a heated labor dispute. COMO was an active presence in strikes, drives for better regulation in the border factories, and research on border workers, but its main contribution to change in the border plants was the raising of important questions about gender and women's issues. Though COMO members were obviously active in the RCA strikes and other struggles in the 1980s, it is difficult to assess the program's impact qualitatively or quantitatively. For thousands of young maquila women, however, the grass-roots organization addressed what no union brought to the fore: the electronics sector's manipulation of gender identity in the search for inexpensive and malleable labor supplies.[17]

Keeping Them Fresh

While COMO struggled to raise the collective consciousness of the young Juárez workers, RCA and the other maquilas sought to keep turnover high enough to prevent the maturation of their employees' attitudes toward their jobs. One of the most profound differences between the various U.S. cases and the Ciudad Juárez case, in fact, was the company's power to maintain its workforce in Mexico the way it would have preferred to keep it in all of the sites: young, female, and inexpensive. In each of the U.S. cities, the seniority clause in the union contract, after it had been won, ensured that workers would be laid off in the reverse order of their length of employment (first hired, last fired), and that they would accrue wage increases and job security as time on the job increased.[18] These provisions allowed employees to develop a sense of history and reciprocal investment with the company in addition to the security of knowing they could not be dismissed if they protested to improve their pay or working conditions. In Juárez, however, the combination of voluntary and forced turnover kept the RCA labor force constantly renewed with recruits who possessed only a minimal commitment to the plant or their jobs.

Ten years after its establishment in Chihuahua, in 1978, the average seniority of the workers at RCA, as in all the border plants, was only two and a half to three years. Employees began as apprentices earning less than minimum wage and after one month could be promoted to the category of plant operator. After a worker's productivity had improved, she could move up through sixteen performance levels. With each promotion, however, explained an RCA manager, the employee's "pay does not change but they gain more positive recognition which can later pay off in a promotion or bonus." Basic labor economics dictated that wages should have crept up as the number of plants grew, the labor market tightened, skills increased, and firms had to compete to attract workers. The problem, as Leslie Sklair writes, could be found in "the *politics* of wages rather than the *economics* of wages." Bargaining between firms over wages was effectively prevented by a "cartel" of maquila executives that imposed strict discipline on plant managers, thus preventing genuine competition for wages and workers. With pay set at the same minimum-wage level throughout the area, the only method of retaining workers was through bonuses, incentives, and benefits, and workers were notorious for continually shopping around the industrial parks for the plant with the marginally better deal during boom times.[19]

Although most of the RCA turnover was a result of technically "voluntary" resignations, the financial incentives to stay were few and the need for time off from work was frequent. Many young women who left their jobs reported plans to get married or to find better opportunities for their children. An

RCA manager explained the self-fulfilling prophecy: female workers do not last at their jobs "because almost all of them are women, they marry and they go." The employees also frequently required rest periods after a grueling six-day workweek at the plant and then an additional shift doing household chores. Others reported leaving because of discontent with low wages, the tediousness of the work, and health problems—deterioration of their eyesight, nervous and respiratory ailments.[20]

Just as workers had few reasons to stay at the plant, the company had an investment in maintaining high turnover rates. The maquila managers had a saying: "Entre más antiguas, más inconformes son" ("The more senior they are, the less compliant they are"), so the profile of the labor force was carefully constructed to avoid the changes in consciousness produced by decades of labor at plants elsewhere. Even a couple of years on the job could take the edge off an employee's enthusiasm: maquila managers throughout the city reported lower productivity and higher absenteeism after the second year of employment.[21]

In the first recorded labor skirmish at RCA, workers tried to break through the turnover system. In the spring of 1977 the employees publicly condemned the company's policy of forcing workers to resign when they reached the age of twenty-five or accumulated five years on the job. The "mass demonstration," however, was quickly and efficiently defused and defeated. RCA's systematic manipulation of turnover clearly indicated that it preferred to absorb the substantial costs of rehiring and retraining personnel rather than allow wages to rise to market levels or allow workers to acquire inefficient habits and "dangerous" levels of commitment to their jobs.[22]

In the absence of meaningful union representation, workers turned to filing grievances directly with the Conciliation and Arbitration Board. Technically, after a worker had made it past the one-month probationary period, she could be dismissed only for "good cause," as defined by Mexican labor law. A worker dismissed without good cause was entitled to three months' salary, twelve additional days per year of seniority, and twenty days of pay for each year worked. Of the 1,255 grievances submitted by individual workers between 1969 and 1978, a phenomenal 97 percent were for unjustifiable dismissal. Of the 1,024 workers who demanded reinstatement, three got their jobs back. The majority got no compensation at all, but 43 percent were granted indemnification (27% complete and 16% partial). Women were particularly active in registering grievances with the board, although fewer than their numbers in the plant would suggest. Between 1969 and 1978, less than 60 percent of all grievances filed against the electronics firms were by women, but the total number of registered grievances may represent only an estimated 10 to 20 percent of those that made it to the board past supervisors or union representatives. One maquila researcher claims that for employees in search of protection from arbitrary dismissal or abuse, the Arbitration Board "represents a losing proposition." [23]

Management's constant battle against absenteeism suggests that RCA's lack of commitment to its workers also limited the employees' fidelity to the company. To get around this problem, executives applied a carrot-and-stick strategy. The stick consisted of severe penalties for those who did not adhere strictly to the work schedule. "Control over absenteeism and tardiness is very important for internal plant discipline," explained an RCA technician. "If you arrive more than ten minutes late, the guard outside the plant is under order to detain you and not let you enter. Then the section chief will show up and at his discretion will decide whether or not to let you enter." Three tardies added up to one absence, and four absences resulted in an "indefensible" suspension. All the disciplinary measures imaginable, however, could not solve the fundamental problem. As an RCA official baldly speculated, "How can the problem of absenteeism be resolved among people that have disgusting jobs, little freedom to make decisions on their own behalf, lack skills, and possess the normal share of human laziness and stubbornness?" [24]

The carrot took the form of rewards for good attendance. A worker with a punctual record over the course of many months received a T-shirt emblazoned with a slogan (in Spanish) such as "RCA and me," "RCA and I are one team," or "I am part of RCA," and won an opportunity to participate in a raffle that might even lead to a free trip into the interior of the country. As in Bloomington, RCA also tried to construct a family atmosphere (*una gran familia*) through a variety of extracurricular activities—team sports, birthday parties, production awards, dances, exercise groups, drill teams, the celebration of festival days, and educational courses. Workers could even enter the plant beauty contest for the title of Miss RCA, the winner to compete against Miss Sylvania, Miss GTE, and so on for the coveted title of Miss Maquiladora; or they could enter the Maquilolimpiada, the Maquila Olympics, and compete in athletic events against company teams from all over the country. In later years, with the revival of the company mascot, the line with the highest production numbers won the "privilege" of displaying a giant stuffed Nipper in their work space.[25]

The Debt Crisis

While turnover kept workers new, dramatic national peso devaluations in 1976, 1982, and 1994 played a crucial role in keeping the RCA employees inexpensive. The growth of the entire BIP, in fact, exhibited a frightening dependency on periodic devaluations as a mechanism for cutting the dollar value of wages and preserving the steady growth of employment in the bor-

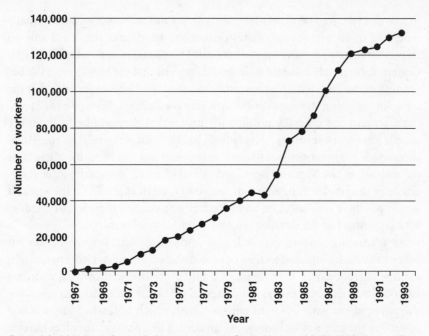

Figure 6.1. Number of maquiladora workers in Ciudad Juárez, 1967–1993. (INEGI, *Estadística de la industria maquiladora de exportación, 1989–1993* [Aguascalientes, 1994], 5; Jorge Carrillo V. and Alberto Hernández, *Mujeres fronterizas en la industria maquiladora* [Mexico City: SEP/CEFNOMEX, 1985], 99; Leslie Sklair, *Assembling for Development* [La Jolla: Center for U.S.-Mexico Studies, University of California, San Diego, 1993], 99.)

der zone. The economist Joseph Grunwald captured the paradox of Third World development and foreign industrial investment: "The key to greater foreign investment in assembly plants is the maintenance of as wide a gap as possible between wages in Mexico and wages in the United States."[26]

As wage rates tended to creep up over time, currency devaluations delivered that key. In Ciudad Juárez, the minimum daily wage followed Mexico's inflation rate as it rose from 102 pesos in late 1976 to 160 in 1980 and finally jumped to 210 pesos in 1981. In dollars, RCA paid only about 57 cents an hour in 1976, but the wage rate had nearly doubled in only five years, to $1.12.[27] With border-zone labor costs at an all-time high (but still a fraction of U.S. wages), maquila managers openly announced that they found the cost pressures threatening to their profitability, and their talk of plant closings and the need for competitiveness with other Third World nations became increasingly open. For the first time since the recession of 1974, when several cities saw an exodus of maquila jobs, employment in the border zone actually dropped between 1981 and 1982 (see Figure 6.1).

With wage costs creeping upward on the border and the "Reagan recession" under way in the United States, RCA temporarily laid off 3,700 workers in March 1982. As a result of a bargain with the union, however, the company paid half of its employees' wages during the layoff and the CTM offered interest-free loans to cover the other half. The secretary general of the CTM, Genaro Ricarte, tried to ease widespread concern that the layoffs were the beginning of the end of RCA's commitment to Juárez. "There is no risk that the company is going to abandon the city," he proclaimed. "Despite the layoff, management has officially notified the union that they will be hiring more people after work resumes." His faith in RCA's word was based on the Mexican president's commitment to devalue the peso just one month earlier. "The devaluation of the Mexican peso," explained Ricarte, "makes the foreign operator in the border zone more attractive to foreign capital." So the workers would get their jobs back, he was sure, but he made no mention of the devastating impact of the devaluation on the employees' earnings.[28]

As a growing custom dictated, just before President López Portillo left office in 1982, he initiated a series of peso devaluations in an effort to reestablish the currency on a firm financial foundation for the incoming administration. The price of Mexico's main export, petroleum, then tumbled, leaving the government with less hard currency with which to finance imports and to service the country's massive foreign debt. The country's finances quickly spiraled out of control as the enormous burden created by government borrowing from international lenders during the previous decade appeared to be pushing Mexico toward default. "What began in 1982 was not just a short-term financial crisis precipitated by rising international interest rates and falling oil prices," explains the political scientist Wayne Cornelius, "but rather a much more fundamental economic and political crisis." As a result of the Mexican tailspin, real wages between 1983 and 1988 dropped 40 percent across the country, to levels not seen since the mid-1960s. Of workers in the largest cities, 62 percent earned less than the already low official minimum wage by the late 1980s.[29]

For workers, the 1980s might as well have been the 1930s—except that there was no federal spending to cushion the blow. The austerity programs initiated to pull Mexico back from the brink of collapse took their heaviest tolls on the country's workers and unemployed: the government set severe limits on wage increases, dramatically cut spending on social programs, loosened price controls on basic commodities, eventually sold off state-owned companies (although it nationalized the banks), and terminated or cut subsidies on key popular goods and services such as gasoline, utilities, and mass transportation.[30] The end result of becoming an international hostage to their own debt crisis was a complete reorientation of Mexican development strategies from a nationalistic economic vision to a neoliberal approach that would place increasing emphasis on loosening government controls as a way to earn desperately needed foreign investment.[31] The government's turn from one of its traditional pillars of support, organized labor, threw into question the unions' weakening alliance with the state apparatus. When the debt crisis struck in 1982, however, the CTM chose to continue to support the administration and to fight inflationary demands from the rank and file rather than engage in open struggle to recover workers' lost wages. In exchange, the government maintained minimal programs to protect workers' purchasing power and offered slight increases in the minimum wage.

Organized labor's tame response to the austerity programs, as Kevin Middlebrook explains, was part of a long history of "pragmatic intra-elite bargaining rather than open confrontation with state authorities." This negotiating strategy led in late 1987 to the Economic and Solidarity Pact, which offered only limited compensation to organized workers but effectively restrained the union membership's demands for their lost income. However brutal to Mexico's workers, the austerity programs proved pivotal in taming runaway inflation by 1989. The CTM leadership recognized that its support from the government depended on its ability to curtail workers' often desperate push for a restoration of their earnings. Strategically, although its members saw their buying power collapse, organized labor's callous commitment to controlling workers' reaction to the austerity programs may have been what allowed what was left of labor's federal institutional framework to survive and the country to recover.[32]

The debt crisis was certainly not triggered on behalf of TNC wage bills, but the workers' nightmare during the 1980s was certainly a dream for foreign capital. As the Mexican economy entered the 1980s, a period known as the "lost decade" throughout Latin America, the slashes in the value of the peso sponsored the single largest rise in BIP employment ever—from 150,687 workers in 1983 to an astonishing 305,253 workers only four years later. "While there is no convincing evidence that the TNCs can bring salvation to the Third World," accurately concluded Leslie Sklair, a noted maquila critic, "in many poor countries the TNCs are seen as responsible for the only bright spots in the economy and society."[33]

Many workers found the unions in general to be of some slight benefit, but most agreed that the unions' goal was to contain rank-and-file opposition to the austerity programs. One woman with four years' seniority at the RCA plant summed up their position: "*Charrismo* [corrupt or sellout unionism] is one of the worst sins we face as workers. The verbal disputes between the authorities and the union haven't lightened the economic burdens we carry. We're vulnerable to being fired at any moment, as happened to several *compañeros* who decided to leave the CTM to join the CROC." But the RCA workers were growing increasingly restless; "they're sensing the growing strength of genuine unionism and they're getting scared."[34] Another RCA worker said that the union could help with occasional bread-and-butter issues, but because of its national commitments, it had no power at the local level. "The union never intervenes in anything in the plant," she said. "We hear almost nothing from the unions, except when they tell us we have to ask for more money or when they dismiss somebody and she has to go to the union so they can help her." The most common sentiment among the employees was that the only thing the union was interested in was siphoning off a percentage of their paychecks in the form of dues.[35]

Recovering Lost Ground

As workers watched their wages fall, paid prices connected to the U.S. dollar, and felt the constraints of a union bent on keeping it all that way, they took part in the first major labor conflict at RCA Juárez in November 1982. The CTM's pragmatism at the national level manifested itself as a basic problem of labor control at the local level as the RCA workers sought to oust both the CTM and the salary caps it supported. Since union democracy had to precede the demand for a restoration of the RCA workers' falling pay, a small number of setmakers began to organize the first of what would be several drives to overthrow the CTM leadership. Although the "vast majority" of the employees wanted to reject the union, reported the local press, the struggle centered on "numerous" activists who organized rallies and threatened work stoppages. They demanded that the collective contract be rewritten, that the union's collection and allocation of dues be clarified, and above all that the CTM leader, Genaro Ricarte, and his executive board be removed. One worker, exasperated by the union members who followed him around and monitored his speech, said, "It's not really that important, the struggle to get the wage increase, in comparison with the removal of Genaro Ricarte, who has been in place almost twelve years without getting any benefits for the workers." Many RCA employees believed that Ricarte was more interested in his new disco and his automobile dealership and other properties than in fighting for the maquila workers. "You can play with a lot of things, but not the workers' hunger," declared Efrén Arellano of the Socialist Workers Party, "and the workers of RCA have undertaken a struggle to defend their buying power."[36]

Still the CTM refused to support the RCA employees' efforts to restore their wages. The union proved more than capable of controlling the incipient democratic movement among the workers, thus confirming the viability of the maquila system's wage caps under even the most austere of economic conditions. The CTM simply signed an agreement to raise the official wage a nominal 13.5 percent and supported RCA's dismissal of four leaders particularly active in the campaign to oust the union. The incentive of the wage increase, however meager, and the fear aroused by the firing of the activists put a halt to the struggle.[37] Types of wage discipline similar to that imposed by the CTM at RCA across the nation were essential elements in reforming the Mexican economy, but it was the workers who bore the direct costs of the government's mismanagement.

Minor protests and major confrontations erupted all along the border in 1982 and 1983, but they did not stop the plummeting cost of labor from fostering dramatic growth in maquila employment.[38] Although a windfall for U.S. corporations, the devaluations severely weakened the hard-currency contributions the BIP brought in to the national coffers. As dollars purchased more labor power, the maquila industry actually brought into the country relatively fewer dollars per worker after the devaluations. In sum, the program grew rapidly, but employment rose less quickly than the peso fell in value.[39] Most important for the trajectory of social change in Juárez, the growth in employment sponsored by falling wages began to restrict a once wide-open labor market. With fewer potential workers competing for the available jobs, *juarenses* found themselves with just a bit more room for negotiation with their employers.

As wages continued to fall throughout the 1980s, the other major weakness in the Mexican political economy, electoral fraud, triggered further demands for pay increases. In July 1986, several states were slated for local and state elections (Baja California Norte, Campeche, Chihuahua, Durango, Michoacán, and Zacatecas), and Chihuahua looked as though it had the best chance of turning the long-dominant Institutional Revolutionary Party (PRI) out of the governor's office. The National Action Party (PAN), a rapidly growing pro-business party with particular strength in the border states, named Francisco Barrio, a former mayor of Juárez and former head of the Bermúdez group, as its candidate for governor. The PAN allied itself with parties to the left of the ruling PRI, in an organization known as the Democratic Electoral Movement, and pledged civil disobedience and hunger strikes if the elections appeared to have been stolen by the PRI. "I'm enchanted to work with any organization or party that is fighting for democracy in our state and our country," the charismatic Barrio declared.[40]

After the ruling PRI announced that it had again "won" all important seats in Chihuahua, a month of popular protest against electoral fraud led to the imposition of martial law in Juárez. Mass demonstrations erupted around the city as soldiers marched in "at bayonet point and declared themselves in charge" of the city. By the second week of July, 25,000 *panistas* marched on the Juárez city hall as military helicopters buzzed overhead. Two days later the thousands of demonstrators marched onto the international bridge and blocked traffic; soldiers fired shots in the air but still they would not disperse. Even the Archdiocese of Chihuahua announced that religious services in sixty-two parishes throughout the state would be canceled to protest the alleged election fraud. Finally, a five-day blockade of the international bridge stopped hundreds of trucks shipping parts and products to and from maquilas. "Please excuse the inconvenience," read one polite protest sign on the international bridge. "We are fighting to save our dignity."[41]

In the midst of the demonstrations, the Juárez papers carried PAN advertisements urging the maquila workers to engage in a week-long series of rolling, thirty-minute ministrikes to protest the electoral fraud. Workers at twenty plants in the city participated in the PAN's protest. Of the thousands of workers at RCA, however, only twenty halted their work—most of them supervisors and lower management personnel, the PAN's primary constituency. RCA quickly dismissed four of the *panistas* and the CTM tried to persuade other workers not to heed the party's call for further shop-floor protests.[42]

Entrepreneurs and managers made up the bulk of the PAN's base, but the small RCA stoppage quickly spilled over to rank-and-file protests against the old problems of salary caps and repressive unions. Many working-class women who participated in the pro-PAN/anti-PRI protests knew very little about the PAN's platform; their self-described goal was simply to defeat those who had been in power for their entire lives. RCA's firing of the strikers triggered an estimated 5,000 out of 5,600 workers to demand, once again, the removal of the union leadership and a restoration of their wages. When the union threw three PAN supporters out of the CTM, the affair escalated to broad-based work stoppages. The company countered with sizable bonuses —the usual incentive that kept wage caps in place—in an effort to avoid seeing the entire plant come to a halt.[43]

Although the bonuses purchased some peace, tensions continued high until October, when the sporadic stoppages and petitions made the labor force unruly enough for even RCA to denounce the union executive board. Fifteen hundred employees stopped work to take advantage of the schism between the company and the union. The CTM countered by deducting the work stoppages from protesters' pay and revoking strikers' seniority benefits. Other Juárez shops joined in the fight, and maquila officials began to fear that the TNCs would flee the city if the sporadic upheavals at RCA and another plant with rebellious workers, Cupones de Oro, were to succeed. Work stoppages, reprisals by CTM officials against the RCA workers, more road blockages, and police intervention became regular occurrences. Finally the executive committee of the Chihuahua state CTM intervened and signed an agreement with the company to pay the 4,700 RCA employees who had taken part in the protests for their time off the job, not to take any more reprisals against the dissidents, and to hold an election for new union leaders. The leadership replacements were again drawn from the CTM old guard, however, and the RCA workers demanded their removal, too. Faced with an inflation rate that continued to devour their wages, the RCA employees demanded a 100 percent wage increase but ended up accepting the union's meager 15 percent increase in the form of bonuses.[44]

The disruptions came to an abrupt halt when GE purchased RCA in 1986. Much as in Bloomington, the new owner went through the plant and introduced a variety of new production technologies, reshuffled workers around the plant, terminated the third shift, cut two assembly lines, and, by March 1987, suspended 1,500 workers, including four supervisors and many line chiefs. Rather than oppose the actions, the union actually facilitated GE's draconian policies, earning it even more enmity among the rank and file. Although employment levels would eventually recover, the massive layoffs reinstated the company's lost discipline over the workers, affirmed the salary caps, and left the CTM in place.[45]

Labor Market and Social Change in Juárez

The failure of the two major pushes for union democracy during the 1980s led many observers to despair over the possibility of changing the maquila labor system. "The history of labor conflicts in the [RCA] plant has been played out in the presence of a union clearly tied to the corporation's positions," reports María Eugenia de la O Martínez. "Each time [of conflict] resulted in an increase in the collaboration of the union for the functioning of the plant."[46] Even though the labor crises only seemed to draw the union closer to the company, the lessons learned during the protests and on the shop floor helped to crystallize a growing awareness and maturity in the RCA labor force.

Marisa González Salazar, a nine-year veteran of RCA's Juárez operation, illustrates the impact that years of industrial work alone can have on a worker's thinking. A bright and articulate young woman, she was recognized by RCA for her leadership potential and quickly promoted to the level of supervisor. The promotion served the dual purpose of separating her from her fellow employees and tapping her skills for the good of the company, but it did not prevent her from trying to organize her co-workers. "The threats were heavy and it pretty much shook up the organizers," she said. "You know it is more difficult to organize and struggle in a transnational firm than in a national company." Surrendering hope, she confessed, "It will never be possible to really win struggles in the maquilas." Although her despair grew from her organizing drive at RCA, her awareness also came directly from the shop floor. It was work itself that forged her political identity and launched her on her post-RCA career as a community activist. "As much as I hated working in those factories, I have to admit that I learned a lot," she said. "I learned that workers can do a lot of self-organizing. I mean, here you have this immense place, with assembly lines running up and down the length of the building. And while it may seen somewhat chaotic, there is a lot of order, a lot of interdependency." Like many of the successful CIO organizers of the 1930s, she had the mobility to see how the entire plant was knit together and how each worker played an indispensable role in production. "You work the lines, and as a group-chief, you get to know more about other areas of the plant," Marisa concluded. "Roaming around, I got to learn that way." Explaining her commitment to activism at COMO, she said, "That is what I think got me to view the world as I do now . . . it really opens up your eyes."[47]

Just as Mary Frances Roll, the personnel manager in Bloomington, claimed that RCA delivered the industrial revolution to the women of southern Indiana, a maquila manager boasted that "we have brought the second industrial revolution to the Mexican-American border. We are again transforming the world by bringing progress to all people, but especially to women."[48] Indeed, the Juárez of the 1980s would have been barely recognizable to anyone present when RCA first selected the city. Not only were over 120,000 people employed by foreign capital in the city by 1990, but they had become increasingly contentious about the terms of their employment. Throughout the 1980s, labor unrest kept cropping up at some of the most important maquilas in the city: protracted conflicts at Acapulco Fashions (1979, 1980), Convertors de México (1980, 1982), Centralab (1981), General Instrument (1982), Cupones de Oro (1986), Banda Grande (1985, 1986), Texcan (1986), and AMF (1986), among dozens of others.[49]

The labor unrest of the 1980s forced a reworking of researchers' understanding of maquila labor as a pliable glut of cheap workers. "In comparison to the 1960s and 1970s," Jorge Carrillo concluded at the beginning of the 1990s, "labor conflicts in the maquiladora industry have become more radical in recent years. . . . Women workers have come to play an increasingly prominent role in struggles for union democracy and improved working conditions." The unions' repression in many of these disputes, rather than keeping workers in line as it had done in the early years, actually redoubled their efforts. Clearly, as the newspapers showed women marching, carrying sticks, and blocking roads around the city, the image of the docile maquila worker lost credibility. "Although young women continue to constitute the majority of the work force in in-bond processing plants," writes Carrillo, "workers' growing experience and combativeness indicate that labor relations in the maquiladora industry may become even more conflictive in the future."[50]

As in Bloomington, part of what fueled the change was the disappearance of the labor glut. By the mid-1980s, growth had been so strong that local leaders even became concerned that the city could not absorb any more TNC investment. The pools of labor began to dry up, industry analysts feared that adequate space simply did not exist for any more growth, and infrastructure appeared to be at the breaking point. "Industrial expansion in Cd. Juárez shall be curtailed in order to avoid the rise of a megalopolis," announced the central government rather prematurely. "Cd. Juárez cannot handle any more assembly plants," echoed the local press. In fact, by 1990 the Parque Bermúdez had grown into the largest industrial park in the world; that corner of Juárez alone contained 46 plants, 49 companies, and 35,000 workers.[51]

The maquila system of high turnover to maintain a labor force of women forever young began to crumble as the growth of employment opportunities forced corporations to shift to efforts to retain their workers. In the late 1970s it was estimated that three eligible women could be found for every maquila operator in the city. By 1987 a local manager was saying, "We're taking anybody that breathes. We used to try to take anyone between the ages of 18 and 25; now we're taking anyone." The running joke among Juárez managers in the 1980s was that personnel managers were driving around town and holding a mirror up in front of anyone they could find. If it fogged up, they hired them. In 1986 one could count 150 maquila want ads per week in the local papers, and by the end of the decade, it was safe to say that unemployment basically did not exist in Ciudad Juárez.[52]

With other sectors of the economy growing alongside the maquilas, women could find opportunities outside the TNCs, in tourism and the burgeoning service sector. Although managers constantly complained about the lack of "maquila-grade" employees, a genuine shortage of assembly operators did not exist in the city; the root of the problem was a shortage of financial incentives to keep people on the job. "Companies' reluctance to raise wages so as to increase the attractiveness of maquila jobs is a primary reason for the so-called maquila-grade labor shortage," concludes Susan Tiano. Because of the artificial "shortage" of women and the arrival of new types of work, such as the manufacture of auto parts, male employment suddenly grew from less than 25 percent to 42 percent of the BIP labor force by 1987.[53]

Although many interested observers began to call for restrictions on the program's growth, the shrinking labor market actually pushed the maturation of the industry. In the 1980s, several Juárez plants, particularly RCA, began to move toward more capital-intensive forms of assembly production, more flexible forms of work organization, and a radical increase in efforts to retain well-trained and desirable employees. The electronics factories started to encompass high-technology investments, greater automation, quality circles, flexible production strategies, an increase in skill levels, a rise in the number of workers per plant, and a diversification of products manufactured. The new forms of work organization and product innovation also blurred the distinction between industrial work performed in the United States and that done in Mexico. "The common denominator among all the electronics companies visited," reported the International Labour Organization in 1986, "was the employers' strategy to produce a new type of worker whose attitude and behavior are different from those previously required."[54]

Indeed, a "new type" of worker not only had to be loyal but willing to share her knowledge as well. "You want to get operators to work at a like rhythm," explained a member of the RCA management team. "In the U.S., if a worker can't function with enough time in a particular assembly sequence, . . . the operators will rebel, they'll complain, make you change it. It will not go unnoticed. In Mexico, the operator is more obedient and won't complain. As a result you have more rejects. We don't want this. The operator can play an important role. If the worker speaks up, we'll listen and make changes if possible." Increases in the technical skills of the maquila workers were evident throughout the city. The need to tap into RCA workers' growing body of knowledge became most evident when a group of line operators actually designed an entire circuit matrix for a new television set that went onto RCA's list of best-selling products.[55]

As one of the oldest major firms in Juárez, RCA became a pioneer in introducing new technologies and developing innovative labor systems in the area. "We are super automated," reported an RCA manager. "This is the highest level of technology plant in our division, and I do mean world-wide."[56] Automatic insertion devices, programmable machinery, the miniaturization of components, and printed circuit boards supplemented new forms of production strategies that required higher levels of initiative and autonomy on the part of the workers. In accordance with the Japanese management strategies that were sweeping the business world, 25 percent of the plant was divided into work teams, authority structures became more diffuse, and responsibility fell from the supervisors down to the workers themselves in order to develop a sense of group fate at the plant. To remind the workers of the new climate of "enforced responsibility," large signs on the wall declared: "Quality is the number one priority in our business, there are no exceptions!" and "Gain confidence through customer satisfaction!" The new system ingeniously encouraged workers to monitor each other's behavior rather than be under the constant supervision of management. An RCA employee explained, "We're trying not to have mistakes and to fulfill the quality [goals], because here we achieve teamwork and respect the others' work." Another echoed, "We're all important, because our job depends on quality."[57]

When the Bloomington workers decided to sacrifice 20-inch television production rather than make concessions in their contract, Thomson had the opportunity to examine its commitment to Ciudad Juárez as well. Management told its plant location expert to find the best location possible for what would soon be the most technologically sophisticated plant in the world for the production of its 20-inch sets. RCA executives told him to put it any-

Petra Guadiana slides a finished and packaged set off the assembly line in Juárez's clean, state-of-the-art TTM plant in 1998. Under a sign proclaiming, "World class is my goal, continuous improvement is my way," workers, prodded by millions of dollars' worth of automated equipment, transform a collection of parts into ready-to-ship television sets in only an hour and a quarter. (Photo copyright © Mark Hume.)

where—anywhere but Juárez. "Yeah, we need one," they told him, "but whatever you do, don't put it in Juárez because of employment, the crowdedness and on and on and on." The location expert roamed around for a couple of months in search of another site, but "it all kept pointing back. As bad as supposedly Juárez was for employment and all of those things," he said, "it was the best place along the border." This time, however, the new plant site had a twist. The state of Chihuahua sold the corporation a nice piece of land outside of town, far from the other industrial parks. Like the company towns of decades past, according to an RCA manager, the nonunion plant "is the control of the area."[58]

When the new Thomson Televisiones de México (TTM) plant started production, it was an amazing spectacle. All of RCA's previous television manufacturing systems had been spread out geographically: Juárez built the prealigned and pretested chassis; Marion, Indiana, or Scranton, Pennsylvania, built the picture tubes; Mocksville, North Carolina, provided the high-end wood cabinets; and Bloomington joined everything together into a completed set. The new just-in-time plant, however, brought all aspects of television manufacturing "into one continuous, integrated assembly line," including skill-intensive plastic-modeling operations. The manufacturing operation, the result of decades of ongoing innovation in the assembly process, was laden, according to Thomson's operations specialist, with "one ton of technology." Parts entered the east side of the building and seventy-five minutes later were "right out the back door directly to the Kmarts and Walmarts" without warehousing or middlemen. By 1995, 3,600 workers, in addition to those in the original factory, staffed the lines at the new plant. Soon it would be a matter of a few days between the arrival of an order at the factory and the shipping of the new sets, manufactured to the retailer's exact specifications.[59] With the increase in skills, innovations in labor relations, and the new technology, the city appeared to be on the path from labor-intensive periphery to a new center of industrial innovation.

Revolt of the "Fallen Workers"

While the just-in-time plant was making history with new production records, history was repeating itself back at the old Parque Bermúdez plant. The austerity program initiated after 1982 and continued after 1988 by President Carlos Salinas de Gortari appeared to have placed the peso on a stable platform. The dollar value of the Juárez maquila workers' pay recovered from its 1986 nadir of 57 cents an hour and finally went back up to $1.47 in 1990. The upward crawl of the dollar value of the workers' wages kept them relatively content through the first half of the 1990s. Unfortunately, the peso was openly acknowledged to be grossly overvalued, and when Salinas devalued it in late 1994, before his departure from office, the action triggered a large-scale flight of particularly volatile investment from Mexico. What was supposed to be a readjustment in financial markets spiraled out of control, and, much as in 1982, practically overnight the maquila workers lost 30 to 40 percent of their purchasing power. As the pro-NAFTA economist Gary Hufbauer explained, the de facto wage cut sponsored by the peso crisis returned maquila labor costs to rock bottom. TNCs in the border zone "are making so much money down there that running a factory in Mexico now . . . is like running a mint. They are making tons of money." [60] As RCA workers watched their pay practically dissolve in their hands one more time, they again stormed the twin barricades of the maquiladoras: salary caps and union intransigence. And this time they won.

By late January 1995, the crisis left RCA workers facing rapidly rising food prices on pay of less than $20 a week (about what they made in 1968). Although the workers were struggling with inordinate financial burdens, the spark that actually ignited the highly volatile situation was the company's shortsighted decision to cut paid vacations from two weeks to one. A disgruntled line worker complained that the plant manager, Hector Barrio (brother of the PAN governor of Chihuahua), "has cut back on many benefits. He always looks for ways to make more money for the owners and he is never for the people." Hearing the news, the first shift of 2,000 angry workers walked off the job on Wednesday, 1 February 1995. Since, as another protester proclaimed, "all the union [leaders] are with the company, not with us," the workers formed their own negotiating team in a strategy designed to circumvent, rather than simply oppose, the CTM. With the vast majority of the employees again on its side, the Democratic Workers' Coalition (Coalición de Trabajadores Democráticos de RCA), as the dissident group was called, demanded a 30 percent wage increase, the removal of corrupt union officials, and the reinstatement of the two-week vacation. Rather than negotiate, the company broke off talks with the independent workers on the second of February and locked the workers out of the plant for the rest of the week. The plant, they announced, would open up the following Monday for those willing to work and interested in keeping their jobs.[61]

Throughout the four-day lockout, dubbed the "revolt of the fallen workers" by participants, employees blocked roads, held rallies, collected contributions to their strike fund, and organized an alternative leadership coalition. In front of the Parque Bermúdez they sat high atop the fence surrounding the plant and led thousands of employees in chants for pay raises and a democratic union. In a swipe at the Arbitration Board, a popular sign demanded "support from impartial and competent authorities." The RCA lockout moved from isolated struggle to a movement when workers at several other plants sought the same objectives. The crisis spilled into the media in Mexico City and became a point of departure for national discussions about the future of democracy, economic development, currency stability, and Mexico's entry into the North American Free Trade Agreement.[62]

The impact of the conflict spread northward, too. The Bloomington plant laid off all its production staff without pay for two days when the firm ran out of television chassis to feed the assembly lines. Never in the history of the two cities' plants had a moment been more ripe for international solidarity, but none was forthcoming. "We don't like [the layoff], but it's what you get when you move stuff to Mexico and pay people a dollar an hour," said Bloomington's chief shop steward, Larry Lake. "We predicted something like this would happen. We fought NAFTA, we stood in the rain and did everything we could to prevent this. But it didn't work. This is what you get. I hate it." It could be argued that the only way for the Bloomington employees to escape the trap set by a globalized labor market was to build a strong floor for wages and working conditions that spanned international boundaries. Rather than rush a portion of the union's funds and personnel to Mexico, however, the Bloomington workers merely complained. They had difficulty envisioning a world far beyond the boundary of Monroe County.[63]

Back in Juárez, the local power structure proved unable to control the protest, and the president of the National Association of Transformation Industries arrived to try to contain the unrest with an old tactic: fomenting fears of capital flight. He proclaimed that "*juarenses* offer the best labor force on the border" and that they had the right to bargain for better wages, but the RCA workers had to remember that they did not compete with North American workers. Their competitors were "employees who earn less per workday in countries such as China, Indonesia, and Taiwan." Crises like the RCA stoppage, he argued, "give Juárez a bad image," and "if the company decides to leave, it could generate problems for the rest of the local maquila industries." Federal and state government officials also made clear to the plant manager that giving in to the workers' demands would break the salary caps in the industry, initiating an inflationary pattern that would push the country back "to the period of the eighties, when prices rose until we had an annual inflation rate of 160 percent."[64]

When the plant reopened on 7 February, strike leaders tried to negotiate with busloads of workers determined to cross the picket lines and enter the plant. Unable to convince many employees that staying off the job was the most effective tactic and fearful of dividing their forces, strike leaders decided to support a return to the job. In an act that resonated back in Camden, however, activists walked to their positions and boldly engaged in a work stoppage inside the plant, in effect a sit-down strike, which rolled through the plant and paralyzed production. The occupation of RCA finally forced management's hand, and by the end of the day the Democratic Coalition had won a 20 percent wage hike, a return of their paid vacation, and the company's commitment to hold free and fair elections. The next month the RCA employees voted out their former CTM officials in favor of the slate of candidates offered by the Democratic Workers' Coalition. Although the raise they won was a compromise, for the first time in the history of the company's presence in Juárez the employees forced the television manufacturer to negotiate directly with their elected representatives and to raise wages above the salary caps.[65]

The Issue of Maquiladora Exceptionalism

Given the common trajectory of social change in all of these sites, an important question remains: Just how new is the working class found under the "new international division of labor"? Several factors suggest more commonality between the United States and Mexico than many observers think. Though the wages paid in Juárez are still a fraction of U.S. rates, they are slightly higher than those offered in the interior of Mexico. Local personnel are being promoted, and a move toward capital investment and flexible production strategies has overthrown the old labor-intensive maquila model. The number of men being employed by the border firms has increased dramatically. Because of RCA's privileged position in the local labor market, the corporation has been able to indulge its preference for female workers, but by 1993 the proportion of male employees in the Juárez maquilas had grown to 45 percent. Since the French conglomerate Thomson Consumer Electronics has bought RCA, its employees in the United States and Mexico even share the experience of working for a foreign employer.[66]

Some factors unique to the Juárez experience, however, do suggest a new era of labor relations and a different type of economic development. The Mexican frontier remains much more an economic zone than a development zone, as backward economic linkages between the border plants and the rest of Mexico—at less than 2 percent—probably remain the most important obstacle to the deepening of local and national development. While NAFTA may suggest that the border will cease to be an enclave as the maquila strategy spreads throughout the country, unless domestic content requirements or incentives are put in place to stimulate the development of local parts suppliers, the country will have a difficult time developing its economic role beyond that of simple supplier of labor.[67]

Yet the new just-in-time TTM plant and General Motors' plans to locate a $13 million engineering and design center in Juárez indicate that some genuine technology transfer is taking place. Ciudad Juárez may actually be evolving from the periphery to a new center of innovation. The third Thomson plant in the city, the one built to take the final Bloomington jobs after the 1998 shutdown, represents a big step in this direction. For RCA-brand production, this event marked the end any sort of "international division of labor," as all manufacturing was centralized in Juárez. The new shop, called Manufacturas Avanzadas, S.A., or MASA, cost $60 million to build and will be responsible for the most sophisticated television assembly processes. Yet a dramatic contrast remains between the "clean, orderly, well-lit and spacious" plants amidst clusters of dusty, windblown houses of cement blocks, plywood, and cardboard.[68]

The maquila exceptionalism question must also address differences in unionization. In Camden, Memphis, and Bloomington, industrial life itself ultimately delivered varying types of democratic organization to the "RCA family." No one can predict the future of Mexican labor politics, but some trends are encouraging. A variety of upheavals in the Mexican political economy—privatization, the liberalization of foreign investment, flexible work arrangements—have weakened the state-oriented unions. Although the country's corporatist structure and the unions' position within it retain a great deal of legitimacy in many popular sectors, it is clearly beginning to crack. Political changes under way foreshadow significant transformations ahead. The recent past, as two historians note, delivered Mexico to a key historic juncture in which the old formulas cast in the revolutionary experience no longer apply to present circumstances. "Mexican society is witnessing the end of a fundamental agreement within itself, a true change of era, that makes us feel both disconcerted and desirous of change," write Héctor Aguilar Camín and Lorenzo Meyer, who see the nation caught between "the inert weight of the past and the magnetic and undefined clamor of the future."[69]

The political changes are becoming increasingly evident. In addition to losing occasional state-level elections, the PRI lost the very important mayor's seat in Mexico City to a long-time opposition candidate, Cuauhtémoc Cárdenas (who many believe really won the presidency in 1988), and pivotal labor federations have begun to crystallize in opposition to the CTM's continued subordination to the national ruling party. The question remains, however, whether unions that are not protected by the state will even be tolerated in the global order. Simply put, the vacuum left by the passing of the old system of labor politics will leave two possibilities in the border zone: renewed militant unions and no unions at all. The political scientist Maria Cook believes the process will hinge on the fate of democratic struggles such as those at Thomson. The transformation ahead, she suggests, is likely to be "complex and conflictive . . . , as dependent on the organizing skills and strategies of unions, parties, and other citizens' groups and their international allies as it is on the responses and actions of Mexico's political elites."[70]

Whatever the outcome on the union front, the wage gap between the two countries is not going to go away soon. The disparity between Juárez and Bloomington dwarfs the differential between Camden and Bloomington in the 1930s and 1940s. After the peso crisis, a Bloomington worker could make in a couple of hours what a Juárez wage earner made in a week. This difference cannot be attributed simply to the lower costs of basic commodities in Mexico, either, for prices along the border are nowhere near low enough to compensate for the shortfall in wages.[71] More than any other factor, a currency so unstable that U.S. inflation rates become all but irrelevant eats away at Mexican workers' buying power and weakens their position vis-à-vis their employers.

Yet maquila employees' wages, benefits, and working conditions are often better than those of most workers in Mexico's domestic sectors. Whether labor on the border can continue to break through the political and economic restraints that served the corporations well in the United States and whether Mexico can harness foreign capital in a constructive developmental strategy rather than a simple cheap-labor approach remain to be seen. Mexican workers find themselves in competition not with counterparts to the north but with those in some more distant place on the globe, where labor is cheaper still. Just as U.S. workers faced Mexico, now Mexicans face the Far East. "Our competition for this location is China," says Terry Burns, manager of Thomson's newest plant. "It's amazing what that country is doing." The tight labor market makes "Help Wanted" signs permanent fixtures outside TCE and most other plants, but the one thing employers avoid at all costs is open bidding over the price of labor. As Burns argues, "if this guy raises his wages," indicating a neighboring factory, "I'm going to raise my wages. Now all we've done is increase the cost to the business. All we'd do is just drive everybody out of here." Having worked in Asia, the plant manager explained how Taiwan "priced itself out of business"—an act he sees as a cautionary tale for the growing unrest in Mexico's workforce.[72]

A comparison of Ciudad Juárez with the U.S. cities, in sum, reveals a very similar but more powerful formula for labor control in Juárez. Understanding capital migration to Mexico in the context of a lengthy history of plant locations and relocations clearly challenges the view that the globalization of capital signals a radical departure from previous systems of labor control. In defining "postmodern labor regimes," for instance, Aihwa Ong identifies a radical new system based on a "local milieu constituted by the unprecedented conjuncture of labor relations and cultural systems, high-tech operations and indigenous values." In areas such as the Mexico-U.S. border, "new techniques operating through the control of social spaces" and fostering a "cultural struggle" are "a distinctive feature of postmodern regimes." Ong's criteria for postmodern labor systems, of course, can easily be met by any of the RCA cities in the twentieth century. In the 1940s, the exotic working-class "other" was merely the white worker in Bloomington, where there was little identifiably "postmodern" about RCA's system of labor relations. Most important, critics such as Ong dismiss the power of such fragmented cultural struggles to lead to genuine structural change.[73] Although the changes that come may not be the ones workers desire, it is exactly the accumulation of subtle transformations at the local level that has played the pivotal role in global economic transformations.

CHAPTER SEVEN

The Distances In Between

In May 1993, Sandy Anderson left Bloomington and boarded a plane bound for Ciudad Juárez. As she headed out through the factory gates to begin her journey, her co-workers urged her to "tell all those blankety-blank Mexicans they've got our jobs!"

The fact that she was on her way to the unfamiliar place where so many RCA jobs had been relocated placed her in a more reflective mood than her angry co-workers. "It's not *their* fault," she said. "If you didn't have a job and someone built a factory here, what would you do? Say, 'I'm not taking those jobs because the Mexican people had them'? You're gonna grab 'em. You know *I* would." Unknowingly Anderson had pinpointed what Bloomington workers had done when RCA arrived in their town from its historic home in Camden, New Jersey, over half a century earlier.[1]

Anderson and the two co-workers who accompanied her belonged to a worker-management quality circle that had won the award for the most significant contribution to productivity and efficiency at the RCA-Thomson television plant. In what was certainly one of the more peculiar prizes that could have been awarded to a group of workers, the company sent them on a tour of Thomson's factories along the Mexican border to, as she put it, "see where our jobs went." Like her traveling companions, Anderson had never before ventured very far outside Indiana. She had never been farther north than Muskegon, Michigan, or farther south than Nashville, Tennessee, or farther west than nearby Vincennes, Indiana. She had never flown before, and the prospect made her nervous. As the jet lifted off from Hoosier soil, Anderson's friends teased her about her frantic thumbing of her New Testament.

In contrast to the workers, with their limited experience of travel, the manager guiding them on their trip had made this flight over fifty times. Unlike many other U.S. trade unionists' exploratory visits to the Mexican border in the NAFTA era, these workers' international adventure was tightly orchestrated by the company, and the delegation remained well insulated from their Mexican counterparts. Staying in posh hotel suites ("almost as big as my house") on the U.S. side of the border, dining in steak houses and tourist restaurants, and bargaining in the curio shops in Juárez left the group with little sense of the Mexicans' life and work. Many smiles and an occasional "*Hola*" or "Hi" was the extent of the workers' transnational interactions. When Anderson pressed their guide for the one piece of information she really wanted—the Mexicans' hourly wage—"he danced around like he was doing the Virginia reel," she explained. "He never did tell me."

Although she had no opportunity actually to speak with any Mexican workers, Anderson still found her visits to the factory floor "amazing" and "fantastic." Her preconceptions of the oppressive conditions in Mexico led her to envision the Juárez operations as "just a bunch of people in a little garage or something," so the reality "really shocked me." The first plant they toured, which had been operating since 1968, "looked like a lot of it used to here [in Bloomington]"—the same equipment, the same rows of young women assembling television chassis. They also visited the just-in-time RCA factory on the outskirts of Juárez, probably the most technologically sophisticated television plant in the world at the time. "They do everything, start to finish," she remarked. "You would have thought this plant would've been sittin' right here" in Bloomington. She wished she could have gone to Honolulu, where winners of the Quality Leadership Program had gone in the past, but she still found the tour interesting. "Now if my job goes, I know where it's at." An employee who won the same award the following year may have captured the experience best. Gazing at Mexican workers on machines formerly in Bloomington, Nelda Stuppy remarked after the news of the final Bloomington shutdown, "My past and future was right there and I didn't realize it."[2]

The trip greatly disturbed Anderson, but her thirty years of labor for RCA allowed her an insightful point of reference from which to critique the future of the North American political economy. Although she had just witnessed the crisis produced by the shutdown of a local food distribution plant and had trouble imagining other employment options, it was the sense of being a disposable part of the "RCA Family" after almost thirty years of dedication to the company that particularly grated on her.[3] "You've worked hard all your life and thought you had a good job, and it doesn't seem to mean a lot," she reflected. "That's what bothers most of us." Her feelings moved from sadness at the memory of her early days at the plant in the 1960s, when over eight thousand workers made TV sets night and day in Bloomington, to anger as she contemplated the politicians whom she held responsible for the workers' plight. "You know, I don't care what Clinton, Bush, any of 'em say, I just think the free trade thing is not going to benefit as many people as it's gonna hurt." The leaders who negotiated NAFTA "never lived on the level of life we live on. You know, like Bush didn't even know how much a loaf of bread costs! And I doubt Clinton does, probably a Big Mac—or they probably just give them to him free because it's him." Uncomfortable about going against the perceived economic wisdom of trade liberalization, she said, "Maybe I'm weird on this too—'cause I'm a factory worker—but I feel . . . that maybe there's gonna be the jobs, but maybe you can't *make* anything. And if you've got all these people that are making three dollars an hour, than what's going to happen with the economy?" Clearly, she concluded as she pointed to the snapshots from her trip to Juárez, "we could not live on what these people live on."

As Sandy Anderson's story suggests, her local history, sense of place, and immediate social relations formed the fundamental source of her strength; she was rooted in her culture, her community, and the geographic space that contained them. When she did look beyond the boundaries of her community, it was to another notion of community, her federal government, to provide some protection from global competition. At the same time, her narrative highlights the vastly different and more expansive space occupied by management. Following a strict economic logic and not hemmed in by social commitments to a particular place or group of people, managers of capital can wield their authority across the economic landscape to their best advantage. RCA's command of mobile capital, therefore, reveals the Bloomington workers' sense of place not as a simple resource but as a pivotal point of vulnerability and exposure. Finally, Anderson's story points to the complexities involved in efforts to build transnational, even transregional solidarity or to find any other solution to the problem of the runaway shop. As the new labor history has shown, the pull of place and community has been a powerful force in labor relations, but the limitations of local identity also create constraints on a more expansive notion of working-class politics in an era in which capital transcends boundaries with complete ease.

Workers across Space

The moral and political aspects of capital migration are not easy to pin down—how can one weigh a group of people who get good jobs against another group that lose them? The economic opportunity afforded to workers in these four communities, often to some of the neediest people in each city, is a much more complex matter than a mean company taking advantage of its workers. The economist Joseph Schumpeter may have summed up the paradox best when he spoke of the "process of creative destruction." A healthy economy, he argued, requires constant renewal through galelike forces that simultaneously wreck the old and make way for the new. Aging industrial orders, he implied, inevitably crumble and rot, but in doing so provide the nutrients and sustenance for the blooming of fresh new economic growth. Taming the process at any single point, according to Schumpeter, would be counterproductive, for attempting to direct a firm's industrial policy or save a particular plant from the ravages of the process would eventually stunt overall growth and devastate the economy as a whole. The arrival of RCA was always good news, but the legacy of its exodus varies from community to community. For Bloomington, even the aftermath will be "creative" as the town completes a *relatively* smooth transition to a service- and technology-based economy. Camden, in contrast, has been unable to recover from the ravages of deindustrialization even after many generations have passed.[4]

Clearly no location has a lock on industrial investment in a free market economy. RCA's migration suggests that any theory that posits static economic and regional divisions will prove inadequate. On the contrary, we have seen how the most marginal parts of the RCA empire evolved into "growth peripheries" when the cheap-labor region—Indiana, for instance—slowly took over all of the functions of the earlier geographic and economic core, even product design and innovation. William Greider's vivid metaphor captures the process:

> Imagine a wondrous new machine, strong and supple, a machine that reaps as it destroys. It is huge and mobile, something like the machines of modern agriculture but vastly more complicated and powerful. Think of this awesome machine running over open terrain and ignoring familiar boundaries. It plows across fields and fencerows with a fierce momentum that is exhilarating to behold and also frightening. As it goes, the machine throws off enormous mows of wealth and bounty while it leaves behind great furrows of wreckage. . . . It is sustained by its own forward motion, guided mainly by its own appetites. And it is accelerating.[5]

These changes were most evident in Bloomington, where a small, obscure branch plant for the production of portable radios evolved into the "Color Television Capital of the World," stripping Camden, formerly the "Radio Capital of the World," of the definitive postwar consumer product. Today, with production terminated in Bloomington and a growing network of plants in northern Mexico, Chihuahua is likely to be the next center of innovation. A new location for production—whether green belt, sun belt, or maquila—cannot be understood simply as a simple "branch" of the old. Although it may begin that way, RCA's path suggests that capital is regenerating and recreating itself on any terms that enable it to do so, and in the process is sponsoring cultural change. As Doreen Massey explains, the entire package of "local histories and local distinctiveness" is "integral" to industrial production and "should be central to any attempt at 'characterizing capital.'"[6]

Although RCA workers may appear to be simple victims, most of them enjoyed the fruits of decades of industrial work and were far from powerless. They raised families, built institutions, negotiated and fought with their employer, and struggled to leave a better world for their children. They asserted authority in countless forms, including appeals to their elected representatives, bargaining sessions with the company, arguments with their national union leaders, and simple forms of day-to-day shop-floor resistance. Mostly they worked very hard. Yet working-class communities and their national representatives have been unable to formulate feasible political restraints on private investment or to forge political bonds with more than a few of the scattered pockets of the global labor market. The local community, once a counterpoint to capital's absolute prerogatives, has been weakened but not destroyed by the increasingly expansive space inhabited by capital in the last half of the twentieth century.

Perhaps the most intriguing aspects of the process are the hidden connections between the various sites, as social changes and actions in one area have had unintended consequences in another. "One of the most distinctive features of the contemporary period," writes the social theorist Anthony Giddens, "is the burgeoning of complex ties between the global and the local, where 'the local' includes not just the regional locality but intimate aspects of our personal lives. . . . A process of global economic development which generates prosperity in one region of the world may bring impoverishment on another." Speaking to the tensions lived by the RCA workers as demands for improved pay and working conditions jeopardize their jobs, Giddens continues, "On a more subtle level, our personal experiences and needs may exist in contradictory relation to the global impact of our actions."[7]

When electrical firms searched for labor across the economic globe, they sought a simple package: low wages, a peaceful industrial relations environment, and an abundance of young, unemployed women. The circumstances that caused a firm to choose a given community, however, were fundamentally transformed by the very presence of the factory. As one of the RCA managers in charge of finding new plant locations explained, these changes become unacceptable to corporate leaders, and once again they search for a new location. Many managers, he said, "say a plant should never be at one location more than twenty years, because of the development of habits, of wage structures, of seniority, and you should move those things every twenty years. . . . There is some sanity, some credibility to that statement." In contrast, he continued, "There are some older manufacturing sites that are still productive. A lot of it has to do with the mentality that had developed in the workforce."[8] The power to decide whether a community's "mentality" was acceptable or not remained the right of the corporation as workers' local actions could be countered with the simple existence of what to them was a distant and abstract alternative to their own place.

The core of the problem is that the wielders of capital have far greater ability than workers to transcend and use space; the cognitive geographies of the two groups were formed under different circumstances and for different purposes. Management is able to manipulate distance to fragment labor's collective power, and the countless variations in the economic topography offer unlimited terrain for corporations to seek out less costly labor or less aggressive working-class communities. By relocating, the corporation can peel back the layers of historical change accumulated at the old site. It can nurture and reinforce social and political tendencies on the local scene, or it can punish them by moving capital out of the area. Command of spatial relations, therefore, becomes a crucial weapon in management's arsenal, and its mobility increases the return on investment and bolsters its ability to contend with competition. The "spatial mobility of capital is pitted against the geographical solidarity of labor," writes Massey. "Capital can make positive use, in a way labor cannot, of distance and differentiation."[9]

A single commonality among the various sites of industrial activity was the uniqueness of their social and cultural reserves and the heterogeneity of their historical experience. From African American workers in Tennessee to Mexicans on the border, history and propinquity allowed the key aspects of community life—family, church, clubs, schools, sports, unions—to form, flourish, and take on the weight and momentum of history. The peculiar commodity that management searches for, labor, is thus place-bound, its consciousness and resistance formed in and by a specific locale. As we have had ample opportunity to observe, we cannot understand the behavior of a corporation without taking into account the social changes that have taken place in its environment. But if working-class strength can be found on the local level, what are the possibilities for a mobilization strategy that transcends its limits?

Community as a Problem

Any definition of "community" depends on a shared network of connections and expectations. Bonds formed within a group of social actors are based on a mutual sense of historical experience and proximity, and they increase in density as further layers of exchange accumulate. The power of simple familiarity—an investment in the consistency of interaction, of predictability—is at the core of a sense of historical and social continuity. Specific obligations, such as economic interdependence or shared membership in organizations, thicken the shared sense of place and fate. Bonds of kinship and friendship link social actors into an even wider web of long-term social networks that reinforce a shared set of principles of social behavior. The density or degree of fragmentation of these social bonds depends on the size, diffusion, and multiplicity of both organized and spontaneous interaction. Pierre Bourdieu refers to *habitus*, or "embodied history, internalized as a second nature and so forgotten as history . . . the active presence of the whole past of which it is a product."[10]

But this is an *internal* definition of community; we must complicate it by looking beyond what a social group proclaims itself to be by examining what it believes it is not. Less obvious than the network of internal social relations are the external aspects of community—the unifying social relations based on opposition to "others"—that tie social actors in a charged tension with other groups. As some existential philosophers argue, humans have the capacity to objectify the world, to see themselves as separate from it rather than as part of it. They do so by "creating a gap, a distance, a space" between themselves and others. But the creation of distance between the individual and his or her "other" in the life world is only one facet of humanity. "To be human is not only to create distances but to attempt to cross them," argues Edward Soja, "to transform primal distance through intentionality, emotion, involvement, [and] attachment."[11] Thus workers' ability to forge an alliance depends on their ability to bridge social distance and make connections with others. Yet this ability is in constant tension with the propensity to place others at a social distance. As the reaction of Sandy Anderson's co-workers to her trip to the border suggests, the desire to bridge the gap of difference can easily dissolve into objectification when one confronts a great geographical distance, competition for jobs, or cultural, racial, or gender difference.

The key to a more profound understanding of community is to see how the experience of outsiders acts as a fundamental adhesive for social identity. As the anthropologists John and Jean Comaroff argue, to define a collective social identity there must invariably be "a marked opposition between 'ourselves' and 'other/s'." The concept of "us" rests on an implicit opposition to others ("them"), which serves as the foundation for social cohesion within a cultural group. The notion of ourselves is therefore formed on and within the local level, and community resources can be mobilized against a variety of others, be they the company, the state, or other communities with which workers find themselves in competition. The psychic distance between the familiar and the unfamiliar, the intimate and the foreign, those with whom you work and those who appear to threaten your livelihood therefore functions to undermine the project of transregional and transnational working-class solidarity just as it simultaneously strengthens the bonds of local social life.[12]

When asked about her life, for instance, Ruth Ann Greene, like many of her colleagues in Bloomington, succinctly captured a story of place: "I was born in Monroe County, my parents were from Monroe County, and I worked at RCA all my life. So there you go."[13] Bob Doty, too, had difficulty seeing beyond the boundaries of largely white Monroe County. When asked about the closure of the Memphis plant, he did not blame the company, global competition, or the competitive pressures the new workers faced; he blamed their color. "The people that they had down there [were] mainly black. I'm not throwin' anything against the blacks because I think just as much of a black person as I do a white or any other nationality. But they worked three or four days and then when they get that wine and then they didn't show up for three or four days, see, until they got ready to go back to work and get some more money to get some more wine with."[14]

Even in Camden, where the intensity of class warfare captured the national spotlight, labor politics remained explicitly local. The RCA unions in New Jersey would "devote an extraordinary amount of time" to join up with their sister unions to create national organizations but "normally showed little interest in organizing unorganized employees into unions"—a task left to inadequately financed national institutions. When UE organizers did make it to Bloomington, their arguments fell on deaf ears. Distance troubled the Juárez workers as well, for their competition was another faraway point on the globe as the specter of Asia haunted labor relations in Mexico. When the Mexicans did make their push against their autocratic union, no support was forthcoming from their colleagues to the north, many of whom continued to believe that the "Made in USA" label would guarantee some sort of job security. After France-based Thomson bought the RCA plants, the Bloomington workers did not take up the study of Spanish in order to communicate with their colleagues in Juárez. Instead they studied French in order to speak with the managers they knew rather than the co-workers they did not.[15]

A definition of "community" that takes account of external as well as internal understandings must give pause to scholars and activists who see transregional and transnational working-class solidarity naturally springing forth from the economic conditions of the globalizing labor market.[16] Such hope must be tempered by the nature of community, the power of *habitus*, and the local sources of social identity. At the same time, as Bourdieu stresses, it is the improvisation and spontaneity within the inherited structure that remolds the past and so shapes the future. If constructive aspects of globalization, such as communication, multiculturalism, and the opportunity for transnational organizing, are internalized through practice, education, and experience, the future contains the possibility of a positive social and political response to the problem of capital mobility.

Clearly, the nation-state offers one transcendent, if volatile, place for mobilization beyond the geographic limits of immediate familiarity. Benedict Anderson coined the term "imagined political community" to explain the mobilizing power of a national image or myth. It is imagined, he writes, "because citizens can never possibly know each other"; and it is a community because "regardless of the actual inequality and exploitation that may prevail . . . , the nation is always conceived as a deep horizontal comradeship." Once industrial capital has achieved a transnational plane of investment, however, even the imagined community of the nation, like the real community where a group of people live and work, can easily run counter to workers' unity. History suggests that the bond forged by an appeal to nationalism has been a far more effective tool of mobilization than a (possibly more objective) conceptual identity—"workers of the world." As industrial capital has left not just local sites but the nation itself, the community whose needs are in tension with those of capital is not just the place defined by a zip code but the imagined community of the nation as well.[17]

The homogenizing forces of the market, Karl Marx once argued, would one day tame the wild card of nationalism. "National differences and antagonisms between peoples are daily more and more vanishing," he posited, "owing to the development of the bourgeoisie, to freedom of commerce, to the world market, to uniformity in the mode of production and in the conditions of life corresponding thereto." As ethno-religious fundamentalism, populist nationalism, and immigrant-bashing appear to be the dark side of globalization, however, the opposite of Marx's assumptions may be true as people search for roots within the placeless flow of capital and ideas.[18]

Strangely enough, if one historian's controversial conclusions are any guide, the role of mass culture may actually offer a glimmer of hope. When Lizabeth Cohen investigated the CIO in Chicago, she found that, contrary to "the usual assumption that mass culture was depoliticizing," it allowed workers "to overcome the cultural fragmentation that had hindered them earlier." Remarkably, "workers who partook of mass culture did not become passive politically, even as they led lives that on the surface at least may have looked increasingly like those of the middle class. . . . Ironically, the broader dissemination of commercial culture . . . may have done more to create an integrated working-class culture than a classless American one."[19] The prospects for a shared identity emerging from mass culture run up against other problems in the global age, however: the concerns that worldwide mass consumerism is simply unsustainable in the global environment and, conversely, that a global glut of poorly paid labor will foster a crisis of underconsumption and possibly a deflationary future.[20]

Five days after the announcement that the Bloomington works was shutting down forever, an unemployed woman attends the local labor council's "Grocery Giveaway." The sign on the wall is one of many indications of the distance between the concerns of local workers and those with whom they are forced to compete for their jobs. (*Bloomington Herald-Times*, June 5, 1964.)

Whatever unfolds, the fragmentation of social space offers capital what Edward Soja calls a "cartography of power and social control" in which the community functions as both a site and a source of resistance but also as the outer limits of workers' geography of social action. Differences in ability to transcend space have economic and political repercussions, and RCA workers' ability to do battle on the community level but only occasionally to move beyond its limitations leaves them vulnerable to competition from workers in other communities for the coveted, if uneven, rewards of private investment. Thus workers' community, the focus of their identity and the locus of their political action, functions as both asset and liability in the game of capital migration and territorial development. The problem laid out by Selig Perlman at the height of the "old labor history" continues to burden workers today. "The solidarity of American labor," he wrote in 1928, "is a solidarity with a quickly diminishing potency as one passes from the craft group,—which looks upon the jobs in the craft as its common property for which it is ready to fight long and bitterly,—to the widening concentric circles of the related crafts, the industry, the American Federation of Labor, and the world labor movement." As the new labor history has shown, working-class communities are often the main actors in social, economic, and political change, but it becomes clear, to play with Marx's famous dictum, that workers "make history under geographical circumstance not of their own choosing."[21]

The Geography of North American Trade Unionism

In historical terms, the differences in the ability of labor and capital to control space have not always been as significant as they are today. Studies of nineteenth-century communities have found that outside interference was often minimal and, in analytic and real terms, the issue remained contained within a specific locale. "Prior to the coming of the railroad and the telegraph," argues the geographer David Harvey, "the powers of capital and labour in terms of the ability to command space were not radically different."[22] When both labor and capital were bounded by the same territorial limits, the contest was head to head. While capitalists learned to locate power in the spaces they controlled, to disempower locations with strong oppositional cultures, and to divide the bargaining power of organized labor, trade unions struggled to overcome regional and locational diversity by building national organizations to keep up with the expanding marketplace.

The task of transcending the social limitations of community has fallen to workers' representatives on the national level. As the market revolution linked isolated communities into a vast national network of economic relations in the nineteenth century, trade unions formed national organizations to fill the political needs of workers whose interests were similar but who were scattered across the map and armed with different resources.[23] Unions achieved the pinnacle of their scope and power in both the United States and Mexico during the postwar period, when organized labor, business, and the federal governments forged class truces known variously as "labor-management accords" and "postwar pacts." After workers' organizational drives in the 1930s and the governments' mobilization of the unions for political support, a period of uneasy and often tumultuous mutual recognition between workers and their companies emerged alongside a variety of state-sponsored industrial relations institutions and regulations. As the early Camden-to-Bloomington migration suggests, the dissolution of those compromises may have been under way as soon as they began, but the postwar settlements nonetheless laid the foundation for a golden age for organized wage earners in both countries.

In the United States, that settlement grew out of struggles for the recognition of industrial unions in the 1930s and 1940s, which by the 1950s had brought over one-third of all nonagricultural workers into the labor movement. With such unprecedented union power coupled with the technocratic milieu of Keynesian economics and the federal regulation of labor relations, unions and management agreed to a variety of formal and informal channels to a historic modus vivendi. Management, for the first time in U.S. history, recognized the right of industrial workers to bargain collectively and conceded an ever-increasing amount of the firm's profits to its workforce. In return, labor retreated from its claim to control shop-floor issues and to contest management's prerogatives, restricted its organization efforts, and abdicated—through force and consent—much of its political vision. As Steve Fraser summarized it, labor underwent a double transformation during the New Deal years: it now had a powerful national voice, but it became less threatening to the political stability of the postwar order as it fell under the purview of national labor organizations and the federal government.[24]

Although Mexican workers' political and economic contexts differed substantially from those of U.S. workers, they too enjoyed a troubled truce. As a popular sector that could be mobilized by revolutionary elites, unions played a pivotal role in the consolidation and growth of a powerful and effective one-party state regime. Paralleling Franklin Roosevelt's successful bid for the CIO's support, President Lázaro Cárdenas mobilized a fragmented and weak labor movement during the 1930s and took popular bold actions such as the nationalization of the oil industry in his struggle to build a viable ruling alliance. Consolidating labor's role as a pivotal social sector in national politics after World War II, the Mexican government provided financial and political subsidies to favored labor organizations to sustain the "Mexican miracle" of postwar stability and growth. The various presidential administrations also resorted to force to demobilize movements that threatened the system and rewarded those that supported the government's policies with access to elective offices, government-subsidized housing, health care, basic commodities, and profit sharing. In an authoritarian version of the formula established in the United States, observes Ian Roxborough, "the state supports the union leaderships against possible insurgent movements within their unions and, in return, union leaders act in a 'statesman-like' manner to secure 'responsible,' moderate wage increases."[25]

The complete dissolution of those uneasy class compromises, so apparent today in both countries, has been a matter of profound concern, but little attention has been paid to the problem of space. Labor leaders are caught between, on the one hand, the need to centralize power in order to bargain effectively with multiplant firms, to seek support from national governments, and to assert authority on the national level and, on the other hand, the need to decentralize power in order to be responsive to members' economic requirements, political interests, and regional social identities. Even in the postwar glory days, unions were still hampered by geographic weakness and, as the remarkable number of wildcat strikes in both countries attests, faced with community resistance to the national discipline necessary to sustain the postwar compromises.

The collective bargaining system and the federated union structure in the United States—unlike the system in parts of Europe, where labor relations are considerably more centralized—made it difficult to project labor issues onto the national stage, where a cohesive working-class identity might be possible. In fact, the very design of the 1935 Wagner Act and the entire American collective bargaining system, according to the social geographer Gordon Clark, was aimed at maintaining the "distinctiveness and legitimacy of local interests over general interests of corporations and unions as national organizations." The fact that the three U.S. sites under investigation here were organized by different unions (UE, IBEW, IUE) demonstrates management's ability to splinter the television workers' bargaining power. The most militant of those unions, the United Electrical Workers, remained geographically isolated in the industrial Northeast—New England, New York, New Jersey, and Pennsylvania—even before Cold War politics destroyed its growing power. The strength of labor, of course, varied radically from region to region. After the failure of Operation Dixie, the CIO's postwar organizing drive, southern elites exploited the South's reputation as a low-wage and nonunion business haven to attract capital and maintain local power structures. The success of that strategy required a commitment to keeping labor politically and economically subdued, as the Crump machinery tried so hard to do in Memphis.[26]

Like the southern states, northern Mexico is distant from traditional locations of union strength, most notably Mexico City. The number of permanently employed workers registered with the Mexican Social Security Institute (IMSS), for instance, grew only about 10 percent in the traditional industrial areas around Mexico City from 1980 to 1986, while in the northern states it jumped dramatically: 67 percent in Chihuahua, 61 percent in Baja California Norte, 50 percent in Tamaulipas, and 25 percent in Nuevo León. Moreover, in a country frequently criticized for its authoritarian, overly centralized system of labor relations, it may actually be the government's ability to keep organized labor divided on the local level (as the CTM-CROC rivalry shows) rather than its strategy of co-opting it on the national level that kept a check on labor's power in Mexico. In sum, economic integration of unionized regions with areas where labor was weaker in each country served to undermine the postwar settlements among business, government, and labor long before the problem spilled over international boundaries.[27]

Traditionally, labor leaders saw the solution to their crumbling position in protectionist terms. In an effort to contain the transnationalization of production, the AFL-CIO exerted its national influence in an attempt to scuttle or at least limit the Border Industrialization Program in the late 1960s and early 1970s. U.S. labor leaders directed their political energies toward terminating tariff provision 807, which they viewed as a subsidy to relocate jobs abroad. The problem was that even without the tariff breaks, offshore production was still immensely profitable. The unions' opposition to the tax loopholes forced the Nixon administration to launch a detailed investigation of the matter, but the report concluded that repeal of 806/807 would neither return jobs to the United States nor slow their exodus. In their next step, the unions rallied behind (and helped to write) the highly protectionist Hartke-Burke Foreign Trade and Investment Proposal of 1973, which included provisions to tax the foreign earnings of U.S. corporations, eliminate the tariff loopholes, and fix the share of the market taken by imports at levels reached in the late 1960s. The argument advanced by Vance Hartke, the bill's sponsor in the Senate, captured labor's new position: "We can no longer afford to export American jobs and technology at the expense of our own industry, all in the name of 'free trade.'" Although the bill was soundly defeated, a variety of other protectionist bills and hearings clamored for Congress's attention throughout the 1970s. By the summer of 1977, a total of six antimaquiladora bills were pending in the Ways and Means Committee.[28]

Even though protectionism appeared to be a ready solution to the globalizing labor market, U.S. trade unionists remained hamstrung by their push for higher tariff barriers. Protectionist restrictions tended to offer little to workers on the community level, and tariffs often actually insulated corporations from competitive pressures and still left management free to squeeze its workforce. Most important, protectionism tended to erect "barriers of ill will" between the wage earners of different nations—particularly those of the First and Third Worlds.[29] The lessons that might have been learned from the migration of capital to the U.S. South—that regulatory mechanisms that ensured an upward, rather than downward, harmonization of regional economies may be the only solution—were lost when it came to formulating strategies for the transnational level. Although the flight of jobs to foreign lands indicated that business and the state had abdicated their ends of the postwar bargains, organized labor continued to try to uphold the entire framework through protectionist measures until a Democratic president put his full weight behind the passage of the North American Free Trade Agreement, signaling the bitter end. The PATCO strike, when President Reagan permanently replaced striking air-traffic controllers, is frequently cited as the symbolic end of labor's political clout. Labor's power had been dwindling since the 1970s, and the passage of NAFTA by a member of "labor's own" party demonstrated just how marginal organized labor had become to the political process. At the same time, NAFTA reinvigorated the labor movement as John Sweeney replaced the stale Lane Kirkland as president of the AFL-CIO, funds went back into organizing, and students and intellectuals were welcomed back into the fold.

No system of cross-border labor regulation materialized until President Bill Clinton revealed the Labor Side Agreement to NAFTA. Even then, the limited regulatory mechanisms put in place were designed to calm workers' fears, not protect their rights.[30] It is worth noting, however, that when the Lyndon Johnson administration tacitly accepted the BIP, it was assumed that some type of transnational regulation would be necessary to placate the protest predicted to come from U.S. unionists. "To reassure American labor that there is no intention of creating sweat shops along the border," reads a confidential memo to the president written in 1967, "there will have to be agreement between both governments to consult together with a view to the maintenance of fair labor standards through both parts of the binational parks."[31] Even though labor consistently lost on the issue of the leaky tariff code, if the fears of BIP proponents are any indication, unions probably did have at least the power to regulate the maquila program. Officials high in the Johnson administration, members of the U.S. Chamber of Commerce, and local business leaders pondered "how to pacify or mollify U.S. labor unions." A highly placed Mexican government official stated, "In the long run, opposition from organized labor could mean the effective scuttling of the whole border industrialization idea. If it brings too much pressure to bear on Washington, we could be in serious trouble."[32] Unfortunately, labor invested its political capital in protectionism in an attempt to insulate itself from Mexican workers who were beyond its imagined community rather than recognizing the fundamental transformations in the continental economy.[33]

As one theorist argues, however, since "communities tend to constitute themselves by excluding difference, the task of a philosophical politics is to conceptualize new forms of association which let the different appear in their midst."[34] Workers and their unions are rising to the occasion as activists struggle to incorporate a feasible balance of community power, national identity, and transnational politics. Cross-border visits, rallies, seminars, conferences, information exchanges, and even organizing efforts were increasingly evident throughout all sectors of the labor movement during and after the anti-NAFTA campaign. The Teamsters, the Farm Labor Organizing Committee, important segments of the United Auto Workers, and UNITE were all pivotal in forging new directions in transnational working-class politics and consciousness. The most active organization involved in cross-border organizing was once again the dissident United Electrical Workers. Although the UE has not represented any RCA workers since it was red-baited out of Camden in 1950, it followed many years of transnational linkages with the dissident Frente Auténtico de Trabajadores (Authentic Workers' Front, or FAT) with a collaborative project to launch the cross-border

Beatriz Luján poses in front of a sign in Juárez announcing "Unionism without Borders." The Thomson/RCA story came full circle when the United Electrical Workers, the original Camden union, launched a collaborative effort with Mexico's independent Authentic Labor Front to promote democratic organizing in Ciudad Juárez. (Photo copyright © Mark Hume.)

Labor Workshop and Studies Center (CETLAC). Opened in Ciudad Juárez in September 1996, the center brought the labor histories of Camden and Juárez full circle and will provide a concrete location for the otherwise placeless concept of transnational labor politics.[35] Even NAFTA's Labor Side Accord, if aggressively wielded against abuses in all three countries of North America, could prove to be a basis for a transnational regulatory regime. In the absence of such tangible projects to bring the other closer, the discourse of globalization, as Michel Foucault observes, "always seems to be inhabited by the other, elsewhere, distant, far away; it is hollowed by absence." Edward Gibbon captures the issue in a different context: "Our sympathy is cold to the relation of distant misery." Even if warmth would serve our own interest.[36]

Space and the Working Woman

Just as the history of workers, communities, and unions can be understood in spatial terms, so can the gender of work. The sexual division of labor, constructed in one location, later deconstructed and then reconstructed in another site, was at the center of the electronics industry's labor recruitment strategies from the Great Depression to the global age. What appears as the extraordinary exploitation of young women in electronics firms around the world is actually a system as old as the electrical industry itself. It is hardly unique to the Third World and can be regarded as pernicious there as it was in the United States. The ability of corporations to manipulate "the comparative advantage of women's disadvantages" into a sexual division of labor of remarkable durability, however, has also meant new economic and social opportunities to thousands of blue-collar women.[37]

Employment at RCA liberated young women from the patriarchal household, but it also left them at the mercy of factory discipline. As Susan Tiano observes, the material benefits of wage labor and the freedom they offered were mitigated by "a labor contract that limit[ed] their autonomy in a different way by subjecting them to capitalist and patriarchal relations in the workplace."[38] As the factory regime played with the existing gender system to create and recreate the cheap-and-docile formula it desired, however, the incorporation of women into wage work also presented the mechanisms for small but important transformations in patriarchy itself. As women entered the factories, the blurring of gender roles broadened the range of behaviors available to both men and women, and money of their own—however limited—gave women increasing freedom to question the domestic division of labor. Even though economic need drew workers into the assembly plants, then, many nonmaterial benefits kept them returning to the lines.[39]

Subtle changes in working-class women's culture were evident throughout RCA's migration. As Fernández-Kelly observed about the young Juárez workers, "individually these women bore an aura of vulnerability, even shyness . . . [but] as a group they could be a formidable sight." When a lone man embarked on a bus full of maquila workers, "he was immediately subjected to verbal attacks similar to those women sometimes experience from men. They chided and they teased him, feeling protected by anonymity and by their numerical strength. They offered kisses and asked for a smile. They exchanged laughing comments about his physical attributes and suggested a raffle to see who would keep him."[40] The same sort of thing happened in Bloomington. When Ken Beasley walked onto the shop floor in the 1960s, he was subjected to a barrage of embarrassing comments as he traversed the female space of the production line. "The women on the chassis assembly lines would whistle and howl at the guys going down the lines—especially the younger ones—and I remember my eyes were very large circles. They'd say, 'Hey, I like your butt!'—pretty embarrassing for a young kid."[41] In the long run, although industrial work certainly does not transform patriarchy, it does slowly undermine the ideological tenets of the cheap-and-docile formula.

Such changes made allegedly docile women in all of the RCA cities more willing participants in the making of North American labor history.

The most interesting aspect of this gendered division of labor was its unsustainability over time. This instability was due partly to the company's decision to bring in technology to perform the labor-intensive work for which women were originally hired, and partly to the fact that labor-intensive assembly work was the first to be relocated to a lower-wage site. Other factors, too, brought changes in the gender of work: the tightening of the labor market, which forced management to hire more men; the bias in seniority rules, which privileged the roles of men; political pressures from women for equal pay; and interventions by the state. The fact that women were the first to be absorbed into electronics assembly and the most disposable workers in the chain of production places women at the heart of the story of both industrialization and deindustrialization. Women at both declining center and growing periphery carry much of the weight of global transformations.

The question that informs much of the maquila literature—whether factory work is good or bad for women—is therefore irrelevant in the face of the more important issue, the quality of their employment.[42] In a region once marked by widespread poverty, more jobs were clearly better than fewer. Although the work was exploitive, mind-numbing, and unstable, although it offered little pay and less chance for advancement, few employees in any of those communities would have liked to see the plants disappear. The central issues in the debate, therefore, ought to be the level of workers' control over the production process, the amount of remuneration they receive, the adequacy of compensatory changes in the domestic sphere, and the assurance that demands placed on the firm will not mean the eventual disappearance of the workplace.

Yet in the overwhelming majority of situations in the four RCA sites, the formal industrial relations systems of the countries concerned took no account of the specific problems of the women workers. Ruth Milkman's concise portrayal of female workers' alienation from labor unions in the postwar United States could as well have been written about Mexican women too. "Women were organized without any particular attention to the fact of their gender," she writes, "but rather as members of occupational groups which happened to be largely female in composition. Because they were organized on these terms, the result of their extensive recruitment over the postwar period is that women are now squarely in but generally still not of the labor movement." As increasing numbers of jobs are becoming feminized, this problem stands out as one of the most glaring failures of the labor movements of both countries. Though women were in the majority at each location, in no instance did a woman hold the top leadership position in any RCA union local.[43]

Toward a Transnational Future

Life space, the space inhabited by conscious actors functioning in the context of their cultures and communities, consists of territory; this is the space where workers struggle and organize. Economic space, in contrast, is abstract and discontinuous. Capital flows into new locations across the economic and social landscape. The global topography over which capital moves, however, is shaped by the consciousness, action, and resistance of workers. Since economic space is highly uneven and ever changing, capital has ample room to pick and choose new locales as a way to reorder class relations on the local level. Corporations can whittle down the bargaining power of unions by ensuring that different unions are installed at different production sites; they can recreate a gendered system of labor control when it comes under challenge from below; and they can reestablish relative tranquillity on the shop floor by moving elsewhere, or simply by threatening to do so. Strong oppositional cultures can be traded for weak, and when the weak grow strong, the search for a new location may begin again. Most important, workers can be relatively effective in pursuing their interests at the local level but can only struggle to keep up with capital's more fluid command of space.

The idea that people have a direct political investment in their immediate place and find what is beyond their surroundings alien and abstract is, of course, not particularly new. C. Wright Mills eloquently captured it in 1959:

> What ordinary [people] are directly aware of and what they try to do are bounded by the private orbits in which they live; their visions and their powers are limited to the close-up scenes of job, family, neighborhood; in other milieux, they move vicariously and remain spectators. And the more aware they become, however vaguely, of ambitions and of threats which transcend their immediate locales, the more trapped they seem to feel.
>
> Underlying this sense of being trapped are seemingly impersonal changes in the very structure of continent-wide societies.[44]

By sustaining the argument that workers' power is simultaneously rooted in their communities and weakened by their inability to transcend its boundaries, I do not go so far as to claim a postmodern conundrum of "placeless power" on the part of capital and "powerless place" on the part of workers. As David Harvey has found, an evolving compression of space and time has created extremely complex political problems for workers and their communities, but the dizzying depoliticization caused by condensed realms of capitalist space is not insurmountable.[45]

Among all the discussions of plant closures and relocations, it is worth noting that there are more industrial workers in the world today than there ever were before—they are now just of different colors, speak different languages, and are in different locations than labor historians have come to expect. If we bracket for a moment the brutality of job losses to specific individuals and communities and take the global perspective of Giovanni Arrighi, the relocation of jobs and investment constitutes not "a reduction in the overall social power of the world proletariat" but merely "a transfer of social power from one segment of the world proletariat to another segment." It is a tipping of fortunes between workers of First and Third Worlds, he argues, in which "the tendency of the first half of the twentieth century towards a spatial polarization of the social power and mass misery of labour in different and separate regions of the world economy has begun to be reversed."[46] As the power relation embedded in industrial investment is relocated, however, the benefits and remuneration accrued by workers in the old site do not follow it. The prerogatives of corporations in the new community must be rechallenged and labor's organizational power reconstituted there. In the interim, the benefits of relocation undoubtedly accrue more to capital than to the new workers.

Since a convergence of wages and regulations in North America appears the likely end product of economic integration, will harmonization be downward to the lowest standards or upward toward the highest? Just as the rise of national corporations in the nineteenth century precipitated the growth of the national regulatory state during the Progressive Era and the New Deal, so the social and economic well-being of the global workforce may now depend on projecting a similar regulatory system to meet the transnational hegemony of corporate capitalism. Cross-border regulations, for instance, could be easily financed by a very small tax on the enormous number of transnational financial transactions that take place every day. The projection of rigorous and meaningful regulatory mechanisms to the transnational level, however complicated, would make the cultural and economic reserves of distant locations less attractive, since they would fall under the same regulatory regime as those of the old site. Although even the most rigorous set of international labor and environmental laws would never prevent a company from moving across regions or nations, a transnational safety net of labor rights and standards would militate against the current process of economic harmonization down to the lowest global common denominator.

International pressure on environmental issues is a case in point. Since NAFTA has forced a degree of transparency into Mexico's environmental regulatory system, inspectors caught Thomson dumping paint, solvents, and shellac into the waste water system and fined the corporation $45,000. "Normally, these industrial people are very powerful," explained Francisco Nuñez, director of Juárez's water sanitation. "The first thing they do is call the governor, who is a friend, [to stop the investigation]." With the breakup of the

PRI's monopoly power and increased pressure from international agencies, however, the new goal is often increased respectability through regulation.[47]

Yet all the transnational regulations thinkable would do little good without an audible voice for working people on the national level. The fulcrum that frequently leveraged workers' hopes in all four RCA communities was the state. The intervention of the NLRB in the UE strike in Camden, the government's signing of contracts that provided jobs during the Cold War buildup in Camden, the development of HDTV, the Mexican government's creation of the Border Industrialization Program, and the Japanese and French governments' promotion of the consumer electronics industries all testify to the pivotal role of the state. Meaningful labor law in both countries that regulated the safety and basic levels of remuneration in the workplace and provided for the right to organize and strike when necessary would allow workers to meet their needs and assert their rights in the workplace without fear of retribution. Legislation that raised the costs of relocation by requiring indemnification to displaced workers or compensation to distressed communities would give working people more political room to assert their needs and make adjustments to the changing industrial landscape. More important, transnational labor regulations would ensure that countries were not constructing, through political repression, a "comparative advantage" of cheap labor as a way to attract foreign capital.

Left to its own devices, however, the global economy appears to be heading for a dismal place. For one commentator, it looms as a horrifying choice between dwindling numbers of low-paying, life-draining jobs in a homogenized, monocultural McWorld and a variety of ethnic and regional jihads as marginalized peoples search for a meaningful social identity amid the prevailing winds of global history. For other observers, the choice will be between "global pillage and global village." Yet another analyst sees in the formula of increased production technology and global labor markets nothing short of "the end of work." "The death of the global labor force is being internalized by millions of workers who experience their own individual deaths, daily, at the hands of profit-driven employers and a disinterested government." As managers of capital lose their allegiance to place and nation, politics becomes a confusing question of "Who is them and who is us?"[48]

A world beyond such demoralizing alternatives requires a complex balance of local, regional, national, and transnational systems of political action and social identity. If cultural diversity, economic growth and development, communication, travel, and other desirable aspects of globalization can be absorbed at the community level through practice, education, and experience, many constructive responses to capital's disproportionate mobility and power become possible. Whether economic integration entails social disintegration as people are forced to compete against distant and unknown others for jobs and resources depends on a variety of projects that are being worked out in communities, workplaces, and executive offices around the world.[49]

On the shop floor, workers may be figuring it all out in their own small ways. After unloading a truckload of chassis that arrived in Bloomington from Juárez, Rocky Gallagher found an envelope taped to the front of the trailer inscribed, "To Our RCA Compadres." Pulling down the envelope and peering in, Rocky found a few loose marijuana joints carefully wrapped for the cross-continental journey. Amused by the anonymous gift, the Bloomington dockworkers headed down to the local minimart on their lunch hour and picked up a small collection of *Playboy* magazines, put them in an envelope, and taped it to the inside wall of the semitrailer for the return trip to their co-workers across the border. Although the moment has passed for Bloomington's RCA workers, it may be on just such tiny transnational acts of faith (however sexist or illegal) that the future of any sort of global working-class politics may depend.[50]

NOTES

Introduction

1. Radio broadcast, "Jobs Today, Gone Tomorrow," *Making Contact*, 7 May 1997, tape recording, National Radio Project, Portola Valley, Calif.

2. Although Helen I. Safa mentions continuity with earlier patterns of the sexual division of labor, her emphasis is on the newness of female employment in conjunction with the international division of labor. "The high rate of female employment [in developing countries] represents a radical departure from the pattern of most multinationals," she writes, "which generally employ men in highly mechanized, capital intensive industry": "Runaway Shops and Female Employment: The Search for Cheap Labor," *Signs* 7 (1981): 419.

3. At best, it must be labeled a "limited capital-labor accord," because it left out so many workers, particularly the unorganized. To this critical weakness we must add the freedom of corporations to relocate away from areas of labor resistance to pools of more controllable labor. See David M. Gordon, "Chickens Home to Roost: From Prosperity to Stagnation in the Postwar U.S. Economy," in *Understanding American Economic Decline*, ed. Michael A. Bernstein and David E. Adler (New York: Cambridge University Press, 1994), 55–61; Bruce Nissen, "A Post–World War II 'Social Accord'?" in *U.S. Labor Relations, 1945–1989: Accommodation and Conflict*, ed. Nissen (New York: Garland, 1990), 191–193. See also Nelson Lichtenstein, "From Corporatism to Collective Bargaining," in *The Rise and Fall of the New Deal Order, 1930–1980*, ed. Steven Fraser and Gary Gerstle (Princeton: Princeton University Press, 1989), 122; David Montgomery, "The New Deal Formula," in his *Workers' Control in America* (New York: Cambridge University Press, 1979), 153–180.

4. Thomas J. Sugrue, *The Origins of the Urban Crisis: Race and Inequality in Postwar Detroit* (Princeton: Princeton University Press, 1996), 6, 127–130.

5. Andrew Herod, "From a Geography of Labor to a Labor Geography: Labor's Spatial Fix and the Geography of Capitalism," *Antipode* 29 (1997): 1–31. For the classic studies of plant location, see Alfred Weber, *Theory of the Location of Industries* (Chicago: University of Chicago Press, 1929); Richard M. Cyert and James G. March, *A Behavioral Theory of the Firm* (Englewood Cliffs, N.J.: Prentice-Hall, 1963); August Losch, *The Economics of*

Location (New Haven: Yale University Press, 1954). More recent work that places an emphasis on labor in the production of space includes the essays in *Organizing the Landscape: Geographical Perspectives on Labor Unionism*, ed. Andrew Herod (Minneapolis: University of Minnesota Press, 1998); Dorene Massey, *Spatial Divisions of Labour: Social Structures and the Geography of Production* (London: Macmillan, 1984); Richard Walker and Michael Storper, "Capital and Industrial Location," *Progress in Human Geography* 5 (1981): 473–509; Richard Peet, "Relations of Production and the Relocation of United States Manufacturing Industry since 1960," *Annals of the Association of American Geographers* 75 (1985): 309–333; Gordon L. Clark, *Unions and Communities under Siege* (New York: Cambridge University Press, 1989).

6. As one analyst explains, "The idea, so prominent in popular globalization literature, that businesses pick up stakes and relocate offshore in the blink of an eye is largely 'globaloney.'" See Kim Moody, *Workers in a Lean World: Unions in the International Economy* (New York: Verso, 1997), 7. Examples of the deindustrialization literature include Michael Wallace and Joyce Rothschild, "Plant Closings, Capital Flight, and Worker Dislocation: The Long Shadow of Deindustrialization," in *Deindustrialization and the Restructuring of American Industry*, ed. Wallace and Rothschild (Greenwich, Conn.: AI Press, 1988); Harry Bluestone and Bennett Harrison, *The Deindustrialization of America* (New York: Basic Books, 1982); David Bensman and Roberta Lynch, *Rusted Dreams: Hard Times in a Steel Community* (New York: McGraw-Hill, 1987); Gijsbert van Liemt, ed., *Industry on the Move: Causes and Consequences of International Relocation in the Manufacturing Industry* (Geneva: ILO, 1992); Charles Craypo and Bruce Nissen, eds., *Grand Designs: The Impact of Corporate Strategies on Workers, Unions, and Communities* (Ithaca: ILR Press, 1993). For community-based industrial retention strategies see Bruce Nissen, *Fighting for Jobs: Case Studies of Labor-Community Coalitions Confronting Plant Closings* (Albany: SUNY Press, 1995), and Staughton Lynd, *The Fight against Shutdowns: Youngstown's Steel Mill Closings* (San Pedro, Calif.: Singlejack Books, 1982). For the gradual process of industrial decline, see Saskia Sassen, *The Mobility of Labor and Capital: A Study in International Investment and Labor Flow* (New York: Cambridge University Press, 1988), 198n.

7. E. P. Thompson, *The Making of the English Working Class* (New York: Vintage, 1963), 9. The now crumbling paradigm of the "new labor history" is covered in Bruce Laurie, *Artisans into Workers* (New York: Hill & Wang, 1989), 3–14; David Brody, "The Old Labor History and the New: In Search of an American Working Class," *Labor History* 20 (1979): 111–126; David Montgomery, "To Study the People: The American Working Class," *Labor History* 21 (1980): 485–512.

8. Leon Fink, "Looking Backward: Reflections on Workers' Culture and Certain Conceptual Dilemmas within Labor History," in Fink, *In Search of the Working Class: Essays in American Labor History and Political Culture* (Urbana: University of Illinois Press, 1994), 186.

9. For example, see Nelson Lichtenstein, *Labor's War at Home: The CIO in World War II* (New York: Cambridge University Press, 1982); Steven Fraser, *Labor Will Rule: Sidney Hillman and the Rise of American Labor* (New York: Free Press, 1991); Melvyn Dubofsky, *The State and Labor in Modern America* (Chapel Hill: University of North Carolina Press, 1994); David Gordon, Richard Edwards, and Michael Reich, *Segmented Work, Divided Workers: The Historical Transformation of Labor in the United States* (New York: Cambridge University Press, 1982). Notable exceptions to the lack of culturalism from the 1930s on are Cohen, *Making a New Deal*; Gary Gerstle, *Working-Class Americanism: The Politics of Labor in a Textile City* (New York: Cambridge University Press, 1989); Robin D. G. Kelley, *Hammer and Hoe: Alabama Communists during the Great Depression* (Chapel Hill: University of North Carolina Press, 1990); Michael Honey, *Southern Labor and Black Civil Rights* (Urbana: University of Illinois Press, 1993). For a postwar exception (histor-

ically and historiographically) see Leon Fink and Brian Greenberg, *Upheaval in the Quiet Zone* (Urbana: University of Illinois Press, 1989). In Mexico and much of the rest of Latin America, the "new labor history" is just emerging. It is very much a First World product, with well-endowed archives and adequate funding. Mexican labor studies also have a strong institutional emphasis, given the unarguable centrality of the state in the labor relations system.

10. The transnational path under consideration here explains only one aspect (assembly) of one set of uniquely competitive and highly labor-intensive products (radios and televisions) out of a vast array of goods and services, ranging from radar systems to portable tape recorders, produced by RCA workers around the world. For an overview of the crises in consumer electronics, see Philip J. Curtis, *The Fall of the U.S. Consumer Electronics Industry: An American Tragedy* (Westport, Conn.: Quorum Books, 1994); Vincent A. LaFrance, "The United States Television Receiver Industry: United States versus Japan, 1960–1980" (Ph.D. diss., Pennsylvania State University, 1985); Susan Walsh Sanderson, *The Consumer Electronics Industry and the Future of American Manufacturing* (Washington, D.C.: Economic Policy Institute, 1989).

1. In Defiance of Their Master's Voice: Camden, 1929–1950

1. *Camden Daily Courier*, 9 January 1920; quoted in Jeffrey M. Dorwart and Philip English Mackey, *Camden County, New Jersey, 1616–1976: A Narrative History* (Camden: Camden County Cultural and Heritage Commission, 1976), 229; William H. McMahon, *South Jersey Towns* (New Brunswick: Rutgers University Press, 1973), 267–270.

2. *Philadelphia Evening Bulletin*, 20 April 1916; *Camden Courier-Post*, 7 and 10 April 1979.

3. *Philadelphia Evening Bulletin*, 8 June 1930, 22 September 1935. A map of the buildings and an account of their history and their use can be found in the RCA Collection, Hagley Museum and Library, Wilmington, Del., file 8, box 1, and file 18, box 3; a useful if celebratory company history of Victor and RCA-Victor is Frank O. Barnum, *"His Master's Voice" in America: Ninety Years of Communication Pioneering and Progress* (Camden, N.J.: General Electric, 1991).

4. The company was officially the Radio Corporation of America, or R.C.A., but often it was referred to merely as Radio during its first decades of operation. In 1967, in an effort to bring its name up to date with the wider variety of products and services the corporation offered, it changed the name to simply the unpunctuated RCA. After Thomson Consumer Electronics (TCE) purchased the corporation in 1986, the consumer electronics manufacturing wing often went by RCA, Thomson, or TCE. RCA continued to be the brand name. Throughout this book I shall use simply RCA, Thomson, and TCE. See Robert Sobel, *RCA* (New York: Stein & Day, 1986), 74.

5. Ibid., 35.

6. Kenneth Bilby, *The General: David Sarnoff and the Rise of the Communications Industry* (New York: Harper & Row, 1986), 102.

7. *New York Times*, 18 April 1930; Bilby, *The General*, 106–107, 114.

8. Victor and its founder, Eldridge Johnson, are discussed in the compilation by Elsie Reeves Fenimore, *Eldridge Johnson (1867–1945) Industrial Pioneer: Founder and President of the Victor Talking Machine Company, Camden, New Jersey* (n.p., 1951) (pamphlet); and Barnum, *His Master's Voice in America*. Dorwart and Mackey, *Camden County*, 247; Sobel, *RCA*, 85–91; *New York Times*, 22 January 1929, 22, 23, and 27 November 1932.

9. Camden County Chamber of Commerce, *Two Hundred and Fiftieth Anniversary, 1681–1931* (Camden, 1931), 68, 75.

10. Leo Troy, *Organized Labor in New Jersey* (Princeton: Van Nostrand, 1965), 46; Dorwart and Mackey, *Camden County*, 57–58, 108–109. The militia was called out in 1919 during violence surrounding a new zoning fare system for Camden's trolleys. See Warren E. Stickle III, "The Apple Sack Campaign of 1919: 'As Wet as the Atlantic Ocean,'" in *A New Jersey Anthology*, ed. Maxine N. Lurie (Newark: New Jersey Historical Commission, 1994), 359.

11. Dorwart and Mackey, *Camden County*, 230.

12. Robert Zieger, *The CIO, 1935–1955* (Chapel Hill: University of North Carolina Press, 1995), 9. As John Bodnar argues, "the labor discontent of most immigrants and their children in the 1930s represented a drift away from the social idealism of the nineteenth century and an affirmation of a pragmatic world view which included the valuation of job security and steady wages as a means to family stability": "Immigration, Kinship, and the Rise of Working-Class Realism in Industrial America," *Journal of Social History* 14 (Fall 1980): 56.

13. Dorwart and Mackey, *Camden County*, 164, 230, 255.

14. *Camden Evening Bulletin*, 22 November 1929. The turning point came in 1938, when the New York Shipbuilding Company won a Navy contract to build the *South Dakota*. Only then did the city begin to pull out of the Depression. See Dorwart and Mackey, *Camden County*, 267.

15. Puzant Henry Jeryan, "High-Speed Radio Production," *Electronics* 8 (December 1935): 515–519. Men were also more involved in tube production than in radio assembly.

16. Only the manufacturing of electric lamps had a higher percentage of women. See the census data in Ruth Milkman, *Gender at Work: The Dynamics of Job Segregation by Sex during World War II* (Urbana: University of Illinois Press, 1987), 14, 26; U.S. Department of Labor, Women's Bureau, *Fluctuation of Employment in the Radio Industry*, Bulletin no. 83 (Washington, D.C.: GPO, 1931), 26–27.

17. "What Women Are Doing in Industry," *Factory Management and Maintenance* 100 (March 1942): 63.

18. Milkman, *Gender at Work*, 15–16; Leslie Sklair, *Assembling for Development: The Maquila Industry in Mexico and the United States* (La Jolla: Center for U.S.-Mexican Studies, University of California, San Diego, 1993), 172.

19. As Susan Tiano argues, "Under the earlier international division of labor, women were marginal to the centers of capitalist production. . . . By contrast, women now constitute the bulk of the assembly work force throughout the world": *Patriarchy on the Line: Labor, Gender, and Ideology in the Mexican Maquila Industry* (Philadelphia: Temple University Press, 1994), 17. The other possibility, that women did the light work involved in electrical manufacturing and men did the heavier work of auto, has several problems. Milkman finds the definitions of heavy and light to be highly variable and inconsistent from plant to plant, from time to time, and from region to region. Moreover, automation of auto production made the physical requirements of the job significantly less important, yet auto companies did not follow the obvious profit-maximizing behavior of hiring more women at lower wages. See Milkman, *Gender at Work*, 7, 12, 25–26.

20. Helen S. Hoeber, "Collective Bargaining by United Electrical, Radio, and Machine Workers," *Monthly Labor Review* 47 (July–December 1938): 69.

21. Sklair points out that "men have no monopoly on fat and clumsy fingers, nor are they unable to play the piano or the violin or perform brain surgery": *Assembling for Development*, 173–174. By the time RCA's sexual division of labor made it to Mexico, wage differentials did not matter, because all workers received the same minimum wage. It was therefore the attitudes of the workforce that RCA sought to shape through its preference for young women, not rates of pay. The term belongs to Art Preis, *Labor's Giant Step: Twenty Years of the CIO* (New York: Pioneer Publishers, 1964).

22. Zieger, *CIO*, 6–7.

23. Dorwart and Mackey, *Camden County*, 259–260. The UE leader Julius Empsak said that the RCA recognition strike established the union's presence on the national level: Julius Empsak interview, transcript, Oral History Collection, Columbia University Libraries, 129; and Ronald L. Filippelli and Mark D. McColloch, *Cold War in the Working Class: The Rise and Decline of the United Electrical Workers* (Albany: SUNY Press, 1995), 33–34.

24. Robert Morris to Franklin D. Roosevelt, 8 August 1933, National Archives, RG 280, box 410, case 182–1723.

25. Donald Winfield Jarrell, "A History of Collective Bargaining at the Camden-Area Plants of the Radio Corporation of America, with Special Attention to Bargaining Power" (Ph.D. diss., University of Pennsylvania, 1968), 44.

26. Work at RCA was much more routinized and mechanized than the heavy-current operations at GE and Westinghouse studied by Ronald Schatz. RCA's workers were often younger and more subject to sporadic employment, and the majority of workers in the home appliance sector were women. Moreover, workers and management in the brand-new radio industry lacked the radical tradition developed at the older heavy-current plants. "The presence of revolutionaries in union leadership in the 1930s," Schatz explains, "was of course a legacy of the left-wing electoral campaigns and strike struggles which had galvanized electrical manufacturing towns between 1906 and 1923." As operations such as GE and Westinghouse made relatively quick peace with the new industrial unions in the 1930s, the violence and volatility of organizing drives in the home appliance sector were reminiscent of the earlier battles in the heavy-current operations. See Schatz, *The Electrical Workers: A History of Labor at General Electric and Westinghouse, 1923–1960* (Urbana: University of Illinois Press, 1983), 63, 80–89. The company's lack of experience in labor relations could also have the opposite outcome; Philco's management gave in to unionization without a fight. See Filippelli and McColloch, *Cold War*, 17–19.

27. The IWW had a very active, dynamic, and interethnic presence on the Delaware waterfront. See Peter Cole, "Shaping Up and Shipping Out: The Philadelphia Waterfront during and after the I.W.W. Years, 1913–1940" (Ph.D. diss., Georgetown University, 1997); Irving Bernstein, *The Turbulent Years* (Boston: Houghton Mifflin, 1970), 103–104; Schatz, *Electrical Workers*, 97.

28. Many labor leaders dismissed the NRA as the "National Run-Around," and few things better explain why than the question of the legality of company unions. The National Labor Board, which was set up to ensure compliance with the National Industrial Recovery Act (NIRA), ruled in favor of exclusive majority representation, while the NRA board sanctioned "non-coercive" company unions. The issue would not be clarified until the passage of the Wagner Act. See Melvyn Dubofsky, *The State and Labor in Modern America* (Chapel Hill: University of North Carolina Press, 1994), 116–119.

29. Steven Fraser, *Labor Will Rule: Sidney Hillman and the Rise of American Labor* (New York: Free Press, 1991), 297; Roy J. Adams, *Industrial Relations under Liberal Democracy* (Columbia: University of South Carolina Press, 1995), 47. The AFL issued federal charters as a mechanism to enroll newly organized industrial locals until they could be divided up into their various appropriate craft unions. Although the tactics differed, the choices of independence and affiliation with the AFL were really two strategies that moved toward the same ends. Locals that sought affiliation with the AFL hoped to gain a large enough number of charters to force the AFL Executive Council to grant them a charter for the entire industry. In a parallel effort, the independents sought first to organize an independent international union, which would eventually force the AFL to admit them. See Ronald L. Filippelli, "UE: The Formative Years," *Labor History* 17 (Summer 1976): 355. For the formation of the UE see Milton Derber, "Electrical Products," in *How Collective Bargaining Works*, ed. Harry A. Millis (New York: Twentieth Century Fund, 1942), 790–793; Jarrell,

"Collective Bargaining," 44–46; James J. Matles and James Higgins, *Them and Us: Struggles of a Rank-and-File Union* (Englewood Cliffs, N.J.: Prentice-Hall, 1974), 55–56.

30. Jarrell, "Collective Bargaining," 48–49.

31. Ibid.; Bernstein, *Turbulent Years*, 608.

32. James Carey to John L. Lewis, 22 June 1936, and William Green to E. T. Cunningham, President, RCA, 19 June 1936, both in CIO files of John L. Lewis, microfilm pt. 1, reel 4, University Publications of America, Frederick, Md. For an officially endorsed overview of the IBEW, see Grace Palladino, *Dreams of Dignity, Workers of Vision: A History of the International Brotherhood of Electrical Workers* (Washington, D.C.: IBEW, 1991).

33. Interestingly, given the future trajectory of RCA's migration, the lobby of the RCA Building, in Rockefeller Center, was the spot where the great Mexican artist Diego Rivera was commissioned by Nelson Rockefeller to paint *Man at the Crossroads*, a huge mural that was to depict humankind's liberation from the tyranny of the machine. When Rivera chose to depict instead the transition from capitalism to socialism and included a portrait of Lenin, a public battle took place between the artist and Rockefeller. Newspaper headlines—"Rivera Perpetrates Scenes of Communist Activity for RCA Walls—and Rockefeller, Jr., Foots the Bill"—escalated the conflict into a national political and artistic controversy. In the end Rockefeller had Rivera's work destroyed (but it was later recreated in Mexico City). See Laurance P. Hurlburt, *The Mexican Muralists in the United States* (Albuquerque: University of New Mexico Press, 1989), 159–174.

34. Bilby, *The General*, 3; James B. Carey, Oral Autobiography, Columbia University Oral History Research Office, transcript, 36–37, 42, 69, 97.

35. *New York Herald Tribune*, 25 June 1936; Johnson's interpretation of section 7a appears to coincide with the "right-to-work laws" of the post–Taft-Hartley era. He believed the labor law needed to be rewritten in such a way that if a majority voted to be represented by a union, then no parallel organization would exist in the plant, but he also sought to eliminate the "distasteful idea" that a worker would have to join a union because the majority wanted to be represented by it. See Hugh S. Johnson, *Blue Eagle from Egg to Earth* (Garden City, N.Y.: Doubleday Doran, 1935), 293–294, 342–343; Dubofsky, *State and Labor*, 112, 117; James Carey statement in U.S. Congress, Senate, *Hearings before a Subcommittee of the Committee on Education and Labor . . . Pursuant to S. Res. 266 (74th Congress), A Resolution to Investigate . . . Interference with the Right of Labor to Organize and Bargain Collectively*, pt. 8, 75th Cong., 1st sess., 11 March 1937, 2930–31 (hereafter *La Follette Hearings*); Richard O. Boyer and Herbert M. Morais, *Labor's Untold Story* (New York: Cameron, 1955), 297–298.

36. Unidentified article on p. 1 of "UE Scrapbook of 1936 RCA Strike," UE Archives, University of Pittsburgh Library; *Camden Courier-Post*, 24 June 1936; *Camden Evening Bulletin*, 24 June 1936.

37. The extensive press coverage of the spectacular four-week strike is collected in the scrapbook assembled by the union. See "UE Scrapbook of 1936 RCA Strike" and the clippings and notes of federal mediators in National Archives, RG 280, box 410, case 182-1723; *New York Times*, 25 June 1936.

38. *La Follette Hearings*, 2880–2882, 2916.

39. A visiting group of prominent civil libertarians observed that Camden authorities "interfered with the conduct of the strike through assaults on strikers, illegal arrests, unnecessary use of force and arbitrarily prescribing rules for picketing," and the courts "upheld many of the illegal arrests, have followed illegal procedure in convicting and sentencing strikers, have passed drastic sentences on strikers for alleged minor offenses and have held strikers under extremely high bail": *Camden Courier-Post*, 21 July 1936. The committee consisted of the American Civil Liberties Union, the New Jersey Civil Liberties Union, the National Committee for the Defense of Political Prisoners, and the League of

Women Shoppers. An NLRB inquiry later found RCA in violation of the Wagner Act through its support of the company union.

40. *Philadelphia News*, 29 June 1936. In the first fifteen days of the strike, 200 strikers were arrested and their bail was set at $225,000. Although numerous complaints had been sworn out against the strikebreakers as well, only six had been recorded by county officials. On one day alone, three and a half weeks into the strike, the police arrested more than one hundred people—many of them supporters from the Philco local—and set bail for the prisoners at over $500,000. By the end of the dispute the union's tab at the Camden Courthouse reached $2 million in bail bills. See telegrams from Joseph Mitton, chairman of the Strike Committee, to President Roosevelt, 16 July 1936, National Archives, RG 280, box 410, case 182–1723.

41. *La Follette Hearings*, 2918–2920; Derber, "Electrical Products," 794; telegram in CIO files of John L. Lewis, microfilm, pt. 1, reel 4.

42. *New Republic*, 5 August 1936.

43. Powers Hapgood to Mary Hapgood, 15 and 17 July 1936, and Hapgood to Mother and Father, 28 July 1936, all in Powers Hapgood Papers, 1935–1940, Manuscripts Department, Lilly Library, Indiana University.

44. "UE Scrapbook"; *Camden Courier-Post*, 24, 25, and 26 June 1936; *Camden Evening Courier*, 27 June 1936; Jarrell, "Collective Bargaining," 224. During the UE's tenure at RCA, 20% of the local's officers were women; some were second and third vice presidents, but most of them were recording and financial secretaries or treasurers. Fifteen percent of the members of negotiating committees were women during the UE period.

45. *Philadelphia Record*, 24 June 1936; *Seventeenth Annual Report of the Radio Corporation of America* (New York: RCA, 1936), 4, Hagley Museum and Library, Wilmington, Del.

46. *Camden Courier-Post*, 24 and 26 June, 17 and 21 July 1936.

47. P. W. Chappell, Department of Labor, to Hon. H. L. Kerwin, 20 July 1936, National Archives, RG 280, box 410, case 182–1723.

48. *Camden Courier-Post*, 22 July 1936. The illegality of RCA's company unionism was confirmed in an NLRB hearing. See *Camden Courier-Post*, 20 July 1936; *New York Times*, 20 July 1936; John L. Lewis to General Hugh S. Johnson, 12 July 1936, in CIO files of John L. Lewis, microfilm, pt. 1, reel 4.

49. *Philadelphia Evening Bulletin*, 27 July 1936. Matles and Higgins, *Them and Us*, 58–59, suggest that it was Johnson's idea to boycott the election, and the wording of the document indicates that there was some sort of plan to subvert the election right from the start. Flyers and leaflets are reprinted in *La Follette Hearings*, 3191, 3193, 2933, 3195; "No Voting" flyer in Hapgood Papers.

50. *Philadelphia Evening Bulletin*, 28 July 1936.

51. National Archives, RG 280, box 410, case 182–1723. Of the 3,163 votes, 3,016 were for the UE and 51 for the ECU; 96 were disqualified.

52. Emphasis added. J. Warren Madden, chairman of the NLRB, pointed out that this phrasing was probably not in accordance with the Wagner Act, and it was later deemed not to be; see NLRB, *Decisions and Orders of the National Labor Relations Board,* vol. 2, *July 1, 1936–July 1, 1937* (Washington, D.C.: GPO, 1937), 159–180, esp. 176; *Camden Courier-Post*, 22 July 1936. As Powers Hapgood explained, "They knew they would be beaten, so they formerly [*sic*] instructed their members not to vote": Hapgood to Mother and Father, 15 August 1936, Hapgood Papers.

53. *La Follette Hearings*, 3195; NLRB, *Second Annual Report*, 115, National Archives, RG 280, box 410, case 182–1723; "Certification of Electrical and Radio Workers at R.C.A. Plant," press release, 9 November 1936, in CIO files of John L. Lewis, microfilm, pt. 1, reel 4. James A. Gross shows the substantial impact this ruling had on the course of the

NLRB in *The Reshaping of the National Labor Relations Board: National Labor Policy in Transition, 1937–1947* (Albany: SUNY Press, 1981), 20–21.

54. *La Follette Hearings*, 3193; Matles and Higgins, *Them and Us*, 159; *Camden Courier-Post*, 16 and 17 July 1936.

55. Dubofsky, *State and Labor*, 144–145.

56. Quoted in Derber, "Electrical Products," 796–797; Matles and Higgins, *Them and Us*, 59.

57. Helen S. Hoeber, "Collective Bargaining by United Electrical, Radio, and Machine Workers," *Monthly Labor Review* 47 (July– December 1939): 67–77; Derber, "Electrical Products," 796–797; Jarrell, "Collective Bargaining," 64. The 1937 RCA-UE contract can be found in National Archives, RG 280, box 410, case 182-1723. Statement of E. D. Bieretz, IBEW assistant president, in *Camden Courier-Post*, 8 July 1936; *Philadelphia Evening Bulletin*, 16 November 1939.

58. Jarrell, "Collective Bargaining," 3, 27–28, 63–74, 77–83.

59. Author's interview with Ed Riedweg, 22 November 1994, Bloomington. Riedweg conflated several events and missed the date of the strike by two years, placing it in 1938; his story is nonetheless reasonably consistent with events, given the fallibility of human memory and the fact that this was the story as it was collectively remembered by RCA management, not a reflection of his personal experiences. He compresses into a single story the strike, the opening of the Bloomington plant, and the relocation of the engineering division, which was moved to Indiana in 1960 after the engineering personnel unionized.

60. Radio Corporation of America, *Report to Employees* (New York, 1949), in the RCA files of the Camden County Historical Collection; Jarrell, "Collective Bargaining," 16–17. Rather than relocate, the company could have redoubled its efforts at union busting, as Philco did. Having conceded the organization of the Philadelphia works early on, Philco's management reversed course and tried to cut wages, return to the forty-hour week, and, if necessary, bust the union in 1938. As the UE leaders realized, "radio manufacturing is one of the sickest branches of our industry," and the competition would clearly drive many of the companies out of business. At the end of a bitter four-month strike/lockout, Philco's workers met most of the company's demands. They did, however, hold on to their union shop. See UERMWA, "Report of the General Officers," August 1938, in Electrical, Radio, and Machine Workers, 1930–42, box 165, FF 10, Labor-Management Documentation Center, Catherwood Library, Cornell University; Filippelli and McColloch, *Cold War*, 42.

61. See, for instance, June Nash and María Patricia Fernández-Kelly, eds., *Women, Men, and the International Division of Labor* (Albany: SUNY Press, 1983); Folker Fröbel, Jürgen Heinrichs, and Otto Kreye, *The New International Division of Labor* (Cambridge: Cambridge University Press, 1980). For a useful corrective, see Soon Kyoung Cho, "The Labor Process and Capital Mobility: The Limits of the New International Division of Labor," *Politics and Society* 14 (1985): 185–222.

62. National Archives, RG 280, box 829, case 209-6734, 24 September 1942; Filippelli and McColloch, *Cold War*, 271.

63. Ben Riskin to James Matles, "Report on Meeting with Local 103 Executive Board on October 20, 1948," N.O., 1975 Access, D/L-1, FF 131, UE Archives; "Brief Submitted to Mayor George E. Brunner, Camden, N.J., by Local 103, UERMWA-CIO," 30 March 1949, UE Archives, C.B., RCA, FF 86, Local 103 Runaway Shops/Unemployment, 1948– March 1949; *Philadelphia Evening Bulletin*, 28 and 31 March 1949.

64. In the context of a rapidly expanding network of production facilities, a variety of subcontracting arrangements, and temporary transfers of manufacturing, tracing the flight of specific jobs to new locations is a difficult task, beyond the capability of union leaders at the time. One example will illustrate the complexity. Camden made the "RF unit," a key component of a television tuner, for all of RCA's production and all of its out-

side contractors, such as Motorola, through the mid-1940s. That production was then transferred to Indianapolis. Not long after that, Bloomington took over RF unit production from Indianapolis and the Standard Coil Company acted as a subcontractor for all of RCA's independent customers. Camden therefore lost two-thirds of its RF unit assembly jobs as of February 1948, but the path of its production branched in several directions. See Ben Riskin to James J. Matles, "Report on Meeting with Local 103," 1 November 1948, D/L-1, FF 131, 1975 access, UE Archives; *Philadelphia Evening Bulletin*, 7 October 1949.

65. "RCA AM Units Scheduled This Month," *Broadcasting*, 11 March 1946, 68; A. F. Inglis, division vice president and general manager, RCA Government and Commercial Systems, "RCA in Camden," speech to Camden Rotary Club, 10 April 1973, in RCA files of the Camden County Historical Collection; "RCA Corporation," *International Directory of Company Histories* (Chicago: St. James Press, 1988), 88–90; and *RCA: Five Historical Views* (New York: RCA, 1971), 10–34.

66. *Philadelphia Evening Bulletin*, 28 January 1946; Schatz, *Electrical Workers*, 154–155; George Lipsitz, *Rainbow at Midnight: Labor and Culture in the 1940s* (Urbana: University of Illinois Press, 1994), 100; Matles and Higgins, *Them and Us*, 144–145. For a more general discussion see Zieger, *CIO*, 212–215.

67. A complete statistical breakdown of the factory's female employment is in the firm interview conducted by the Women's Bureau of the Department of Labor, in National Archives, RG 86, box 610, Research for Report no. 197. The reasons listed for the decline in female employment when other factories were hiring women were: the cabinet department had been eliminated as war work increased; the commercial radio business had suffered an overall decline; and the company had experienced an increase in "short orders," for which it was more practical to assign skilled men to carry the tasks all the way through to completion "rather than to break women in." Each of these reasons is compatible with the relocation argument: the cabinet factory was relocated to Pulaski, Va.; radio assembly was in Bloomington, among other cities; and the increase in "short-order work" was facilitated by the relocation of the labor-intensive work. See also ibid., RG 280, box 829, case 209-6734, 24 September 1942. For postwar figures on RCA employment, see ibid., box 1901, case 462-921, 12 April 1946; Jarrell, "Collective Bargaining," 221.

68. Earl Fox to James Matles, 30 September 1948, D/L-1, FF 141, District 1, Local 103, Correspondence, UE Archives; memorandum, 21 May 1946, ibid., FF 139.

69. David Roediger, "The Crisis in Labor History: Race, Gender and the Replotting of the Working Class Past in the United States," in Roediger, *Towards the Abolition of Whiteness* (London: Verso, 1994), 70; Doreen B. Massey, *Spatial Divisions of Labour: Social Structures and the Geography of Production* (London: Macmillan, 1984), 85; Michael Storper and Richard Walker, *Capitalist Imperative: Territory, Technology, and Industrial Growth* (New York: Basil Blackwell, 1989), 10, 181.

70. Of the 5,539 votes cast out of a possible 5,776 in the election of 18 May 1950, 2,857 were cast for the IUE and 2,532 for the UE; 30 were cast against both unions; and 120 ballots were challenged: *Radio Corporation of America, Victor Division*, 90 NLRB 1989 (1950); Jarrell, "Collective Bargaining," 55; Schatz, *Electrical Workers*, 226, 232. For how the earlier divisions in the UE later revealed themselves in the Cold War, see Filippelli and McColloch, *Cold War*. Research suggests that the UE's commitment to racial and sexual equality, in addition to anticommunism, may have undermined the union's support among white male ethnic workers. See Gerald Zahavi, "Passionate Commitments: Race, Sex, and Communism at Schenectady General Electric, 1932–1954," *Journal of American History* 83 (1996): 548.

71. Jarrell, "Collective Bargaining," 19–20; Nelson Lichtenstein, *Labor's War at Home: The CIO in World War II* (New York: Cambridge University Press, 1982), 234. Jarrell uses the following anecdote to argue that labor militancy and unionization had nothing to do

with the decentralization of production: "One union leader . . . encouraged members of his division to accept a substantial cut in incentive rates to prevent production of certain component parts from being moved out of Camden. Despite the cut in rates, the production was moved out with no little loss in prestige for the union leader involved in bringing about the acceptance of the wage cut." Clearly, however, the threat of moving production can be nearly as effective a labor-control technique as the relocation of production itself and hardly proves that RCA's decision to relocate was not due to the labor climate in the city.

72. *Philadelphia Evening Bulletin*, 8 July 1962; *Philadelphia Inquirer*, 22 June 1969; *Camden Courier-Post*, 7 October 1975.

73. *Philadelphia Inquirer*, 9 September 1979; also see the *Inquirer*'s series on Camden's problems on 13–17 April 1970; and *City of Camden's Twenty Year Analysis: 1971–1991* (Camden: Department of Administration and Finance, 1971). The politics of race and deindustrialization in the immediate postwar period are well addressed in Thomas J. Sugrue, *The Origins of the Urban Crisis* (Princeton: Princeton University Press, 1996).

74. Walt Whitman, "I Dream'd in a Dream," in *Complete Poetry and Selected Prose* (Boston: Houghton Mifflin, 1959), 96.

75. After General Electric bought RCA, including the Aerospace group, in 1985, Camden County and the State of New Jersey sought to revitalize the industry's commitment to the city. In 1991, GE built a modern administrative and engineering building on the site of some of the old RCA buildings. Finally, in 1993, the defense contractor Martin Marietta bought GE Aerospace for $3 billion, and one year later Martin Marietta and Lockheed announced their $10 billion merger. See *Camden Courier-Post*, 12 December 1985; 20 March 1991; 31 August 1994. Right down the waterfront from RCA's old docks another urban renewal project, an aquarium, has opened, but few tourists are willing to venture through Camden to visit it. Most take a nostalgic ferry ride from Philadelphia to visit the new tourist site.

2. "Anything but an Industrial Town": Bloomington, 1940–1968

1. Robert Doty, interview by R. T. King, 5 September 1980, interview 80-57, transcript, Indiana University Oral History Project (hereafter IUOHP), 2–7.

2. In number of persons on relief, Monroe Country ranked third highest of ninety-two counties in Indiana from 1933 to 1937. Rankings were determined from various publications of the Governor's Commission on Unemployment Relief, including State Department of Public Welfare, *Statistical Survey of Public Assistance in Indiana*, November 1937. For an overview of Monroe County's development, see Louis Orzack, "Employment and Social Structure: A Study of Social Change in Indiana" (Ph.D. diss., Indiana University, 1953).

3. Indiana was one of nine states that had abdicated responsibility for relief but did help with administrative costs. Four other states paid nothing for relief. See Roger Biles, *A New Deal for the American People* (De Kalb: Northern Illinois University Press, 1991), 112. For numbers of workers on relief see William E. Leuchtenburg, *Franklin D. Roosevelt and the New Deal* (New York: Harper & Row, 1963), 124–130.

4. *Bloomington Evening World*, 22 February 1940.

5. Ibid., 22 and 23 February 1940; *Bloomington Daily Telephone*, 22 February 1940.

6. Doty interview, 7.

7. *Bloomington Daily Telephone*, 29 January 1924.

8. Orzack, "Employment and Social Structure," 80–87. Showers Brothers also built a huge factory in Burlington, Iowa, and bought a chair factory in nearby Bloomfield, In-

diana. See Roland E. Williams, "Major Industrial Trends of Bloomington, Indiana" (Ph.D. diss., Indiana University, 1962), 29; James F. Leins, "The History and Development of the Showers Brothers Company" (M.A. thesis, Indiana University, 1938), 58; and Williams, "Major Industrial Trends," 29–31; Orzack, "Employment and Social Structure," 113–134; *United States Census, 1940*, vol. 2, pt. 2: *Population* (Washington, D.C.: GPO, 1940), 793. Donald Hansen, a banker, and John Pardue, a worker at Showers, volunteered the same explanation for the demise of the furniture company. See John Oscar Pardue, interview by R. T. King, 26 August 1980, interview 80-54, transcript, and Donald Hansen, interview by R. T. King, 21 August 1980, transcript, both in IUOHP; *Bloomington Evening World*, 13 March 1940.

9. Joseph Batchelor, *An Economic History of the Indiana Oolitic Limestone Industry*, Indiana Business Studies no. 27 (Bloomington: Indiana University, 1944), 257, 324, 352; *United States Census, 1940*, vol. 2: *Mineral Industries* (Washington, D.C.: GPO, 1940), 60.

10. Jessamyn West, *The Witch Diggers* (New York: Harcourt Brace, 1951), 5.

11. Quoted in Joint Committee on the Economic Report, 82d Congress, 1st sess., *Underemployment of Rural Families* (Washington, D.C.: GPO, 1951), 26.

12. Indiana Employment Service, *Labor Market Developments Report: For Bloomington, Indiana, Labor Market Area* (Indianapolis, June 1943), 22; U.S. Employment Service, War Manpower Commission, *Summary Report on Adequacy of Labor Supply: For Bloomington–Burns City, Indiana, Labor Market Area* (Indianapolis, October 1943), 7; Orzack, "Employment and Social Structure," iv.

13. Henry Boxman, interview by R. T. King, 28 August 1980, interview 80-56, transcript, IUOHP; Jane Chestnutt, interview by Emilye Crosby, 27 February 1990, interview 90-107, tape, ibid.

14. Pardue interview.

15. All figures come from interviews with Mary Frances Roll, who surveyed job opportunities for women in Bloomington for the Indiana State Employment Service in the late 1930s. With this knowledge base, she was selected as the only local member of management at RCA Bloomington. She also provided the title of this chapter. See interview of Mary Frances Roll by Robert Barrows, 10 February 1977, interview 77-4, transcript, IUOHP. Also see "Local Labor Market Survey for the Bloomington–Bedford–Burns City, Indiana, Area" (mimeo), a report prepared by the U.S. Employment Service, Federal Security Agency, Social Security Board (August 1942); Ruth Ann Greene interview by Emilye Crosby, 4 October 1990, interview 90-108, tape, IUOHP.

16. George W. Starr, *Industrial Development of Indiana* (Bloomington: Indiana University School of Business Administration, 1937), 51; Pardue interview.

17. Batchelor, *Indiana Oolitic Limestone Industry*, 139, 143, 250, 261–263, 312–318. Among the many craft unions active in the stone belt were the International Association of Marble, Slate, and Stone Polishers; the International Union of Operating Engineers; the International Brotherhood of Blacksmiths, Drop Forgers, and Helpers; the International Association of Machinists; and the Quarry Workers' International Union, for all quarry workers not eligible for any of the other unions. In 1937 a jurisdictional dispute led the Quarry Workers to vote to affiliate with the CIO, but members said that they thought they were voting for an AFL industrial charter.

18. Orzack, "Employment and Social Structure," 139; Henry F. Boxman of the chamber of commerce found the theory "exaggerated": Boxman interview, 10.

19. Roll interview by Barrows, 6; Mary Frances Roll, interview by Emilye Crosby, 21 February 1990, interview 90-113, tape, IUOHP. Without RCA, the *Bloomington Daily Telephone* editorialized on 22 March 1940, local workers "must go through a period of hardship, with public relief staving off want and hunger, and finally they must leave Bloomington and go to other cities in search of jobs."

20. Williams, "Major Industrial Trends," 19–29; Virginia M. Savage and Pamela F. Service, "A Brief History of Monroe County, Indiana," Monroe County Historical Society Museum, n.d., 6; Pardue interview, 12; Mary Frances Roll interview by R. T. King, 18 August 1980, interview 80-50, transcript, IUOHP, 28–29.

21. Williams, "Major Industrial Trends," 55, 18; *Bloomington Daily Telephone*, 22 February 1940; Roll interview by King, 5.

22. *Bloomington Daily Telephone*, 22 February 1940; Sylvia S. Lotman, "An Evaluation of Test Scores, Behavior during Test Performance, and Interview in Selecting Radio Workers" (M.A. thesis, Indiana University, 1944), 32; Robert Brookshire, interview by R. T. King, 19 August 1980, interview 80-51, transcript, IUOHP, 2, 6; Roll interview by Crosby; Roll interview by Barrows.

23. For wage comparisons see Report to Mr. Clarence M. Mitchell, Negro Employment and Training Section, Office of Production Management, 28 November 1942, in Regional Archives, Philadelphia, RG 211, box 24-353, ser. 278, folder "RCA Camden"; Firm Interview for Report no. 197, National Archives, RG 86, box 610; Roll interview by King, 7; National Archives, RG 280, box 1824, case 445-6475, 31 March 1945.

24. Brookshire interview.

25. *Bloomington Daily Telephone*, 22 February and 18 April 1940; Boxman interview, 15; *Bloomington Evening World*, 22 and 23 February 1940.

26. Author's interview with Anna Belle Van Hook (formerly Ooley), 22 March 1994, Bloomington; Chestnutt interview; Roll interview by Barrows, 8.

27. Author's interview with Alyce Hunter, 21 March 1994, Bloomington; Joska Hoke interview by Emilye Crosby, 3 April 1990, tape recording, interview 90-110, IUOHP. The family metaphor in U.S. labor relations is problematic, as it begs the question of reference: who has authority, who is parent and who is child, who is contained within the fraternal circle and who is not? The metaphor is further complicated by the fact that RCA regularly referred to its workforce as the "RCA family" and the company newsletter was the *RCA Victor Family News*. For use of the metaphor writ large, see Jacquelyn Dowd Hall, James Leloudis, Robert Korstad, Mary Murphy, Lu Ann Jones, and Christopher B. Daly, *Like a Family: The Making of a Southern Cotton Mill World* (Chapel Hill: University of North Carolina Press, 1987).

28. Roll interview by King, 27–28.

29. Doty interview, 247; author's interview with Hunter; *RCA Victor Family News* (Bloomington), September 1946.

30. Roll interview by Crosby; Greene interview. According to a study conducted at RCA Bloomington, however, management's logic was actually counterproductive. Management wanted single young women, according to the employment manager, because "they wouldn't have distracting influences [such as husbands and children] to keep them away from the job." Yet none of the workers who took jobs because they needed the money "to support children, to help pay for a farm, husband not making enough money," were found to be unsatisfactory. Older workers, rather than the eighteen-to-twenty-eight-year-olds they preferred, were found to have better attendance records and longer tenure at the plant. See Roll interview by King, 7; Lotman, "Evaluation of Test Scores."

31. Doty interview, 11, 18–19; Greene interview; minutes of International Brotherhood of Electrical Workers, Local 1424, Bloomington; Hunter interview by Crosby.

32. Bob Kirkwood to David Scribner, 7 July and 1 August 1944, Red Dot 136, FF "IBEW RCA," United Electrical Workers Archives, University of Pittsburgh Library; NLRB cases 9-R-1483 and 9-7-1484, 30 September 1944, National Office Records, Red Dot, box 17, FF "R.C.A. (Bloomington, Ind.)," ibid. With 95% of the plant voting, 79% of the workforce cast their ballots for the IBEW.

33. Memorandum, Ben Riskin to All RCA Locals and Organizers, 31 July 1946, FF "RCA Miscellaneous," Red Dot 267, UE Archives. Offering further evidence of the relationship between skill and unionization, the UE organizer did try to break the tool shop off as a separate bargaining unit because of the UE support there. See RG 25, Box 3945, Case 9-R-1483, RCA Bloomington, National Archives.

34. UE Organizers' Bulletin, 31 March 1950, Red Dot 136, FF "IBEW: Constitution and By-Laws," UE Archives.

35. Beatrice Henderson, Robert Norris, and Louis Watson, interview by Emilye Crosby, 4 April 1990, tape recording, IUOHP; Crosby interview; Chestnutt interview; Doty interview.

36. Author's interview with Bob Norris, 22 March 1994, Bloomington; Henderson / Norris / Watson interview.

37. Author's interview with Hunter; Greene interview.

38. Lisa Kannenberg, "The Impact of the Cold War on Women's Trade Union Activism: The UE Experience," *Labor History* 34 (1993): 312–314; and Ruth Milkman, *Gender at Work: The Dynamics of Job Segregation by Sex during World War II* (Urbana: University of Illinois Press, 1987), 74–83.

39. Some Bloomington women who had taken on traditionally male jobs did have to give them up to men. Ruth Ann Greene lost her inspection job after the war —"When the men started drifting back, they got those jobs, and we went back to crimping and soldering"—and the plant did shut down for 41 days for reconversion. The statistics are from Milkman, *Gender at Work*, 112–118.

40. Doty interview, 14.

41. *Bloomington Herald-Telephone*, 1, 2, 3, and 4 August 1950. Norris also explained that balance was important: "You can't keep them out too long, otherwise your people will turn against you."

42. Robert Sobel, *RCA* (New York: Stein & Day, 1986), 133, 150; *Television Digest and FM Reports*, 6 October 1945 and 30 August 1947; "RCA and Television," *Fortune*, September 1948.

43. Sobel, *RCA*, 160–164; Federal Communications Commission, *Color Television Hearings, 3, 4 May 1950* (Washington, D.C.: G.P.O., 1950); E. W. Engstrom, *RCA: Five Historical Views*, pt. 2 (Cherry Hill, N.J. : RCA, 1978), 13.

44. Sobel, *RCA*, 164–166.

45. W. C. Miller to Herman B. Wells, 12 May 1950, Wells Papers, Indiana University. Production actually began in Camden and sojourned briefly in Indianapolis before landing in Bloomington.

46. *Television Digest and FM Reports*, 30 August 1947. For an overview of sales growth in the industry, see *Electronic Industries*, 30 January 1963, and Wickham Skinner and David Rogers, *Manufacturing Policy in the Electronics Industry* (Homewood, Ill.: Irwin, 1968), 60.

47. Elizabeth Shelton, interview by Mary Stevens, February 1979, IUOHP, 3.

48. Williams, "Major Industrial Trends," 36; author's interview with Thomas F. Whitten, 17 November 1994, Indianapolis.

49. Robert O. Harvey, *Land Uses in Bloomington, Indiana, 1818–1950* (Bloomington: School of Business, 1951), 41–43; author's interviews with Bill Cook, 18 March 1994, and Darrell "Bear" Clayton, 21 March 1994, Bloomington; Delbert C. Miller, "A History of Sarkes Tarzian, Inc." (mimeo, n.d.).

50. Williams, "Major Industrial Trends," 39–51; Miller, "Sarkes Tarzian"; Arthur J. Olsen, interview by Vincent Giroux, 21 February 1979, transcript, IUOHP, 45; *Bloomington Herald-Telephone*, 21 June 1961.

51. Indiana Department of Commerce, Agriculture, Industry, and Public Relations, *Indiana Plant Location Fact Book* (Indianapolis, 1961); Vasilios Basil Kafiris, *Indiana Manufacturing Growth Patterns, 1958–1967* (Indianapolis: Indiana Department of Commerce, 1969), 198–202; Williams, "Major Industrial Trends," 21. Joining seventeen other states at the time, Indiana passed a right-to-work law on 1 March 1957, eliminating the possibility that employees could be required to join a union as a condition of employment. See Fred Witney, *Indiana Labor Relations Law* (Bloomington: Indiana University School of Business, 1960), 81–90.

52. Michael Storper and Richard Walker, *The Capitalist Imperative: Territory, Technology, and Industrial Growth* (New York: Basil Blackwell, 1989), 188–189, 86, 180–181; *RCA in Indiana,* January 1961, brochure in the RCA files of the Indiana Room, Bloomington Public Library.

53. "RCA Victor: All Operations Now Centered in Indiana," *Indiana Business and Industry,* December 1960, 8–10; author's interview with Ed Riedweg, 22 November 1994, Bloomington; Whitten interview; Donald Winfield Jarrell, "A History of Collective Bargaining at the Camden Area Plants of the Radio Corporation of America, with Special Attention to Bargaining Power" (Ph.D. diss., University of Pennsylvania, 1968), 38.

54. *RCA Victor Family News* (Bloomington), September 1946; *Bloomington Herald-Telephone,* 21 June 1961, 17 June 1964; Roll interview by Crosby.

55. Roll interview by Crosby; *RCA Victor Family News* (Bloomington), March 1947.

56. Roll interview by Barrows, 18; Doty interview, 36.

57. Author's interview with Ken Beasley, 18 March 1994, Bloomington. "Not that way today," he explained. "People are much more serious about their jobs."

58. Roll interview by Barrows, 16.

59. The program began in 1934 and is still in use today. See Joseph H. Quick, ed., *The Detailed Work-Factor Manual for Time Standards Analysis,* 9th ed. (Moorestown, N.J.: WOFAC, 1969), 1-1; for the early history of its development see Joseph H. Quick, "Motion-Time Standards," *Factory Management and Maintenance* 103 (May 1945): 97–108.

60. Harry Braverman, *Labor and Monopoly Capital: The Degradation of Work in the Twentieth Century* (New York: Monthly Review Press, 1974), 173–179; Quick, *Detailed Work-Factor Manual*; author's interview with David "Rocky" Gallagher and Mary Gallagher, 19 November 1994, Bloomington; Cook interview; author's interview with E. B. Pruitt, 19 March 1994, Bloomington; Beasley interview.

61. Recorded minutes, Local 1424, International Brotherhood of Electrical Workers, Bloomington; Pruitt interview. Bill Doty (interview, 32–33) recalled finding a woman on the line who had begun menstruating without protection. She had begged the foreman to let her leave the line, but the "weirdo foreman" paid no attention to her. The relief operator was tied up and the group leader was not around, so when the shop steward found out she had been left there in her state for over an hour, he walked over and pulled the cord to shut the line down. The foreman, who "must have had ears like radar," came running over, ready to "whip" the shop steward right there. Some women recalled that they had to keep "old shorts and stuff" in the dispensary because this type of thing continued to happen during the hectic time when production was at its peak.

62. Author's interviews with Judy Cross, 18 and 21 March 1994, Bloomington.

63. Hoke interview.

64. *Bloomington Herald-Telephone,* 5, 6, and 8 June 1964; Clayton interview; Cook interview.

65. *Bloomington Herald-Telephone,* 12 June 1964.

66. Ibid., 11 June 1964.

67. Cook interview; *Bloomington Tribune,* 27 October 1966.

68. *Indiana Daily Student,* 27 and 28 October 1966; *Bloomington Herald-Telephone,* 7,

28, and 29 October 1966; Doty interview; Cross interview; Betty Doty interview by R. T. King, 5 September 1980, transcript, interview 80-58, IUOHP.

69. *Indiana Daily Student*, 27 and 28 October 1966; *Bloomington Herald-Telephone*, 7, 28, and 29 October 1966; Doty interview; Cross interview. Few of the workers I interviewed remembered much about the strikes, and they seemed shocked when I showed them newspaper pictures of the violence. The four years of strike activity do not fit with their perception of the plant's overall peaceful history.

70. *Bloomington Star-Courier*, 13 July 1967; *Bloomington Herald Tribune*, 3 June and 3 and 5 July 1967.

71. Among the things that had faded from the plant manager's memory was the title of the Johnny Paycheck song: "Take This Job and Shove It."

72. Riedweg interview.

73. Doty interview, 30.

74. *Indianapolis Star*, 16 June 1965, 11 January 1966; *Bloomington Herald-Telephone*, 16 June 1965, 24 January 1966.

3. Bordering on the Sun Belt: Memphis, 1964–1971

1. *Memphis Commercial Appeal*, 21 December 1965, 1 January 1966.

2. Ibid., 8 and 16 January 1966; Donald E. Pursell, William R. Schriver, and Roger Bowlby, "Trade Adjustment Assistance: An Analysis of Impacted Worker Benefits on Displaced Workers in the Electronics Industry," Center for Manpower Studies, Memphis State University, 1974, 11.

3. Michael Honey, *Southern Labor and Black Civil Rights: Organizing Memphis Workers* (Urbana: University of Illinois Press, 1993), 15–20.

4. Gavin Wright, *Old South, New South: Revolutions in the Southern Economy since the Civil War* (New York: Basic Books, 1986), 52; Robert A. Sigafoos, *Cotton Row to Beale Street: A Business History of Memphis* (Memphis: Memphis State University Press, 1979), 86. See also Honey, *Southern Labor*, 23.

5. Sigafoos, *Cotton Row*, 72; David M. Tucker, "Black Pride and Negro Business in the 1920s: George Washington Lee of Memphis," *Business History Review* 43 (1969): 437; James C. Cobb, *Industrialization and Southern Society, 1877–1984* (Lexington: University Press of Kentucky, 1984), 32.

6. Sigafoos, *Cotton Row*, 194; George B. Tindall, *The Emergence of the New South, 1913–1945* (Baton Rouge: Louisina State University Press, 1967), 527. Crump paid African Americans' poll taxes under the presumption that they would then vote for the candidate of Crump's choice. See David M. Tucker, *Memphis since Crump: Bossism, Blacks, and Civic Reformers, 1948–1968* (Knoxville: University of Tennessee Press, 1980), 22–39; and William D. Miller, *Mr. Crump of Memphis* (Baton Rouge: Louisiana State University Press, 1964)—uncritical and financed by the Crump family, but the only biography available.

7. Honey, *Southern Labor*, 135–136, 150–152.

8. Lucy Randolph Mason, *To Win These Rights: A Personal Story of the CIO in the South* (New York: Harper, 1952), 104; Tucker, *Memphis since Crump*, 54–55; Honey, *Southern Labor*, 184–191, 209.

9. See Bob Korstad and Nelson Lichtenstein, "Opportunities Found and Lost: Labor Radicals and the Early Civil Rights Movement," *Journal of American History* 75 (1988): 786–811; Michael Honey, "Unionism and Racial Justice in Memphis," in *Organized Labor in the Twentieth-Century South*, ed. Robert Zieger (Knoxville: University of Tennessee Press, 1991), 151–152.

10. Wright, *Old South, New South*, 243; Honey, *Southern Labor*, 281.

11. Ray Marshall, "The Old South and the New," in *Employment of Blacks in the South: A Perspective on the 1960s*, ed. Marshall and Virgil L. Christian Jr. (Austin: University of Texas Press, 1978), 7–8; Pursell, et al., "Trade Adjustment Assistance," 6; Wright, *Old South, New South*, 257.

12. James C. Cobb, *The Selling of the South: The Southern Crusade for Industrial Development, 1936–1990* (Urbana: University of Illinois Press, 1993), 235; *Memphis Commercial Appeal*, 21 December 1965; *Memphis Press-Scimitar*, 21 December 1965.

13. Ronald E. Carrier and William R. Schriver, *Plant Location Analysis: An Investigation of Plant Locations in Tennessee* (Memphis: Memphis State University, 1969), 148. More firms chose Tennessee because of low cost and availability of labor than because of raw materials and market considerations combined. In 1965 the average hourly wage in durable goods in Memphis was $2.16; in the United States it was $2.79: U.S. Department of Labor, *Employment and Earnings: States and Areas, 1939–1972* (Washington, D.C.: G.P.O., 1974); Thomas M. Carroll, David H. Ciscel, and John E. Gnuschke, "Determinants of Wage Rates in Memphis, Tennessee: 1962–1975," *Mid-South Quarterly Business Review* 18 (July 1980): 12–13.

14. *Memphis Press-Scimitar*, 11 January 1966; author's interview with Thomas F. Whitten, 17 November 1994, Indianapolis; *Memphis Commercial Appeal*, 11 and 17 January 1966.

15. *Memphis Commercial Appeal*, 6 January 1966; "Summary of Prospect, Radio Corporation of America, 8 August 1962," in Sanford Correspondence, North Carolina State Archives, Raleigh.

16. *Memphis Commercial Appeal*, 21 December 1965; *Memphis Press-Scimitar*, 21 December 1965.

17. *Memphis Press-Scimitar*, 9 February 1966, 21 December 1965; *Memphis Commercial Appeal*, 21 December 1965.

18. *Memphis Commercial Appeal*, 22, 24, 30, 31 December 1965, 4 and 11 January 1966; *Memphis Press-Scimitar*, 21 and 23 December 1965.

19. Thomas W. Collins and David H. Ciscel, "An Analysis of the RCA Television Assembly Plant in Memphis: Why It Closed," *Mid-South Quarterly Business Review* 14 (April 1976): 4; *Memphis Commercial Appeal*, 17 January 1966; Whitten interview.

20. *Memphis Commercial Appeal*, 20 January and 6 February 1966.

21. *Memphis Press-Scimitar*, 30 May 1966; *Memphis Commercial Appeal*, 6 February 1966.

22. *Memphis Press-Scimitar*, 15 June 1966, 14 October 1966; David Ciscel and Tom Collins, "The Memphis Runaway Blues," *Southern Exposure* 4 (1976): 145.

23. Gordon M. Freeman to Paul Jennings, 15 July 1966, IUE Archives, Rutgers University, RA II, box 86, folder 40, "RCA-NLRB Memphis," and box 84, "RCA Conference Board Minutes—18–20 October 1965." Thomas Whitten confirmed in my interview with him that this had indeed been the company's strategy.

24. *Memphis Commercial Appeal*, 16 June and 17 August 1966; *Memphis Press-Scimitar*, 17 July and 17 August 1966.

25. See the collection of campaign leaflets issued by both sides in the IUE Archives, RA II, box 86, folder 40, "RCA-NLRB Memphis"; *Memphis Commercial-Appeal*, 7 October 1966.

26. "The RCA-Bloomington Tragedy," *IUE Local 730 News*, in IUE Archives, RA II, box 86, folder 40, "RCA-NLRB Memphis"; *Memphis Commercial Appeal*, 17 December 1966.

27. D. H. Bartholomew to International President, IUE, 18 November 1968, in IUE Archives, RA II, box 175, folder 42, "Local 730, IUE-AFL-CIO."

28. Pursell et al., "Trade Adjustment Assistance," 19.

29. Quoted in Ciscel and Collins, "Runaway Blues," 147.

30. Pursell et al., "Trade Adjustment Assistance," 19–21; Ciscel and Collins, "Runaway Blues," 147–148.

31. *Memphis Commercial Appeal*, 10, 11, and 24 March 1967; *Memphis Press-Scimitar*, 10, 11, and 23 March 1967.

32. D. H. Bartholomew to International President, IUE, 18 November 1968, in IUE Archives, RA II, box 175, folder 42, "Local 730, IUE-AFL-CIO."

33. Pat Hanna quoted in Pursell et al., "Trade Adjustment Assistance," 291.

34. J. Edwin Stanfield, *In Memphis: More than a Garbage Strike* (Atlanta: Southern Regional Council, 1968), suppl. I, 1.

35. For an overview of the strike, see Joan Turner Beifuss, *At the River Stand: Memphis, the 1968 Strike, and Martin Luther King* (Brooklyn: Carlson, 1989).

36. Quoted in Honey, *Southern Labor*, 289.

37. Pursell et al., "Trade Adjustment Assistance," 23.

38. Virgil Grace, Local 730 President, to G. J. Rooney, Personnel Manager, 18 June 1968, IUE Archives, RA II, box 175, folder 42, "Local 730, IUE-AFL-CIO."

39. *Wall Street Journal*, 3 June and 18 August 1970; *Memphis Commercial Appeal*, 3 June 1970.

40. *Memphis Press-Scimitar*, 22 October 1970; *Memphis Commercial Appeal*, 3, 22, and 23 October 1970, 2 December 1970; *Wall Street Journal*, 30 October 1969, 6 January 1970, 27 March 1970.

41. *Memphis Press-Scimitar*, 2 and 10 December 1970; Ciscel and Collins, "Runaway Blues," 149.

42. *Memphis Press-Scimitar*, 2 and 14 December 1970, 2 February 1971.

43. Ciscel and Collins, "Runaway Blues," 3. A researcher on the scene after the shutdown remarked, "The black women were the ones who mostly said something about competition; the whites said poor production. They tended to blame it on the employees, meaning, I think, a latent thing that blacks were probably the root of it. Some of them said the plant closed because blacks stood around with their hands in their pockets": Pursell et al., "Trade Adjustment Assistance," 288.

44. See Collins and Ciscel, "Analysis of the RCA Television Assembly Plant," 3–7.

45. U.S. Tariff Commission, *Television Receivers: Production and Maintenance Workers at RCA Corp. Plant, Memphis, Tenn.: Report to the President on Worker Investigation No. TEA-W-70*, Tariff Commission Publication 76 (Washington, D.C.: GPO, 1971), 10–21.

46. U.S. Tariff Commission, *Economic Factors Affecting the Use of Items 807.00 and 806.30 of the Tariff Schedule of the United States: Report to the President on Investigation 332–61 under Section 332 of the Tariff Act of 1930* (Washington, D.C.: GPO, 1970), 15–18; idem, *Television Receivers: Production and Maintenance Workers*, 16.

47. See Peter Donohue, "'Free Trade' Unions and the State: Trade Liberalization's Endorsement by the AFL-CIO, 1943–1962," *Research in Political Economy* 13 (1992): 54–64; U.S. Tariff Commission, *Television Receivers: Production and Maintenance Workers*, 3–9, and *Television Receivers and Certain Parts Thereof: Report to the President on Investigation No. TEA-I-21 under Section 301(b) of the Trade Expansion Act of 1962* (Washington, D.C.: GPO, 1971), A-3.

48. U.S. Tariff Commission, *Television Receivers: Production and Maiantenance Workers*, 3–9.

49. Patricia A. Wilson, *Exports and Local Development: Mexico's New Maquiladoras* (Austin: University of Texas Press, 1992), 53.

50. Human Relations Committee to workers, 15 September 1969, IUE Archives, RA II, box 175, folder 42 "Local 730, IUE–AFL-CIO"; Louis Vick to Richard Scupi, 21 January 1971, ibid.; Ciscel and Collins, "Runaway Blues," 5.

51. Pursell et al., "Trade Adjustment Assistance," 265–266.

52. Ibid.; *Memphis Commercial Appeal*, 5 November 1971.

53. The problem of effective trade adjustment assistance did not improve in the decades to come. See Ross Koppel and Alice Hoffman, "Dislocation Policies in the USA: What Should We Be Doing?" *Annals* 544 (March 1996): 121.

54. William R. Schriver, Roger L. Bowlby, and Donald E. Pursell, "Evaluation of Trade Readjustment Assistance to Workers: A Case Study," *Social Science Quarterly* 57 (December 1976): 553.

55. Hanna interview, 296, 287, 291; Pursell et al., "Trade Adjustment Assistance," 270.

56. *Memphis Press-Scimitar*, 31 March 1971, 7 September 1972, 9 August 1973, 9 November 1974, 17 and 18 April 1975. After sitting empty for years, the old RCA building finally became a parts warehouse for Caterpillar Tractors. See Tucker, *Memphis since Crump*, 160; Sandra Vaughn, "Memphis: Heart of the Mid-South," in *In Search of the New South: The Black Urban Experience in the 1970s and 1980s*, ed. Robert D. Bullard (Tuscaloosa: University of Alabama Press, 1989), 111–113; Honey, *Southern Labor*, 290.

57. Cobb, *Selling of the South*, 268; James C. Cobb, "Beyond Planters and Industrialists: A New Perspective on the New South," *Journal of Southern History* 54 (February 1988): 45–68; Wright, *Old South, New South*, 273.

4. The New Industrial Frontier: Ciudad Juárez, 1964–1978

1. "Boundary" is the political line; the concept of "frontier" has a more zonal, social connotation. This dualism has often led theorists to see a standard evolutionary development from frontier to boundary, but the frontier quality of a border zone tends to persist long after the linear boundary is established. See Peter Sahlins, *Boundaries: The Making of France and Spain in the Pyrenees* (Berkeley: University of California Press, 1989), 2–4; Gloria Anzaldúa, *Borderlands/La Frontera: The New Mestiza* (San Francisco: Aunt Lute Books, 1987), 3.

2. David J. Weber, *The Spanish Frontier in North America* (New Haven: Yale University Press, 1992), emphasizes the history of the zone as a social and political frontier; Raul A. Fernandez, *The United States–Mexico Border: A Politico-Economic Profile* (Notre Dame: University of Notre Dame Press, 1977), tends to see the area as a place where economic systems clash; Rodolfo Acuña, *América ocupada: Los chicanos y su lucha de liberación* (Mexico City: ERA, 1976), emphasizes the power of nationalism in the region; Tom Barry, Harry Browne, and Beth Sims, *The Great Divide: The Challenge of U.S.–Mexico Relations in the 1990s* (New York: Grove Press, 1994), offers a solid introduction to the First and Third World interests that conflict along the border.

3. Daniel D. Arreola and James R. Curtis, *The Mexican Border Cities: Landscape Anatomy and Place Personality* (Tucson: University of Arizona Press, 1993), 77.

4. Donald Baerresen, *The Border Industrialization Program of Mexico* (Lexington, Mass.: Heath-Lexington Books, 1971), 23.

5. INEGI, *Estadística de la industria maquiladora de exportación, 1989–1993* (Mexico City, 1994), 2.

6. Robert H. Schmidt and William J. Lloyd, "Patterns of Urban Growth in Ciudad Juárez," in *The Social Ecology and Economic Development of Ciudad Juárez*, ed. Gay Young (Boulder: Westview, 1986), 24–25. The Spanish sought, with mixed results, to establish a "frontier of inclusion" of Native Americans, whereas the Anglo-Americans sought a "frontier of exclusion" of the indigenous population. See Patricia Nelson Limerick, *The Legacy of Conquest: The Unbroken Past of the American West* (New York: Norton, 1987), 226; Oscar J. Martínez, *Border Boom Town: Ciudad Juárez since 1848* (Austin: University of Texas Press, 1978), 9.

7. Friedrich Katz, "Labor Conditions on Haciendas in Porfirian Mexico: Some Trends and Tendencies," *Hispanic American Historical Review* 54 (February 1974): 31–37.

8. Limerick, *Legacy of Conquest*, 229.

9. President Juárez took refuge in the town in 1865–66 to escape the French intervention.

10. Quoted in Martínez, *Border Boom Town*, 25. The *zona libre* did continue in Baja California Norte, the most remote border state, throughout the twentieth century.

11. Mario T. García, *Desert Immigrants: The Mexicans of El Paso, 1880–1920* (New Haven: Yale University Press, 1981), 235.

12. Arreola and Curtis, *Mexican Border Cities*, 90–96; Martínez, *Border Boom Town*, 30.

13. Edward L. Langston, "The Impact of Prohibition on the Mexican–United States Border: The El Paso–Ciudad Juárez Case" (Ph.D. diss., Texas Tech University, 1974), 244–245; Martínez, *Border Boom Town*, 63.

14. Josiah McC. Heyman, *Life and Labor on the Border: Working People of Northeastern Sonora, Mexico, 1886–1986* (Tucson: University of Arizona Press, 1991), 4–5.

15. Oscar J. Martínez, "Chicanos and the Border Cities: An Interpretative Essay," *Pacific Historical Review* 46 (February 1977): 91–101.

16. Peter Baird and Ed McCaughan, "Hit and Run," *NACLA's Latin America & Empire Report* 9 (July–August 1975): 4; Jorge Durand and Douglas Massey, "Mexican Migration to the United States: A Critical Review," *Latin American Research Review* 27 (1992): 6; Richard B. Craig, *The Bracero Program* (Austin: University of Texas Press, 1971), 23; and the best study of the program is Ernesto Galarza, *Merchants of Labor: The Mexican Bracero Story* (Charlotte, N.C.: McNally & Loftin, 1964). The INS official is quoted in Martínez, *Border Boom Town*, 113.

17. Vicki Ruiz, "By the Day or the Week: Mexicana Domestic Workers in El Paso," in *Women on the U.S.–Mexican Border: Responses to Change*, ed. Ruiz and Susan Tiano (Boston: Allen & Unwin, 1987), 61, 65–69; see also the series "Special Report: The Border," which ran in the *El Paso Herald-Post* in the summer of 1983; and Vicki Ruiz, "Working for Wages: Mexican Women in the Southwest, 1930–1980," Working Paper no. 19, Southwest Institute for Research on Women, University of Arizona, 1984.

18. Antonio Ugalde, *The Urbanization Process of a Poor Mexican Neighborhood* (Austin: University of Texas, 1974), 10, 38–41; Nestor A. Valencia, "Twentieth-Century Urbanization in Latin America and a Case Study of Ciudad Juárez" (M.A. thesis, University of Texas at El Paso, 1969), 90–91; Instituto Nacional de la Vivienda, *Estudio de viviendas en la zona fronteriza del norte* (Mexico City, 1967), 9–20.

19. In 1970 the population reached 424,135; in 1980, 567,365. Reliable employment statistics are notoriously difficult to obtain. Some observers claim that unemployment ran as high as 40 to 50 percent; see Peter Baird and Ed McCaughan, *Beyond the Border: Mexico and the U.S. Today* (New York: NACLA, 1979), 129.

20. Lauro Pallares Rodríguez, "Análisis sobre la viabilidad económica de tres industrias en Ciudad Juárez" (tesis de licenciado, UNAM, 1966), 35; Alicia Castellanos, *Ciudad Juárez: La vida fronteriza* (Mexico City: Nuestro Tiempo, 1981), 168.

21. Richard H. Hancock, *The Role of the Bracero in the Economic and Cultural Dynamics of Mexico: A Case Study of Chihuahua* (Stanford: Hispanic American Society, 1959), 121; *Programa Nacional Fronterizo* (Mexico City: PRONAF, 1961), 11–16 (for a collection of *juarenses*' opinions about their relationship with El Paso, see Castellanos, *Ciudad Juárez*, 185–186); *Comercio Exterior de México* 7 (July 1961): 2; Banco Nacional de México, "Economic Importance of Mexican Townships Bordering with U.S.A.," *Review of the Economic Situation of Mexico* 37 (June 1961): 8.

22. For comments by the Mexican minister of finance on the limits of the strategy of import substitution industrialization and the alternative offered by the export strategy that

emerged in the 1960s, see L. Antonio Aspra, "Import Substitution in Mexico: Past and Present," *World Development* 5 (1977): 111–123.

23. Kevin Middlebrook, *The Paradox of Revolution: Labor, the State, and Authoritarianism in Mexico* (Baltimore: Johns Hopkins University Press, 1995), 209–22. Although nationalist industrialization gave popular sectors a voice in the corporatist structure of Mexican politics, the rising tide of import substitution industrialization actually increased economic and social inequality. Inflated exchange rates, balance-of-payments problems, corruption, inefficient domestic industries, and an inability to export manufactured goods would lead to crisis in the 1980s.

24. Antonio J. Bermúdez, *Recovering Our Frontier Market: A Task in the Service of Mexico*, trans. Edward Fowlkes (Mexico City: Eufesa, 1968), 14, 105, 142 (translation modified); Antonio J. Bermúdez, interview by Oscar J. Martínez, 21 June 1974, transcript, Institute of Oral History, University of Texas at El Paso.

25. PRONAF, *Programa Nacional Fronterizo: Ciudad Juárez, Chihuahua* (Mexico City, 1963), 31; C. Daniel Dillman, "Urban Growth along Mexico's Northern Border and the Mexican National Border Program," *Journal of Developing Areas* 4 (July 1970): 501–505; *Comercio Exterior de México* 7 (April 1960): 10.

26. Bermúdez, *Recovering Our Frontier Market*, 27–29.

27. Alfonso Lugo to C. Lic. Noé Palomárez López, 8 July 1963, Ciudad Juárez, Archivo Municipal, Correspondencia del Ayuntamiento, quoted in Martínez, *Border Boom Town*, 198n (translation modified).

28. Craig, *Bracero Program*, 183; Anna-Stina Ericson, "Economic Development in the Mexican Border Areas," *Labor Developments Abroad*, June 1967, 33. *Ejidos* are lands held in common by communities and apportioned to be worked by specific individuals or worked by the community as a whole. Millions of acres were distributed as *ejidos* by President Lázaro Cárdenas in the 1930s during the most extensive agrarian reform in Mexican history. See Jorge Bustamante, "Maquiladoras: A New Face of International Capitalism on Mexico's Northern Frontier," in *Women, Men, and the International Division of Labor*, ed. June Nash and María Patricia Fernández-Kelly (Albany: SUNY Press, 1983), 233; Baird and McCaughan, *Beyond the Border*, 130–131; *Wall Street Journal*, 29 January 1963. See also Ronald B. Greenens, "Economic Adjustments to the Termination of the Bracero Program" (Ph.D. diss., University of Arkansas, 1967).

29. *El Paso Times*, 27 May 1980.

30. One facilitator of the program challenged the consensus view by arguing that the end of the bracero program had nothing to do directly with the development of the Border Industrialization Program, referring to the bracero program as "an after-the-fact rationalization." Yet the general pressures associated with unemployment were part of the overall problem the city leaders sought to address through the program, and most researchers and actors present at the time believe it to have been a pivotal factor.

31. *San Antonio Express-News*, 9 November 1969, quoted in Leslie Sklair, *Assembling for Development: The Maquila Program in Mexico and the United States* (La Jolla: Center for U.S.-Mexican Studies, University of California, San Diego, 1993), 101–102; Augusta Dwyer, *On the Line: Life on the U.S.–Mexican Border* (London: Latin American Bureau, 1994), 17.

32. The idea of the "twin plants" persisted for years, even though very few maquiladora operations had "twins" on the U.S. side of the border. Although almost all maquilas still had home operations somewhere in the United States, of the twelve electronics firms in El Paso, only four had twins in Ciudad Juárez. See A. Van de Ende and H. Haring, "Sunbelt Frontier and Border Economy: A Field-Work Study of El Paso" (working paper, Center for Inter-American and Border Studies, University of Texas at El Paso, 1983), 23. The idea was proposed in Arthur D. Little de México, S.A., *Industrial Opportunities for Ciudad Juárez: Report to the National Frontier Program of Mexico* (1964), 1–4, 28–29. For the de-

velopment of Puerto Rico, see Pedro A. Caban, "Industrial Transformation and Labour Relations in Puerto Rico: From 'Operation Bootstrap' to the 1970s," *Journal of Latin American Studies* 21 (1989): 559–591; for the connection between Bolin and Operation Bootstrap, see Baird and McCaughan, *Beyond the Border*, 131.

33. El Paso Industrial Development Corporation, *International Twin Plant Concept Fact Book* (El Paso, November 1968), 4.

34. Aureliano González-Vargas, former mayor of Juárez, assisted in establishing the program through his friendship with Presidents Gustavo Díaz Ordaz and Luis Echeverría; see *El Paso Times*, 27 May 1980.

35. *El Paso Times*, 21 May 1965; *Wall Street Journal*, 25 May 1967.

36. The tariff exemptions, as we saw in Chapter 3, allowed the reimportation of goods with a tariff to be charged only on the value added abroad. For discussions about the program within the Johnson administration, see Harry R. Turkel, "Report to the President on U.S. Mexican Border Trade Problems," 15 March 1967, 4–5, and Raymond Telles, "Memorandum for the President," 9 June 1967, 1–2, both in Memos and Miscellaneous, box 60, Mexico Country File, National Security Files, Lyndon Baines Johnson Presidential Library, Austin, Tex.

37. Jorge Carrillo Viveros and Alberto Hernández, "La mujer obrera en la industria maquiladora: El caso de Ciudad Juárez" (tesis profesional, Universidad Nacional Autónoma de México, 1982), 163.

38. Sklair, *Assembling for Development*, 99.

39. Quoted in Dwyer, *On the Line*, 16.

40. Sklair, *Assembling for Development*, 101–102, 111, 137n; interview with William Mitchell in *El Paso Herald-Post*, 24 April 1976.

41. Fulton Freeman, Introduction to Baerresen, *Border Industrialization Program of Mexico*, xii–xiii; airgram, U.S. Embassy to State Department, 4 February 1968; Anna-Stina Ericson, "An Analysis of Mexico's Border Industrialization Program," *Monthly Labor Review* 12 (May 1970), 40; Sklair, *Assembling for Development*, 48.

42. U.S. Tariff Commission, *Economic Factors Affecting the Use of Items 807.00 and 806.30 of the Tariff Schedules of the United States: Report to the President on Investigation 33-61 under Section 332 of the Tariff Act of* 1930, Publication 339 (Washington, D.C.: GPO, 1970), 66; Baerreson, *Border Industrialization Program of Mexico*, 24; Harold O. Walker, "Border Industries with a Mexican Accent," *Columbia Journal of World Business* 4 (January–February 1969): 25; Anthony Spaeth, "Maquila Boom," *Forbes*, 10 December 1979, 102.

43. "Labor's Big Push for Protectionism," *Fortune*, March 1973; Baird and McCaughan, "Hit and Run," 13.

44. John Charles Cassidy, "The Location of Foreign Direct Investment: The U.S. Offshore Electronics Industry in Mexico" (Ph.D. diss., University of Pennsylvania, 1979), 223. Evidence from another firm, Bloomington's Sarkes Tarzian, confirms the pattern. The independently owned tuner producer, which had spun off of RCA's operation in Bloomington, was one of the largest and most ambitious of the maquiladora operations in the late 1960s. The aggressively antiunion employer had followed a migratory track similar to RCA's. Movement of operations from Bloomington to the southern region (with plants in Clarksdale, Miss.; Clarendon, Ark.; and Brownsville, Tex.) was followed by a series of relocations to the border zone. By 1973 Tarzian had maquiladoras in Piedras Negras, Nuevo Laredo, Zaragoza, and Ciudad Acuna. Some evidence suggests that each of these moves was forced by increased labor militancy and a squeeze from competition as Tarzian shut down all its Bloomington electronics facilities in the decade following several unionization attempts at the plant. After a failed union vote in 1956, another in 1963, and again in 1966, the IBEW filed unfair labor practice charges that included accusations of distributing anti-union material, threatening employees with loss of their jobs, intimidating and bribing workers, using unfair and unhealthy work procedures against pro-union

employees, company spying, threatening employees with discharges and other reprisals, and blatant manipulation of the organization process through coercion and false promises to the workers. The NLRB found the company guilty of unfair labor practices, but the board was overruled on appeal. The company's notoriety continued in the border cities as well. Management boasted that "having two plants in different Mexican states means it's harder to be dictated to." Their performance in the BIP earned them a reputation as *maquiladoras golondrinas,* or "swallow plants," because they quickly flew away without warning. For the U.S. side of the story, see the collection of documents in Delbert C. Miller, "The History of Sarkes Tarzian, Inc.: The Story of Sarkes and Mary Tarzian and the Industrial Company They Built" (unpublished manuscript, n.d.), in the Indiana Room of the Bloomington Public Library; for the Mexican side, see Baird and McCaughan, "Hit and Run," 18–19.

45. Cassidy, "Location of Foreign Direct Investment," 223.

46. U.S. Commission for Border Development and Friendship, *Mexican Program of Border Industrialization* (El Paso, 1968), 7.

47. It is unclear to what extent the BIP factories drew further migrants into the border zone, but it does not appear to have been a strong pull force in and of itself. Mitchell R. Seligson and Edward J. Williams, *Maquiladoras and Migration: Workers in the Mexico–United States Border Industrialization Program* (Austin: University of Texas Press, 1981), found that between 5 and 16 percent of all BIP workers migrated specifically to work in the maquilas. Many firms, including RCA, required residence in the city for at least six months before a person was eligible for hire, so the people who were actually working in the factories did not include the most recent immigrants. María Patricia Fernández-Kelly, *For We Are Sold, I and My People: Women and Industry in Mexico's Frontier* (Albany: SUNY Press, 1983), 58–69, points to the complexity of the issue. Most of the maquila workers she surveyed were born in northern cities and had lived there an average of 14 years. Most migrant workers in the United States were men traveling alone; they had left their families behind, many of them in the border area. The subtlety of the process was revealed by a new maquila worker interviewed by Fernández-Kelly: she had asked a relative to move up to Juárez to take care of her children while she worked in the factory. Thus employment in a maquila increased the pressure to migrate in indirect ways. See also Cruz Arcelia Tanori Villa, *La mujer migrante y el empleo: El caso de la industria maquiladora en la frontera norte* (Mexico City: Instituto Nacional de Antropología e Historia, 1989). Both the U.S. and Mexican governments hoped that the program would slow migration to the United States by creating "a wall of jobs"; that hope appears unlikely to be fulfilled. See Francisco Rivera-Bátiz, "Can Border Industries Be a Substitute for Immigration?" *American Economic Review* 76 (May 1986): 263–268.

48. Baerresen, *Border Industrialization Program of Mexico,* 23–32; Sklair, *Assembling for Development,* 37–39; U.S. Department of Labor, *Employment and Earnings: States and Areas, 1939–1972* (Washington, D.C.: GPO, 1974).

49. Donald Baerresen, ed., *Mexico's Border Assembly Program* (Laredo: Institute for International Trade, Laredo State University, 1979), 103; El Paso Chamber of Commerce, *Proximity for Progress: El Paso/Juárez Twin Plant Handbook* (El Paso, 1981), sec. 2.1.

50. Rosario Hernández (pseudonym), 1978, interview by María Patricia Fernández-Kelly, tape recording, Institute of Oral History, University of Texas at El Paso.

51. INEGI, *Estadística de la industria maquiladora de exportación, 1975–1986* (Mexico City, 1988). The requirements listed here are from an RCA recruitment campaign advertised in *El Fronterizo* (Ciudad Juárez), 6 November 1980.

52. María Patricia Fernández-Kelly, "Las maquiladoras y las mujeres I," *Los Universitarios,* March 1979, 139–140.

53. Baerresen, *Border Industrialization Program of Mexico,* 34–35.

54. Sklair, *Assembling for Development*, 167. One of the most sophisticated of the analysts, Susan Tiano, argues, "The new international division of labor is replicating on a global scale the gender-based divisions within and between the domestic and capitalist modes of production": *Patriarchy on the Line: Labor, Gender, and Ideology in the Mexican Maquila Industry* (Philadelphia: Temple University Press, 1994), 30–47. As we have seen, the gendered divisions have historically been part of the labor strategies of the electronics industry, not a new development associated with the new international division of labor. What is consistent within the industry, however, can be quite new for the society. Viewed from the perspective of national development rather than that of industrial strategy, the change from ISI employment to assembly work in a transnational corporation does indicate a profound change in the gendered division of industrial labor for Mexico. From the perspective of developing nations, the change was from the extraction and processing of primary commodities to the provision of cheap labor to TNCs. See the comparison in Altha J. Cravey, "The Changing Relationship of the State, Market and Household: Industrial Strategies in Mexico" (Ph.D. diss., University of Iowa, 1993). See also Helen Safa, "Runaway Shops and Female Employment," *Signs* 7 (1981): 418–433.

55. Middlebrook, *Paradox of Revolution*, 106. See also Ruth Berins Collier and David Collier, *Shaping the Political Arena: Critical Junctures, the Labor Movement, and Regime Dynamics in Latin America* (Princeton: Princeton University Press, 1991), 239–242.

56. Víctor Manuel Durand Ponte, "The Confederation of Mexican Workers, the Labor Congress, and the Crisis of Mexico's Social Pact," in *Unions, Workers, and the State in Mexico*, ed. Kevin J. Middlebrook (La Jolla: Center for U.S.-Mexican Studies, University of California, San Diego, 1991), 87. Both confederations came under the umbrella of the Labor Congress in 1966, when numerous organizations signed a "Pact of Definitive and Permanent Unity of the Working Class," but the CTM maintained its dominance. See Middlebrook, *Paradox of Revolution*, 149–151. For a comparison of Mexican labor law with the corresponding laws of the United States and Canada, see Commission for Labor Cooperation, *Preliminary Report to the Ministerial Council on Labor and Industrial Relations Law in Canada, the United States, and Mexico* (Dallas, 1996).

57. Quoted in Michael Van Waas, "The Multinationals' Strategy for Labor: Foreign Assembly Plants in Mexico's Border Industrialization Program" (Ph.D. diss., Stanford University, 1981), 286–287.

58. *El Fronterizo* (Ciudad Juárez), 27 and 28 November 1976; Jorge Carrillo, *Dos décadas de sindicalismo en la industria maquiladora de exportación: Exámen en las ciudades de Tijuana, Juárez y Matamoros* (Mexico City: Universidad Autónoma Metropolitana–Iztapalapa/Miguel Ángel Porrúa, 1994), 130–132; Jorge Carrillo and Alberto Hernández, *Mujeres fronterizas en la industria maquiladora* (Mexico City/Tijuana: SEP/SEFNOMEX, 1985), 144.

59. *El Correo* (Ciudad Juárez), 30 December 1969; María Eugenia de la O Martínez, *Innovación tecnológica y clase obrera* (Mexico City: Universidad Autónoma Metropolitana–Iztapalapa/Miguel Ángel Porrúa, 1994), 124.

60. Carrillo, *Dos décadas de sindicalismo*, 8–12; Altha J. Cravey, "Cowboys and Dinosaurs: Mexican Labor Unionism and the State," in *Organizing the Landscape: Geographical Perspectives on Labor Unionism*, ed. Andrew Herod (Minneapolis: University of Minnesota Press, 1998), 77.

61. See José Luis Canchola P., "Maquiladoras, consentidas del Estado," paper presented at the Seminario sobre la Industria Maquiladora en Baja California, Tijuana, 1979; Fernández-Kelly, *For We Are Sold*, 144–150.

62. Devon G. Peña, "Class Politics of Abstract Labor: Organizational Forms and Industrial Relations in the Mexican Maquiladoras" (Ph.D. diss., University of Texas, Austin, 1983), 271–272.

63. *El Paso Herald-Post*, 30 December 1969; airgram, U.S. Embassy to Department of State, 4 June 1971; *El Paso Times*, 20 February 1975.

64. Although labor activism had become a major problem for the maquila managers— particularly in Nuevo Laredo—it was generally reported that "the two relatively inactive labor unions in Ciudad Juarez have not presented any serious problems"; see Peter G. Van der Spek, "Mexico's Booming Border Zone: A Magnet for Labor-Intensive American Plants," *Inter-American Economic Affairs* 24 (Summer 1975): 40; *El Correo* (Ciudad Juárez), 30 October 1974. One study predicted the need for a worker to be created every six minutes, and another claimed the need for an additional 105,000 "qualified" workers between 1975 and 1977: *El Correo* (Ciudad Juárez), 29 May and 9 August 1975.

65. Author's interview with Thomas F. Whitten, Indianapolis, 17 November 1994.

66. Van Waas, "Multinationals' Strategy," 348–349; Norma Iglesias Prieto, *Beautiful Flowers of the Maquiladora: Life Histories of Women Workers in Tijuana*, trans. Michael Stone with Gabrielle Winkler (1985; Austin: University of Texas Press, 1997).

67. Bermúdez interview. The term is Susan Marie Christopherson's in "Family and Class in the New Industrial City" (Ph.D. diss., University of California, Berkeley, 1983).

5. Moving toward a Shutdown: Bloomington, 1969–1995

1. Robert Doty, interview by R. T. King, 5 September 1980, interview 80-57, transcript, Indiana University Oral History Project (hereafter IUOHP,), Bloomington, 40–41; author's interview with Bill Cook, Bloomington, 18 March 1994. Workers' quiescence in a plant shutdown or layoff period is not uncommon. See Dale Andrew Hathaway, "The Politics of Deindustrialization: An Explanation of Worker Quiescence Based on Responses to the Decimation of Pittsburgh's Steel Industry in the 1980s" (Ph.D. diss., Cornell University, 1990). Even one of the most celebrated political efforts at industrial retention, launched in Youngstown, Ohio, was energized by clerical leaders rather than labor organizations and required tremendous efforts to overcome the demoralization that accompanied the disappearance of the arena of struggle itself, the plant. See Staughton Lynd, *The Fight against Shutdowns: Youngstown's Steel Mill Closings* (San Pedro, Calif.: Singlejack Books, 1982). For a comparison of community responses to capital flight, see Charles Craypo and Bruce Nissen, eds., *Grand Designs: the Impact of Corporate Strategies on Workers, Unions and Communities* (Ithaca: ILR Press, 1993).

2. The dichotomy of center and growth periphery is discussed in Michael Storper and Richard Walker, *The Capitalist Imperative: Territory, Technology, and Industrial Growth* (New York: Blackwell, 1989), 86, 180–181, 188–189.

3. Compare, for instance, Peter Drucker, "The Rise of Production Sharing," *Wall Street Journal*, 15 March 1977, and Folker Fröbel, Jürgen Heinrichs, and Otto Kreye, *The New International Division of Labor: Structural Unemployment in Industrialised Countries and Industrialisation in Developing Countries* (Cambridge: Cambridge University Press, 1980).

4. These tensions are discussed in Leslie Sklair, *The Sociology of the Global System: Social Change in Global Perspective* (Baltimore: Johns Hopkins University Press, 1991), particularly 102–104.

5. Elizabeth Shelton, interview by Mary L. Stevens, 3 February 1979, transcript, IUOHP, Bloomington; author's interview with Judy Cross, 21 March 1994, Bloomington; author's interview with Sandy Anderson, 22 March 1994, Bloomington.

6. Joseph Grunwald and Kenneth Flamm, *The Global Factory: Foreign Assembly in International Trade* (Washington, D.C.: Brookings, 1985), 222. In a period of relatively generous benefits, 71,700 were found to be fully eligible for benefits and 3,200 only partially

so. RCA was also not beyond doctoring the numbers of laid-off workers. When management announced the first 1,500 positions to be terminated, Ruth Anne Greene pored back over the list and found that they had actually terminated 2,100 operators. In an effort to maintain good community relations, the company frequently downplayed the number laid off and exaggerated the number rehired. "When they lay off they fib and when they call back they fib," she concluded. See Ruth Anne Greene interview by Emilye Crosby, 1990, tape recording, IUOHP, Bloomington; *Bloomington Herald-Times*, 7 October 1971.

7. For an overview of early developments in Taiwan, see Robert Che-Tong Chen, "The Electronics Industry in Taiwan: A History and Analysis" (Ph.D. diss., Santa Clara University, 1974).

8. *Television Digest*, 21 January 1980. See also Vincent A. LaFrance, "The United States Television Receiver Industry: United States versus Japan, 1960–1980" (Ph.D. diss., Pennsylvania State University, 1985), 267. The four major parts of a television set are the picture tube, which had always been made in factories specifically set up for glassblowing and sophisticated assembly; the tuner, a subassembly frequently bought from an outside supplier until electronic tuning made it a relatively simple part; the chassis, which contains the bulk of the circuitry, subassemblies, and components; and the cabinet, which houses the other parts. The chassis represents the bulk of the labor-intensive operations for assembly plants.

9. Author's interview with Emil B. Pruitt, 19 March 1994, Bloomington; Robert Brookshire, interview by R. T. King, 19 August 1980, interview 80–51, transcript, IUOHP, Bloomington, 7.

10. Author's interview with Alyce Hunter, 21 March 1994, Bloomington. Many interviewees told similar tales about processing foreign production, and like feelings were expressed about the products from Memphis. Author's interview with Bob Norris, 22 March 1994, Bloomington; Brookshire interview; Anderson interview; Beatrice Henderson, Robert Norris, and Louis Watson, interview by Emilye Crosby, 4 April 1990, tape recording, IUOHP, Bloomington. The Mexican workers, of course, could do the job. See Harley Shaiken, *Mexico in the Global Economy: High Technology and Work Organization in Export Industries* (La Jolla: Center for U.S.-Mexican Studies, University of California, San Diego, 1990).

11. LaFrance, "United States Television Receiver Industry," 79, 95, 228–229.

12. Ibid., 77, 317–318; Jonathan David Levy, "Diffusion of Technology and Patterns of International Trade: The Case of Television Receivers" (Ph.D. diss., Yale University, 1981), 71–72. Figures on Bloomington are from Thomson Consumer Electronics productivity calculations, July 1991, in papers of IBEW Local 1424, Bloomington; and U.S. Department of Labor, Bureau of Labor Statistics, *Productivity Measures for Selected Industries, 1958–1985*, Bulletin 2277 (1987), 243.

13. Author's interview with Thomas F. Whitten, 17 November 1994, Indianapolis.

14. *Television Digest*, 19 September 1966; LaFrance, "United States Television Receiver Industry," 273, 336, 354–356. RCA still received $50 million each year from Japanese firms for the licensing of color TV technologies begun in the 1960s.

15. Cross interview; author's interview with Kay Oliver, 18 March 1994, Bloomington.

16. Hunter interview; author's interview with Ken Beasley, 18 March 1994, Bloomington; *Indianapolis News*, 3 April 1990. The speedup and the high technology may have caused one death at the plant. When a cargo elevator jammed, a worker under pressure to keep production moving tried to fix it rather than wait for repair personnel. His rash act triggered an electronic beam that caused the elevator to fall, crushing his skull. The employee, John Craig, "may have pushed too hard at times . . . to keep television sets rolling down the line," a co-worker said. The press suggested that pressures from "cheap Mexican

labor" and "sagging sales projections" may have played a role in Craig's attempts to keep the line moving. The State of Indiana fined the company $20,000 for safety violations after the incident. See *Bloomington Herald-Times*, 19 and 20 September 1990, 22 February 1991.

17. Mary Frances Roll, interview by R. T. King, 18 August 1980, interview 80-50, transcript, IUOHP, Bloomington, 20.

18. IBEW report quoted in La France, "United States Television Receiver Industry," 80; Cross interview; Shelton interview, 45; Cook interview.

19. Shelton interview, 38–39; *Indiana Daily Student*, 30 July 1977.

20. Equal Employment Opportunity Commission, *First Annual Digest of Legal Interpretations, July 2, 1965, through July 1, 1966* (Washington, D.C., 1966), 15, 17. Almost everybody I interviewed remembered the checks for back pay. See, among others, Anderson interview; Cross interview; Betty Doty interview by R. T. King, 5 September 1980, transcript, interview 80-58, IUOHP, Bloomington; Shelton interview; Robert Doty interview. GE had replaced "men's" and "women's" categories by "heavy" and "light" decades earlier, under the UE. See Ruth Milkman, *Gender at Work: The Dynamics of Job Segregation by Sex during World War II* (Urbana: University of Illinois Press, 1987), 81–83.

21. Betty Doty interview, 9–11, 15; Anderson interview; Cross interview.

22. "25 Year Club 7th Annual Ceremonies," program, 11 November 1971, in Alyce Hunter's possession.

23. Cross interview; author's interview with David "Rocky" and Mary Gallagher, 19 November 1994, Bloomington.

24. Shelton interview, 8; Beasley interview.

25. Shelton interview; Cross interview; Cook interview.

26. Joska Hoke interview by Emilye Crosby, 3 April 1990, tape recording, interview 90-110, IUOHP, Bloomington.

27. In the end, the four antiheroes prevail over the college kids in a grueling relay bicycle race. The group's solidarity gives way to personal triumph as the main character is admitted into college after winning the race. Although the four friends swore they would stick together, the fate of the other three boys fades from the story as the film focuses on Dave's success. Even Dave's father, who has maintained throughout the film that he does not need a college education to support his family, takes up riding his own bicycle in celebration of his son's upward mobility.

28. For an analysis of the 1980 and 1990 census data sets, see Indiana Workforce Development, *Highlights: Monroe County* (Indianapolis, 1993) and *Job Service Openings and Starting Wages Report: Bloomington* (Indianapolis, October 1992–September 1993).

29. Beasley interview.

30. Robert Sobel, *RCA* (New York: Stein & Day: 1986), 199–216.

31. Kenneth Bilby, *The General: David Sarnoff and the Rise of the Communications Industry* (New York: Harper & Row, 1986), 1; A. F. Ehrbar, "Splitting Up RCA," *Fortune*, 22 March 1982, 62; LaFrance, "United States Television Receiver Industry," 485–486.

32. Beasley interview; *Indianapolis News*, 23 September 1986, 6 January 1987; *Indiana Business Journal*, 27 April 1987; *Indianapolis Star*, 20 December 1985; *Bloomington Herald-Telephone*, 9 October and 17 December 1986, 13 February and 24 March 1987.

33. Cook interview; Cross interview; Beasley interview; Oliver interview; *Indianapolis News*, 25 August 1987. See also author's interview with Ed Riedweg, 22 November 1994, Bloomington.

34. *Indianapolis News*, 25 August 1987, 3 April 1990; *Indianapolis Star*, 27 and 28 July 1987; *Bloomington Herald-Times*, 18 October 1990; Gallagher interview; Beasley interview.

35. *Bloomington Herald-Times*, 18 October 1990; *New York Times*, 13 September 1990, 7 April and 23 October 1994.

36. *Courier-Tribune*, 14 January 1973; *Bloomington Herald-Telephone*, 14 January 1973, 18 March 1980, 27 September 1981; *Indianapolis Star*, 22 March 1981.

37. *Indianapolis Star*, 23 November 1984; *Indianapolis News*, 15 November 1984. The strategy behind the development of SelectaVision is discussed in Margaret B. W. Graham, *RCA and the Videodisc: The Business of Research* (New York: Cambridge University Press, 1986).

38. *Indiana Daily Student*, 12 and 19 April 1984; *Bloomington Herald-Times*, 5, 19, and 29 April 1984; Cross interview; Cook interview.

39. *Bloomington Herald-Times*, 5 March 1989; *Indiana Business Journal*, July 1992; *Indianapolis News*, 6 October 1992.

40. See the review of HDTV in Kenneth D. Springer, "High-Definition Television: New World Order or Fortress America?" *Law and Policy in International Business* 24 (1993): 1309–1341.

41. Robert Reich explores the politics of "zero-sum nationalism" and "impassive cosmopolitanism" in *The Work of Nations* (New York: Vintage, 1991), 301–315; *Indianapolis News*, 8 January and 22 February 1993; *Bloomington Herald-Times*, 16 March 1993, 18 December 1997; author's interview with Philip G. McCabe, 20 November 1994, Bloomington. On the development and competition between the consortia, see *New York Times*, 26 January 1990; *Wall Street Journal*, 26 January 1990; *Washington Post*, 25 May 1993.

42. For a discussion of labor and the NAFTA debate, see William A. Orme, Jr., *Understanding NAFTA: Mexico, Free Trade, and the New North America* (Austin: University of Texas Press, 1996); Ian Robinson, *North American Trade as if Democracy Mattered* (Washington, D.C./Ottawa: CCA and ILRERF, 1993); Ricardo Grinspun and Maxwell A. Cameron, *The Political Economy of Free Trade* (New York: St. Martin's Press, 1993); Jefferson Cowie, "National Struggles in a Transnational Economy," *Labor Studies Journal* 4 (Winter 1997): 3–32.

43. An excellent analysis of the side accord and the alternatives is Lance Compa, "Another Look at NAFTA," *Dissent* (Winter 1997): 45–50.

44. Cook interview; U.S. Congress, Office of Technology Assessment, *U.S.-Mexico Trade: Pulling Together or Pulling Apart?* (Washington, D.C.: GPO, 1992), 166.

45. *Indianapolis Star*, 22 August 1990; *Indianapolis News*, 22 August 1990, 21 July 1992; *Bloomington Herald-Times*, 22 and 30 August 1990. An overview of events leading up to the final shutdown of Zenith is in *AFL-CIO News*, 20 February 1995; *Television Digest*, 7 February 1994.

46. "Conveyor" (Thomson Consumer Electronics press release), 23 March 1994.

47. *Bloomington Herald-Times*, 26 March 1994; "Conveyor," 23 March 1994. The "RCA Dome" became a focal point for discontent as the company continued to move jobs to Mexico. The Indiana state AFL-CIO leafleted the NCAA Final Four men's basketball championships with fliers calling Thomson "The Terminator" for saying *adiós* to American jobs. Even sportscasters, who would not use a corporate logo unless the company had bought advertising time on the network, used any name except RCA Dome. Finally, the Indiana legislature passed a bill that allowed it to raise taxes to avoid using the RCA name. See *Indianapolis Star*, 5 March and 5 April 1997.

48. *Bloomington Herald-Times*, 24, 25, and 26 March 1994; 6, 15, and 26 April 1994; 3 May 1994.

49. Ibid., 28 January 1998.

50. "Conveyor," February 13, 1997. The 15-month advance notification of the shutdown far exceeded the federal mandate under the Worker Adjustment and Retraining Notification (WARN) Act, which required only 60 days' written notice of a large-scale termination or layoff. For a short period, it looked as though the Bloomington workers might be saved, at least temporarily, by another buyout. Thomson Multimedia, the parent

company of Thomson Consumer Electronics, tried to sell the heavily indebted firm to the Korean firm Daewoo. The price tag of only one franc and assumption of the corporation's staggering debt outraged the French public. Critics in the Socialist Party declared "total opposition" to the government's "savage" privatization policies, and Gaullist parties attacked the deal as handing France over to Korea. This response, in combination with accusations of corruption, scuttled the deal. See *Washington Post*, 11 November and 7 December 1996; *Bloomington Herald-Times*, 16 February 1997.

51. *Bloomington Herald-Times*, 17 February 1997, 2 and 31 March 1997, 3 July 1998.

52. *Indiana Courier-Journal*, 28 May 1997; *Bloomington Herald-Times*, 20 December 1996, 16 February 1997, 26 January 1998. Ruth Milkman, in her study of GM auto workers, shows that those who accepted the company's buyout offer "expressed little nostalgia for the days they had worked at GM-Linden, with the important exception of the African-American respondents. Many did miss the high pay and excellent benefits that they had enjoyed at GM, but most felt that escaping from the plant's daily humiliations was adequate compensation for their losses in those areas": *Farewell to the Factory: Auto Workers in the Late Twentieth Century* (Berkeley: University of California Press, 1997), 134–135. The wages and benefits at Thomson, of course, will be sorely missed, but only with time will the former RCA workers be able to evaluate the freedom from driving 3,000 screws into the backs of hundreds of television sets before lunch or unboxing and placing on the line 240 television cabinets each hour.

53. *Indiana Daily Student*, 19 and 22 June 1997, 8 September 1997; *Bloomington Herald-Times*, 14 August and 30 September 1997.

54. *Bloomington Herald-Times*, 14 February and 29 March 1997; *Indiana Daily Student*; 18 February 1997.

6. The Double Struggle: Ciudad Juárez, 1978–1998

1. This narrative is derived from the data on a single anonymous questionnaire, no. 185, administered at RCA on 19 October 1978, among the data set collected by María Patricia Fernández-Kelly, in Fernández-Kelly Collection, Institute for Policy Studies, Johns Hopkins University; INEGI, *Estadística de la industria maquiladora de exportación, 1975–1986* (Mexico City: Secretaría de Programación y Presupuesto, 1988), table 3.

2. Devon G. Peña, *The Terror of the Machine: Technology, Work, Gender, and Ecology on the U.S.-Mexico Border* (Austin: University of Texas Press, 1997), 6.

3. María Eugenia de la O Martínez, *Innovación tecnológica y clase obrera: Estudio de caso de la industria maquiladora electrónica R.C.A. Ciudad Juárez, Chihuahua* (Mexico City: Universidad Autónoma Metropolitana–Itztapalapa/Miguel Ángel Porrúa, 1994), 90–92, 94; author's interview with Sandy Anderson, 22 March 1994, Bloomington; *Bloomington Herald-Times*, 28 January 1998.

4. Devon Peña, "*Tortuosidad*: Shop Floor Struggles of Female Maquiladora Workers," in *Women on the U.S.-Mexico Border: Responses to Change*, ed. Vicki L. Ruiz and Susan Tiano (Boston: Allen & Unwin, 1987), 130, 137, 140.

5. O Martínez, *Innovación tecnológica*, 135.

6. Important exceptions are Altha J. Cravey, "The Changing Relationship of the State, Market, and Household: Industrial Strategies in Mexico" (Ph.D. diss., University of Iowa, 1993), which compares the traditional domestic industrial workers in Mexico with export workers in the border zone. Studies that capture change over time in a single place on the border include Josiah McC. Heyman, *Life and Labor on the Border: Working People of Northeastern Sonora, Mexico, 1886–1986* (Tucson: University of Arizona Press, 1991), and

Alicia Castellanos, *Ciudad Juárez: La vida fronteriza* (Mexico City: Nuestro Tiempo, 1981), both of which offer rich historical perspectives on working-class life on the border.

7. Survey data from Jorge Carrillo V. and Alberto Hernández, "La mujer obrera en la industria maquiladora: El caso de Ciudad Juárez" (tesis profesional, UNAM, 1982) ($n = 476$); María Patricia Fernández-Kelly, *For We Are Sold: Women and Industry in Mexico's Frontier* (Albany: SUNY Press, 1983) ($n = 510$); Devon G. Peña, "The Class Politics of Abstract Labor: Organizational Forms and Industrial Relations in the Mexican Maquiladoras" (Ph.D. diss., University of Texas, 1983) ($n = 223$). A useful comparative chart of available data is in Jorge Carrillo, *Dos décadas de sindicalismo en la industria maquiladora de exportación: Examen en las ciudades de Tijuana, Juárez y Matamoros* (Mexico City: Universidad Autónoma Metropolitana–Iztapalapa/Miguel Ángel Porrúa, 1994), 90. Data on RCA workers calculated from 120 survey questionnaires extracted from the sample of 510 conducted by María Patricia Fernández-Kelly in 1978, Fernández-Kelly collection, Institute for Policy Studies, Johns Hopkins University.

8. Kathleen A. Staudt, "Economic Change and Ideological Lag in Households of Maquila Workers in Ciudad Juárez," in *The Social Ecology and Economic Development of Ciudad Juárez,* ed. Gay Young (Boulder: Westview, 1986), 101–105, 110–112. The survey data were collected from 5,000 households in Ciudad Juárez by the Universidad Autónoma de Ciudad Juárez; the studies in the Young collection are based on a sample of 1,236 questionnaires from that data set.

9. A basic guide to labor law for plant operators can be found in Jorge Millan, Mario Perera, and Jon Lowe, "The ABC's of Mexican Labor Relations," *Twin Plant News,* May 1990, 40–43; Edward George, "Impact of the Maquilas on Manpower Development and Economic Growth on the U.S.-Mexico Border" (paper presented at the meeting of the North American Economics and Finance Association, Montreal, 1986), 22.

10. Staudt, "Economic Change," 104–105.

11. See the discussion of the cultural changes sponsored by maquila employment and the complexities of prostitution in Fernández-Kelly, *For We Are Sold,* 133–150, especially 142–144.

12. Susan Marie Christopherson, "Family and Class in the New Industrial City" (Ph.D. diss., University of California, Berkeley, 1982), 13; Fernández-Kelly, *For We Are Sold,* 56.

13. Conversation with Gustavo de la Rosa Hickerson, Ciudad Juárez, 1994.

14. Peña, *Terror of the Machine,* 138–139.

15. Devon Peña, "Class Politics of Abstract Labor," 461. See Paulo Freire, *Pedagogy of the Oppressed* (New York: Continuum, 1993 [1970]).

16. Kathleen Staudt, "Programming Women's Empowerment: A Case from Northern Mexico," in *Women on the U.S.-Mexican Border: Responses to Change,* ed. Vicki L. Ruiz and Susan Tiano (Boston: Allen & Unwin, 1987), 159–161, 171.

17. Gay Young, "Gender Identification and Working-Class Solidarity among Maquila Workers in Ciudad Juárez," Working Papers on Women in International Development no. 124, Michigan State University, 1986, 12–13; María Patricia Fernández-Kelly, "Alternative Education for Maquiladora Workers," *Grassroots Development,* nos. 6/7 (Spring 1983), 41–46. For a very enthusiastic and detailed overview of the course of COMO's development, see Peña, *Terror of the Machine,* 135–173.

18. The entire seniority system was often circumvented by temporary contracts with workers that precluded the state protections.

19. Leslie Sklair, *Assembling for Development: The Maquila Program in Mexico and the United States* (La Jolla: Center for U.S.-Mexican Studies, University of California, San Diego, 1993), 67; emphasis his. The seniority figure, calculated from personnel figures given to Jorge Carrillo by RCA, matches the findings of five other studies conducted

between 1978 and 1983, which showed the average seniority in the border industries to be about three years. See Carrillo, *Conflictos laborales en la industria maquiladora* (Tijuana: CEFNOMEX, 1985), 19.

20. Quoted in Jorge Carrillo and Alberto Hernández, *Mujeres fronterizas en la industria maquiladora* (Mexico City/Tijuana: SEP/CEFNOMEX, 1985), 136; Fernández-Kelly, *For We Are Sold*, 67–68.

21. Quoted in Peña, "Class Politics of Abstract Labor," 90–92.

22. *El Diario de Juárez*, 18 and 19 July 1977; *El Fronterizo* (Ciudad Juárez), 12 May and 19 July 1977. In 1981, 90% of all labor conflicts brought before the labor board were for unjustified dismissals; see *El Correo* (Ciudad Juárez), 21 January 1981; *El Fronterizo* (Ciudad Juárez), 12 March 1981; Carrillo and Hernández, "La mujer obrera," 90–92; Fernández-Kelly, *For We Are Sold*, 67–68; Sklair, *Assembling for Development*, 179.

A series of articles in *Twin Plant News*, the publication for maquila managers, tried to explain the high turnover rate. Although the worker-interviewees told the management consultant/author that they wanted more money, the researcher concluded that high turnover was essentially a "social" problem that needed to be solved within the plant. See *Twin Plant News*, March, April, and June 1990. G. W. Lucker, "The Hidden Costs of Worker Turnover: A Case Study in the Maquila Industry," *Journal of Borderlands Studies* 2 (Spring 1987): 93–98, calculated that a plant of 375 workers with a turnover rate of 8.1% per month cost the company $60,000 and encouraged the corporations to see Mexico as a "cheap labor country."

23. Carrillo and Hernández, *Mujeres fronterizas*, 176–183; Peña, "Class Politics of Abstract Labor," 80, 82–83.

24. Carrillo and Hernández, *Mujeres fronterizas*, 135.

25. See, for instance, *El Universal* (Ciudad Juárez), 9 September 1982; Carrillo y Hernández, *Mujeres fronterizas*, 135–136; Peña, "Class Politics of Abstract Labor," 93n; O Martínez, *Innovación tecnológica*, 99; *Bloomington Herald-Times*, 26 January 1998.

26. Joseph Grunwald and Kenneth Flamm, *The Global Factory: Foreign Assembly in International Trade* (Washington, D.C.: Brookings, 1985), 245.

27. *Twin Plant News*, January 1987, 48.

28. *El Universal* (Ciudad Juárez), 2, 13, and 15 March 1982; *Diario de Juárez*, 11 and 30 March 1982. For currency values, see Grunwald and Flamm, *Global Factory*, 159; and Carrillo, *Dos décadas de sindicalismo*, 124.

29. Wayne Cornelius, *The Political Economy of Mexico under de la Madrid: The Crisis Deepens, 1985–1986* (La Jolla: Center for U.S.-Mexican Studies, University of California, San Diego, 1986), 1; Kevin Middlebrook, *The Paradox of Revolution: Labor, the State, and Authoritarianism in Mexico* (Baltimore: Johns Hopkins University Press, 1995), 214–215, 257–258; Sklair, *Assembling for Development*, 72.

30. These cuts came in addition to the 1977 legislation passed under the López Portillo administration to provide additional investment incentives and to make Mexico more competitive with other Third World countries. Employees regarded as "inefficient" could be dismissed without severance pay, management gained more say over pay and working conditions, the 30-day sub-minimum-wage probationary period was extended to 90 days, and the social security responsibilities of the companies were reduced.

31. The relationship between neoliberalism, authoritarianism, and prospects for democracy are well analyzed in Maria Lorena Cook, Kevin J. Middlebrook, and Juan Molinar Horcasitas, "The Politics of Economic Restructuring in Mexico: Actors, Sequencing, and Coalition Change," in *The Politics of Economic Restructuring: State-Society Relations and Regime Change in Mexico*, ed. Cook, Middlebrook, and Horcasitas (La Jolla: Center for U.S.-Mexican Studies, University of California, San Diego, 1994), 33–40.

32. Middlebrook, *Paradox of Revolution*, 265; Francisco Zapata, *El sindicalismo mexicano frente a la restructuración* (Mexico City: Colegio de México, Instituto de Investigaciones de las Naciones Unidas para el Desarrollo Social, 1995), 153–154, points to the tradeoff organized labor made during the restructuring period which helped maintain its role within the state; Enrique de la Garza Toledo, "The Restructuring of State-Labor Relations in Mexico," in Cook et al., *Politics of Mexican Restructuring*, 214–216, agrees on the CTM's traditional response but emphasizes a new brand of corporatism in Mexico which will place more emphasis on negotiations at the level of the firm rather than the state; Middlebrook, *Paradox of Revolution*, 269.

33. INEGI, *Estadística de la industria maquiladora, 1975–1986*, table 1; Leslie Sklair, *Sociology of the Global System: Social Change in Global Perspective* (Baltimore: Johns Hopkins University Press, 1991), 102; Sklair, *Assembling for Development*, 68.

34. Dalia Barrera Bassols, *Condiciones de trabajo en las maquiladoras de Ciudad Juárez* (Mexico City: Instituto Nacional de Antropología e Historia, 1990), 75. The popular term *charrismo* can be traced to the government-supported railroad union leader Jesús Díaz de León and his successful scheme to undercut the radical and independent railroad workers' unions in 1948. The event was called *el charrazo* after his penchant for rodeo and horsemanship (which made him a *charro*, or horseman). "Sellout" unionism has been called *charrismo* ever since.

35. See the series of interviews in O Martínez, *Innovación tecnológica*, 174–176. The general impression of unions held by maquila workers throughout the city was mixed. When asked if unions functioned as they thought they should perform, 50% of Juárez workers said yes. Of the 38% who responded with an unambiguous no, most believed that Juárez unions favored the company or did nothing at all, and the majority of the workers without a union in their plant did not want one. Of the remaining 12%, 4% believed that unions did their jobs "more or less" and 8% did not know; 49% belonged to the CTM, 20% to the CROC, 1 to a company union, and 29% did not know to which central they belonged. See Guillermina Valdés-Villalva, "Perfil obrero maquila en Cd. Juárez" (unpublished COMO survey, 1989), tables 48–58.

36. *El Universal* (Ciudad Juárez), 4 and 10 November 1982; *El Diario de Juárez*, 6, 7, and 9 November 1982, 1 June 1983.

37. *El Universal* (Ciudad Juárez), 4 and 10 November 1982; *El Diario de Juárez*, 6, 7, and 9 November 1982, 1 June 1983.

38. In Reynosa the 7,000-odd workers at Zenith, RCA's major competitor, faced a similar crisis of wage erosion. They asked for a wage increase and when the union did not respond, they set up a blockade outside the plant. Fidel Velázquez, CTM's president, happened to be at the border at the time and settled the dispute by guaranteeing free elections. The Zenith employees voted in their democratic slate, including four women on the union committee, but the CTM voided the election. A subsequent hunger strike by the leadership ended in police violence against the workers. That was the end of the struggle. See Sklair, *Assembling for Development*, 135.

39. Ibid., 65–67, 72. The *Maquiladora Newsletter*, August 1986, examined the problem. In the first quarter of 1986, value added in dollars grew only 2% over the first quarter of 1985, but to obtain such growth, the maquilas had to increase their value added by 34% in constant pesos over the same period.

40. *El Paso Times*, 5 July 1986; Alejandra Salas-Porras, "Maquiladoras y burguesia regional," *El Cotidiano* (Ciudad Juárez), special issue 1 (1987), 51–58. The local politics of these changes are exceedingly complex. Barrio was elected mayor of Juárez in 1983 on the PAN ticket. Jaime Bermúdez, head of the Grupo Bermúdez, supported Barrio at the time. Though Miguel de la Madrid's administration had moved toward decentralization, the

president pushed Bermúdez to run as the PRI candidate for governor against Barrio. Some observers argue that Bermúdez only temporarily defected from the PAN to draw attention and power to the maquila facilitators. During the protests, however, the Bermúdez properties were frequently targeted as symbols of the ruling elite.

41. See the detailed coverage of events every day of July 1986 in *El Diario de Juárez* and *El Universal* (Ciudad Juárez), plus *El Paso Times*, 3, 5, 11, 12, 15, 20, 26, 28, 29, and 30 July 1986. As the historian Oscar Martínez explained, the PRI's tactic was to "'smash Barrio once and for all.'. . . Hence the crude, blatant tactics in taking the election. But Barrio now becomes the injured party. In my view the PRI's tactics backfired": *El Paso Times*, 16 July 1986. Indeed, Barrio returned to win the governorship the next term.

42. Carrillo, *Dos décadas de sindicalismo*, 236–237.

43. Yemile Mizrahi, "Rebels Without a Cause? The Politics of Entrepreneurs in Chihuahua," *Journal of Latin American Studies* 26 (1994): 139. A full one-third of the maquila workers continued to support the ruling PRI. Only 4% declared themselves to be supporters of Cuauhtémoc Cárdenas's PRD, the left-wing opposition party widely thought to have won the 1988 elections. About one-third of the workers polled had no political sympathies, but 31% backed the right-wing PAN. The majority of the workers believed Salinas had stolen the elections. See Valdés-Villalva, "Perfil obrero," tables 71, 78, 84; Dalia Barrera Bassols and Lilia Venegas Aguilera, *Testimonios de participación popular femenina en la defensa del voto, Ciudad Juárez, Chihuahua, 1982–1986* (Mexico City: Instituto Nacional de Antropología e Historia, 1992), 59; Carrillo, *Dos décadas de sindicalismo*, 236–238.

44. Carrillo, *Dos décadas de sindicalismo*, 236–238; O Martínez, *Innovación tecnológica*, 124–126; *Diario de Juárez*, 25, 26, 27, and 28 October 1986; *El Fronterizo* (Ciudad Juárez), 25, 26, 27, 28, and 29 October 1986.

45. *Semanario Ahora* (Ciudad Juárez), March 1987.

46. O Martínez, *Innovación tecnológica*, 126.

47. Much of the interview is transcribed in Peña, "Class Politics," 465–467; Peña, *Terror of the Machine*, 147.

48. Fernández-Kelly, *For We Are Sold*, 134.

49. Carrillo, *Dos décadas de sindicalismo*, 146. An index to the major strikes can be found on 203–238.

50. Jorge Carrillo V., "The Evolution of the Maquiladora Industry: Labor Relations in a New Context," in *Unions, Workers, and the State in Mexico*, ed. Kevin Middlebrook (La Jolla: Center for U.S.-Mexico Studies, University of California, San Diego, 1991), 238. For a more detailed discussion of the gender aspects of the situation, see Leslie Salzinger, "Producing Gender, Engendering Production: The Constitution and Control of Ciudad Juárez's Maquiladora Workforce," a paper delivered at the Center for U.S.-Mexican Studies, University of California, San Diego, 17 November 1993.

51. *El Fronterizo* (Ciudad Juárez), 26 March 1984. A list of the largest industrial parks compiled by Conway Data Business Park Survey was reported in *El Paso Herald-Post*, 6 November 1990.

52. Lisa M. Catanzarite and Myra H. Strober, "The Gender Recomposition of the Maquiladora Workforce in Ciudad Juárez," *Industrial Relations* 32 (Winter 1993): 141; Ciudad Juárez management interviews in Salzinger, "Producing Gender, Engendering Production"; George, "Impact of the Maquilas," 25. As late as 1989, 81% of 273 workers surveyed had had their jobs no more than two to three years. See Valdés-Villalva, "Perfil obrero," table 22. The estimate is from María Patricia Fernández-Kelly, "Mexican Border Industrialization: Female Labor Force Participation and Migration," in *Women, Men, and the International Division of Labor*, ed. June Nash and Fernández-Kelly (Albany: SUNY Press, 1983), 220.

53. Catanzarite and Strober, "Gender Recomposition," 134, 145; Jeffrey T. Brannon

and William G. Lucker, "The Impact of Mexico's Economic Crisis on the Demographic Composition of the Maquiladora Labor Force," *Journal of Borderland Studies* 4 (1990): 39–70; Susan Tiano, *Patriarchy on the Line: Labor, Gender, and Ideology in the Mexican Maquila Industry* (Philadelphia: Temple University Press, 1994), 164. Government tax policy complicates the issue of raises. All "unskilled operators" are paid the same minimum wage, as the marginal tax rates on earnings above the minimum wage are very high and workers earning more than the minimum for their grade end up paying a high penalty tax on that portion of their earnings. Managers can circumvent the problem by upgrading personnel, but they prefer to offer a variety of tax-free fringe benefits.

54. Leonard Mertens and Laura Palomares, "El surgimiento de un nuevo tipo de trabajador en la industria de alta tecnología: El caso de la electrónica" (Mexico City: International Labour Organization, 1986), 33. The probability of high-technology production and investment in the border zone, despite its workers' alleged low level of skill, is well examined in Harley Shaiken, *Mexico in the Global Economy: High Technology and Work Organization in Export Industries* (La Jolla: Center for U.S.-Mexican Studies, University of California, San Diego, 1990).

55. Peña, *Terror of the Machine*, 59 (Philip G. McCabe expressed similar sentiments in my interview with him, 20 November 1994, Bloomington); COMO, "Primer taller de análisis sobre aprendizaje en la producción y transferencia de tecnología en la industria de maquila de exportación" (Ciudad Juárez: CEFNOMEX, 1984), mimeo, found that 52% of women had made a change in machinery or a product in order to increase production, 48% had performed some form of "engineering" work, 20% had made changes to the production system, and 90% did regular maintenance on tools and machinery—all at standard operator's wages. See also Devon Peña, "Skilled Activities among Assembly Line Workers in Mexican-American Border Twin Plants," *Campo Libre* 2, nos. 1–2 (1984): 189–207; Peña, "Class Politics," 328, 341n.

56. Quoted in Peña, *Terror of the Machine*, 59.

57. *Boletín QLP* (RCA-Thomson, Ciudad Juárez), 19 August 1988; O Martínez, *Innovación tecnológica*, 103, 107–114; *El Universal* (Ciudad Juárez), 15 April 1982, 25 July 1983, 12 September 1985, 13 September 1986.

58. McCabe interview. This was the first time a corporation had been allowed to buy land rather than lease it. The state of Chihuahua, McCabe commented, was "moving into the twenty-first century."

59. Ibid. Of course, just-in-time production is very vulnerable to labor unrest, since there are no parts or finished products in the warehouses that can be shipped when production is stopped. See Andrew Sayer, "New Developments in Manufacturing: The Just-In-Time System," *Capital and Class* 30 (Winter 1986): 43–72.

60. Carrillo, *Dos décadas de sindicalismo*, 124; *Chicago Tribune*, 20 April 1995, quoted in Sarah Anderson, John Cavanagh, and Jonathan Williams, *Workers Lose, CEOs Win (II): The Widening Wage Gap Between U.S. Executives and Their U.S. and Mexican Workers* (Washington, D.C.: Institute for Policy Studies, 1995).

61. *El Norte de Juárez*, 1, 2, 4, and 6 February 1995; *Diario de Juárez*, 3, 4, and 5 February 1995; *El Paso Times*, 2 and 3 February 1995.

62. *El Financiero* (Mexico City), 6 February 1995; *La Jornada*, 19 February 1995; *New York Times*, 1 and 9 February 1995; *Norte de Juárez*, 7 February 1995.

63. *Bloomington Herald-Times*, 3 February 1998. Before these events I asked Bill Cook, Local 1424's elected business agent, if the union would offer support to the Mexican workers in the event of a strike. He said that such a decision would have to come from the union's International office. Efforts toward transnational solidarity had been well under way in Camden's original UE, but no such leadership emerged at the old craft-based IBEW.

64. *Diario de Juárez*, 7 and 8 February 1995.

65. Ibid., 7, 8, and 9 February 1995; *El Paso Times*, 7 and 9 February 1995; Coalition for Justice in the Maquiladoras, *1994 Annual Report* (San Antonio, 1995), 14; *La Jornada* (Mexico City), 19 February 1995. The plant manager, the brother of the governor, earned more than U.S.$100,000 a year. It is worth noting that the length of time between plant opening and first overt labor conflict was the same in Bloomington and in Ciudad Juárez: 26 years.

66. Evaluation criteria for analyzing the industry are drawn from Sklair, *Assembling for Development*, 244–254; INEGI, *Estadística de la industria maquiladora de exportación, 1989–1993* (Aguascalientes, 1994), 5.

67. Patricia A. Wilson, *Exports and Local Development: Mexico's New Maquilas* (Austin: University of Texas Press, 1992), 125, lays out the important policy strategies for connecting local networks of businesses and manufacturers to meet the needs of TNCs as a path to deepen developmental strategies based on foreign investment.

68. *El Paso Times*, 8 February 1995; *Bloomington Herald-Times*, 26 January 1998.

69. Héctor Aguilar Camín and Lorenzo Meyer, *In the Shadow of the Mexican Revolution: Contemporary Mexican History, 1910–1989*, trans. Luis Alberto Fierro (Austin: University of Texas Press, 1993), 267.

70. Maria Cook, "Mexican State-Labor Relations and the Political Implications of Free Trade," *Latin American Perspectives* 22 (Winter 1995): 87–93; Héctor De la Cueva, "Cracks in PRI Unionism," *NACLA Report on the Americas* 30 (January/February 1997): 16–27; Francisco Zapata, "¿Crisis del sindicalismo en México?" *Revista Mexicana de Sociología* 56 (January–March 1994): 79–88.

71. *Before* the peso crisis, a market-basket survey of U.S. and maquila auto workers expressed the difference in dramatic terms. A North American UAW worker could buy a gallon of milk with 11.1 minutes of work; one in the border zone had to work 146.3 minutes for the same milk. A pound of fresh whole chicken required 4.5 minutes in the United States, 87.0 minutes in Juárez; for a dozen eggs the price in labor was 4.1 vs. 69.8 minutes. For further details see Ruth Rosenbaum, *Market Basket Survey: A Comparison of the Buying Power of Maquiladora Workers in Mexico and UAW Assembly Workers in GM Plants in the U.S.* (San Antonio: Coalition for Justice in the Maquiladoras, 1994). This study completely undermines the argument, advanced by William A. Orme Jr., that the wage difference is reduced to only 3:1 when the low productivity of Mexican workers is factored into the equation. See Orme, *Understanding NAFTA: Mexico, Free Trade, and the New North America* (Austin: University of Texas Press, 1996), 125–128.

72. *Bloomington Herald-Times*, 26 January 1998; *Chicago Tribune*, 29 November 1998.

73. Aihwa Ong, "The Gender and Labor Politics of Postmodernity," *Annual Review of Anthropology* 20 (1991): 280–281, 284; Devon Peña takes a similar perspective. "Maquiladoras are postmodern factory systems . . . characterized by fragmented and partialized labor processes, by multinational workforces, and by a pastiche-like organization culture": *Terror of the Machine*, 46.

7. The Distances In Between

1. Author's interview with Sandy Anderson, 22 March 1994, Bloomington; Carolyn Carmichael, "Quantum Leapers Trip to El Paso/Juárez," *CE Horizon*, 27 May 1993.

2. *Bloomington Herald-Times*, 26 January 1998.

3. Despite well-organized community opposition, Bloomington's Wetterau Foods distribution center shut down in March 1994, throwing 350 employees out of work.

4. Joseph A. Schumpeter, *Capitalism, Socialism, and Democracy* (New York: Harper, 1942), 81–86. The Camden case is immensely complicated by the issue of race as it surfaced

after World War II. For a similar case, see Thomas J. Sugrue, *The Origins of the Urban Crisis: Race and Inequality in Postwar Detroit* (Princeton: Princeton University Press, 1996).

The argument that the social change sponsored by the presence of the plant itself was an important factor in the eventual relocation of production appears to fly in the face of another classic economic theory—Raymond Vernon's idea of the product life cycle. A firm manufacturing a new product, his theory predicts, requires a high degree of flexibility in order to make quick changes in the design, and needs rapid communication between customers, suppliers, and producers. A new product is also relatively insulated from competitive pressures so the firm can afford to pay higher wages. As the product matures in its life cycle and demand increases, however, manufacturing becomes standardized, competitors enter the market, and the need for communication, skill, and flexibility in production declines. Once a company has used its skilled workforce to standardize, automate, and perfect the manufacturing process of a certain product, Vernon's argument goes, the work may then be shifted to a peripheral location where the various factors of production are cheaper. He first applied his idea specifically to the radio industry, which decentralized from the New York metropolitan area to midwestern branch plants and then to international investment in the developing world—patterns that appear to explain RCA's movement of its radio and television production from Camden to Bloomington in 1940 and then from Bloomington to Juárez in the 1970s. The product life cycle can be complemented with a social history life cycle of production in the community. See Raymond Vernon, "International Investment and International Trade in the Product Cycle," *Quarterly Journal of Economics* 80 (May 1966): 190–207; and Vernon, *Metropolis 1985: An Interpretation of the Findings of the New York Metropolitan Region Study* (Cambridge: Harvard University Press, 1960); see also Seev Hirsch, "The United States Electronics Industry in International Trade," in *The Product Life Cycle and International Trade*, ed. Louis T. Wells (Cambridge: Division of Research, Graduate School of Business Administration, Harvard University, 1972), 40; discussion in Michael Storper and Richard Walker, *The Capitalist Imperative: Territory, Technology, and Industrial Growth* (New York: Basil Blackwell, 1989), 119–122; and Jonathan David Levy, "Diffusion of Technology and Patterns of International Trade: The Case of Television Receivers" (Ph.D. diss., Yale University, 1981), 188–189. On the breakdown of the traditional paradigms in international trade theory, see Richard Harris, "New Theories of International Trade and the Pattern of Global Specialization" in *Industry on the Move: Causes and Consequences of Industrial Location in the Manufacturing Industry*, ed. Gijsbert van Liemt (Geneva: International Labour Organization, 1992), 25–50.

5. William Greider, *One World, Ready or Not: The Manic Logic of Global Capitalism* (New York: Simon & Schuster, 1997), 13.

6. Doreen Massey, *Spatial Divisions of Labour: Social Structures and the Geography of Production* (London: Macmillan, 1984), 85, 59. See also Gordon L. Clark, *Unions and Communities under Siege* (New York: Cambridge University Press, 1989), 9.

7. Anthony Giddens, Foreword to *NowHere: Space, Time, and Modernity*, ed. Roger Friedland and Deirdre Boden (Berkeley: University of California Press, 1994), xii.

8. Author's interview with Philip G. McCabe, 20 November 1994, Bloomington.

9. Massey, *Spatial Divisions of Labour*, 57.

10. Pierre Bourdieu, *The Logic of Practice* (Stanford: Stanford University Press, 1980), 56, 65. See also Craig Calhoun, *The Question of Class Struggle: Social Foundations of Popular Radicalism during the Industrial Revolution* (Chicago: University of Chicago Press, 1982), 157–158.

11. Edward Soja, "Ontological Space," in his *Postmodern Geographies: The Reassertion of Space in Social Theory* (London: Verso, 1989), 132.

12. John Comaroff and Jean Comaroff, *Ethnology and the Historical Imagination*

(Boulder: Westview, 1992), 51. The concept of "psychic distance" was originally developed to explain and quantify the factors that prevented firms from learning about, understanding, and trading with other foreign firms. Essentially, something other than pure geographic distance was needed to explain the uneven distribution of world trade even when market prices might dictate buying or selling with a certain country. A similar pattern holds for the labor movement: cultural and national differences make others more distant than the imperatives of their material needs for joint action might otherwise dictate. See Kjell A. Nordstrøm and Jan-Erik Vahlne, "Is the Globe Shrinking? Psychic Distance and the Establishment of Swedish Sales Subsidiaries during the Last 100 Years," in *International Trade: Regional and Global Issues*, ed. Michael Landeck (New York: St. Martin's Press, 1994), 41–42.

13. Ruth Ann Greene, interview by Emilye Crosby, 10 April 1990, interview 90-108, tape recording, Indiana University Oral History Project (hereafter IUOHP), Bloomington.

14. Robert Doty, interview by R. T. King, interview 80-57, 5 September 1980, transcript, IUOHP, Bloomington, 30; this contemporary passage speaks to the historical continuity of the ideas presented in David Roediger, *Wages of Whiteness: Race and the Making of the American Working Class* (London: Verso, 1991).

15. Donald Winfield Jarrell, "A History of Collective Bargaining at the Camden-Area Plants of the Radio Corporation of America, with Special Attention to Bargaining Power" (Ph.D. diss., University of Pennsylvania, 1968), 120–121; Anthony Spaeth, "The Maquila Boom," *Forbes*, 10 December 1979, 102. The Mexican workers also consistently referred to Bloomington as "Baltimore."

16. For an extraordinarily successful example of community-based transnational solidarity at Ravenswood Steel, see Andrew Herod, "The Practice of International Labor Solidarity and the Geography of the Global Economy," *Economic Geography* 71 (October 1995): 341–364.

17. Benedict Anderson, *Imagined Communities: Reflections on the Origin and Spread of Nationalism* (London: Verso, 1991), 6–7. For an elaboration of national interest and the anti-NAFTA fight, see Jefferson Cowie, "National Struggles in a Transnational Economy: A Critical Analysis of U.S. Labor's Response to NAFTA," *Labor Studies Journal* 21 (Winter 1997): 3–32. On the tension between capital and community, see Barry Bluestone and Bennett Harrison, *The Deindustrialization of America: Plant Closings, Community Abandonment, and the Dismantling of Basic Industry* (New York: Basic Books, 1982): 15–21.

18. Karl Marx and Friedrich Engels, *The Communist Manifesto* (New York: Penguin, 1967), 102. Marx contradicts himself with regard to Ireland: there, he argues, the bourgeoisie heighten national conflict by using nationalism as an ideological tool to distract workers' attention from class antagonisms; see Michael Lowy, "Marxists and the National Question," *New Left Review* 96 (March–April 1976): 81–100. Migration and capital mobility are two sides of the same low-wage, labor-control coin. Whether the sweatshops go to Mexico or immigrants come to the unregulated garment district of Los Angeles or New York, the end is the same. Both moves can also foment nationalist backlashes against foreigners. See the important study by Saskia Sassen, *The Mobility of Capital and Labor* (Cambridge: Cambridge University Press, 1988); and for the migratory system within the United States, see Jacqueline Jones, *The Dispossessed: America's Underclasses from the Civil War to the Present* (New York: Basic Books, 1992).

19. Lizabeth Cohen, *Making A New Deal: Industrial Workers in Chicago, 1919–1939* (New York: Cambridge University Press, 1990), 357.

20. See Greider, *One World, Ready or Not*.

21. Soja, *Postmodern Geographies*, 63; Selig Perlman, *A Theory of the Labor Movement* (New York: Macmillan, 1928); Storper and Walker, *Capitalist Imperative*, 227.

22. David Harvey, *The Condition of Postmodernity: An Enquiry into the Origins of Cultural Change* (Cambridge, Mass.: B. Blackwell, 1989), 235–239.

23. This is the argument in Lloyd Ulman, *Rise of the National Trade Union: The Development and Significance of Its Structure, Governing Institutions, and Economic Policies* (Cambridge: Harvard University Press, 1955).

24. Steve Fraser, "The Labor Question," in *The Rise and Fall of the New Deal Order*, ed. Fraser and Gary Gerstle (Princeton: Princeton University Press, 1989), 55–78. See also Nelson Lichtenstein, *Labor's War at Home: The CIO in World War II* (New York: Cambridge University Press, 1982), 242; and his "From Corporatism to Collective Bargaining," in Fraser and Gerstle, *Rise and Fall of the New Deal Order*, 122; David Gorden, Michael Reich, and Richard Edwards, *Segmented Work, Divided Workers: The Historical Transformation of Work in the United States* (New York: Cambridge University Press, 1982); David Montgomery, "The New Deal Formula," in his *Workers' Control in America* (New York: Cambridge University Press, 1979), 153–180.

25. Ian Roxborough, *Unions and Politics in Mexico: The Case of the Automobile Industry* (New York: Cambridge University Press, 1984), 27. This is Roxborough's portrayal of the "typical view" of a weak and ineffectual labor movement; he argues that the Mexican labor movement is actually more diverse and threatening than most observers believe.

26. Stephen Amberg, "The Contrasting Consequences of Institutions and Politics: Labor and Industrial Relations in the United States and Germany," *Political Power and Social Theory* 10 (1996): 195–227; Gordon L. Clark, *Unions and Communities under Siege: American Communities and the Crisis of Organized Labor* (New York: Cambridge University Press, 1989), 58; Ronald W. Schatz, *The Electrical Workers: A History of Labor at General Electric and Westinghouse, 1923–1960* (Urbana: University of Illinois Press, 1983), 63. Today, however, the UE is the single most active union in transnational organizing efforts. For the South see James C. Cobb, *The Selling of the South: The Southern Crusade for Industrial Development, 1936–1990* (Urbana: University of Illinois Press, 1993), particularly chap. 4.

27. The exception in Mexico is the eastern border state of Tamaulipas; see Edward J. Williams and John T. Passé-Smith, *The Unionization of the Maquiladora Industry: The Tamaulipan Case in National Context* (San Diego: Institute for Regional Studies of the Californias at San Diego State University, 1992). For an understanding of geographical aspects of new and old industrialization strategies, see Altha Cravey, "Changing Relationship of the State, Market, and Household: Industrial Strategies in Mexico" (Ph.D. diss., University of Iowa, 1993). Statistics are from Laurence Whitehead, "Mexico's Economic Prospects: Implications for State-Labor Relations," in *Unions, Workers, and the State in Mexico*, ed. Kevin J. Middlebrook (La Jolla: Center for U.S.-Mexican Studies, University of California, San Diego, 1991), 64.

28. The debate and testimony are collected in U.S. Tariff Commission, *Economic Factors Affecting the Use of Items 807.00 and 806.30 of the Tariff Schedule of the United States: Report to the President on Investigation No. 332–61 under Section 3332 of the Tariff Act of 1930* (Washington, D.C.: GPO, 1970); *Congressional Record* 117, pt. 25 (28 September 1971): 5136; Oscar J. Martínez, *Border Boom Town* (Austin: University of Texas Press, 1978), 138.

29. Harry Browne and Beth Sims, *Runaway America: U.S. Jobs and Factories on the Move* (Albuquerque: Resource Center Press, 1993), 95.

30. Jefferson Cowie and John D. French, "NAFTA's Labor Side Accord: A Textual Analysis," *Latin American Labor News* 9 (1993–94): 5–8.

31. Harry R. Turkel, Report to the President on U.S.-Mexican Border Trade Problems, 15 March 1967, Mexico Country File, vol. 3, Document 77e, NSF files, Lyndon B. Johnson Library, Austin, Tex.

32. John H. Christman, "Border Industries Foster New Jobs, More Exports," *Mexican-American Review* 36 (February 1968): 12, 15; Ambassador Orville Freeman, Introduction to Donald Baerresen, *The Border Industrialization Program of Mexico* (Lexington, Mass.: Heath-Lexington Books, 1971), xii; Irwin Ross, "Labor's Big Push for Protectionism," *Fortune*, March 1973, 169. For an analysis of U.S. labor's 1986 campaign against the maquilas and section 807, see El Colegio de la Frontera Norte, "Aspectos económicos y políticos del debate sobre las maquiladoras en Estados Unidos" (a report to the governor the State of Chihuahua) (Tijuana, 9 March 1987), mimeo; with specific reference to electronics see William Bywater, "The Impact of the Maquiladora Program on the Mexican and U.S. Workers and the Role of the U.S. Commerce Department in Promoting U.S. Investment in Mexico" (Washington, D.C.: International Union of Electronic, Electrical, Technical, Salaried, and Machine Workers, 25 November 1986).

33. Later trade liberalization plans did make the linkages between trade and labor rights. The Generalized System of Preferences, the Caribbean Basin Initiative, the Overseas Private Investment Corporation, and section 301 of the Omnibus Trade and Competitiveness Act of 1988 all made an explicit, if difficult to use, connection between trade and labor rights.

34. Seyla Benhabib, "Democracy and Difference: Reflections on Rationality, Democracy, and Postmodernism," unpublished manuscript, 1994, 30, quoted in Nicola Lacey, "Community in Legal Theory: Idea, Ideal, or Ideology?" *Studies in Law, Politics, and Society* 15 (1996): 105.

35. The center was launched in conjunction with the Teamsters and the equally small and creative Mexican union FAT. The success of the dissident unions in the UE-FAT alliance begs the question of the distance between the AFL-CIO and the CTM, as well as the Canadian Labour Congress. For the problems involved in these three labor centrals' efforts to find common ground during the NAFTA battles, see John D. French, Jefferson Cowie, and Scott Littlehale, *Labor and NAFTA: A Briefing Book* (Durham: Duke-UNC Program in Latin American Studies, 1994).

36. Foucault is quoted in Friedland and Boden, *NowHere*, 13; Gibbon is quoted in William Appleman Williams, *The Great Evasion* (Chicago: Quadrangle, 1964), 56. For the prospects of transforming the current side accord into a more potent weapon, see Lance Compa, "Another Look at NAFTA," *Dissent* (Winter 1997): 45–50; and Stephen Herzenberg, "Switching Tracks: Using NAFTA's Labor Agreement to Move toward the High Road," Border Briefing 2, Interhemispheric Resource Center/International Labor Rights Fund (Albuquerque, N.M., May 1996).

37. I borrow the term from Lourdes Arizpe and Josefina Aranda, "The 'Comparative Advantages' of Women's Disadvantages: Women Workers in the Strawberry Export Business in Mexico," *Signs* 7 (1981): 453–473.

38. Susan Tiano, *Patriarchy on the Line: Labor, Gender, and Ideology in the Mexican Maquila Industry* (Philadelphia: Temple University Press, 1994), 222–225.

39. Ibid., 58.

40. María Patricia Fernández-Kelly, *For We Are Sold: Women and Industry in Mexico's Frontier* (Albany: SUNY Press, 1983), 131–132.

41. Author's interview with Ken Beasley, 18 March 1994, Bloomington.

42. Leslie Sklair, for instance, argues that "the practical dilemma is whether women and girls are better off outside or inside the factories": *Assembling for Development: The Maquila Industry in Mexico and the United States* (La Jolla: Center for U.S.-Mexican Studies, University of California, San Diego, 1993), 168.

43. Ruth Milkman, "Women Workers, Feminism, and the Labor Movement since the 1960s," in *Women, Work, and Protest: A Century of U.S. Women's Labor History*, ed. Milkman (Boston: Routledge & Kegan Paul, 1985), 302. Fernández-Kelly agrees that unions in

Ciudad Juárez have been reluctant "to include in their agenda issues that are particularly relevant to women": *For We Are Sold*, 148.

44. C. Wright Mills, *The Sociological Imagination* (New York: Oxford University Press, 1959), 3.

45. Jeffrey Henderson and Manuel Castells, "Techno-economic Restructuring, Socio-political Processes and Spatial Transformation: A Global Perspective," in *Global Restructuring and Territorial Development*, ed. Henderson and Castells (London: Sage, 1987), 7; Harvey, *Condition of Postmodernity*.

46. Giovanni Arrighi, "Marxist Century, American Century: The Making and Remaking of the World Labour Movement," *New Left Review* 179 (1990): 51–52. The labor lawyer Thomas Geoghegan writes, "I worry about the Third World. Not the Third World 'over there,' but the Third World down the street": *Which Side Are You On? Trying to Be for Labor When It's Flat on Its Back* (New York: Farrar, Straus & Giroux, 1991), 218.

47. Clark W. Reynolds, "Will a Free Trade Agreement Lead to Wage Convergence? Implications for Mexico and the United States," in *U.S.-Mexico Relations: Labor Market Interdependence*, ed. Jorge Bustamante, Reynolds, and Raúl A. Hinojosa Ojeda (Stanford: Stanford University Press, 1992), 477–486; Terry Collingsworth, J. William Goold, and Pharis Harvey, "Time for a Global New Deal," *Foreign Affairs*, January/February 1994, 8–14. TCE's violation of environmental standards is covered in *Los Angeles Times*, 30 June 1997.

48. Benjamin R. Barber, *Jihad vs. McWorld* (New York: Times Books, 1995); Jeremy Rifkin, *End of Work: The Decline of the Global Labor Force and the Dawn of the Post-Market Era* (New York: Putnam, 1995), 197; Jeremy Brecher and Tim Costello, *Global Village or Global Pillage: Economic Reconstruction from the Bottom Up* (Boston: South End Press, 1994); and Robert Reich, *Work of Nations: Preparing Ourselves for 21st-Century Capitalism* (New York: Knopf, 1995). Immanuel Wallerstein also argues that in the twenty-first century, "the class struggle will be a race struggle." See his response to Charles Tilly in "Response: Declining States, Declining Rights?" *International Labor and Working-Class History* 47 (Spring 1995): 27.

49. Todd A. Eisenstadt and Cathryn L. Thorup use the formulation to discuss immigration issues in *Caring Capacity versus Carrying Capacity: Community Responses to Mexican Immigration in San Diego's North County* (La Jolla: Center for U.S.-Mexican Studies, University of California, San Diego, 1994), vii.

50. Discussion with Rocky Gallagher, November 1994, Bloomington.

BIBLIOGRAPHY

Archives and Personal Papers

Camden County Historical Association, Camden, New Jersey.
El Centro de Orientación de la Mujer Obrera Papers, El Colegio de la Frontera Norte, Ciudad Juárez, Chihuahua.
Hagley Museum and Library, Wilmington, Delaware.
Powers Hapgood Papers, Manuscript Department, Lilly Library, Indiana University.
Indiana Room, Bloomington Public Library, Bloomington, Indiana.
International Brotherhood of Electrical Workers, Local 1424, Bloomington, Indiana. Papers and meeting minutes.
International Union of Electrical Workers Archives, Rutgers University.
Lyndon Baines Johnson Papers, University of Texas, Austin.
Johnson/RCA Victor Museum, Dover, Delaware.
Junta de Conciliación y Arbitraje, Ciudad Juárez, Chihuahua.
John L. Lewis Papers (microfilm), University Publications of America, Frederick, Maryland.
National Archives, Suitland, Maryland.
RCA Files, Memphis Room, Shelby County Public Library, Memphis, Tennessee.
RCA Files, Monroe County Historical Society, Bloomington, Indiana.
Regional Archives of the National Archives, Philadelphia, Pennsylvania.
Special Collections, University of Texas at El Paso.
United Electrical Workers Archives, University of Pittsburgh Library.
Urban Archives, Temple University.
Herman B. Wells Papers, Indiana University.

Periodicals

Bloomington Herald-Telephone
Bloomington Herald-Times

Bloomington Evening World
Bloomington Star-Courier
Bloomington Tribune
Camden Courier-Post
Comercio Exterior de México
El Correo (Ciudad Juárez)
El Diario de Juárez
Electronics Industries
El Fronterizo (Ciudad Juárez)
El Norte de Juárez
El Paso Herald-Post
El Paso Times
Indianapolis News
Indiana Daily Student
La Jornada (Mexico City)
Memphis Commercial Appeal
Memphis Press-Scimitar
New York Times
Philadelphia Evening Bulletin
Philadelphia Inquirer
Philadelphia Record
RCA Victor Family News (Bloomington)
Television Digest
Television Digest and FM Reports
Twin Plant News (Ciudad Juárez)
El Universal (Ciudad Juárez)
Wall Street Journal

Interviews

Sandy Anderson. Interview by the author, 22 March 1994, Bloomington. Tape recording.

Pauline Archer. Interview by Emilye Crosby, 4 April 1990, interview 90–105, Indiana University Oral History Program, Bloomington (hereafter IUOHP). Tape recording.

Ken Beasley. Interview by author, 18 March 1994, Bloomington. Tape recording.

Antonio J. Bermúdez. Interview by Oscar J. Martínez, 21 June 1974, University of Texas at El Paso Institute of Oral History. Transcript.

Henry Boxman. Interview by R. T. King, 28 August 1980, interview 80–56, IUOHP. Transcript.

Robert Brookshire. Interview by R. T. King, 19 August 1980, interview 80–51, IUOHP. Transcript.

James B. Carey. Oral autobiography, Columbia University Oral History Research Office.

Jane Chestnutt. Interview by Emilye Crosby, 27 February 1990, interview 90–107, IUOHP. Tape recording.

Darrell "Bear" Clayton. Interview by the author, 21 March 1994, Bloomington. Tape recording.

Bill Cook. Interview by the author, 18 March 1994, Bloomington. Tape recording.

Judy Cross. Interview by the author, 18 and 21 March 1994, Bloomington. Tape recording.

Betty Doty. Interview by R. T. King, 5 September 1980, interview 80–58, IUOHP. Transcript.

Robert Doty. Interview by R. T. King, 5 September 1980, interview 80–57, IUOHP. Transcript.

Julius Empsak. Interview, Oral History Collection, Columbia University Libraries. Transcript.

David "Rocky" Gallagher and Mary Gallagher. Interview by the author, 19 November 1994, Bloomington. Tape recording.

Frank and Lucile Godsey. Interview by R. T. King, 27 August 1980, interview 80–55, IUOHP. Transcript.

Ruth Ann Greene. Interview by Emilye Crosby, 4 October 1990, interview 90–108, IUOHP. Tape recording.

Pat Hanna. Interview by Donald E. Pursell, William R. Schriver, and Roger Bowlby, 3 January 1974, in Pursell, Schriver, and Bowlby, "Trade Adjustment Assistance: An Analysis of Impacted Worker Benefits on Displaced Workers in the Electronics Industry." Memphis: Center for Manpower Studies, Memphis State University, 1974.

Donald Hansen. Interview by R. T. King, 21 August 1980, IUOHP. Transcript.

Beatrice Henderson, Robert Norris, and Louis Watson. Interview by Emilye Crosby, 4 April 1990, IUOHP. Tape recording.

Alyce Hunter. Interview by Emilye Crosby, 13 March 1990, IUOHP. Tape recording.

———. Interview by the author, 21 March 1994, Bloomington. Tape recording.

Joska Hoke. Interview by Emily Crosby, 3 April 1990, interview 90–110, IUOHP. Tape recording.

John D. Leffler. Interview by R. T. King, 22 August 1980, IUOHP. Transcript.

Maquiladora workers. Interviews by María Patricia Fernández-Kelly, 25 hours of tape recordings with anonymous interviewees, set no. 435 (access restricted), Institute of Oral History, University of Texas at El Paso.

Philip G. McCabe. Interview by the author, 20 November 1994, Bloomington. Tape recording.

Bob Norris. Interview by the author, 22 March 1994, Bloomington. Tape recording.

Kay Oliver. Interview by the author, 18 March 1994, Bloomington. Tape recording.

Arthur J. Olsen. Interview by Vincent Giroux, 21 February 1979, IUOHP. Transcript.

John Oscar Pardue. Interview by R. T. King, 26 August, 1980, interview 80–54, IUOHP. Transcript.

E. B. Pruitt. Interview by the author, 19 March 1994, Bloomington. Tape recording.

Ed Riedweg. Interview by the author, 22 November 1994, Bloomington. Tape recording.

Mary Frances Roll. Interview by Robert Barrows, 10 February 1977, interview 77–4, IUOHP. Transcript.

———. Interview by Emilye Crosby, 21 February 1990, interview 90–113, IUOHP. Tape recording.

———. Interview by R. T. King, 18 August 1980, interview 80–50, IUOHP. Transcript.

Elizabeth Shelton. Interview by Mary Stevens, February 1979, IUOHP. Transcript.

Anna Belle Van Hook (formerly Ooley). Interview by the author, 22 March 1994, Bloomington. Tape recording.

Thomas F. Whitten. Interview by the author, 17 November 1994, Indianapolis. Tape recording.

Bert Wisely. Interview by the author, 17 March 1994, Bloomington. Tape recording.

Dissertations, Theses, and Unpublished Studies

Carrillo V., Jorge, and Alberto Hernández. "La mujer obrera en la industria maquiladora: El caso de Ciudad Juárez." Tesis profesional, Universidad Nacional Autónoma de México, 1982.

Cassidy, John Charles. "The Location of Foreign Direct Investment: The U.S. Offshore Electronics Industry in Mexico." Ph.D. diss., University of Pennsylvania, 1979.

Chen, Robert Che-tong. "The Electronics Industry in Taiwan: A History and Analysis." Ph.D. diss., Santa Clara University, 1974.

Christopherson, Susan Marie. "Family and Class in the New Industrial City." Ph.D. diss., University of California, Berkeley, 1983.

Cole, Peter. "Shaping Up and Shipping Out: The Philadelphia Waterfront during and after the I.W.W. Years, 1913–1940." Ph.D. diss., Georgetown University, 1997.

Cravey, Altha J. "The Changing Relationship of the State, Market, and Household: Industrial Strategies in Mexico." Ph.D. diss., University of Iowa, 1993.

George, Edward. "Impact of the Maquilas on Manpower Development and Economic Growth of the U.S.-Mexico Border." Paper presented to the North American Economics and Finance Association Conference, Montreal, 1986.

Greenens, Ronald B. "Economic Adjustments to the Termination of the Bracero Program." Ph.D. diss., University of Arkansas, 1967.

Hathaway, Dale Andrew. "The Politics of Deindustrialization: An Explanation of Worker Quiescence Based on Responses to the Decimation of Pittsburgh's Steel Industry in the 1980s." Ph.D. diss., Cornell University, 1990.

Jarrell, Donald Winfield. "A History of Collective Bargaining at the Camden Area Plants of the Radio Corporation of America, with Special Attention to Bargaining Power." Ph.D. diss., University of Pennsylvania, 1968.

King, George Davis. "The Industrialization of Indiana, 1860–1920." Ph.D. diss., Indiana University, 1963.

LaFrance, Vincent A. "The United States Television Receiver Industry: United States versus Japan, 1960–1980." Ph.D. diss., Pennsylvania State University, 1985.

Langston, Edward L. "The Impact of Prohibition on the Mexican-United States Border: The El Paso–Ciudad Juárez Case." Ph.D. diss., Texas Tech University, 1974.

Leins, James F. "The History and Development of the Showers Brothers Company." M.A. thesis, Indiana University, 1938.

Levy, Jonathan David. "Diffusion of Technology and Patterns of International Trade: The Case of Television Receivers." Ph.D. diss., Yale University, 1981.

Lotman, Sylvia S. "An Evaluation of Test Scores, Behavior during Test Performance, and an Interview in Selecting Radio Assembly Workers." M.A. thesis, Indiana University, 1944.

Mertens, Leonard. "El surgimiento de un nuevo tipo de trabajador en la industria de alta tecnología: El caso de la electrónica." Paper presented at the conference "Crisis, Proceso de Trabajo, y Clase Obrera," sponsored by the International Labor Organization, Xalapa, Veracruz, 1987.

Miller, Delbert C. "The History of Sarkes Tarzian, Inc.: The Story of Sarkes and Mary Tarzian and the Industrial Company They Built." Bloomington, n.d.

Mitchell, Jacquelyn. "Preliminary Report on the Impact of Mexico's Twin Plant Industry along the U.S.-Mexico Border." El Paso: Organization of United States Border Cities, 1977. Mimeo.

Mutlu, Servet. "Interregional and International Mobility of Industrial Capital: The Case of the American Automobile and Electronics Companies." Ph.D. diss., University of California at Berkeley, 1979.

Orzack, Louis. "Employment and Social Structure: A Study of Social Change in Indiana." Ph.D. diss., Indiana University, 1953.

Pallares Rodríguez, Lauro. "Análisis sobre la viabilidad económica de tres industrias en Ciudad Juárez." Tesis licenciado, Universidad Nacional Autónoma de México, 1966.

Peña, Devon G. "The Class Politics of Abstract Labor: Organizational Forms and Industrial Relations in the Mexican Maquiladoras." Ph.D. diss., University of Texas, 1983.

Ruiz, Vicki. "Working for Wages: Mexican Women in the Southwest, 1930–1980." Working Paper no. 19. Tucson: Southwest Institute for Research on Women, University of Arizona, 1984.

Salzinger, Leslie. "Producing Gender, Engendering Production: The Constitution and Control of Ciudad Juárez's Maquiladora Workforce." Paper presented at the Center for U.S.-Mexican Studies, University of California, San Diego, 1993.

Savage, Virginia M., and Pamela F. Service. "A Brief History of Monroe County, Indiana." Monroe County Historical Society Museum, n.d.

Soukup, William Raymond. "Strategic Response to Technological Threat in the Electronics Components Industry." Ph.D. diss., Purdue University, 1979.

Valencia, Nestor A. "Twentieth-Century Urbanization in Latin America and a Case Study of Ciudad Juárez." M.A. thesis, University of Texas at El Paso, 1969.

Van de Ende, Arthur A. P. M., and Henk A. Haring. "Sunbelt Frontier and Border Economy: A Field-Work Study of El Paso." Working paper, Center for Inter-American and Border Studies, University of Texas at El Paso, 1983.

Van Waas, Michael. "The Multinationals' Strategy for Labor: Foreign Assembly Plants in Mexico's Border Industrialization Program." Ph.D. diss., Stanford University, 1981.

Williams, Rolland Edward. "The Major Industrial Trends of Bloomington, Indiana." M.A. thesis, Indiana University, 1963.

Young, Gay. "Gender Identification and Working-Class Solidarity among Maquila Workers in Ciudad Juárez." Working Paper on Women in International Development no. 124. Michigan State University, 1986.

Government Publications and Agency Reports

Arthur D. Little de México, S.A. "Industrial Opportunities for Ciudad Juárez: Report to the National Frontier Program of Mexico." Mexico City, 1964. Mimeo.

Camden, City of. *City of Camden Twenty-Year Analysis: 1971–1991*. Camden: Department of Administration and Finance, 1991.

Camden County Chamber of Commerce. *Two Hundred and Fiftieth Anniversary, 1681–1931*. Camden, 1931.

Chávez, Armando. *Programa nacional fronterizo*. Mexico City: PRONAF, 1961.

El Paso Chamber of Commerce. *Proximity for Progress: El Paso/Juárez Twin Plant Handbook*. El Paso, 1981.

El Paso Industrial Development Corporation. *International Twin Plant Concept Fact Book*. El Paso, 1968.

Equal Employment Opportunity Commission. *First Annual Digest of Legal Interpretations, July 2, 1965, through June 1, 1996*. Washington, D.C.: GPO, 1966.

Federal Communications Commission. *Color Television Hearings, 3, 4 May 1950*. Washington, D.C.: GPO, 1950.

Governor's Commission on Unemployment Relief. *State Department of Public Welfare, Statistical Survey of Public Assistance in Indiana*. Indianapolis, 1937.

Indiana Department of Commerce, Agriculture, Industry, and Public Relations. *Indiana Plant Location Fact Book*. Indianapolis, 1961.

———. Economic Research Division. *Indiana Community Profiles*. Indianapolis, 1969.

Indiana Employment Service. "Labor Market Developments Report: For Bloomington, Indiana, Labor Market Area." Indianapolis, 1943.

Indiana Workforce Development. "Highlights: Monroe County." Indianapolis, 1993.

———. "Job Service Openings and Starting Wages Report: Bloomington." Indianapolis, 1993.

INEGI. *Estadística de la industria maquiladora de exportación, 1975–1986*. Mexico City: Secretaría de Programación y Presupuesto, 1988.

———. *Estadística de la industria maquiladora de exportación, 1989–1993*. Aguascalientes, 1994.

Instituto Nacional de la Vivienda. *Estudio de viviendas en la zona fronteriza del norte*. Mexico City, 1967.

Kafiris, Vasilios Basil. *Indiana Manufacturing Growth Patterns, 1958–1967*. Indianapolis: Indiana Department of Commerce, 1969.

National Labor Relations Board. *Decisions and Orders of the National Labor Relations Board*. Vol. 2. Washington: GPO, 1937.

Nieda, Frederick von, and Arthur M. Taylor, eds. *Industrial Camden, New Jersey*. Camden: Works Progress Administration, 1937.

PRONAF. *Programa Nacional Fronterizo: Ciudad Juárez*. Mexico City, 1963.

Pursell, Donald E., William R. Schriver, and Roger Bowlby. "Trade Adjustment Assistance: An Analysis of Impacted Worker Benefits on Displaced Workers in the Electronic Industry." (Under U.S. Department of Labor contract.) Center for Manpower Studies, Memphis State University, 1974.

Ryle, Patricia. *An Economic Profile of Camden County*. Camden, N.J.: New Jersey Department of Labor, 1978.

Secretaría de Industria y Comercio. *La frontera norte: Diagnóstica y perspectivas*. Mexico City, 1975.

———. *Zona fronteriza norte de México: Viabilidad industrial*. Mexico City, 1974.

———. Dirección General de Industrias. *Programa de industrialización de la frontera norte de México*. Mexico City, 1968.

United States Commission for Border Development and Friendship. *Mexican Program of Border Industrialization*. El Paso: CODAF/4, 1968.

United States Congress. Joint Committee on the Economic Report, 82d Cong., 1st sess. *Underemployment of Rural Families*. Washington, D.C.: GPO, 1951.

———. Office of Technology Assessment. *U.S.-Mexico Trade: Pulling Together or Pulling Apart?* Washington, D.C.: GPO, 1992.

———. Senate. Subcommittee of the Committee on Education and Labor. *Hearings before a Subcommittee of the Committee on Education and Labor . . . Pursuant to S. Res. 266 (74th Congress), A Resolution to Investigate . . . Interference with the Right of Labor to Organize and Bargain Collectively*, pt. 8, 75th Cong., 1st sess., 11 March 1937, 2930–31 (*La Follette Hearings*).

United States Department of Commerce. *Census of Manufactures*. Washington, D.C.: GPO, 1967, 1982, 1992.

United States Department of Labor. *Employment and Earnings: States and Areas, 1939–1972*. Washington, D.C.: GPO, 1974.

———. *Handbook of Labor Statistics: 1975 Reference Edition*. Washington, D.C.: GPO, 1975.

———. *Handbook of Labor Statistics, 1980*. Washington, D.C.: GPO, 1980.

———. Women's Bureau. *Fluctuation of Employment in the Radio Industry*. Bulletin no. 83, 1931.

United States Employment Service. Federal Security Agency, Social Security Board. *Local Labor Market Survey for the Bloomington–Bedford–Burns City, Indiana, Area*. Washington, D.C.: GPO, 1942.

———. War Manpower Commission. *Summary Report on Adequacy of Labor Supply: For Bloomington–Burns City, Indiana, Labor Market Area*. Washington, D.C.: GPO, 1943.

United States Tariff Commission. *Color Television Report*. Washington, D.C., 1980.

———. *Economic Factors Affecting the Use of Items 807.00 and 806.30 of the Tariff Schedules of the United States: Report to the President on Investigation 332-61 under Section 332 of the Tariff Act of 1930*. Washington, D.C., 1970.

———. *Television Receivers: Production and Maintenance Workers at RCA Corp. Plant, Memphis, Tenn.: Report to the President on Worker Investigation No. TEA-W-70*. Publication 76. Washington, D.C., 1971.

———. *Television Receivers and Certain Parts Thereof: Report to the President on Investigation No. TEA-121*. Publication 436. Washington, D.C., 1971.

Works Progress Administration. *The Labor Force of the Philadelphia Radio Industry in 1936*. Philadelphia Labor Market Studies, Report No. P-2, 1938.

Secondary Works

Acuña, Rodolfo. *América ocupada: Los chicanos y su lucha de liberación*. Mexico City: ERA, 1976.

Adams, Roy. *Industrial Relations under Liberal Democracy*. Columbia: University of South Carolina Press, 1995.

Aguilar Camín, Héctor, and Lorenzo Meyer. *In the Shadow of the Mexican Revolution: Contemporary Mexican History*. Trans. Luis Alberto Fierro. Austin: University of Texas Press, 1993.

Amberg, Stephen. "The Contrasting Consequences of Institutions and Politics: Labor and Industrial Relations in the United States and Germany." *Political Power and Social Theory* 10 (1996): 195–227.

Anderson, Benedict. *Imagined Communities: Reflections on the Origin and Spread of Nationalism*. London: Verso, 1991.

Anderson, Sarah, John Cavanagh, and Jonathan Williams. *Workers Lose, CEOs Win (II): The Widening Wage Gap between U.S. Executives and Their U.S. and Mexican Workers*. Washington, D.C.: Institute for Policy Studies, 1995.

Anzaldúa, Gloria. *Borderlands/La Frontera: The New Mestiza*. San Francisco: Aunt Lute Books, 1987.

Arizpe, Lourdes, and Josefina Aranda. "The 'Comparative Advantages' of Women's Disadvantages: Women Workers in the Strawberry Export Business in Mexico." *Signs* 7 (1981): 453–473.

Arreola, Daniel D., and James R. Curtis. *The Mexican Border Cities: Landscape Anatomy and Place Personality*. Tucson: University of Arizona Press, 1993.

Arrighi, Giovanni. "Marxist Century, American Century: The Making and Remaking of the World Labour Movement." *New Left Review* 179 (1990): 29–63.

Aspra, L. Antonio. "Import Substitution in Mexico: Past and Present." *World Development* 5 (1977): 111–123.

Baerresen, Donald W. *The Border Industrialization Program of Mexico*. Lexington, Mass.: Heath-Lexington Books, 1971.

———, ed. *Mexico's Border Assembly Program*. Laredo: Institute for International Trade, Laredo State University, 1979.

Baird, Peter, and Ed McCaughan. *Beyond the Border: Mexico and the U.S. Today*. New York: North American Congress on Latin America, 1979.

———. "Hit and Run: U.S. Runaway Shops on the Mexican Border." *Latin America and Empire Report* 9 (July–August 1975).

Bakaly, Charles G., and William J. Isacson. *Diversion of Work: Plant Relocations, Inter-Plant Work Transfers, Subcontracting, and Importing*. New York: Harcourt Brace Jovanovich, 1983.

Barber, Benjamin J. *Jihad vs. McWorld*. New York: Times Books, 1995.

Barnum, Frank O. *His Master's Voice in America: Ninety Years of Communication Pioneering and Progress*. Camden, N.J.: General Electric, 1991.

Baron, Ava. "Gender and Labor History." In *Work Engendered: Toward a New History of American Labor*, ed. Ava Baron. Ithaca: Cornell University Press, 1991.

Barrera Bassols, Dalia. *Condiciones de trabajo en las maquiladoras de Ciudad Juárez*. Mexico City: Instituto Nacional de Antropología e Historia, 1990.

Barrera Bassols, Dalia, and Lilia Venegas Aguilera. *Testimonios de participación popular femenina en la defensa del voto, Ciudad Juárez, Chihuahua*. Mexico City: Instituto Nacional de Antropología e Historia, 1992.

Barry, Tom, Harry Browne, and Beth Sims. *The Great Divide: The Challenge of U.S.-Mexico Relations in the 1990s*. New York: Grove Press, 1994.

Batchelor, Joseph. *An Economic History of the Indiana Oolitic Limestone Industry*. Indiana Business Studies no. 27. Bloomington: Indiana University, 1944.

Beifuss, Joan Turner. *At the River I Stand: Memphis, the 1968 Strike, and Martin Luther King*. Brooklyn: Carlson, 1985.

Bell, Daniel. *The Coming of Post-Industrial Society*. New York: Basic Books, 1973.

Bensman, David, and Roberta Lynch. *Rusted Dreams: Hard Times in a Steel Community*. New York: McGraw-Hill, 1987.

Bermúdez, Antonio J. *Recovering Our Frontier Market: A Task in the Service of Mexico*. Trans. Edward Fowlkes. Mexico City: Eufesa, 1968.

Bernstein, Irving. *The Turbulent Years: A History of the American Worker, 1933–1941*. Boston: Houghton Mifflin, 1970.

Bilby, Kenneth. *The General: David Sarnoff and the Rise of the Communications Industry*. New York: Harper & Row, 1986.

Biles, Roger. *A New Deal for the American People*. De Kalb: Northern Illinois University Press, 1991.

Bluestone, Barry, and Bennet Harrison. *The Deindustrialization of America: Plant Closings, Community Abandonment, and the Dismantling of Basic Industry*. New York: Basic Books, 1982.

Bodnar, John. "Immigration, Kinship, and the Rise of Working-Class Realism in Industrial America." *Journal of Social History* 14 (Fall 1980): 45–65.

Bolin, Richard. "Border Industries: A Rebuttal." *Mexican-American Review*, March 1971, 21–23.

———. "Border Industry Facts for 1973." *Mexican-American Review*, September 1973, 14–23.

Bourdieu, Pierre. *The Logic of Practice*. Stanford: Stanford University Press, 1980.

Boyer, Richard O., and Herbert M. Morais. *Labor's Untold Story*. New York: Cameron Associates, 1955.

Brannon, Jeffrey T., and William G. Lucker. "The Impact of Mexico's Economic Crisis on the Demographic Composition of the Maquiladora Labor Force." *Journal of Borderland Studies* 4 (Spring 1989): 39–70.

Braverman, Harry. *Labor and Monopoly Capital: The Degradation of Work in the Twentieth Century*. New York: Monthly Review Press, 1974.

Brecher, Jeremy, and Tim Costello. *Global Village or Global Pillage: Economic Reconstruction from the Bottom Up*. Boston: South End Press, 1994.

Brody, David. "The Old Labor History and the New: In Search of an American Working Class." *Labor History* 20 (1979): 111–126.

———. *Workers in Industrial America: Essays on the Twentieth-Century Struggle*. New York: Oxford University Press, 1980.

Browne, Harry, and Beth Sims. *Runaway America: U.S. Jobs and Factories on the Move*. Albuquerque: Resource Center Press, 1993.

Bustamante, Jorge. "Maquiladoras: A New Face of Capitalism on Mexico's Northern Frontier." In *Women, Men, and the International Division of Labor*, ed. June Nash and María Patricia Fernández-Kelly, 224–256. Albany: SUNY Press, 1983.

Caban, Pedro A. "Industrial Transformation and Labour Relations in Puerto Rico: From 'Operation Bootstrap' to the 1970s." *Journal of Latin American Studies* 21 (1989): 559–591.

Cahn, Bill. *Mill Town: A Dramatic Pictorial Narrative of the Century-Old Fight to Unionize an Industrial Town*. New York: Cameron & Kahn, 1954.

Calhoun, Craig. *The Question of Class Struggle: Social Foundations of Popular Radicalism during the Industrial Revolution*. Chicago: University of Chicago Press, 1982.

Carr, Barry. "Crossing Borders: Labor Internationalism in the Era of NAFTA." In *Neoliberalism Revisited: Economic Restructuring and Mexico's Political Future*, ed. Gerald Otero. Boulder: Westview, 1996.

Carrier, Ronald E., and William R. Schriver. *Plant Location Analysis: An Investigation of Plant Locations in Tennessee*. Memphis: Memphis State University, 1969.

Carrillo V., Jorge. *Conflictos laborales en la industria maquiladora*. Tijuana: CEFNOMEX, 1985.

———. *Dos décadas de sindicalismo en la industria maquiladora de exportación: Examen de Tijuana, Ciudad Juárez, y Matamoros*. Mexico City: Universidad Autónoma Metropolitana–Iztapalapa/Miguel Ángel Porrúa, 1989.

———. "The Evolution of the Maquiladora Industry: Labor Relations in a New Context." In *Unions, Workers, and the State in Mexico*, ed. Kevin J. Middlebrook, 213–241. La Jolla: Center for U.S.-Mexican Studies, University of California, San Diego, 1991.

———. *Restructuración industrial: Maquiladoras en la frontera México– Estados Unidos*. Mexico City: Consejo Nacional para la Cultura y las Artes, Colegio de la Frontera Norte de México, 1989.

Carrillo V., Jorge, and Alberto Hernández. *Mujeres fronterizas en la industria maquiladora*. Mexico City: Secretaría de Educación Pública, 1985.

Carroll, Thomas M., David H. Ciscel, and John E. Gnuschke. "Determinants of Wage Rates in Memphis, Tennessee: 1962–1975." *Mid-South Quarterly Business Review* 18 (July 1980): 12–15.

Castellanos, Alicia G. *Ciudad Juárez: La vida fronteriza*. Mexico City: Nuestro Tiempo, 1981.

Catanzarite, Lisa M., and Myra H. Strober. "The Gender Recomposition of the Maquiladora Workforce in Ciudad Juárez." *Industrial Relations* 32 (Winter 1993): 133–147.

Cho, Soon Kyoung. "The Labor Process and Capital Mobility: The Limits of the New International Division of Labor." *Politics and Society* 14 (1985): 185–222.

Christman, John H. "Border Industries Foster Jobs." *Mexican-American Review* 36 (February 1968).

Ciscel, David, and Tom Collins. "The Memphis Runaway Blues." *Southern Exposure* 4 (January–February 1976): 143–149.

Clark, Gordon L. *Unions and Communities under Siege: American Communities and the Crisis of Organized Labor*. New York: Cambridge University Press, 1989.

Cobb, James C. *The Selling of the South: The Southern Crusade for Industrial Development, 1936–1990*. Urbana: University of Illinois Press, 1993.

———. "The Sunbelt Southern Industrialization in Regional, National, and International Perspective." In *Searching for the Sunbelt: Historical Perspectives on a Region*, ed. Raymond A. Mohl. Knoxville: University of Tennessee Press, 1990.

Cohen, Lizabeth. *Making a New Deal: Industrial Workers in Chicago*. New York: Cambridge University Press, 1990.

Collier, Ruth Berins, and David Collier. *Shaping the Political Arena: Critical Junctures, the Labor Movement, and Regime Dynamics in Latin America*. Princeton: Princeton University Press, 1991.

Collingsworth, Terry, J. William Goold, and Pharis Harvey. "Time for a Global New Deal." *Foreign Affairs*, January/February 1994, 8–14.

Collins, Thomas W., and David H. Ciscel. "An Analysis of the RCA Television Assembly Plant in Memphis: Why It Closed." *Mid-South Quarterly Business Review* 14 (April 1976): 3–7.

Comaroff, John, and Jean Comaroff. *Ethnology and Historical Imagination*. Boulder: Westview, 1992.

Compa, Lance. "Another Look at NAFTA." *Dissent* 4 (Winter 1997): 45–50.

Cook, Maria Lorena, Kevin J. Middlebrook, and Juan Molinar Horcasitas. "The Politics of Economic Restructuring in Mexico: Actors, Sequencing, and Coalition Change." In *The Politics of Economic Restructuring: State-Society Relations and Regime Change in Mexico*, ed. Cook, Middlebrook, and Horcasitas, 3–52. La Jolla: Center for U.S.-Mexican Studies, University of California, San Diego, 1994.

Cornelius, Wayne. *The Political Economy of Mexico under de la Madrid: The Crisis Deepens, 1985–1986*. La Jolla: Center for U.S.-Mexican Studies, University of California, San Diego, 1986.

Cowie, Jefferson. "National Struggles in a Transnational Economy: A Critical Analysis of U.S. Labor's Campaign against NAFTA." *Labor Studies Journal* 21 (Winter 1997): 3–32.

Cowie, Jefferson, and John D. French. "NAFTA's Labor Side Accord: A Textual Analysis." *Latin American Labor News* 9 (1993–94): 5–8.

Craig, Richard B. *The Bracero Program*. Austin: University of Texas Press, 1971.

Craypo, Charles, and Bruce Nissen, eds. *Grand Designs: The Impact of Corporate Strategies on Workers, Unions, and Communities*. Ithaca: ILR Press, 1993.

Derber, Milton. "Electrical Products." In *How Collective Bargaining Works*, ed. Harry A. Millis. New York: Twentieth Century Fund, 1942.

Dex, Shirley. *The Sexual Division of Work: Conceptual Revolutions in the Social Sciences*. New York: St. Martin's Press, 1985.

Dillman, Daniel C. "Urban Growth along Mexico's Northern Border and the Mexican National Border Program." *Journal of Developing Areas* 4 (July 1970): 487–508.

Donohue, Peter. "'Free Trade' Unions and the State: Trade Liberalization's Endorsement by the AFL-CIO, 1943–1962." *Research in Political Economy* 13 (1992): 1–73.

Dorwart, Jeffery M., and Philip English Mackey. *Camden County, New Jersey, 1616–1976: A Narrative History*. Camden: Camden County Cultural and Heritage Commission, 1976.

Dubofsky, Melvyn. *The State and Labor in Modern America*. Chapel Hill: University of North Carolina Press, 1994.

Dunnett, Peter J. S. *The World Television Industry: An Economic Analysis*. London: Routledge, 1990.

Durand, Jorge, and Douglas Massey. "Mexican Migration to the United States: A Critical Review." *Latin American Research Review* 27 (1992): 3–40.

Durand Ponte, Victor Manuel. "The Confederation of Mexican Workers, the Labor Congress, and the Crisis of Mexico's Social Pact." In *Unions, Workers, and the State in Mex-*

ico, ed. Kevin J. Middlebrook, 85–104. La Jolla: Center for U.S.- Mexican Studies, University of California, San Diego, 1991.

Ehrbar, A. F. "Splitting Up RCA." *Fortune*, 22 March 1982.

Eisenstadt, Todd A., and Cathryn L. Thorup. *Caring Capacity versus Carrying Capacity: Community Responses to Mexican Immigration in San Diego's North County*. La Jolla: Center for U.S.-Mexican Studies, University of California, San Diego, 1994.

Elson, Diane, and Ruth Pearson. "Nimble Fingers Make Cheap Workers: An Analysis of Women's Employment in Third World Export Manufacturing." *Feminist Review*, no. 7 (Spring 1981), 87–107.

Engstrom, E. W. *RCA: Five Historical Views*. Cherry Hill, N.J.: RCA, 1978.

Ericson, Anna-Stina. "An Analysis of Mexico's Border Industrialization Program." *Monthly Labor Review* 93 (May 1970): 33–40.

———. "Economic Development in the Mexican Border Areas." *Labor Developments Abroad* 12 (June 1967): 1–8.

Fatemi, Khosrow, ed. *The Maquiladora Industry: Economic Solution or Problem?* New York: Praeger, 1990.

Faue, Elizabeth. "Gender and the Reconstruction of Labor History." *Labor History* 34, nos. 2–3 (1993), 169–177.

Fernandez, Raul. *The United States–Mexico Border: A Politico-Economic Profile*. Notre Dame: University of Notre Dame Press, 1977.

Fernández-Kelly, María Patricia. "Alternative Education for Maquiladora Workers." *Grassroots Development*, nos. 6/7 (1983), 41–46.

———. "Contemporary Production and the New International Division of Labor." In *The Americas in the New International Division of Labor*, ed. Steven E. Sanderson, 206–225. New York: Holmes & Meier, 1985.

———. *For We Are Sold, I and My People: Women and Industry in Mexico's Frontier*. Albany: SUNY Press, 1983.

———. "Las maquiladoras y las mujeres I." *Los Universitarios*, March 1979.

Filippelli, Ronald L. "UE: The Formative Years." *Labor History* 17 (Summer 1976): 351–371.

Filippelli, Ronald L., and Mark D. McColloch. *Cold War in the Working Class: The Rise and Decline of the United Electrical Workers*. Albany: SUNY Press, 1995.

Fink, Leon. "Looking Backward: Reflections on Workers' Culture and Certain Conceptual Dilemmas within Labor History." In *In Search of the Working Class: Essays in American Labor History and Political Culture*, ed. Leon Fink, 175–200. Urbana: University of Illinois Press, 1994.

Fink, Leon, and Brian Greenberg. *Upheaval in the Quiet Zone*. Urbana: University of Illinois Press, 1989.

Fraser, Steve. "The Labor Question." In *The Rise and Fall of the New Deal Order, 1930-1980*, ed. Steve Fraser and Gary Gerstle. Princeton: Princeton University Press, 1989.

———. *Labor Will Rule: Sidney Hillman and the Rise of American Labor*. New York: Free Press, 1991.

Freire, Paulo. *Pedagogy of the Oppressed*. Trans. Myra Berger Ramos. New York: Herder & Herder, 1970.

French, John D., Jefferson Cowie, and Scott Littlehale. *Labor and NAFTA: A Briefing Book*. Durham: Duke–University of North Carolina Program in Latin American Studies, 1994.

Fröbel, Folker, Jürgen Heinrichs, and Otto Kreye. *The New International Division of Labor: Structural Unemployment in Industrialised Countries and Industrialisation in Developing Countries*. Cambridge: Cambridge University Press, 1980.

Galarza, Ernesto. *Merchants of Labor: The Mexican Bracero Story*. Charlotte, N.C.: McNally & Loftin, 1964.

García, Mario T. *Desert Immigrants: The Mexicans of El Paso, 1880–1920*. New Haven: Yale University Press, 1981.

Garza Toledano, Enrique de la. "The Restructuring of State-Labor Relations in Mexico." In *The Politics of Economic Restructuring: State-Society Relations and Regime Change in Mexico*, ed. Maria Lorena Cook, Kevin J. Middlebrook, and Juan Molinar Horcasitas, 195–217. La Jolla: Center for U.S.-Mexican Studies, University of California, San Diego, 1994.

Geoghegan, Thomas. *Which Side Are You On? Trying to Be for Labor When It's Flat on Its Back*. New York: Farrar, Straus & Giroux, 1991.

Gereffi, Gary. "Development Strategies and the Global Factory." *Annals* 505 (September 1989): 92–104.

Gerstle, Gary. *Working-Class Americanism: The Politics of Labor in a Textile City*. New York: Cambridge University Press, 1989.

Giddens, Anthony. "Foreword." In *NowHere: Space, Time, and Modernity*, ed. Roger Friedland and Deirdre Boden. Berkeley: University of California Press, 1994.

———. *Modernity and Self-Identity: Self and Society in the Late Modern Age*. Stanford: Stanford University Press, 1991.

Goldfield, Michael. *The Decline of Organized Labor in the United States*. Chicago: University of Chicago Press, 1987.

Goldfinger, Nat. "The Case for Hartke-Burke." *Columbia Journal of World Business* 8 (Spring 1973): 22–26.

González Montes, Soledad, Olivia Ruiz, Laura Velasco, and Ofelia Woo, eds. *Mujeres, migración, y maquila en la frontera norte*. Mexico City: El Colegio de México and El Colegio de la Frontera Norte, 1995.

Gordon, David, Richard Edwards, and Michael Reich. *Segmented Work, Divided Workers: The Historical Transformation of Labor in the United States*. New York: Cambridge University Press, 1982.

Graham, Margaret B. W. *RCA and the Videodisc: The Business of Research*. New York: Cambridge University Press, 1986.

Greider, William. *One World, Ready or Not: The Manic Logic of Global Capitalism*. New York: Simon & Schuster, 1997.

Grunwald, Joseph, and Kenneth Flamm. *The Global Factory: Foreign Assembly in International Trade*. Washington, D.C.: Brookings, 1985.

Gutman, Herbert. *Work, Culture, and Society in Industrializing America*. New York: Knopf, 1976.

Hall, Jacquelyn Dowd, James Leloudis, Robert Korstad, Mary Murphy, Lu Ann Jones, and Christopher B. Daly. *Like a Family: The Making of a Southern Cotton Mill World*. Chapel Hill: University of North Carolina Press, 1987.

Halsel-Gilliam, Frances V. *A Time to Speak: A Brief History of the Afro-Americans of Bloomington, Indiana, 1865–1965*. Bloomington: Pinus Strobus Press, 1985.

Hancock, Richard H. *The Role of the Bracero in the Economic and Cultural Dynamics of Mexico: A Case Study of Chihuahua*. Stanford: Hispanic American Society, 1959.

Harris, Nigel. *The End of the Third World: Newly Industrializing Countries and the Decline of an Ideology*. New York: Penguin, 1987.

Harris, Richard. "New Theories of International Trade and the Pattern of Global Specialization." In *Industry on the Move: Causes and Consequences of International Relocation in the Manufacturing Industry*, ed. Gijsbert van Liemt, 25–50. Geneva: International Labour Organization, 1992.

Hart, Jeffrey A. *The Consumer Electronics Industry in the U.S.: Its Decline and Future Revival*. Bloomington: Indiana Center for Global Business, School of Business Administration, Indiana University, 1988.

Hartmann, Heidi. "The Historical Roots of Occupational Segregation: Capitalism, Patriarchy, and Job Segregation by Sex." In *Women and the Workplace*, ed. Martha Blaxall and Barbara Benton Reagan. Chicago: University of Chicago Press, 1976.

Harvey, David. *The Condition of Postmodernity*. Cambridge: Blackwell, 1990.

Harvey, Robert O. *Land Uses in Bloomington, Indiana, 1818–1950*. Bloomington: School of Business Administration, Indiana University, 1951.

Henderson, Jeffrey, and Manuel Castells. "Techno-economic Restructuring, Sociopolitical Processes, and Spatial Transformation: A Global Perspective." In *Global Restructuring and Territorial Development*, ed. Henderson and Castells, 1–17. London: Sage, 1987.

Herod, Andrew. "From a Geography of Labor to a Labor Geography: Labor's Spatial Fix and the Geography of Capitalism." *Antipode* 29 (1997): 1–31.

———. "The Practice of International Labor Solidarity and the Geography of the Global Economy." *Economic Geography* 71 (October 1995): 341–364.

———, ed. *Organizing the Landscape: Geographical Perspectives on Labor Unionism*. Minneapolis: University of Minnesota Press, 1998.

Heyman, Josiah McC. *Life and Labor on the Border: Working People of Northeastern Sonora, Mexico, 1886–1986*. Tucson: University of Arizona Press, 1991.

Hirsch, Seev. "The United States Electronics Industry in International Trade." In *The Product Life Cycle and International Trade*, ed. Louis T. Wells. Cambridge: Division of Research, Graduate School of Business Administration, Harvard University, 1972.

Hoeber, Helen S. "Collective Bargaining by United Electrical, Radio, and Machine Workers." *Monthly Labor Review* 47 (July 1938): 67–77.

Hoerr, John P. *And the Wolf Finally Came: The Decline of the American Steel Industry*. Pittsburgh: University of Pittsburgh Press, 1988.

Honey, Michael K. *Southern Labor and Black Civil Rights: Organizing Memphis Workers*. Urbana: University of Illinois Press, 1993.

———. "Unionism and Racial Justice in Memphis." In *Organized Labor in the Twentieth-Century South*, ed. Robert Zieger, 135–151. Knoxville: University of Tennessee Press, 1991.

Hurlburt, Laurance P. *The Mexican Muralists in the United States*. Albuquerque: University of New Mexico Press, 1989.

Iglesias Prieto, Norma. *Beautiful Flowers of the Maquiladora: Life Histories of Women Workers in Tijuana*. Trans. Michael Stone with Gabrielle Winkler. 1985. Austin: University of Texas Press, 1997.

Jenkins, Rhys. *Transnational Corporations and Uneven Development: The Internationalization of Capital and the Third World*. London: Methuen, 1987.

Jeryan, Puzant Henry. "High-Speed Radio Production." *Electronics* 8 (December 1935): 515–519.

Johnson, Hugh S. *Blue Eagle from Egg to Earth*. Garden City, N.Y.: Doubleday, Doran, 1935.

Jones, Jacqueline. *The Dispossessed: America's Underclass from the Civil War to the Present*. New York: Basic Books, 1992.

Kannenberg, Lisa. "The Impact of the Cold War on Women's Trade Union Activism: The UE Experience." *Labor History* 34, nos. 2–3 (1993): 309–323.

Katz, Friedrich. "Labor Conditions on Haciendas in Porfirian Mexico: Some Trends and Tendencies." *Hispanic American Historical Review* 54 (February 1974): 1–47.

Kelley, Robin D. G. *Hammer and Hoe: Alabama Communists during the Great Depression*. Chapel Hill: University of North Carolina Press, 1990.

Kessler-Harris, Alice. "Just Price, the Free Market, and the Value of Women." *Feminist Studies* 14 (Summer 1988): 235–250.

Koppel, Ross, and Alice Hoffman. "Dislocation Policies in the USA: What Should We Be Doing?" *Annals* 544 (March 1996): 111–126.

Korstad, Robert, and Nelson Lichtenstein. "Opportunities Found and Lost: Labor Radicals and the Early Civil Rights Movement." *Journal of American History* 75 (1988): 786–811.

Laurie, Bruce. *Artisans into Workers*. New York: Hill & Wang, 1989.

Leuchtenburg, William E. *Franklin D. Roosevelt and the New Deal*. New York: Harper & Row, 1963.

Lichtenstein, Nelson. "From Corporatism to Collective Bargaining." In *The Rise and Fall of the New Deal Order, 1930–1980*, ed. Steve Fraser and Gary Gerstle. Princeton: Princeton University Press, 1989.

———. *Labor's War at Home: The CIO in World War II*. New York: Cambridge University Press, 1982.

Limerick, Patricia Nelson. *The Legacy of Conquest: The Unbroken Past of the American West*. New York: Norton, 1987.

Linvill, John G., ed. *The Competitive Status of the U.S. Electronics Industry: A Study of the Influences of Technology in Determining International Industrial Competitive Advantage*. Washington, D.C.: National Academic Press, 1984.

Loper, David T. "Low-Wage Lures South of the Border." *American Federationist* 76 (June 1969): 1–7.

Losch, August. *The Economics of Location*. New Haven: Yale University Press, 1954.

Lowy, Michael. "Marxists and the National Question." *New Left Review* 96 (March–April 1976): 81–100.

Lucker, G. W. "The Hidden Costs of Worker Turnover: A Case Study in the Maquila Industry." *Journal of Borderlands Studies* 2 (Spring 1987): 93–98.

Lynd, Staughton. *The Fight against Shutdowns: Youngstown's Steel Mill Closings*. San Pedro: Singlejack Books, 1982.

Mandel, Ernest. *Late Capitalism*. London: New Left Books, 1975.

Marshall, Ray, and Virgil L. Christian Jr., eds. *Employment of Blacks in the South: A Perspective on the 1960s*. Austin: University of Texas Press, 1978.

Martínez, Oscar J. *Border Boom Town: Ciudad Juárez since 1848*. Austin: University of Texas Press, 1978.

———. "Chicanos and the Border Cities: An Interpretive Essay." *Pacific Historical Review* 46 (February 1977): 85–106.

———. "The Foreign Orientation of the Ciudad Juárez Economy." In *The Social Ecology and Economic Development of Ciudad Juárez*, ed. Gay Young, 141–151. Boulder: Westview, 1986.

Marx, Karl, and Friedrich Engels. *The Communist Manifesto*. New York: Penguin, 1967.

Mason, Lucy Randolph. *To Win These Rights: A Personal Story of the CIO in the South*. New York: Harper, 1952.

Massey, Doreen. *Spatial Divisions of Labor: Social Structures and the Geography of Production*. London: Macmillan, 1984.

Matles, James J., and James Higgins. *Them and Us: Struggles of a Rank-and-File Union*. Englewood Cliffs, N.J.: Prentice-Hall, 1974.

Middlebrook, Kevin. *Paradox of Revolution: Labor, the State, and Authoritarianism in Mexico*. Baltimore: Johns Hopkins University Press, 1995.

Milkman, Ruth. *Farewell to the Factory: Auto Workers in the Late Twentieth Century*. Berkeley: University of California Press, 1997.

———. *Gender at Work: The Dynamics of Job Segregation by Sex during World War II*. Urbana: University of Illinois Press, 1987.

————, ed. *Women, Work, and Protest: A Century of U.S. Women's Labor History*. Boston: Routledge & Kegan Paul, 1985.

Miller, William D. *Mr. Crump of Memphis*. Baton Rouge: Louisiana State University Press, 1964.

Mills, C. Wright. *The Sociological Imagination*. New York: Oxford University Press, 1959.

Millstein, James E. "Decline in an Expanding Industry: Japanese Competition in Color Television." In *American Industry in International Competition: Government Policies and Corporate Strategies*, ed. John Zysman and Laura Tyson. Ithaca: Cornell University Press, 1983.

Mizrahi, Yemile. "Rebels Without a Cause? The Politics of Entrepreneurs in Chihuahua." *Journal of Latin American Studies* 26 (1994): 137–158.

Montgomery, David. "To Study the People: The American Working Class." *Labor History* 21 (1980): 485–512.

————. *Workers' Control in America*. New York: Cambridge University Press, 1979.

Moody, Kim. *Workers in a Lean World: Unions in the International Economy*. New York: Verso, 1997.

Nash, June, and María Patricia Fernández-Kelly, eds. *Women, Men, and the International Division of Labor*. Albany: SUNY Press, 1983.

Neufeld, Maurice F. "The Sense of History and the Annals of Labor." In *Proceedings of the Fourteenth Annual Meeting, New York City, December 28 and 29, 1961*, ed. Gerald G. Somers. New York: Industrial Relations Research Association, 1962.

Nissen, Bruce. *Fighting for Jobs: Case Studies of Labor-Community Coalitions Confronting Plant Closings*. Albany: SUNY Press, 1995.

————. "A Post–World War II 'Social Accord'?" In *U.S. Labor Relations, 1945–1989: Accommodation and Conflict*, ed. Nissen. New York: Garland, 1990.

Nordström, Kjell A., and Jan-Erik Vahlne. "Is the Globe Shrinking? Psychic Distance and the Establishment of Swedish Sales Subsidiaries during the Last 100 Years." In *International Trade: Regional and Global Issues*, ed. Michael Landeck. New York: St. Martin's Press, 1994.

North American Congress on Latin America. "Electronics: The Global Industry." *NACLA's Report on the Americas* 11 (April 1977).

O Martínez, María Eugenia de la. *Innovación tecnológica y clase obrera: La industria maquiladora electrónica R.C.A. Ciudad Juárez, Chihuahua*. Mexico City: Universidad Autónoma Metropolitana–Iztapalapa/Miguel Ángel Porrúa, 1994.

Ong, Aihwa. "The Gender and Labor Politics of Postmodernity." *Annual Review of Anthropology* 20 (1991): 279–309.

Orme, William A., Jr. *Understanding NAFTA: Mexico, Free Trade, and the New North America*. Austin: University of Texas Press, 1996.

Palladino, Grace. *Dreams of Dignity, Workers of Vision: A History of the International Brotherhood of Electrical Workers*. Washington, D.C.: International Brotherhood of Electrical Workers, 1991.

Peet, Richard. "Class Struggle, the Relocation of Employment, and Economic Crisis." *Science and Society* 48 (1984): 38–51.

————. "Relations of Production and the Relocation of United States Manufacturing Industry since 1960." *Annals of the Association of American Geographers* 75 (1985): 309–333.

Peña, Devon G. "Las Maquiladoras: Mexican Women and Class Struggle in the Border Industries." *Aztlán* 11, no. 2 (Fall 1980): 160–229.

————. "Skilled Activities among Assembly Line Workers in Mexican-American Border Twin Plants." *Campo Libre* 2, nos. 1–2 (1984): 189–207.

————. *The Terror of the Machine: Work, Technology, Gender, and Ecology on the U.S.-Mexico Border*. Austin: Center for Mexican-American Studies/University of Texas Press, 1997.

————. "*Tortuosidad*: Shop-Floor Struggles of Female Maquiladora Workers." In *Women on the U.S.-Mexican Border: Responses to Change*, ed. Vicki Ruiz and Susan Tiano, 129–154. Boston: Allen & Unwin, 1987.

Perlman, Selig. *A Theory of the Labor Movement*. New York: Macmillan, 1928.

Preis, Art. *Labor's Giant Step: Twenty Years of the CIO*. New York: Pioneer, 1964.

Quick, Joseph H. "Motion-Time Standards." *Factory Management and Maintenance* 103 (May 1945): 97–108.

————, ed. *The Detailed Work-Factor Manual for Time Standards Analysis*. Moorestown, N.J.: WOFAC, 1969.

Radio Corporation of America. *Report to Employees*. New York, 1949.

Radnor, Michael, Barbara Collins, Liam Fahey, Robert Beam, and Bala V. Balachandran. *The U.S. Consumer Electronics Industry and Foreign Competition*. Evanston, Ill.: Northwestern University for U.S. Department of Commerce, 1980.

Reich, Robert. *The Work of Nations: Preparing Ourselves for 21st-Century Capitalism*. New York: Knopf, 1995.

Reschenthaler, Patricia. *Postwar Readjustment in El Paso, 1945–1950*. Southwestern Studies 6. El Paso: Texas Western Press, 1968.

Rifkin, Jeremy. *The End of Work: The Decline of the Global Labor Force and the Dawn of the Post-Market Era*. New York: Putnam, 1995.

Rivera-Batiz, Francisco. "Can Border Industries Be a Substitute for Immigration?" *American Economic Review* 76 (May 1986): 263–268.

Robinson, Ian. *North American Trade as If Democracy Mattered*. Washington, D.C.: International Labor Rights, Education, and Research Fund; Ottawa: Canadian Centre for Policy Alternatives, 1993.

Roediger, David. "The Crisis of Labor History: Race, Gender, and the Replotting of the Working-Class Past in the United States." In *Towards the Abolition of Whiteness*, ed. Roediger. London: Verso, 1994.

————. *The Wages of Whiteness: Race and the Making of the American Working Class*. London: Verso, 1991.

Rosenbaum, Ruth. *Market Basket Survey: A Comparison of the Buying Power of Maquiladora Workers in Mexico and UAW Assembly Workers in GM Plants in the U.S.* San Antonio: Coalition for Justice in the Maquiladoras, 1994.

Ross, Irwin. "Labor's Big Push for Protectionism." *Fortune*, March 1973.

Roxborough, Ian. *Unions and Politics in Mexico: The Case of the Automobile Industry*. New York: Cambridge University Press, 1984.

Ruiz, Vicki. "By the Day or the Week: Mexicana Domestic Workers in El Paso." In *Women on the U.S.-Mexico Border: Responses to Change*, ed. Ruiz and Susan Tiano, 61–76. Boston: Allen & Unwin, 1987.

Safa, Helen. "Runaway Shops and Female Employment." *Signs* 7 (1981): 418–433.

Sahlins, Peter. *Boundaries: The Making of France and Spain in the Pyrenees*. Berkeley: University of California Press, 1989.

Salas-Porras, Alejandra. "Maquiladoras y burguesia regional." *El Cotidiano*, special issue 1 (1987): 51–58.

Sanderson, Susan Walsh. *The Consumer Electronics Industry and the Future of American Manufacturing: How the U.S. Lost the Lead and Why We Must Get Back in the Game*. Washington, D.C.: Economic Policy Institute, 1989.

Sassen, Saskia. *The Mobility of Labor and Capital: A Study in International Investment and Labor Flow*. New York: Cambridge University Press, 1988.

Sayer, Andrew. "New Developments in Manufacturing: The Just-In-Time System." *Capital and Class* 30 (Winter 1986): 43–72.

Schatz, Ronald W. *The Electrical Workers: A History of Labor at General Electric and Westinghouse, 1923–1960.* Urbana: University of Illinois Press, 1983.

Schmenner, Roger W. *The Location Decisions of Large, Multiplant Companies.* Cambridge: Joint Center for Urban Studies of MIT and Harvard University, 1980.

Schmidt, Robert H., and William J. Lloyd. "Patterns of Urban Growth in Ciudad Juárez." In *The Social Change and Economic Development of Ciudad Juárez*, ed. Gay Young, 23–45. Boulder: Westview, 1986.

Schoenberger, Erica. "Multinational Corporations and the New International Division of Labor: A Critical Appraisal." *International Regional Science Review* 11 (1988): 105–119.

Schriver, William R., Roger L. Bowlby, and Donald E. Pursell. "Evaluation of Trade Readjustment Assistance to Workers: A Case Study." *Social Science Quarterly* 57 (December 1976): 547–556.

Schulman, Bruce J. *From Cotton Belt to Sunbelt: Federal Policy, Economic Development, and the Transformation of the South, 1938–1980.* New York: Oxford University Press, 1991.

Schumpeter, Joseph A. *Capitalism, Socialism, and Democracy.* New York: Harper, 1942.

Schwartzman, David. *The Japanese Television Cartel: A Study on Matsushita v. Zenith.* Ann Arbor: University of Michigan Press, 1993.

Seligson, Mitchell A., and Edward A. Williams. *Maquiladoras and Migration: Workers in the Mexico–United States Border Industrialization Program.* Austin: University of Texas Press, 1981.

Shaiken, Harley. *Mexico in the Global Economy: High Technology and Work Organization in Export Industries.* La Jolla: Center for U.S.-Mexican Studies, University of California, San Diego, 1990.

Sigafoos, Robert A. *Cotton Row to Beale Street: A Business History of Memphis.* Memphis: Memphis State University Press, 1979.

Skinner, Wickham. *Manufacturing Policy in the Electronics Industry.* Homewood, Ill.: Irwin, 1968.

Sklair, Leslie. *Assembling for Development: The Maquila Industry in Mexico and the United States.* La Jolla: Center for U.S.-Mexican Studies, University of California, San Diego, 1993.

———. *Sociology of the World System: Social Change in Global Perspective.* Baltimore: Johns Hopkins University Press, 1991.

Sobel, Robert. *RCA.* New York: Stein & Day, 1986.

Soja, Edward. *Postmodern Geographies: The Reassertion of Space in Critical Social Theory.* London: Verso, 1989.

South, Robert B. "Transnational 'Maquiladora' Location." *Annals of the Association of American Geographers* 80 (1990): 549–570.

Southall, Roger, ed. *Trade Unions and the New Industrialization of the Third World.* Pittsburgh: University of Pittsburgh Press, 1988.

Spaeth, Anthony. "Maquila Boom." *Forbes*, 10 December 1979, 102–104.

Springer, Kenneth D. "High-Definition Television: New World Order or Fortress America?" *Law and Policy in International Business* 4 (1993): 1309–1341.

Stanfield, J. Edwin. *In Memphis: More than a Garbage Strike.* Atlanta: Southern Regional Council, 1968.

Starr, George W. *Industrial Development of Indiana.* Bloomington: School of Business Administration, Indiana University, 1937.

Staudt, Kathleen. "Economic Change and Ideological Lag in Households of Maquila Workers in Ciudad Juárez." In *The Social Ecology and Economic Development of Ciudad Juárez*, ed. Gay Young, 97–120. Boulder: Westview, 1986.

————. "Programming Women's Empowerment: A Case from Mexico." In *Women on the U.S.-Mexican Border: Responses to Change*, ed. Vicki L. Ruiz and Susan Tiano, 155–173. Boston: Allen & Unwin, 1987.

Stern, J. "Consequences of Plant Closure." *Journal of Human Resources* 7 (January 1973): 3–25.

Stickle, Warren E., III. "The Apple Sack Campaign of 1919: 'As Wet as the Atlantic Ocean.'" In *A New Jersey Anthology*, ed. Maxine N. Lurie. Newark: New Jersey Historical Commission, 1994.

Storper, Michael, and Richard Walker. *The Capitalist Imperative: Territory, Technology, and Industrial Growth*. New York: Basil Blackwell, 1989.

Sugrue, Thomas J. *The Origins of the Urban Crisis: Race and Inequality in Postwar Detroit.* Princeton: Princeton University Press, 1996.

Thompson, E. P. *The Making of the English Working Class*. New York: Vintage, 1963.

Tiano, Susan. *Patriarchy on the Line: Labor, Gender, and Ideology in the Mexican Maquila Industry*. Philadelphia: Temple University Press, 1994.

Tindall, George B. *The Emergence of the New South, 1913–1945*. Baton Rouge: Louisiana State University Press, 1967.

Troy, Leo. *Organized Labor in New Jersey*. Princeton: Van Nostrand, 1965.

Tucker, David M. "Black Pride and Negro Business in the 1920s: George Washington Lee of Memphis." *Business History Review* 43 (1969): 435–451.

————. *Memphis since Crump: Bossism, Blacks, and Civic Reformers, 1948–1968*. Knoxville: University of Tennessee Press, 1980.

Ugalde, Antonio. *The Urbanization Process of a Poor Mexican Neighborhood*. Austin: Institute for Latin American Studies, University of Texas, 1974.

Ulman, Lloyd. *Rise of the National Trade Union: The Development and Significance of Its Structure, Governing Institutions, and Economic Policies*. Cambridge: Harvard University Press, 1955.

Van der Spek, Peter G. "Mexico's Booming Border Zone: A Magnet for Labor-Intensive Industries." *Inter-American Economic Affairs* 24 (Summer 1975): 33–47.

Vaughn, Sandra. "Memphis: Heart of the Mid-South." In *In Search of the New South: The Black Urban Experience in the 1970s and 1980s*, ed. Robert D. Bullard. Tuscaloosa: University of Alabama Press, 1989.

Vernon, Raymond. "International Investment and International Trade in the Product Cycle." *Quarterly Journal of Economics* 80 (May 1966): 190–207.

————. *Metropolis 1985: An Interpretation of the Findings of the New York Metropolitan Region Study*. New York: Cambridge University Press, 1960.

Walker, Harold O. "Border Industries with a Mexican Accent." *Columbia Journal of World Business* 4 (January–February 1969): 25–32.

Walker, Richard, and Michael Storper. "Capital and Industrial Location." *Progress in Human Geography* 5 (1981): 473–509.

Wallace, Michael, and Joyce Rothschild, eds. *Deindustrialization and the Restructuring of American Industry*. Greenwich, Conn.: AI Press, 1988.

Wallerstein, Immanuel. "Response: Declining States, Declining Rights." *International Labor and Working-Class History* 47 (Spring 1995): 24–27.

Weber, Alfred. *Theory of the Location of Industries*. Chicago: University of Chicago Press, 1929.

Weber, David J. *The Spanish Frontier in North America*. New Haven: Yale University Press, 1992.

West, Jessamyn. *The Witch Diggers*. New York: Harcourt Brace, 1951.

Whitehead, Laurence. "Mexico's Economic Prospects: Implications for State-Labor Relations." In *Unions, Workers, and the State in Mexico,* ed. Kevin J. Middlebrook, 57–83. La Jolla: Center for U.S.-Mexican Studies, University of California, San Diego, 1991.

————. "Tigers in Latin America?" *Annals* 505 (September 1989): 142–151.

Williams, Edward J., and John T. Passé-Smith. *The Unionization of the Maquiladora Industry: The Tamaulipan Case in National Context.* San Diego: Institute for Regional Studies of the Californias, San Diego State University, 1992.

Wilson, Patricia A. *Exports and Local Development: Mexico's New Maquiladoras.* Austin: University of Texas Press, 1992.

Winters, Jeffrey A. *Power in Motion: Capital Mobility and the Indonesian State.* Ithaca: Cornell University Press, 1996.

Witney, Fred. *Indiana Labor Relations Law.* Bloomington: School of Business Administration, Indiana University, 1960.

Wright, Gavin. *Old South, New South: Revolutions in the Southern Economy since the Civil War.* New York: Basic Books, 1986.

Young, Gay, and Susan Christopherson. "Household Structure and Activity in Ciudad Juárez." In *The Social Ecology and Economic Development of Ciudad Juárez,* ed. Young, 65–95. Boulder: Westview, 1986.

Zahavi, Gerald. "Passionate Commitments: Race, Sex, and Communism at Schenectady General Electric, 1932–1954." *Journal of American History* 83 (1996): 514–548.

Zapata, Francisco. "¿Crisis del sindicalismo en México?" *Revista Mexicana de Sociología* 56 (January–March 1994): 79–88.

————. *El sindicalismo mexicano frente a la restructuración.* Mexico City: Colegio de México, Instituto de Investigaciones de las Naciones Unidas para el Desarrollo Social, 1995.

Zieger, Robert. *The CIO, 1935–1955.* Chapel Hill: University of North Carolina Press, 1995.

ACKNOWLEDGMENTS

While I was gathering material for this book, adventures awaited around every corner. Two chapters and the computer containing them were stolen in San Diego, I totaled a brand-new car outside the Hagley Museum and Library, plainclothes police in Mexico questioned me about my interest in RCA, and I became a fine connoisseur of friends' couches across North America. Perhaps the most surreal episode was the moment when, having hitchhiked from Juárez to a friend's house in Las Cruces, I sat, dusty and tired, watching the billionaire Ross Perot defend "workers' interests" against the Democrat Al Gore during the NAFTA debate—on an RCA television set, of course, made not far from where I sat.

At the end of such a journey, it is a privilege to reflect on the many folks who offered their assistance and whose acquaintance made the journey worthwhile. Each challenging twist in the road seemed to produce generous people ready with advice, resources, and encouragement. I welcome the opportunity to thank them here.

Many people who read, commented on, and influenced the shape of earlier drafts of these chapters have been cherished friends. Georg Leidenberger carefully scrutinized the first incarnation of the book and was not only one of my most perceptive critics but a constant friend and confidant in both Chapel Hill and Mexico City. Michael Trotti read key parts of the book and, most important, has been a supportive friend and a fabulous neighbor. I was privileged to share an office at the University of California, San Diego, with Susie Porter, whose incredible warmth, humor, and critical engagement helped sustain the long hours of the writing process. People often knew where to find us by the laughter emanating from our wing of the building. Many thanks to the constructive criticism I received at the Writing Workshop of the

Center for U.S.-Mexican Studies at UC San Diego, particularly the group's facilitator and the Center's insightful director, Kevin Middlebrook. Members of the Duke–University of North Carolina (UNC) Working Group on Labor and Free Trade—particularly John French, Mark Healey, and Scott Littlehale—had a profound impact on my thinking on the many issues into which we delved. Nelson Lichtenstein and Lance Compa both gave the complete manuscript a serious, respectful, and engaged reading. I am deeply grateful for their comments and encouragement.

Many people graciously shared their files and notes during the course of my research or went beyond the call of duty by finding sets of documents for me. Thanks to Jorge Carrillo, David H. Ciscel, Emilye Crosby, María Patricia Fernández-Kelly, Alyce Hunter, Erik Leaver of the Inter-Hemispheric Resource Center, Local 1424 of the International Brotherhood of Electrical Workers, María Eugenia de la O Martínez, and Socorro Tabuenca at El Colegio de la Frontera Norte in Ciudad Juárez. Professional archivists proved to be key allies. Particular thanks to James Cassedy of the National Archives, the staffs of the Indiana Room at the Monroe County Library in Bloomington and the Mississippi Room of the Shelby County Library in Memphis, Jim Cole at the Mississippi Valley Historical Collection at Memphis University, Claudia Rivers of Special Collections at the University of Texas at El Paso, David Rosenberg at the UE archives at the University of Pittsburgh, and Ralph Bingham and Jim Quizzel at the IUE Archives at Rutgers University. I am particularly grateful to all the RCA workers and managers who allowed me to discuss their work lives with them at home, on the job, or at the union hall.

Chasing a corporation all over the continent also made it necessary for me to impose on many generous people for couches to crash on. For opening up their homes, sharing food, beer, and coffee, and making my extended stays enjoyable, thanks to Yael Bitrán, Kristin Bull, Ernesto Chávez, Jeff Gould, Tracy K'Meyer, Georg Leidenberger, Christine Lux, Margo Michaels, Peach Silbert, and Michael Trotti. For advice, tips, and leads on where to turn next, I thank Altha Cravey, Alejandro Lugo, Zulma Méndez, Leslie Salzinger, Peter Seybold, Leslie Sklair, the staffs of the Center for U.S.-Mexican Studies, the Department of History at UNC, and the School of Industrial and Labor Relations at Cornell University. Thanks also to Carla Freeman, Tami Friedman, Pat Huber, Fred Krissman, Ken Maffitt, David Myhre, Brian Mulligan, Gigi Peterson, Alicia Rouveral, and Hobie Tinkler for support, criticism, and good fun; to Billy, Bob, and Bruce for musical fuel for the writing of labor history; and to Rhonda Hartman for teaching me so much about determination and perseverance. Helen Verwey stood ready with support at a number of critical junctures. Thanks to my friend Bill Bamberger, who not only taught me something about respect for working people but also provided the cover photograph. Detours on this journey have frequently been up the sides of rocks or mountains, and a special thanks goes to all the folks with whom I shared a climbing rope over the past fifteen years; they allowed me to get so far away from the business at hand that at times I thought I might not choose to return—a wonderful gift.

This project certainly would not have proceeded without generous funding from several organizations. An Off-Campus Research Fellowship from the Graduate School of the University of North Carolina at Chapel Hill launched the research, and it was sustained by the Albert J. Beveridge Award of the American Historical Association, a grant from the New Jersey Historical Commission, and a Mowry Award from the UNC Department of History. A Foreign Language and Area Studies (FLAS) Fellowship from the U.S. Department of Education awarded by the Institute for Latin American Studies at UNC allowed me to hone my language skills in Mexico City. A Research-in-Residence Fellowship at the Center for U.S.-Mexican Studies at the University of California, San Diego provided ideal circumstances in which to write, present my findings, and exchange ideas with an engaging group of specialists and a staff of the finest caliber. UNC's Latin American Studies also consistently provided travel funds so that I might share my findings at a variety of scholarly conferences. Finally, the Doris Quinn Fellowship from the UNC Department of History allowed me to remain in residence at the Center for U.S.-Mexican Studies as a guest scholar for another wonderful year.

Teaching at Cornell's School of Industrial and Labor Relations, I enjoyed not only wonderful institutional support and great students but good-natured encouragement from all of the historians while I finished the manuscript. Particular thanks go to the school's dean, Ed Lawler, for his generous assistance. When I was still in New Mexico, Maria Cook sent a well-timed message asking me to get moving and submit the manuscript to Cornell University Press, and I am most grateful that when I did, it ended up in the hands of the editor in chief, Fran Benson. Fran's enthusiasm for the project even rekindled my own interest in it. I simply cannot imagine a better partner in the project of publishing. Further appreciation goes to Barbara Salazar for a rigorous job of editing the manuscript.

At a time when many students complain about the stifling confines of academic research, I am indebted to a group of scholars who gave me plenty of latitude to pursue many paths and make my own mistakes. It was in a seminar with Chuck Bergquist that I first conceived of this project; I hope it is a small testament to his skill as a teacher and vision as a historian. Jacquelyn Dowd Hall provided me with my first serious introduction to women's history, and I can only continue to struggle to live up to her standards of subtlety of analysis and deftness of craft. Peter Coclanis befriended me the day I arrived in Chapel Hill and served as a guide not only on intellectual issues but also through the hazards of professional academic life. John French was one of this book's most dedicated enthusiasts. As a collaborator on other projects and a promoter of this one, he has been a good-humored friend and inspirational scholar. Finally, Leon Fink, my primary adviser, proved to be an adventurous intellectual in a profession that prizes the academic conformist. He never raised the issue of the disciplinary boundaries I was violating, and my deep respect for his willingness to plunge into unexplored territory continues unabated. He recognized the relevance of this research when it was only a vague idea and has been a good friend and advocate ever since.

My parents' little home in the hills was always a welcome retreat. My father continues his unflinching support, but I regret that my mother did not live to see that, as she deeply believed, the circuitous path I had chosen was actually leading someplace. Finally, Janis Whitlock has lived with this project only slightly less intimately than I have. Her patience, perseverance, and faith in me have often come at the expense of the stability and rootedness she has craved. While I have been on the road with RCA, her own work, fueled by an expansive sense of what is possible for society, has continued to change lives in countless wonderful ways that she can only begin to see. Bringing little Aliya into the world has opened up even more amazing new realms to explore. It is to Janis, and the love, commitment, and unyielding sense of adventure we have conspired to maintain, that this book is dedicated.

JEFFERSON COWIE

Ithaca, New York

INDEX